Additional Praise for *Adnan's Story*

The 2017 American Book Award Winner from the Before Columbus Foundation • A *Washington Post* Notable Nonfiction Book for 2016 • A Goodreads Best of 2016 Nonfiction Finalist • A Kobo Best Book of 2016

"Essential reading . . . Chaudry's passion clearly drives *Adnan's Story*. But it's the mix of media skills and legal education that makes her book such an illuminating firsthand report from the front lines of social media change."
—*The Baltimore Sun*

"Any *Serial* fan should eat up this heavily researched book."
—*New York Post*

"*Adnan's Story* should satisfy those who can't get enough of this perplexing case."
—*Newsday*

"You'll find yourself tearing through the book as quickly as you binged on episodes of the podcasts."
—*Bustle*

"As stories of wrongful convictions go, *Adnan's Story* is hands down a certain winner."
—*New York Journal of Books*

"Chaudry is uniquely qualified to tell this story."
—Elle.com

"A skillfully written account of injustice that will have wide appeal to fans of *Serial* and readers of human interest stories."
—*Library Journal*

"Readers new to the story will have no trouble following—the narrative is outlined extensively from the beginning—and podcast listeners will find plenty of previously undisclosed material."
—*Publishers Weekly* (starred review)

"A page-turner . . . [Chaudry's] writing is clear, eloquent, and engaging, and her case is convincing."
—*Kirkus Reviews* (starred review)

"Rabia put her heart and soul [into this]. This is *Serial* come to life. If you liked the podcast, you will love this book."
—Daisy Khan, Women's Islamic Initiative in Spirituality and Equality (WISE)

ADNAN'S STORY

ADNAN'S STORY

The Search for Truth and Justice After *Serial*

———————•———————

RABIA CHAUDRY

 ST. MARTIN'S GRIFFIN NEW YORK

ADNAN'S STORY. Copyright © 2016, 2019 by Rabia Chaudry. All rights reserved. Printed in the United States of America. For information, address St. Martin's Press, 175 Fifth Avenue, New York, NY 10010.

www.stmartins.com

Designed by Steven Seighman

The Library of Congress has cataloged the hardcover edition as follows:

Names: Chaudry, Rabia, author.
Title: Adnan's story : the search for truth and justice after Serial / Rabia Chaudry.
Description: New York, NY : St. Martin's Press, 2016. | "First Edition." | Includes index.
Identifiers: LCCN 2016024062 | ISBN 9781250087102 (hardcover) | ISBN 9781250087119 (ebook)
Subjects: LCSH: Syed, Adnan, 1981– | Murderers—Maryland—Baltimore—Case studies. | Murder—Investigation—Maryland—Baltimore—Case studies. | Judicial error— Maryland—Baltimore—Case studies. | Criminal justice, Administration of—Maryland— Baltimore—Case studies.
Classification: LCC HV6248.S87 C43 2016 | DDC 364.152/3092 [B]—dc23
LC record available at https://lccn.loc.gov/2016024062

ISBN 978-1-250-14654-0 (trade paperback)

Our books may be purchased in bulk for promotional, educational, or business use. Please contact your local bookseller or the Macmillan Corporate and Premium Sales Department at 1-800-221-7945, extension 5442, or by email at MacmillanSpecialMarkets@macmillan.com.

First St. Martin's Griffin Edition: March 2019

10 9 8 7 6 5 4 3 2 1

For the millions in history imprisoned unjustly.
For those who fight for the helpless.

For Aunty, Uncle, Yusuf, and Tanveer, who lived
this nightmare alone for seventeen years.
For Adnan, who gives us all the hope we need to fight
for him, however long it may take.

For Hae.

Bismillah.

CONTENTS

———•———

ADNAN'S STORY

INTRODUCTION

———————•———————

Malik reported: Amir Az-Zubair would stop speaking whenever he heard thunder and he would say, "Glory to Him who said: The thunder exalts His praise as well as the angels from fear of Him," (*Quran* 13:13). Then Amir would say, "This is a strong warning to the people of the earth."

Imam Malik, "Muwatta," 8th century B.C.E.

When Adnan was convicted, it thundered three times. The day was bright and sunny, but as we sat there clutching our hands while the foreman pronounced the verdicts, it thundered.

February 25, 2000, was a Friday, which was a good sign. Fridays are auspicious for Muslims. It is a blessed day, our day of sermons and congregational prayer, the day we start all new things with a "bism`illah," invoking the name of God.

I sat with Adnan's mother, Aunty Shamim, while other members of the community were scattered behind us. Aunty looked straight ahead stoically, a scarf draped over her head, sitting shoulder to shoulder with her oldest son. I prayed silently as the jury was brought in. On the other side of the wooden railing, Adnan stood with his lawyer. Tall and skinny, facial hair coming in sparsely over his pale face, he was barely entering manhood.

The foreman rose.

On the first count, murder in the first degree: guilty. It thundered and we all turned our heads, looking out the courtroom windows at the clear skies, stunned.

On the second count, kidnapping by fraud: guilty. Then it thundered a second time and we again turned our faces, scanning the sunny outdoors, confused.

On the third count, robbery: guilty. It thundered again. This time I only glanced outside, keeping my face turned toward Adnan's slight figure, paralyzed. By the time the fourth count was read, false imprisonment, I had tuned out, my ears filled with the rush of blood.

Closing arguments had been made only a few hours earlier; we had just begun contemplating where to eat lunch when we were called back to the courthouse. A verdict had been reached. A fast and hard verdict. The weekend loomed ahead after all.

The bailiff approached Adnan and closed cuffs around his wrists and ankles, the same ones he had worn shuffling in and out of court day after day. There were audible gasps and sobs, some escaping me as I rocked back and forth in my seat, repeating "no, no, no . . ." This was not actually happening. We were told this was not going to happen.

Then Adnan turned to us—his mother, his brother, his friends, his community—and said, "It's ok. I didn't do it. Allah knows I didn't do it."

Adnan Syed was seventeen when he was arrested for the murder of his former girlfriend Hae Min Lee in 1999 in the suburbs of Baltimore, Maryland. He was convicted and sentenced to life plus thirty years. My younger brother Saad's best friend, Adnan is like a brother to me, and for seventeen years now my family and I have stood by him as he has maintained his innocence.

I was in law school when Adnan was arrested and still a student when he was convicted. I was never Adnan's lawyer. But my life has remained tethered to Adnan through an abiding belief that he is innocent.

In 2013, after exhausting almost all appeals, I contacted Sarah Koenig, a producer at *This American Life*. Her subsequent investigation turned into the podcast *Serial,* an international phenomenon and the most successful podcast ever produced.

Serial told a riveting who-done-it tale in such a masterful way that some people did not realize it was a true story even after the twelve episodes ended. The story it told was true, but it wasn't the whole truth, or the whole story.

The success of the podcast was understandable, if not completely expected. This is a story constructed of dozens and dozens of layers, an array of odd characters, malfeasance and misjudgments, and the aligning of all that can go wrong, and must go wrong, to convict an innocent person. But the real allure of *Serial* was the man at the center of the story, Adnan. Listeners were left wondering, week after week, about who he really was.

Serial presented two options. Adnan was either an innocent, wrongfully convicted young man who had suffered a great travesty of justice. Or he was a cold-blooded psychopathic murderer, driven by either jealousy or brutal religious beliefs, who had managed to manipulate his loved ones into believing his innocence for fifteen years.

This book will tell the stories *Serial* didn't and address issues of justice, bigotry, faith, community, devastation, healing, and hope from the point of view of Adnan and those who support him. I am here to tell Adnan's story as, after so many years of living it and studying it, I see it. But more importantly, to give Adnan his own voice back. Throughout the book, Adnan's own contributions will do just that.

Adnan Syed

10.10.13

Dear Ms. Koenig,

I received your letter today. Thank you for taking the time to write, and also for sending the stamp & paper. This prison does not allow us to receive those items, so it should have been mailed back to you. I appreciate your considering that I may have been low on supplies, but I am very fortunate to have family & friends that have always taken care to make sure I have everything I need. So I have no problem being able to correspond with you.

My attorney Justin Brown wrote me last week regarding his initial conversation with you. He described the things you two spoke about, and he advised me that it would be a good idea to pursue this with you. I wrote him back that I agreed, and I intend to call him as soon as I can so he & I can discuss it some more.

I did have some questions, but most were answered when I received your letter. It made sense that Rabia contacted you and sought your assistance. Aside from my mother & father, I don't think there is anyone who has fought more to prove my innocence. For many years, she has urged me to contact someone from the media, but I have always been very reluctant to do so. The reason being that all the media coverage of my case has been negative, and I did not think any good would come of it. I understood that it would always be a gamble, because if the person did not believe I was innocent, then it would just be another negative report. However, Justin mentioned in his letter that you stated you would not do the story unless you believed I was innocent. And that really allayed my concerns.

I'll be honest with you Ms. Koenig. After about 15 years of studying my case, I can't point to something and say "This proves I didn't commit this crime." I could describe certain elements of the prosecution's case that (to me) are pretty unbelievable. I'm not sure exactly what you do know about my case. You wrote that you had read some of the transcripts and spoke with several people involved in the case. I don't want to assume what you know, and I think this letter would end up a mess if I tried to explain the things that occurred in my case that prevented me from having a fair trial. I think the thing that frustrates me the most is the Timetable the State presented. Between Jay Wilds's several (completely different) statements and the State's's varying theories, it is not easy to piece together. But in the second trial, the Prosecutor (in closing arguments) summed it up using the records of my cell phone. Basically, they narrated a series of events (according to Jay Wilds) and pointed to an entry on the cell phone record at a certain time as proof of the event. Just as human DNA is used to place a person at a certain location, the cell phone records were used (to me) as a form of technological

DNA, to place me at a certain place and time. Which sounds pretty good, on the surface. But if you were to backtrack and trace the footsteps of the prosecutor's theory, using the cells and times as a marker, I believe it is physically impossible for me to have committed this crime.

Essentially, the theory was that I committed the murder by 2:36 pm on 1/13/99. (Exact time placed on phone call) Now, school lets out at 2:15pm, so that leaves 21 minutes. Which may seem like a long time, but it is virtually impossible if you consider the following facts:

1. The final bell rings at 2:15pm, but you can't just leave and jump in the car. There are 1500 other students filling the hallways and stairwells of a 4-story building.

2. Students are not allowed to park in front of the school building. We had to park in the back. There were strict rules about that. The back parking lot of Woodlawn High School is enclosed within a bus loop (you could Google Map it). At 2:15am, every car in that back parking lot is encircled by a ring of buses loading up. You can't leave until the buses leave. And they wait 10-15 minutes before they fill up and leave.

3. The route to the Best Buy parking lot (where the State eventually settled on as the murder scene) traverses several stoplights and major intersections. There are numerous school buses, and there is a large Social Security Building next door to the school. There is a ton of traffic at that time. Those intersections are packed. So even though the Best Buy is about 1-1¾ miles away, it is nowhere near a quick trip (at that time of the day).

4. The State presented that the murder took place in the parking lot of the Best Buy. Now, please keep in mind that at the time, I was 17 years old, like 5'11", 155 lbs. Hae was 18, 5'8", 140 lbs. She was a big, strong and athletic girl. She was voted as one of the best field hockey players in all of Baltimore County, and she was a Varsity lacrosse player. How in the world, within a few moments (according to the prosecutor's timeline) am I able to manually strangle Hae (sustaining no scratch marks, bruises, abrasions etc. on me) [in fact, forensic evidence was found on her body, and the State's expert said in his opinion it did not come from me] remove here body from the car, carry it to the trunk, and place her in there, in broad daylight at 2:30 in the afternoon? And then I walk into the Best Buy lobby and call Jay Wild's and tell him to come meet me there? I asked Ms. Gutierrez over and over to please have someone try to prove that all this would be impossible to do in 21 minutes. But she declined to pursue it. And it has always bugged me for years, cause I am 100% sure that if someone tried to do it, it would be impossible.

I'm not sure if you know anything about all of this, so maybe it is confusing. I have a page with the phone records the prosecutor used, and also a page with the transcript lines to detail their Timeline (from the closing argument) It could really be confusing trying to get it from the entire transcripts, cause you'd be jumping back and forth. Justin did a really amazing outline of the trial transcripts as part of his transcript review for my appeal. I've always used my notes, but now I use his summary if I'm looking for something particular. I'm going to ask him if he will give you a copy, cause I think it would make it easier for you to find something in the transcript. I'm also going to try send you a copy of the thing I have in case they may be helpful.

Ms. Koenig, I am not really sure what I should write you about. I guess it would be a really big help if you told me what you wanted to know. I do want to take some time and tell you about Hae & I.

We met on the first day of 9th grade. We sat next to each other in Biology class. It was a table of 4, and the 2 other seats were occupied by Irina ████ and Emily ████. It was funny amongst us because Hae was Korean, Emily was Hispanic, Irina was Russian, and I was Pakistani. Things were cool, until we had our first quiz. It was basically just a bunch of terms we had to memorize. So I memorized all of them, and got a 19/20. Hae got a 17/20, and Irina & Emily both got, like, 15/20's. Mind you, these are some really smart people, and I'm the dumb jock at the table. Anyway, they go off on me and said I must have cheated with a cheat sheet or something, cause no way could I have done better than them.

Hae snatched my paper and compared it to theirs, and because we all got 1 of the same questions wrong, she concluded I must have copied of their papers. One of them said, "I bet you don't know any of these." I reply, "Go ahead and ask me." Now, we're getting kind of loud and part of the class is getting involved, joining in. So they start asking me the questions, "What is osmosis?, What does the suffix -ose indicate? etc." I answer each one right, and the girls are groaning while a couple of guys are cheering me on. So finally they concede, and now we're giving each other high-fives and making a big commotion. The teacher yells at us to be quiet, and when I turn around, I'm smiling from ear to ear. The three of them are glaring at me something fierce. And that's how Hae and I first got to know each other.

We became casual friends throughout our 9th grade year. We had some classes together, but outside of class we never socialized or saw each other. In our 10th grade year, I didn't see her and heard through the grapevine that she moved to California. She was back for 11th grade, and we had some of the same classes together. Close to the end of the school year, I asked Hae to the prom. She said yes, and we started spending time with each other afterward.

We would do teenager stuff. Go to McDonalds after school, go to movies, the mall, etc. We talked on the phone every night, late into the night. Neither of our families knew about our relationship (in the beginning). We became intimate very early on, and since we couldn't go to either of our homes, we used to go to motels and spend the day there. It progressed over the summer, but it started to get difficult because of our families. We were both close to our families, and it was hard to keep it a secret. Both of us would get in trouble, and her mother made her stay in the city with her for a few weeks. So it wore on us both, but Hae took it really hard. Before our senior year, Hae decided to end the relationship, saying it would be better for us to not have to have problems with our families. I was upset, but I accepted here decision, and we remained friends. One night (about 2-3 weeks later)I was at fashion show at UMBC. She paged me and told me she wanted to get back together. So we dated for a several more weeks, but the family stuff kept coming up. So she broke it off again at the end of October. I was upset again, but by then it was clear that it was really getting to be a mess with our parents. We remained really close friends.

After our relationship ended, we would talk to each other on the phone and still hang out at school. She started seeing someone at her job, and I was spending time with several different girls. We were close enough and had the kind of friendship that she told me about getting in trouble for spending the night at her boyfriends, and I told her about hanging out with one girl while getting a phone call on my cell phone from another. (This was a few months after we broke up)We were close enough that I could tease her about being "a hot Asian chick dating an older white dude" and she would tease me back about being a "Pakistani Gigolo" messing around with different girls at the same time. In fact, one of the girls whom I had spend the night with (the week of Jan 13th) was ███████████. Hae particularly teased me about her because she overheard █████ telling someone in class that now I was no longer with Hae, she was going to try and hook up with me. I told Ms. Gutierrez about all of this, and I gave her the names of several of the girls so that she could call them to show I wasn't some dangerous weirdo who was depressed or stalking Hae. But Ms. Gutierrez didn't pursue it. And I think it would've been important to show that at trial.

A few weeks before she disappeared, Hae called me to pick her up from her job. Her car had broken down, and she asked me for a ride home. When I went to pick her up, her boyfriend was there, and we met. So our friendship was enough that she felt comfortable calling me about 10:00 at night to take her home, even though her boyfriend was right there. A few days later, a couple of us wanted lunch from McDonalds, and I drove her car to pick the food up. I mention these things to you Ms. Koenig so you can have an idea of our relationship and friendship afterwards. I never, not one time screamed at Hae, threatened her, abused her verbally or physically, fussed her out, not ever. We had our disagreements and arguments, as anyone would. But I never did anything to make her feel afraid of me. More importantly, she never told anyone I ever did any of these things. Not <u>one</u> of her friends ever told anyone or came to court and testified that the saw anything like that, or that Hae said anything to them like that. And even more important, in her entire diary, she never mentions any of these things. And she wrote extensively about our relationship. Ms. Gutierrez had a copy of it, and it now is with the files at my parent's house.

I've watched a lot of TV over the past 15 years. I always try to catch the investigative news programs like Dateline, 20/20, Snapped, 48 Hours Mystery, etc. I've probably seen over 200 episodes with husband/wife, boyfriend/girlfriend cases. And while they all had different aspects, in almost every one where it was a case of "scorned love" (and not life insurance or affairs) there is always something where the dude has a history of violent/abusive behavior behavior with the lady. Or she had told one of her friends that she was afraid of him or felt threatened. Especially if it was a younger guy. Whereas an older guy may have the presence of mind to mask his true intentions and bide his time, a younger guy would not have the maturity. I've never seen a story of a 17-year old guy murdering his 18-year old girlfriend. I have seen stories of serious violence and abuse between teenage boyfriend/girlfriend, but there is always a history of abuse. A case that comes to mind is the Yeardley Love and George Hughely case in the Univ. of Virginia. There was a history of abuse and she had expressed fear to many of her friends.

My point is that I do not fit the pattern at all of any of these profiles, so either I'm the first 17-year old guy in history who pretended to by my ex-girlfriend's friend for several months after we broke up, apply to colleges, plan to graduate, work as an EMT, play sports in school, hang out and be intimate with numerous girls, and then all of a sudden one day, out of the blue, decide to commit murder. I asked Ms. Gutierrez time and time again why she couldn't emphasize this in her defense, but she said none of that stuff really mattered.

Hae was one of the kindest, sweetest, just all-around most beautiful people I've ever known. She treated me with all the love and respect in the world. I loved her when we dated for several months, and I loved her as a friend after that. I never, ever would have wished her any harm nor did I have any desire to harm her. I had absolutely nothing to do with her murder. I mentioned in the beginning that I couldn't really point to anything that said, "This proves I didn't do it." Well, I also feel that no one could point to anything in my case and say "This proves I did it." And that is what frustrates me the most about working to clear my name: I have to disprove something that was never really proven in the beginning.

According to the State, I committed the murder between 2:15pm - 2:36pm. When I was arrested, I received a letter from a girl named Asie McClain. In it, she mentioned being in the Public Library with her boyfriend & his best friend. And that she saw me and spoke with me between 2:20pm - 2:40pm. I gave this to Ms.

Gutierrez immediately, and requested she contact Asia McClain. ███████████ later, I followed up with her about it. She replied that she had checked it out, but nothing came of it. I questioned her again, and she told me it didn't pan out, and we were moving on. I took her word for it. However, at the end of trial, I found out she never contacted Asia McClain (through Rabia). When I confronted her, she said, "We have to focus on the appeal." And remember what I said about the timeline; that the State presented the cell phone records to pinpoint exact time? Well, at the exact time the Prosecutor said the murder was taking place, I was sitting in the library with Asia McClain and two others. And at least she (at the time) was willing to come forward. But Ms. Gutierrez never contacted her. More importantly, Asia McClain mentioned she spoke to the librarian about security cameras. In 2010, Justin Brown contacted the Baltimore County Public Library people about it, and they sent him a letter stating the librarian said she remembered security cameras at the time.

I don't believe it's so far-fetched to think that if Asia McClain had testified at trial it would've caused a different outcome. And while we can't say the security footage would still have existed from 1-13-99 to 3-2-99 (the time when I told Ms. Gutierrez), at least she could've tried. But she didn't, now who knows what could've happened.

I'm not sure if any of this is helpful at all. I don't know exactly what you need me to do. I'm willing to answer any questions you have. I'm able to use the phone between 12-1pm in the afternoon each day. If you want me to call you, you just have to tell me which #. I spoke to a Lieutenant about the visit you mentioned. In order for me to have any visitor, I have to submit the full name and address that is on the visitor's driver's license. Obviously, I can understand you'd be reluctant to send me that information. It's weird to even ask you something like that. I don't know if they would make an exception because you are a reporter. You could call and ask. Other than that, I can't do anything else. I've included a copy of the visiting form so you could see for yourself. If you do talk to someone, and they provide a solution, it would be best to write down their name and the day and time of the conversation. A lot of times one person will say one thing and you could drive all the way up here and still be turned away.

Finally Ms. Koenig, I just want to say that I if I wasn't innocent, I wouldn't waste your time. I wouldn't waste Rabia's time, Justin Brown's time, or my parent's time. I would not be sitting around and allowing people to waste valuable time and resources trying to help me. I had nothing with Hae's murder. She was one of my best friends.

I'm sorry this was so long and jumped from one subject to another. In the future I'll try hard to make sure to keep it more organized. But if you decide not to pursue this, thank you anyway for the time you have spent so far.

Sincerely,
Adnan Syed

CHAPTER 1

STAR-CROSSED LOVERS

———•———

We decreed on the Children of Israel that whoever kills a soul,
unless for another killing or for spreading corruption in the land,
it is as if he had slain mankind entirely.
And whoever saves one—it is as if he had saved mankind entirely.
Holy Quran 5:32

Leakin Park is beautiful and quiet. Heavily wooded, yet nestled amid densely populated urban neighborhoods in West Baltimore, its three hundred acres adjoin Gwynn Oak Park seamlessly, forming over a thousand acres of nature in the middle of a city not known for outdoor beauty. Other than a hushed flow of water, its peace is disturbed only by cars passing through on Franklintown Road.

To horror film aficionados Leakin Park should look familiar—the sequel to the cult classic *Blair Witch Project* was partially filmed there. It may have been the park's reputation that drew the filmmakers to it. Leakin Park is a notorious dumping ground for bodies. The remains of at least sixty-eight murdered people have been found there in the past five decades, most recently in November 2012.

You wouldn't know to look at it, though.

In summertime the brambles, vines, and thorny creepers are in abundance, making it difficult to forge a path from where we enter the park back to the Dead Run Stream. The stream is low and gentle this day, but has the potential to surge up forcefully. A century ago it powered grist, cloth, and paper mills, joined by its sister stream, Gwynn Falls, both of which eventually drop eastward into the Patapsco River and then the Chesapeake Bay.

Today Dead Run Stream babbles softly over a rocky bed, cutting through the park's ravine, nearly parallel to the road roughly a hundred yards south of it.

On this sweltering summer day I'm trying to figure something out about Leakin Park. As I head inside on no discernible path, fighting through brambles, I'm followed closely by a soil expert from the U.S. Department of Agriculture, who hauls a shovel and had the forethought to keep high rubber boots in her car. I have asked for her help in determining the terrain type. My younger daughter is with us. At six years old, the idea of the woods is more appealing to her than the reality, and after encountering a few prickly brushes she refuses to go on. I pick her up and try to shelter her from the reaching, spiky foliage as we move under the shade of red oaks and American beeches.

It is cooler inside the park than a few dozen yards away on the road, which is in the sun. But the stillness of the park belies the tangible humidity seeping through our clothing, filling the air and the gaps between us.

Beyond the brambles, a rough path about a foot across becomes noticeable as we approach a fallen tree to our right. The tree is about forty feet long and parallel to the stream. In previous visits I witnessed at least half a dozen "tourists" stomp back to the tree to have their picture taken with it.

But it's the wrong tree.

I turn to the left and begin following the stream westward.

We go up a slight incline and there I set my daughter down. She's still frightened, grasping my legs. A mound rises up to my left, covering God knows what, with a filthy, nearly unrecognizable piece of carpet on top of it. The last time I was here the carpet lay flat. Now it's been pushed to one side, perhaps more "tourists" trying to figure out what's underneath.

I point to a spot a few feet behind it, at a massive fallen tree, unmoved for decades. Its roots spread in the air, claw-like, nearly reaching the stream. Large rocks and manmade concrete chunks lie scattered, and pieces of a corroded metal frame poke out from the ground.

From here, the road seems distant. We are shielded from view.

Under the very center of the tree is a hollow in the earth. It dips from one side of the tree to the other, like a cozy bowl perfectly formed, nearly four feet across. A shallow bed of soft dirt, leaves, and moss.

I wipe the sweat from my face, pushing back the hair that escaped my scarf, and nod toward it.

"That's it. That's where Hae's body was found."

Woodlawn High School in Woodlawn, Maryland, is in western Baltimore County, not the city of Baltimore. But the distance to the city, where the murder rate in 1999 was nearly a homicide a day, is just a few miles. Established in the 1920s, Woodlawn High is now one of the largest public schools in the county, and one of the most diverse.

It has also been prone to violence. Shootings, stabbings, and murder were not unusual in Woodlawn. And though the high school boasts a robust Science, Technology, Engineering and Mathematics (STEM) magnet program, a police presence at and around the school has not been uncommon.

On January 7, 1999, a fifteen-year-old was stabbed repeatedly by another student in the stairwell of the school, the culmination of a long-standing grudge. He was rushed to the hospital where he was treated and survived. The other student was arrested, and the rest of the school went about its day. That was Woodlawn.

While the majority of the student population is and has always been African American, the establishment of a mosque, the Islamic Society of Baltimore, in its vicinity has meant a growing number of local Muslim families and Muslim students at Woodlawn. The mosque eventually became surrounded by neighborhoods with dozens of South Asian Muslim families, including Syed Rahman's.

Rahman and his wife and three sons lived a brisk fifteen-minute walk from the mosque. He was a state employee, and his wife, Shamim, ran a home-based daycare center in the basement of their modest two-level home. They had emigrated from Peshawar, the capital of Pakistan's North-West Frontier Province, now called Khyber Pakhtunkhwa, where ethnic Pashtuns constitute the majority. Rahman and Shamim were Pashtun; their sons, Tanveer, Adnan, and Yusuf, were born in the United States.

The Rahmans were devout and simple people, raising their sons to be involved at the mosque, without television and other external influences at home. To Western sensibilities they might be considered "fundamentalists." To us, they were just conservative but kindly people.

The neighborhood they lived in was part of a modest subdivision peppered with Muslim families, a subdivision my own parents moved to in 1997. Like other Pakistanis and Muslims in the area, the Rahmans became acquaintances we ran into every so often, and as is traditional South Asian custom, my siblings and I called them "Uncle" and "Aunty" out of affection and respect.

My parents first moved to the Baltimore area in 1994 to the mostly white suburb of Ellicott City but moved closer to the mosque, and the city, in 1997. I had gotten married in 1996 while still in college and moved to northern Virginia, and my younger sister, Siddrah, was attending the University of Maryland Baltimore County (UMBC) and living on campus. Our younger brother, Saad, was still in high school and living at home. The move meant Saad would have to switch from the very safe, suburban high school he attended, Mount Hebron, to Woodlawn High. But my mother worried about the school's reputation for drugs and violence, and managed to find a way to keep Saad in the Ellicott City school.

Although Saad never attended Woodlawn High, he got to know many of the local Muslim kids who did through the mosque, where they gathered almost every evening to play basketball. This is how he met Adnan Syed, the Rahman's middle son, and how our family came to know Adnan as Saad's best friend— a gangly, bespectacled kid who most of us thought was too sweet to be my alpha male, sports-jock brother's friend.

In January of 1999 I was in my second year of law school at the George Mason School of Law in Virginia, where I lived with my two-year-old daughter, husband, and nearly a dozen in-laws from Pakistan. It wasn't supposed to be that way, but shortly after my wedding I was told that we would be living in a traditional joint-family system. Mine was no ordinary, set-up-by-the-parents Pakistani marriage. I had met, fallen in love with, and married a student from Pakistan completely on my own. It had taken three years to convince my parents, my mother in particular, to let the marriage take place. After that, I was in no position to complain to my family that I was now badly stuck living with his parents, two grown brothers, their wives, the child of one of them, and a younger sister, all in the same house. Badly stuck not only because I had fought for this relationship in the face of my own family's resistance but also because within two weeks of marriage it was clear that my new marriage was deeply troubled.

My in-laws set the terms of my life. I could attend law school as long as I took care of my family responsibilities, which meant it was my job to cook for the entire extended family twice a day. I had to attend law school in the evenings.

My weeks were exhausting. I woke in the morning, bathed and fed my little girl, made a curry or some such thing for the family's lunch, and ran to my internship at a local law firm from 9:00 a.m. to 2:00 p.m. Then I returned home, spent a couple of hours with my daughter, made dinner, and left for law school by five o'clock. I often returned home around eleven and spent the night hours, after the house had fallen quiet, doing my homework. Most nights I fell asleep around 3:00 a.m. Then I was back up at seven o'clock to start the day over.

By Friday I was in desperate need of respite, and what saved me was being able to come home to my parents in Baltimore every weekend. I told them nothing of my home life, but showed up every Friday night with my daughter in tow and stayed until Sunday evening. Those two days of peace every week kept me sane and got me through the toughest years of my life. And it was during those visits that I first learned that a young local girl, a student at Woodlawn High School named Hae Min Lee, was missing.

Wednesday, January 13, 1999, was a rather mild day for winter in Baltimore, with temperatures reaching into the fifties, though in the weeks prior a number of snowstorms had hit the area.

That year eighteen-year-old Hae Min Lee was a senior at Woodlawn High. A star student-athlete, she played both lacrosse and field hockey, managed the boy's wrestling team, worked part-time at LensCrafters, and maintained excellent grades, with a 3.8 GPA as part of the school's Magnet Program. The students in the program were close. Adnan, Krista Meyers, Debbie Warren, Rebecca (Becky) Walker, Stephanie McPherson, Laura Estrada, Hae's best friend Aisha Pittman, and a few others hung out constantly. By all accounts Hae was a popular, hard-working, independent young woman. Her diary reveals an impassioned teenager focused on her studies and intense romantic love.

Hae was born in South Korea and migrated with her mother and brother to the United States when she was in middle school. She lived in the Woodlawn area with her mother, grandparents, young brother, and two cousins. There were rumors of a stepfather (or ex-fiancé) in California, where Hae, her brother, and mother spent a few months during her sophomore year. There were also conflicting stories about her biological father, who may or may not have ever been in the United States.

That Wednesday morning, January 13, 1999, Hae left home for school around 7:00 a.m. Her grandmother saw her get into her gray Nissan Sentra and drive away, not knowing it would be the last time she would see her granddaughter alive.

Classes started early at Woodlawn, at 7:45 a.m., and students began arriving by 7:30. According to school records and classmate accounts, Hae came to school on time that day. She was the teacher's assistant in her first-period French class. The rest of her day, though, is hard to piece together—inexplicably, statements weren't taken from students and teachers until long after she disappeared.

What is certain is that Hae left school sometime after dismissal at 2:15 p.m. It was her responsibility to pick up her six-year-old cousin from Campfield Early Learning Center, less than four miles away, by 3:15 p.m. every day. But that day her cousin was left stranded.

According to trial testimony, Hae's younger brother, Young Lee, received a phone call from Campfield around 3:30 p.m., asking that someone come to pick up the girl. Young called his grandfather to go retrieve his cousin, then called Hae's workplace and best friend, Aisha Pittman, looking for her. When he was unable to find her, he told their mother that Hae had not made it to Campfield and was missing. After two hours the family called the police, panicked.

An officer from the Baltimore County Police arrived within the hour, began calling Hae's friends, and, having taken details from the family, opened a missing person's investigation. One of the people he called that night was Adnan Syed.

Back in the spring of 1998, prom season was quickly approaching. Adnan and Hae were friends, and neither had a date for the junior prom. Adnan was over six feet tall, dark, handsome, played football and ran track, and charmed the girls. Hae was no less popular and ambitious—tall, athletic, outgoing, attractive, warm, and friendly is how her classmates described her. So when a friend suggested that Adnan ask Hae to the prom, he went for it, and Hae said yes.

For the next ten months Adnan and Hae were deeply, madly in love. Hae chronicled her relationship with Adnan in a diary, begun on April 1, 1998, when she bought a notebook during a French class field trip to a Monet exhibit.

By the second entry, made the same day, she mentions her plan to go to the prom with Adnan and writes with a smiley face, "I think I just might love him."

By April 7th the diary reveals the kind of challenges this new relationship faced from the very beginning. When Hae's grandmother asked who Hae was going to prom with, she was apparently not happy with the answer.

4/7/98

Someone please smack me! What the fuck am I doing?!?! I am pushing Adnan away! Damn my grandma + mother. Shit! I can't get close, and he can't get close to me. This is really fucked up! He is way too sweet + all! What is happening? I can't believe things are about to blow up in my face 'sigh' my life's a bitch

The challenge wasn't one-sided, though; on Adnan's end, any and all romantic relationships (outside of marriage) were a hard and fast cultural no-no.

I feel comfortable making the claim that all teenagers lie to their parents. All of them. They just lie about different things. When you're the first-generation child of American Muslims (or South Asians, or Arabs, or Asians in general), you most definitely lie about dating.

Unfortunately for Adnan, his mother was excellent at catching his lies—and persistent. She had a keen sense of her sons, and she knew this one had an eye for the girls. She would catch him on the phone talking to young women, note the mileage on his car to see if he had traveled farther than the school, and go through his belongings to find some evidence that he had girls in his life.

Eventually she found out about Hae, but not yet. Adnan and Hae had already planned how they would evade parental detection by getting dressed at their friends' homes and then meeting up at the prom.

Adnan was crowned Prom Prince. But his Princess wasn't Hae that night, it was Stephanie McPherson, a longtime friend of Adnan's. Stephanie was an athlete and a beauty who had a playful, flirtatious relationship with her close friend Adnan, often sitting in his lap during class despite having a boyfriend. When Adnan and Stephanie were crowned, Hae initially felt jealous, which she notes in her diary, but then Adnan did something remarkable.

As the K-Ci & JoJo song, "All My Life," played for the Prince and Princess's first dance, Adnan began dancing with Stephanie. Hae took a picture of them and went to have a seat next to a friend, feeling a bit bothered but trying to act natural. Just then, Adnan broke off the dance with Stephanie and came to take Hae to the dance floor.

"10 seconds later guess who danced with me and not w/Stephanie? ADNAN!! Now how can I not fall in love with this guy!" writes Hae. That act of devotion from Adnan pushed them from dating to boyfriend-girlfriend, and later that night at the Baltimore Harbor, outside of a Cheesecake Factory, they had their first kiss. But Hae knew it wouldn't be an easy path. In the same entry she writes that "I keep on falling deeper and deeper into him. He's the cutest, sweetest, and coolest guy, and he loves me!!! The bad thing is we have to keep things secret . . . sigh. But it's ok because love conquers all!"

Hae wasn't the only one falling head over heels in love. This was Adnan's first serious romantic relationship, and he was truly smitten.

Everyone knew about Adnan's deep attachment to Hae; he made no attempts to hide it, giving Hae flowers, gifts, cards, frequently writing poems and letters. They were publicly romantic, holding hands, cuddling, kissing at school, and at the same time supportive of each other's pursuits and success. If there was a power couple at Woodlawn, it was Adnan and Hae.

Unfortunately, Hae predicted wrong—love did not conquer all, and Adnan and Hae continued to deal with family members who were deeply unhappy about their relationship. In May 1998 Hae notes in her diary that she "hates" her grandparents but determines they won't stop her from being with Adnan. Hae was

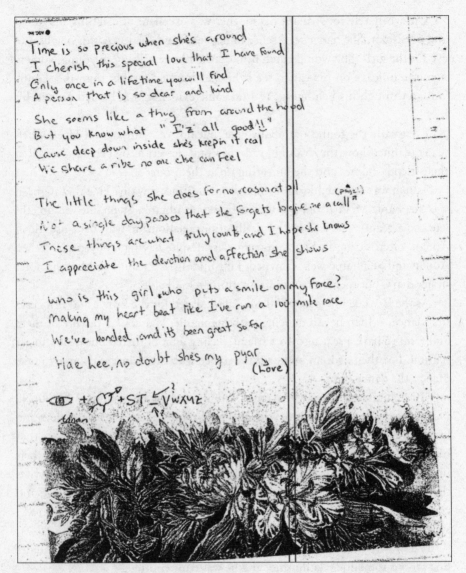

Time is so precious when she's around
I cherish this special love that I have found
Only once in a lifetime you will find
A person that is so dear and kind

She seems like a thug from around the hood
But you know what " I'z all good'!! "
Cause deep down inside she's keepin it real
We share a vibe no one else can Feel

The little things she does for no reason at all   (page!)
Not a single day passes that she forgets to give me a call"
These things are what truly counts and I hope she knows
I appreciate the devotion and affection she shows

who is this girl, who puts a smile on my Face?
making my heart beat like I've run a 100 mile race
We've bonded, and its been great so far

Hae Lee, no doubt she's my pyar
                                            (Love)

Undated poem written by Adnan for Hae

strong-willed and fiercely independent and she refused to give up on the relationship, all the while acknowledging that she had no idea where it would go because of the people "against" them—primarily Adnan's mother. Adnan was no more willing to give up their love.

Adnan would secretly visit Hae at her home in the middle of the night so her family wouldn't know. Sneaking out of his house after his parents fell asleep, Adnan would meet Hae at her basement window and talk through it, sometimes

Undated letter from Adnan to Hae, remainder of letter missing from files

for hours, exchanging whispers so no one would hear them. Sometimes they would meet in her grandfather's car, again hiding from her family. But secrecy isn't easy to maintain. Hae wrote in her diary about a time that Adnan called her home and the phone rang. "I'm going to be in MAD trouble." Later in the relationship Hae expresses regrets for having given Adnan five months of her life, not because she didn't love him, but because she could not be honest with her family about their relationship: "Because I have lost myself . . . in love, in embrace, and in lies. All the lies I told my mother, my family . . . its going to haunt me tonight . . . I love my mother, always have+always will. But . . . why have I been deceiving her for months?"

When Hae's grandparents replace the home's cordless phone with a corded one to stop her "excessive use" of it, she's struck by their decision and realizes the lengths they are having to go to because she's a "troublesome g-child."

The stress in their relationship wasn't limited to family opposition, however. Hae began to feel deep doubt and even guilt about their relationship, pointing to Adnan's religion and culture repeatedly as the real issue standing between them. She's confronted by their English teacher who tells her Adnan used to be so religious the previous year, but now he's changed because of her.

For a couple of pages Hae writes about her discomfort at being an obstacle between Adnan and his faith.

And for good reason. Hae was Adnan's first sexual relationship. They became intimate not long after they began dating. They would have sex in the car in Patapsco State Park. Once school started they found a closer spot to hook up, the rear parking lot of a Best Buy store. At times they would stop there before Hae had to take off to pick up her cousin from elementary school.

The potential immorality of these things weighed on Hae. Calling for a week-long break to assess the relationship, Hae writes, "It irks me to know I'm against his religion. He called me a devil a few times. I know he was only joking, it's somewhat true . . . I hate that. It's like making him choose between me and his religion."

In July Adnan accompanied his father to a Muslim conference in Texas. He called Hae a number of times and Hae cried from missing him. Over the phone he explained how important his faith was, that it meant life to him, and still, he said, he would never leave her. This reassured her for a bit, until weeks later when he said that one day he would have to choose between her and his religion.

From that point it seems Hae started to mentally prepare herself for the day their relationship would end.

"And when it comes down to choosing . . . I'm going to let him go his way. If you have to deny yourself a part of you for love . . . then that's not good. I really couldn't care less since my religion means shit to me. But to him, his religion guides his life."

The internal back-and-forth within Hae persists throughout their relationship—she is almost daily swinging between undying love and doubt in her diary. But whatever her inner struggles were, and however these issues impacted their bond, externally they didn't come off as any more or less tumultuous and passionate than other teenagers in love. Across the board, classmates and friends described them as deeply affectionate, happy, and loving.

When their senior year began in September, Hae was positively ecstatic. Having just gotten her driver's license, about to get her own car and a job, and thrilled in her relationship she says, "Have you ever been so happy that a pin would burst you open??? I have. Oh my goodness . . . how can I love him more? But the most amazing thing is that I keep on loving him more and more w/each passing moment."

That same week she heartbreakingly wrote, "Nothing can go wrong, and nothing ever will."

The euphoria was short lived, as Adnan got busier and had less time for Hae. That fall he began playing football and working as an ambulance technician, hoping to one day have a career in medicine. Hae began working at LensCrafters, further cutting into their time together. And then came the now infamous homecoming dance.

For months Aunty Shamim had been trying to convince her husband that Adnan was in a serious relationship with a girl at school. Uncle either didn't believe it or, quite frankly, didn't care. Regardless, he did his best to deflect Aunty's anxiety by telling her it wasn't true, that she was worked up over nothing. But word of the homecoming dance got around through the "Aunty grapevine": Muslim moms in the area warned other moms about the dance.

Adnan, of course, snuck off anyway. Having rented a tuxedo, he changed at a friend's house before picking up Hae. Back home, a showdown was happening between his parents.

Tanveer, Adnan's brother, remembers coming home and hearing his mother argue with his father. All these months he had dismissed her, but tonight she would prove to him that it wasn't all in her head. Adnan was with a girl—and at a dance no less. Enough was enough, and now her husband had to take this seriously.

They bundled eight-year-old Yusuf into the car and headed to the dance. Yusuf remembers staying in the parking lot, trying to hide behind the car in embarrassment as his parents went in.

Aunty and Uncle asked some students at the entrance to go find their son and tell him his parents wanted to speak to him. Adnan showed up after a few minutes. Aunty Shamim took him by the hand and led him to the car. Hae didn't come out with Adnan, and according to Aunty, she never saw or spoke to her.

Not to be outdone by his mother, though, as soon as they returned home Adnan grabbed a bike and took off, in his tuxedo. He biked the mile and a half to school, pedaling as fast as he could because he knew that Hae was there alone, her night ruined.

Hae doesn't write about this night in her diary, though many of her friends later attested that she was deeply insulted and upset.

This event may have been a last straw of sorts for Hae, a clear indication that a relationship with Adnan meant pitting herself against his family and faith, a fight she did not want. Adnan joked about the incident with Saad and other mosque friends, laughing at his parents. Other Muslim kids got it, how crazy parents can be. Under the laughter, though, was embarrassment and regret that the girl he loved had been subjected to all this in front of her friends and teachers, no less. According to a mutual friend and classmate, Krista Meyers, Adnan was mortified about the entire ordeal.

In November Hae decides enough is enough and calls the relationship off. It wasn't a painless breakup—a note written at that time from Hae to Adnan suggests he didn't take it well, that instead of accepting her decision gracefully, he was acting like a child, ignoring and being cold to her.

She writes, "You know, people break up ALL THE TIME. Your life is NOT going to end. You'll move on and I'll move on."

Adnan wasn't angry, but he was hurt, deeply hurt, that Hae decided to end things because of what happened at the homecoming dance. That wasn't his fault, and he did his best to make it up to her. He came back to the dance, spent the rest of the night with her, apologizing for his parents. He loved Hae. He couldn't just instantly revert to being friends the way she wanted. He couldn't believe that *she* was upset that he was acting cold. She had made a unilateral decision, saying "I really couldn't give a damn about whatever you wanna say" and he was stuck with that. Her note seems stern and final, but internally Hae was conflicted. She writes, "Who would have thought we would end like this? Who would have imagined the kind of pain that comes with a broken heart? I know I'm doing the right thing . . . Oh screw it, I still love you. I would give any and everything to be in your arms."

Adnan and Hae got back together again briefly after the breakup, giving it one last chance.

12/3 (12am)
[. . .] School is pretty ok and all, and most importantly, I love Adnan. To me, it's so much of a surprise. [. . .] I feel like I can't love him anymore than I already do. But everytime I see his smile, my heart melt like the day of the Prom, when I knew I was falling in love with him. When I close my eyes, I swear I see his smiling face and see him mouth those three words that sends my heart spining. This is a true + a genuine love filled with caring, warmth, + occasional desires ☺ But nothing can turn my heart

away from him, cause he has my heart. [. . .] I love you Adnan . . . and every moment we spend together, closer we are to that day when I'll wake up in your arms to find myself complete and my life fulfilled. To us . . . alwayz.

But a few days later, Hae's diary shows her heart is wandering. By early December 1998, another young man has caught her eye: Don.

Don Clinedinst had baby-blue eyes, dirty blond hair, and a red Camaro. He was three years older than Hae and worked with her at LensCrafters. Hae and Adnan were still together, but her infatuation began the first time she laid eyes on Don in the break room.

On December 6th she writes about not being able to get Don out of her mind. She loves Adnan, she insists, but she has a serious crush on Don. She compares the two in her diary, her tall, dark, handsome but immature boyfriend and the polar opposite mature, light-eyed white boy with the crooked smile. She's torn and confused.

She writes, "I would have to die twice before I find someone who loves me as much as he does. I love you, Adnan . . . so much . . . but why Don?"

For days and days Hae goes back and forth, naming all the reasons she loves Adnan but longing for Don. She finally tells Adnan and then breaks off their relationship in mid-December. They stay friends, but it's clear that her romantic focus is now completely on Don. Hae has made her decision.

The breakup is hard on Adnan, who still loves Hae, the first love of his life. He writes, "I've known some of the happiest times with you Hae, and I've also known some of the saddest times, the hardest of which I'm going through right now. When this pain will end, I have no idea."

A friend and classmate, Ja'uan Gordon, later tells the police that Adnan was upset and teary—it was unexpected because he thought they were through the worst of it, though he knew they had been losing steam since the homecoming dance. At the same time Adnan also knew there wasn't much of a future for them. He was more ready to move on than he realized—it was all too intense for a high school romance, and after all, they still cared about each other as friends, college was not far off in the distance, and with college came college girls.

At the end of the month, Adnan and Don come face-to-face when Hae has a minor accident in the snow. Her car skids as she takes an exit ramp, hitting a curb and damaging the car. She calls Adnan, who drives to the mall to take a look. He's inspecting the car when Don happens to leave the mall, heading to his own car, which is parked nearby. Adnan and Don spend a few minutes in small talk, sizing each other up.

Hae comes out of the mall, having finished up work, and both Adnan and Don advise her not to drive the car, the damage making it risky. Don then leaves and Hae gets a ride home with Adnan, which is not odd at all to anyone who knows them. They're still close, and now tease each other about their respective love lives. Adnan joked to others about checking Don out and feeling better after having seen him. At Christmas Adnan gets Hae a frame that says "best friends" and she gets him a jacket. There is seemingly no animosity between the two; instead there seems to be a sense of relief that they no longer have to fight to stay in a difficult and dead-end relationship.

For about a month now, Hae has been making her interest known to Don, who says she was the one pursuing him. On December 31, 1998, the relationship finally takes off. Having picked Adnan up from work and then dropped him off, Hae feels a sudden urge to swing by the mall. Don isn't supposed to be working that day, but she's happy and surprised to see his car in the lot and him walking toward it. They chat, flirt, he lets her drive his Camaro. But most importantly, they agree to go on their first date.

That night is equally notable for Adnan, who meets a girl at a New Year's Eve party. Nisha Tanna is a beautiful Indian-American high school senior from Silver Springs, Maryland, about thirty miles from Baltimore. They dance together, exchange numbers, and plan to meet up sometime soon.

Hae spends New Year's Eve at Aisha Pittman's house, along with a group of friends and classmates. She falls asleep there and rushes to get to work the next day by 9:00 a.m. Don is already there when she arrives.

After work, Hae and Don drive to Aberdeen, Maryland, over forty miles away, to dine at The Olive Tree, an Italian restaurant. Hae writes about her crab cake dinner and their fun conversation. After dinner they drive back to the mall where her car is parked and sit and talk, while she hopes he'll kiss her. He doesn't.

Hae understands, writing that "he's too much of a gentleman for that."

Her next diary page is full of Don's name written repeatedly, with flourishes, underlines, in all directions. On the top she notes his cell phone number and then writes, "127 Dons," the number of times she's written his name.

They go out again on January 6, this time to the movies. Sometime around the 10th Hae tells Aisha, who later tells Becky, that she got into a fight with her mother and spent the night at Don's place. Hae's uncle reports the same thing a couple of weeks later.

Don doesn't mention this when he's questioned later, but on Tuesday, January 12, 1999, according to Don, she spends the evening at his home. Don recalls her being in a good mood, though she had said she was fighting with her mother.

According to Don, Hae returns home and calls him around midnight. As she is speaking to him, she gets another call. It's Adnan, telling her to guess where he's calling from. Hae takes a couple of guesses and then gets it right—a new cell phone! She takes down his number and says she'll call him later that night, but Adnan tells her not to worry about it. He is out right now but is heading home to go to bed.

Then, according to Adnan and others he told, she asks him a question that may haunt him for years to come.

Did he think it was possible that they would ever get back together?

Adnan says no, he didn't think so. They were better as friends.

The call was short, less than a minute and a half, and then Hae returns to her call with Don. He remembers speaking to her until close to 3:00 a.m, and then she writes another journal entry, one that perhaps belies her question to Adnan, or is a reaction to his response, before going to sleep herself. "I love you Don. I think I have found my soulmate. I love you so much. I fell in love with you the moment I opened my eyes to see you in the break room for the first time."

Those would be the last words Hae Min Lee ever wrote in her diary.

Adnan:

It was a day in the spring of our 11th grade year that I asked Hae if she would go to the Junior Prom with me. We were sitting on the steps behind the school, and I was really nervous as I began to talk. As she listened, it seemed she was trying to hold back a smile. It soon turned into a giggle, and then finally she was full-on laughing as I stammered through my words. She broke in before I could finish, and I'll never forget what she said:

"Oh my God, Adnan, you sound like the biggest dork! Yes, I'll go to prom with you, but I have to get to lacrosse practice sometime this year! Can we speed this up a bit, PLEASE?"

Of course, she said all this with that beautiful smile of hers, and I couldn't help but laugh at myself. She had this amazing ability to put you at ease, and all my nervousness had faded away.

Prior to us beginning to date, Hae and I had been casual friends. We had some of the same classes together, and we would always share a joke with each other. But I don't recall ever spending time with her outside of school. After our Junior Prom, however, we began to have long conversations on the phone each night.

It would usually take place fairly late at night. We would wait for our mothers to go to sleep, and then one of us would page the other, and then call the weather service. That way, when the other person would call, the audible ringer would never be activated, i.e., the phone wouldn't ring. The person receiving the call would already be on the line with the weather recording, and could just click over using the call-waiting feature. Many nights, we would talk on the phone until 3:00 or 4:00 a.m.

We were always mindful of the fact that our mothers would be upset it they knew about any of this. They both had very strict opinions on dating; and neither of us could have a boy/girl call the house. If it were to happen, it would cause a big hassle. We had both grown accustomed to our conservative house rules, however, and we knew how to navigate around them.

Our relationship progressed that summer in a typical, teenage fashion. Hae was a wonderful person; smart, beautiful, and caring. We'd go out to eat, go to the movies, and do all the normal things high-school kids do. We spent almost every day of that summer together. We had our small disagreements, but never any huge arguments or fights. We both treated each other with a great deal of love and respect.

Toward the end of the summer, it did begin to become a bit hectic with our mothers. They had both grown suspicious, and we found ourselves in the position of having to evade their attention and their questions. It came to a point where Hae decided we should take a break, around the time when school began.

Our subsequent break-ups would follow a similar pattern over the next few months. Something would happen with one of our families, and Hae would make the decision to call a halt to our dating. Some time would pass, and then she would initiate us getting back together again. I would be pretty sad at those times, but Hae always made sure I understood that it wasn't due to us; rather, it was because of our family situations. And she always went out of her way to be a caring and compassionate person to me. During the times we were split up, we always remained on good terms; being friendly, loving, and respectful toward each other.

Our final break-up was probably the least difficult, as by then it was clear that it would be a constant problem at home. The writing was on the wall, so to speak. It was a decision that made sense, and we had grown so close that our relationship easily transitioned into an amazing friendship.

We would spend time in school together, always joking and laughing. There were times where we socialized outside of school, in mixed company. We were comfortable enough with each other that we would confide in each other about who we were seeing or interested in. She would tease me about some girl whose phone number I told her I got, laughingly insisting that I had just received the number to Pizza Hut. And I would kid her right back for being interested in an older guy.

There was one incident in particular, I think, that really demonstrates the closeness of our friendship. One night it was snowing, and Hae had accidentally driven her car into the cinderblock base of a light pole. It happened in the parking lot of the mall where she worked. She paged me, and asked if I could come pick her up and take her home.

When I arrived, one of her co-workers was with her. His name was Don, and he was the guy she had mentioned that she was interested in dating. She introduced us, and we had a brief conversation as we looked over her car. He had offered to give Hae a ride home, but she had declined. Eventually we left, and during the drive to her home, Hae asked what my impressions of Don were. I responded that he seemed like a very nice guy, and I was impressed that he was concerned enough to offer to give her a ride home. I then proceeded to ask her if he had a twin sister, so we could both date older people. She laughed at that, and we both kept joking with each other for the rest of the drive to her home.

And that was really the tone of our friendship after we stopped dating. There wasn't any anger, resentment, pettiness, or anything negative like that. We cared enough to just want the other to be happy. Our relationship was built on love and respect, and those qualities carried over to our friendship. I think a lot of people have a huge misconception that we wanted to get married, have children together, or planned to run away if our parents didn't approve, and so forth. It was never so dramatic as that. We just really enjoyed each other, and it was very easy to transition from boyfriend/girlfriend to friends. And the fact that we began seeing other people afterward was not some big mystery to solve, so why would we jump back into the same stressful situation we just left.

The new people we were seeing didn't have the same strict family settings that we had. And anyone who has experienced this will tell you that it is easy to accommodate one strict mother, but it is almost impossible for a relationship to work with two . . .

VANISHED: MISSING HAE

———•———

Know that if the whole world gathered together to help you,
they could not unless God had decreed so.
And if the whole world gather together to harm you,
they could not unless God had decreed so.
The pens have been lifted, and the pages have dried.

Prophet Muhammad, Sunan al Tirmidhi

The jurisdiction of the Baltimore County Police Department (BCPD) is a full 612 square miles, surrounding the City of Baltimore, and it has ten precincts. The Woodlawn Precinct 2 is on Windsor Mill Road.

Officer Scott Adcock wasn't assigned to Woodlawn. He was assigned to the 3rd precinct, Garrison (now called Franklin), and he was out on routine patrol on the afternoon of January 13, 1999. Around 6:00 p.m. he was dispatched to a local home to respond to a call about a missing girl, Hae Min Lee.

When he arrived at Hae's home, Officer Adcock met with her fifteen-year-old brother, Young Lee. The officer made note of Hae's routine and her car model, and then asked for relevant telephone numbers. Adcock called the LensCrafters store in Owings Mills, where Hae was scheduled to work that evening, then called Aisha Pittman, Hae's best friend. Hae's mother had called Aisha earlier looking for Hae, and Aisha reached out to other classmates and friends—Becky Walker, Krista Meyers, and Adnan—to ask about Hae. No one had seen her.

The officer then attempted to get in touch with Hae's new boyfriend, Don. Young had retrieved Hae's diary from her bedroom (she knew her brother snuck peeks at it) to look for clues about her plans that evening and for Don's number.

Young dialed a number scribbled on her last entry from the night before. But Don didn't pick up the phone, Adnan did.

Young initially assumed he had reached Don, and when he realized that he had actually called Adnan, handed the phone to the detective.

Adnan recalls the phone call, and that it was in the evening, after school. Aisha had already called him to tell him Hae's family was looking for her and that she had spoken to a police officer. Officer Adcock asked Adnan if he had seen Hae and Adnan replied that he had seen her at school but not since. Adcock asked Adnan for his date of birth, address, and full name.

Adnan was high when he got the phone call. After breaking his Ramadan fast with a quick bite, he had lit up. He remembers feeling panicked at speaking to a police officer in this condition; he thought maybe the cop would want to meet him while he was high as a kite. But he didn't. He had other calls to make. The call to Adnan was brief: there were three incoming calls to Adnan's phone around six o'clock that night, two less than a minute long, and one lasting a bit over four minutes. Adcock's call was one of them, but there is no way to verify which one because no one—not the police, prosecution, or defense—ever retrieved the incoming call numbers in his call records.

Adnan remembers another detail: when the phone rang, he reached over from the driver's seat to get his cell phone from the car's glove compartment. He wasn't alone. He had to reach past his passenger, Jay Wilds.

It always seemed strange to me that the police would open a missing person's investigation for an eighteen-year-old with a car, pager, job, and new boyfriend within hours of her disappearing. After all, Hae was technically an adult. In fact, as of 2005, numerous jurisdictions in Maryland did mandate a twenty-four-hour waiting period before accepting adult missing person's reports. This was eventually changed through legislation that banned all such waiting periods throughout the state, a change unrelated to Hae's case.

While such a waiting period may not have been the Baltimore County Police Department's procedure in 1999, filing a missing person's report within two hours—even before the police had spoken to Hae's current boyfriend—seems highly unusual. But roughly seven months prior, another eighteen-year-old girl had disappeared from Woodlawn and been found killed.

Jada Denita Lambert disappeared one day on her way to work at a local mall. She was found when an anonymous call to 911 alerted the police that there was a young woman's body in a shallow stream in Red Herring Park in the northeast part of Baltimore City. Jada was fully clothed but missing all of her personal property. An autopsy would later confirm she had been raped and strangled.

At the time that Hae disappeared, Jada's murder was yet unsolved. On the one hand, fear of a serial killer may have prompted a quick response by authorities to Hae's not showing up. On the other hand, Jada disappeared in Baltimore

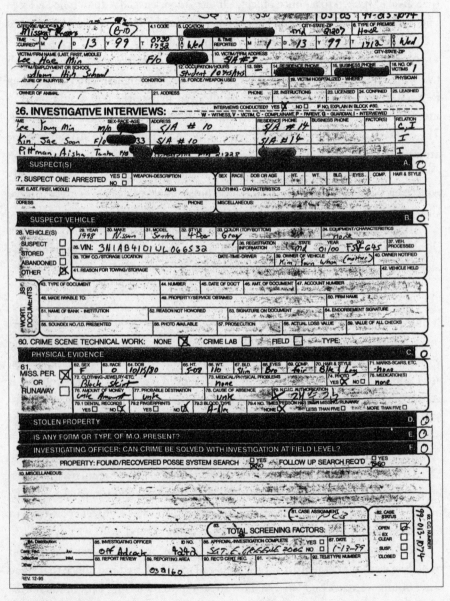

Original missing person's report

City. Her case was never with BCPD, so maybe the County Police never even knew about her.

According to Adcock's testimony, the rest of his evening was devoted to filing the necessary paperwork for the case and trying to connect with Don.

The report prepared for that evening's activities identifies Hae as "victim," another thing that has always struck me as odd this early on in a case.

Back at headquarters that evening Officer Adcock enters Hae's information from the missing person's report into the NCIC, the National Crime Information Center, a massive FBI-run database.

But Adcock makes a mistake; he fails to enter Hae's car information from his written report. These are vital details. After all, Hae disappeared along with her car.

Around 1:30 a.m. on the 14th, about ten hours after Hae disappeared, Officer Adcock is finally able to reach Don.

The report is extraordinarily short. It reads, "I spoke to victim Lee's boyfriend Mr. Donald Robert Clinedinst III, DOB [redacted], M/W. Mr. Clinedinst advised that he does not know the whereabouts of Ms. Lee. Mr. Clinedinst advised that he talked to Ms. Lee last on 1/12/99. It should be noted that I spoke to Mr. Clinedinst on 1/14/99 at 0130 hours."

An additional report taken by another officer notes that Don had not *seen* Hae since January 12th, a slight difference from Adcock's report, which notes they hadn't spoken since then. Still, there are no details as to Don's whereabouts on that day, whether he and Hae had plans to meet, and neither report mentions that he spoke with Hae into the early morning hours of January 13th, though that may be what he meant when he said he spoke to her on the 12th. After the conversations the police do not go meet with him.

By 2:30 a.m. on the 14th, the parking lots of local hotels, motels, and high schools have been searched for Hae and her car, and the sheriff's office of Harford County, the county where Don lives over thirty miles away, has also been alerted with requests to check the area for her vehicle. But no clue as to her whereabouts emerges.

At 2:48 a.m. Hae's car plates are run through the NCIC system, something that generally happens in two instances: a patrol officer runs the plates of a suspicious car he or she spots, or because the officer, having been alerted to keep a lookout for a car with these plates, uses the query as a method to "save" the plate numbers on their system. The query can be run two ways, through mobile terminals that are actually in the patrol cars themselves, or by calling into headquarters and having a dispatcher run the plates for you.

The 2:48 a.m. query was run through the Harford County Emergency

DATE	TIME	TERMINAL ID	ORI	AGENCY
011499	0248	HC69	MD013143N	Harford Co. Emergency Operation
011499	0446	ZBER	MD0030627	Baltimore Co. P. D. MDT311
011599	0324	ZBAS	MD00301N5	Baltimore Co. P. D. MDT168
012999	1027	BC4A	MD0030121	Baltimore Co. P. D.
020499	0335	ZBAK	MD00301M7	Baltimore Co. P. D. MDT160
020499	0944	ZBFT	MD0030676	Baltimore Co. P. D. MDT349

The six times Hae's license plates were run through the NCIC system

Services dispatch in response to a "Be On the Look Out" (BOLO) alert from BCPD; a second query run through the NCIC system came from a Baltimore County terminal at 4:46 a.m. Over the following two weeks, Hae's plates will be run through the NCIC system four more times, all from Baltimore County Police terminals.

The first two times the plates are run, it seems certain that they were in response to the BOLO; but the last two queries run on her plates, both on February 4th, seem to indicate something else entirely. Not just to a layperson, but also to law enforcement officers who reviewed the data. The checks are done a number of weeks after the original BOLO was issued, which means they were probably not run in order to "save" the numbers. They are also done by two different mobile terminals, at 3:35 a.m. and 9:35 a.m. respectively, which raises the likelihood that two different police officers on consecutive patrols came across Hae's vehicle and ran the plates.

If that is actually what happened, the tragedy of it is that these officers would have gotten no indication that this car was connected to an investigation. Those queries would have returned nothing. Adcock's failure to enter Hae's car information from the missing person's report into the NCIC system means there was no alert connected to her tags.

It won't be until February 10 that the database is revised to include the missing car information and actually link it to the missing person's case, but then the VIN, the vehicle identification number, is entered incorrectly. On February 20th, the VIN is corrected. But her plates are never run again.

Quite an investigative failure by any measure.

In the early morning hours of January 14th, not long after Officer Adcock spoke with Don and shortly after Harford and Baltimore County Police had checked the area for Hae's car, things got more complicated.

Shortly before sunrise, a storm hit Baltimore and brought the city to a halt for days.

Overnight, the region had frozen over. From Baltimore to Washington, D.C., trees were coming down left and right, covered in heavy, solid ice, and roads had become treacherous, deadly, with over an inch of frozen cover in some places.

The National Weather Service reported, "After a half to three-quarter inch of ice accumulated on trees and wires, 40 mph winds was enough to bring many of them down. Trees fell on cars, houses, utility lines and roads. The Governor declared a state of Emergency in Harford, Baltimore, Carroll, Howard and Montgomery Counties. About a half a million customers were without power and 800 pedestrians were reported injured from falls on ice."

Emergency rooms were packed with patients who had fallen or suffered a car accident, while newspapers reported hundreds of downed power lines and the struggle of emergency services to respond to storm-related injuries and calls. People were calling it the worst storm in years.

While Governor Parris Glendenning ordered a state of emergency in six Maryland counties, Baltimore was hit worse than southern areas in the storm's path—temperatures dropped lower in the city than in other parts of the state, down to 18 degrees Fahrenheit, well below the freezing point.

This storm may have impacted the early investigation significantly. Not only were police resources stretched to meet emergency needs, but on January 14th and 15th, Thursday and Friday, school was closed. The following Monday was the Martin Luther King holiday, and school was also closed. This meant that Hae's classmates and friends, who may have ordinarily been a bit more concerned about her not appearing at school for those three days, were essentially enjoying their time off because of the weather.

This, remember, was a time before every teenager had a cell phone. Most of their contact was either at school or over landlines, many of which were down because of the weather. The kids Adcock contacted on the evening of the 13th didn't take much notice of Hae's failure to show up at home or work that day because they knew that Hae was deeply in love with her new boyfriend and also had been having trouble at home; she could easily be weathering the actual and familial storm with him. And it also was common for the group of friends to get calls from parents, or other friends, searching for one of them. They figured Hae's family was doing the same. So it wasn't until they returned to school after the five-day break the following Tuesday that they realized Hae was still missing.

Still, many of them assumed Hae was with Don, and one of them, Debbie

Warren, was so sure she was with him that she made it her business to find out. Debbie, also a Magnet Program student, set up a fake e-mail account to reach out to Don. She had met him once when she went to the movies with him, Hae, and Aisha. But for this covert operation, she wanted to fish for information about Hae without revealing her identity, believing "he was hiding her."

After communicating a couple of times over e-mail she fessed up to her identity and they agreed to speak over the phone. That conversation, much to the surprise of police at a later interview, lasted seven hours. They spoke primarily about Hae, and over the course of those hours, her concern that Don had something to do with her disappearance diminished. He seemed genuinely upset and worried about Hae, mentioned that perhaps Adnan had something to do with her being missing, and by the time their conversation was over Debbie felt that she "knew him." She crossed him off her suspect list.

It wasn't until the first week after Hae's disappearance that her friends and classmates began to worry in earnest about her. Aisha Pittman, her best friend, kept the Magnet Program kids apprised of the situation

According to students and friends of Adnan and Hae, some of whom would go on to become witnesses, there was nothing unusual in Adnan's behavior after Hae's disappearance. These were the last few months of senior year, and many of these top students had already completed the credits needed to graduate. Many were taking part-time classes, working elsewhere, or just not showing up as frequently.

After it became clear that Hae hadn't just taken off for a few days, and when the media began reporting her disappearance, Adnan started to worry. He had no relationship with Hae's family, they were opposed to their relationship after all, and couldn't call her house. But Hae's girlfriends were calling to check in with the family, and often in class there would be discussions during which Adnan was now becoming visibly upset and concerned. Aisha would also page Hae every so often, with no response.

At school the kids started to think that perhaps Hae, upset with her mother, had taken off for California to live with her stepfather. The California rumors further muddied the waters for Hae's classmates and friends.

In the report of an interview with police on March 26th, 1999, Debbie is asked who started the California rumors. She responds, unsure, "Um, I don't know that for sure, probably me and Ayesha [sic] cause we were the only ones who knew um, that she had family up there that she could possibly been living with, um, some people had asked and you know just about every day someone would ask us, and you know, where we thought she was."

But a January 27th police interview makes it clear that Aisha wasn't the root of the rumor.

The report reads, "Hae told Aisha that she had problems with her mom, but it was nothing that would make her leave. Hae talked about California, but she never talked about going there."

Aisha's remarks are isolated, in an otherwise extremely brief report, and seem to indicate that she was asked specifically by the police about the possibility that Hae could have gone to California, meaning this was a theory they were exploring, perhaps because Don had mentioned something similar to the authorities in an earlier interview.

In a January 22nd interview with a detective, Don, independently and unprompted, stated that although Hae had no plans to go anywhere, she had mentioned living in California in the past and said she'd like to live there again one day.

Could it be that Debbie and Don's seven-hour conversation took place before January 22nd, and in that conversation Debbie was the one who suggested Hae may have gone to California? Or was it the other way around? Was Don the original source of the rumor?

It's doubtful that Debbie would go to such lengths to investigate whether Hae was with Don if she thought California was a possibility. And the first time any mention of Hae's interest in California appears in any of the documents is Don's January 22nd interview. It seems, then, that the root of the rumor that Hae might be in California was Don himself, and the rumor spread with the help of the police, who asked others about it, and Debbie, who began mentioning it at school after their marathon chat. It is entirely possible that Don offered this information because Hae had indeed mentioned it to him. But it seems unlikely to me that Hae, who was planning and had paid for a trip to France with her class, according to her French teacher, who was about to graduate from high school, who never mentioned it in her diary, and who was newly in love, would consider just taking off to California. But the idea that she might have left gave her friends, who were confused and worried about her disappearance, something to hold on to. The trail of this story, however, leads back to Don, and the police weren't the only place he planted this seed.

Enter the intrepid investigatory services of the Enehey Group.

"The Enehey Group offers its clients services unparalleled in Investigative Research today. Combining a personal approach with the latest information gathering technology and techniques, we strive to provide our services while maintaining complete confidentiality at all times."

An Enehey Group's investigative report about Hae's disappearance submitted to the Baltimore City Police begins with a list of a mind-bogglingly diverse array of services provided by the agency:

> *Business investigations, missing persons investigations, computer fraud investigations, industrial counterespionage, translations and interpreting, software design, market design, genealogical investigations, historical investigations, compiling psychological and behavioral profiles, consulting on educational issues for emotionally challenged and disadvantage youth, and Pro Bono cases for law enforcement*

Notwithstanding consultants, in all meaningful respects for Adnan's case, the Enehey Group seems to be comprised of exactly one person—Mandy Johnson.

Ms. Johnson's portfolio has since expanded even further. She is now also a self-published novelist focusing on espionage, terrorism, and the Middle East.

In January 1999, Tae Su Kim, a Baltimore-area Korean-American business owner, brought in the Enehey Group (Johnson was apparently a family friend) to investigate his missing niece.

The five-page report on Hae begins with basic information. It notes that the missing person's file is with the Baltimore County Police Department, assigned to one Detective Sgt. Joe O'Shea, who took over the case from Officer Adcock. Mandy Johnson, the report notes, has a good relationship with O'Shea; she is in contact with him daily, and she has been sharing her investigative findings with him.

The findings are limited, but interesting. Hae's family has provided full access to Hae's belongings, including her diary and computer. Hae's room appears to have been searched, a routine investigatory procedure, since the report notes that Hae has "left behind her Korean passport and diary."

Johnson tracks down Hae's e-mail accounts and her AOL username, and indicates that she was known to spend time on Asian chat rooms.

While the report notes that Hae's profile has last been checked on January 16, three days after Hae disappeared, it makes no mention of who may have checked the account or who knew of Hae's Asian chat room activity. The interests and likes Hae lists in her online profile show that they've been entered after she began dating Don: "Looking in his blue gray eyes, fast cars like his Camaro, driving to BelAir, selling glasses and her beauty, spending as much time as possible in the lab. Occupation: Part-time sales, Full-time Girlfriend."

Johnson notes that Hae ends her profile with, "I love you and miss you Donnie."

Johnson was astute enough to profile Hae's ex-boyfriend and interview her current boyfriend. But her assessment of Adnan relies on Hae's diary and perhaps her talks with others, though that's unclear. She never meets with or speaks to Adnan directly. How she comes to the conclusion that Adnan is "known to be possessive and domineering but not necessarily violent" isn't explained, but it portends the role she will ultimately play in his fate.

The treatment of Don, whom Mandy interviewed, is entirely benign. Calling him mature and articulate, she spends no time on his background or ethnicity, as she had with Adnan, or even the kind of relationship he had with Hae. Instead, the short write-up of Johnson's interview with Don focuses on his knowledge of where Hae may have gone. Again California comes up, and this time he also mentions a friend of Hae's, which doesn't appear anywhere else in the record, saying she might be at this friend's home. When asked how Hae might travel to California, Don says that she might park at the "satellite parking facility" of the local airport, BWI, and fly from there. Either that, or drive all the way to California.

We don't have a precise date for this report, or for when Johnson spoke to Don, but we can deduce that it was after Detective O'Shea spoke to him on January 25th and before the first week of February, since the report notes that Johnson will notify long-distance truck drivers at the Port of Baltimore in the first week of February so missing person posters can be posted at rest stops in the area. The detectives will also meet with the family during the first week of February, and then the media will be alerted.

Other undertakings that the report indicates are completed or planned: various police jurisdictions have been alerted, airline reservations checked, Asian chat lines to be randomly monitored, Hae's diary to be analyzed, and Korean community members and religious organizations notified.

I have to note here the oddity of an independent investigator, who is not even a licensed private investigator or a former law enforcement officer, becoming so deeply involved in a law enforcement matter. Still, it does seem for all intents and purposes that Johnson was working as a representative for the family to coordinate many aspects of the missing person's investigation. In fact, she may have been doing more than the police themselves in some regard. All very commendable—with one significant exception.

A memo written months later indicates that this involvement may have ultimately derailed the investigation, something we won't discover until fifteen years later.

On January 22, about a week after Hae disappeared, Detective O'Shea gives Don a call. The report taken of this conversation, which is not written up until February 11, is much more extensive than the report taken by Officer Adcock a week prior.

This time, Don tells the police that Hae had spent the evening of the 12th with him. Don's parents are divorced and he lives with his father, which is where Hae must have been visiting him. Hae returned to her home late at night and had spoken with him on the phone until about 3:00 a.m. He says Hae was scheduled to work on the 13th from six to ten o'clock p.m. and that she was going to call him afterward, apparently to meet up. This is the first time Don's own whereabouts on the 13th are mentioned. He says that he was "lent out," that he filled in for someone else at a store he doesn't usually work at, the Hunt Valley LensCrafters.

He tells O'Shea that he worked there from about 9:00 a.m. to 6:00 p.m. and arrived home around seven o'clock, at which point his father told him to call the Owings Mills store. When Don called, he was told that Hae had not shown up for work. His colleagues must have told him the police were looking for Hae, and yet Adcock wasn't able to get in touch with Don until 1:30 a.m. that night. Don didn't attempt to call Hae's family, or page Hae, or reach out to the police himself.

The police never actually visit the Hunt Valley store, or ask for Don's timesheets or pay stubs to verify that he was working there on that day. Instead, they verify Don's whereabouts from the manager at the Owings Mills store, a woman named Cathy Michel, who met with O'Shea on February 1st. The report from that day is short, but precise.

So precise, in fact, that it seems Michel must have been reading off of Don's timecard from January 13 because she cites the exact times he arrived and left work. That is the extent of the police verification of Don's alibi. After a February 4th meeting, they never call or visit him again.

It is not until months later that anyone attempts to actually get a copy of Don's employment records for that day, but the document produced by LensCrafters turns out to raise more questions than it answers.

Over the next few days O'Shea attempts to get a handle on what Hae's plans and activities were for the afternoon she disappeared. He first interviews Adnan on January 25th. Adnan tells him that he last saw Hae on the 13th at school, during school hours, after which he went to track. Adnan tells him he didn't see Hae leave school, that school was closed for the next two days, and he had no idea where she was. Adnan explains that while they had been in a relationship they had kept it private because of their families, and that they had broken up but remained good friends. The detective has a few calls with Adnan and schedules a meeting with him, a meeting that was to take place without the presence of his parents because Adnan felt uncomfortable discussing the relationship in front of them. The meeting is set for February 10th, but never takes place because of an unexpected development.

O'Shea then interviews both Aisha and Debbie over the next couple of days, January 27th and 28th, trying to determine Hae's last known movements. Aisha reports she last saw Hae on the 13th at 2:15, when school was dismissed, and that she was in good spirits. Debbie says she last saw Hae at around 3:00 p.m., near the gym, and that Hae told her she was going to see Don at the mall. But neither Aisha nor Debbie actually saw her leave the school.

It isn't until February 1st that a flurry of activity seems to indicate that foul play is suspected and the police are looking at possible suspects.

O'Shea takes a trip to Woodlawn High to meet and interview a number of people, including the French teacher, Hope Schab, track coach Gerald Russell, and athletic trainer and teacher Inez Butler. His questions for Schab are about Adnan and Hae's relationship. Schab mentions that the only trouble she knew of between Adnan and Hae happened at the homecoming dance, but that they were still friends. Russell is asked whether Adnan attended track practice on the 13th and he's unsure—he doesn't take attendance and recalls that it was Ramadan, and during Ramadan athletes are required to attend practice but don't have to run.

Butler's statement seems to contradict what others have said. According to her, she last spoke to Hae on the 13th and Hae was upset, having problems at home, and wanted to contact her father in California. Butler also recounts that Hae told her she would not be at the wrestling match that evening, the first time a wrestling match is mentioned.

The wrestling match becomes more of a focus, and part of the case narrative, with a later discovery of a note Hae has written. But ultimately it will turn out that, like so many other witnesses, Butler is not remembering the right day.

February 1 is the same day O'Shea checks in with Cathy Michel at Lens-Crafters in Owings Mill and she confirms Don's alibi, and then the detective calls Adnan again. This time, however, he raises a question that he had not asked previously.

Did Adnan ask Hae for a ride after school that day? According to Adcock's report on the 13th Adnan told the officer that he was going to be getting a ride from her, but he ran late and she got tired of waiting and must have left. Adnan denies telling Adcock this, saying he had his own car and didn't need a ride that day. It is odd that O'Shea didn't bring this issue up with Adnan previously. This raises the question of whether that prior report did in fact contain that information initially, or it was added later. There is also the possibility that Adnan, who sometimes got a ride with Hae to the far side of the school for track practice, didn't really consider that "a ride." It could be simple miscommunication. Perhaps he assumed the police meant an off-campus ride, which he normally didn't ask for because he usually had his car and because he knew Hae had to pick up her cousin. Did he forget that he asked for a ride? Then there is the possibility that Adnan did ask for a ride, but later, worried about the implication, he lied to the police about it.

The thing was this: Adnan did have his own car, but he didn't have it with him during much of the day on January 13. He had loaned it to Jay Wilds, his friend Stephanie's boyfriend and his go-to guy for weed, and hadn't gotten it back until after track practice. Whether or not he had asked Hae for a ride after school, while the car was with Jay, this issue will come back to haunt Adnan.

On their February 1, 1999, school visit, the police didn't just question some of the staff; they deputized one in particular to find out intimate details about Adnan and Hae's relationship.

Hope Schab, the twenty-seven-year-old French teacher, was not much older than her students. She considered Hae, who worked as a student assistant in her French class, to be a friend. So when the police asked Schab to question students about things like where Adnan and Hae would meet for sex, she didn't hesitate. She made a list of questions, and word eventually got back to Adnan that his sex life was the subject of Schab's queries. But he didn't just hear it, he saw the actual list of questions in Debbie's school planner when be borrowed it, and, according to Debbie, he returned the planner without the list, insinuating that he took them. Adnan doesn't remember this incident, but he thinks it could be possible because he would have been shocked to have seen it, though on the other hand he doesn't give much stock to Debbie's statements

At this point Adnan had been twice contacted by the police, the night that Hae disappeared by Officer Adcock, and then on February 1st by Detective O'Shea. The sudden whispers about him at school were unsettling; he was already deeply concerned by Hae's disappearance, and now a teacher was digging around about his sex life. The last thing he needed was word to get back to his parents, who had no idea that he and Hae had been sexually involved. Not even his Muslim friends knew that, at least no one other than his best friend, my brother, Saad. But now a teacher, of all people, was asking his friends, including those who went to the same mosque and whose mothers knew his mother, about where he'd been having sex with Hae.

Community gossip moved at lightning speed. The prospect of his mother finding out that he'd been having sex was terrifying, as it would be to any level-headed seventeen-year-old Pakistani kid.

According to Schab, Adnan approached her and asked her, rather politely, to stop prying into his sex life. He told her he "would appreciate it" if she stopped asking questions around the school because it could potentially cause problems with his parents. He had no idea that the police had asked her to ask those questions, but assumed that she was playing sleuth herself.

It's both interesting and telling that the official police report doesn't mention the role Schab was asked to play. But both Schab and Debbie Warren will testify to this less than a year later.

REPORT OF INVESTIGATION

NAME OF SUBJECT	DATE SUBMITTED
SCHAB, HOPE	02/14/99

	TYPE OF INVESTIGATION
	LEE MISSING PERSON 99-013-1074

NOTICE: THE INFORMATION CONTAINED IN THIS REPORT IS HIGHLY CONFIDENTIAL. DISSEMINATION OF INFORMATION TO ANY PERSON WITHOUT A NEED TO KNOW IS STRICTLY FORBIDDEN.

REPORT OF FINDINGS:

INTERVIEWED: SCHAB, HOPE

WHITE FEMALE, DOB ██████

████████████████

TELEPHONE ██████

RELATION: FORMER TEACHER OF HAE LEE

On 02/01/99 the assigned interviewed Ms. Hope Schab. Ms. Schab said Hae works for her as a teacher's aide and Hae was a student in Ms. Schab's French class. Ms. Schab said Hae was excited about a trip to France which is planned for 06/99. Ms. Schab said she could not think of any reason why Hae would leave without telling anyone.

Ms. Schab said the only problem Hae had at school was at the Homecoming dance. Hae went to the dance with Adnan and Adnan's parents came to the school. They were upset that Adnan was with Hae and they had to be asked to leave.

Ms. Schab said Adnan and Hae were still friends. Hae was very happy about her relationship with Donald Clinedinst and always talked about him.

On February 2nd the police contact authorities in Hayward, California, and ask them to visit Hae's mother's ex-boyfriend or fiancé (reports are conflicting about the relationship) who Butler was presumably referring to as Hae's father. They check in with him, and do a sweep of the area for her car, but find nothing.

On February 3rd, the detective checks to see if Adnan is listed in MILES, the Maryland Interagency Law Enforcement System, an online database. His records are clear. O'Shea does not check on anyone else.

On February 4th, the *Baltimore Sun* puts out a request for information on Hae:

Hae Min Lee, who lived with family members was last seen about 3 p.m. January 13th at Woodlawn Senior High School, where she was a student. After school she was supposed to pick up her 6-year-old niece and go to work, police said, but she did not do either.

It's fair to assume the newspaper was given this information by the police, so at that point their theory was certainly that (1) Hae was at school until 3:00 p.m. and (2) she had plans to work that night, not attend a wrestling match.

Once the police take the case public, they begin actively organizing searches for Hae and her car. On February 6th, police search the areas around Woodlawn High with dogs, and follow the banks of the western part of Dead Run Stream into Leakin Park.

Two days later, on February 8th, Adnan calls Detective O'Shea, which we know from his cell phone records, but there are no notes of that conversation anywhere. It is possible the phone call was regarding their meeting scheduled for the 10th. Also on the 8th, nearly a month after Hae's disappearance, O'Shea retrieves Hae's computer from her family, and the Computer Crimes Unit issues a subpoena to America Online for records connected to Hae's e-mail accounts.

Clearly the police are now looking for communications from or to Hae leading up to January 13th. But this line of inquiry will come to a screeching halt, and frustratingly be completely forgotten, because on February 9, 1999, the body of a young woman is discovered in Leakin Park.

Adnan:

After January 13, the next two days were snow days, and then it was the weekend. We talked about it in school that first week, and there was a general assumption Hae was either staying with her boyfriend, or perhaps she went to California. She had spent her sophomore year in California, and we all knew that her father and other family members/friends lived there. As far as her missing school; well, that really was not an issue for most of us who were in the Magnet Program. We had accumulated enough credits to graduate by the beginning of our senior year. Some of us would take half-days, or even skip the whole day together. We may have had jobs or internships to attend, or we may have just gone somewhere and hung out.

Going into the second week was when we all became more concerned because no one had heard from her. We all knew that Hae's mother had called the police on the first day. And the officer had contacted several of us. Any notion that something was really wrong was belied by the knowledge that Hae was someone who always had it together, and surely she was all right. I remember thinking, "Man, Hae's gonna be in so much trouble with her Mom when she gets home."

By the third week, that worry had turned to fear. No one knew what to think. Krista and Aisha would call Hae's house every day and speak to her family, to see if there was any news. The rest of us would talk to Krista and Aisha to find out if there was anything they had learned. But there was never anything for them to pass on to us.

CHAPTER 3

A BODY

———————•———————

Verily we belong to God and to Him we shall return.

Holy Quran 2:156

Alonzo Sellers is no stranger to the law. His list of charges is robust, including an occasional assault here and there, but mostly they reveal that he suffers from a rather colorful compulsion. Between 1994 and 2015, Sellers had been charged with indecent exposure eight times, once jangling his junk whilst completely in the buff right in front of a female police officer. Sellers is a habitual streaker.

In 1999, Sellers was forty years old and worked as a groundskeeper at Coppin State University in Baltimore, less than five miles from his home in Gwynn Oak, Maryland. The total travel time, during non-rush hours, was approximately fifteen minutes.

On February 9, 1999, Sellers was at work when he found himself in need of a plane to shave down a doorframe. He decided to go home and fetch one that afternoon.

According to Sellers, he arrived home, grabbed a twenty-two-ounce beer and the plane he needed, and headed back. He was in his truck, traveling west on Franklintown Road. A few miles from the college he felt the call of nature—the beer having run its course—so he pulled over.

Police reports don't indicate where he pulled over. There was no space on his side of the road. There was a small place to pull over on the opposite side, where he ended up making his discovery.

But he didn't stay by the side of the road. Ostensibly searching for a place to urinate, he wandered more than a hundred feet into the woods north of the road, the ground covered in places by spots of snow and ice, and he came to a stop at a large fallen tree close to the water. A video taken by Adnan's attorney Cristina Gutierrez months later in September 1999, found easily on YouTube, shows the trek Sellers would have taken on this particularly cold day—the temperature hovered between 30 and 40°F—an unlikely slog for a simple leak.

Then, according to Sellers, he stepped over the tree, unzipped his pants, and froze. He had nearly stepped on something.

Peeking through the dirt, a few yards from the stream and close to the log, was a patch of black hair. A bit of white fabric poked up through the dark earth next to the hair. A few feet farther, a small mound rose up slightly, the outline of a hip, dipping back into the dirt.

**POLICE DEPARTMENT
BALTIMORE, MARYLAND**

DET. GREG MACGILLIVARY
2-9-99
BODY IN PARK
FEMALE BODY
IN WOODS

CHIEF COLLINS
COPPIN ST. SECURITY
CHIEF. T/P 383-5634

SUBJECT NAMED
ALONZO SELLERS
FOUND BODY WHILE
TAKING A PISS.

MARCUS

Sellers zipped his pants up, forgetting to urinate, and made his panicked way back to the road and his truck.

On that bitingly cold February day, far from the road, between a stream and a dead tree in Leakin Park, Sellers had found a body.

Chief of Security Ronald Collins from Coppin State College called Baltimore City's Police Homicide Unit at approximately 1:20 p.m. on February 9, 1999, to report Sellers' discovery. According to Sellers, he had raced back to work, upset and unnerved. Shortly afterward Detectives Greg MacGillivary and William Ritz arrived at Coppin to meet Sellers, and he directed them to the 4400 block of Franklintown Road. The detectives, accompanied by Sellers, made their way to Leakin Park, where he led them to his horrid find.

The city surveyor, Phillip Buddemeyer, would later testify that he nearly stepped on the body, it was so difficult to see. The sun had begun to set, which may have added to his trouble in seeing what pictures of the burial site, taken with floodlights set around the perimeter, clearly show—a partially buried female body. In the light of day, when Sellers had been there hours earlier, it may have been much more apparent.

The body lay nearly parallel to the far side of a forty-foot tree, also referred to as a log in the records, hidden from the road. The head pointed southeast, feet pointed northwest, and both log and body were at a roughly 45-degree angle from the road, the farthest end reaching toward Dead Run Creek.

The victim was announced DOA at 1400 hours.

As dusk fell, the crime scene unit began excavating the body, brushing away the few inches of gathered earth to uncover, bit by bit, the slender frame of a young Asian woman.

She lay on her right side, her left leg on top of her right leg, her torso slightly twisted so that her head was turned facing downward at a 45-degree angle from the ground. Her head almost rested on her outstretched right arm, as if asleep. Her right arm didn't lie flat, instead it angled upward, bent at the elbow, and her right hand poked through the dirt, slender, small fingers frozen in the air. A single large rock had been placed on that arm, maybe to force it down, an indication that perhaps the body (or at least that arm and hand) were in rigor when she was left there.

Her left arm was twisted behind her, bent at 90 degrees, her left hand resting against her back.

She was clothed, but her clothing was disheveled. She wore a white jacket over a gray-blue blouse and, from photographs though not mentioned in reports,

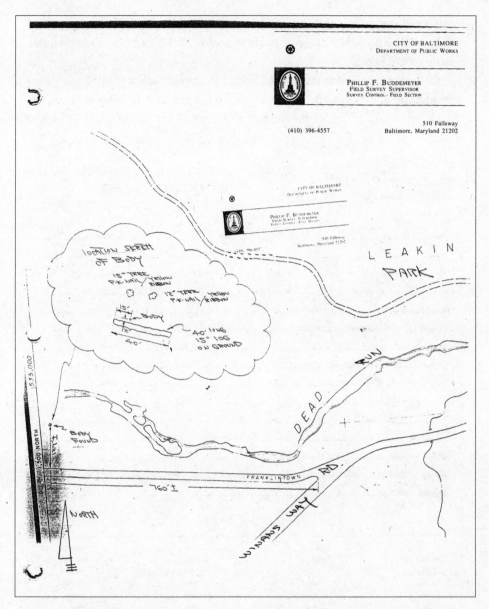

Crime scene sketch

a white knit shirt inside of that, both of which were bunched up in the front. Under the blouse her bra was pulled above her breasts, exposing them. Her long black skirt was gathered above her waist, she wore underwear, and her pantyhose were mostly intact, with a few small but distinct tears. She had no shoes on, but wore a white metal school ring, a second white metal interlocking ring, and two necklaces—a gold one with a charm and a silver one with a heart pendant.

If anything, it was abundantly clear that she was not carefully placed into this spot. The body was in an unnatural position. She had been dumped and hastily covered over.

The body was taken to the Chief Medical Examiner's office where it was properly identified, though the police must have immediately suspected who it was. It took some effort for the medical examiner to get partial prints from the

---

OFFICE OF THE CHIEF MEDICAL EXAMINER
STATE OF MARYLAND
111 PENN STREET
BALTIMORE, MARYLAND 21201

BODY RECEIPT RECORD

Name _____ UNK 99-029 _____ Date 2-9-99

Address _____ Zip _____

Age _____ Race W Sex F Height _____ Weight _____ Decomp. _____

Insp. _____ Autopsy number _____ Medical examiner _____

Time case started _____ A.M. P.M. Assistant _____ Photograph _____

Viewable _____ Not viewable _____ Biohazard _____ because of _____

Pronounced by Det. Carew _____ Date 2-9-99 Time 1400 A.M. P.M.

Baltimore City X County _____ DME _____

Received from Phila. MK _____ Date 1/99 Time 5:05 A.M. P.M.

Agency/Firm X Scid

Scene 4400 N. Franklintown RD

Hospital _____ Funeral home _____

OCME investigator _____

Received at OCME by William Caldwell _____ Date _____ Time A.M. P.M. _____

Searched at OCME by // //

Personal effects of _____

Hat ____	Shorts ____	Wallet ____	Bracelet ____
O/Coat ____	U/clothes ____	License ____	Dentures ____
S/Coat ____	Slip ____	Cash ____	Comb ____
Jacket ____	B/suit ____	Coins ____	Knife ____
Sweater ✓	Hose ✓	Credit cards ____	Glasses ____
Blue Shirt ✓	Shoes ____	Keys ____	Other:
T-Shirt ____	Boots ____	Watch ____	____
Blouse ____	Hosp. gwn. ____	Rings 2 on Rt Hand	____
Dress ____	Pajamas ____	Necklace ✓ on Body	____
Pants ____	NONE ____	Earrings ____	NONE ____

Released by _____ , OCME Date _____ Time A.M. P.M. _____

Released to _____ Firm _____

Clothing: none ____ destroyed ____ held by _____ released with body ____

Valuables: none ____ Effects released to _____

body, which were compared to latent prints from the Lee home. The victim had sustained blunt force trauma to two parts of her head, the rear right portion and right side, causing "focal and poorly delineated right occipital subgaleal and right temporalis muscle hemorrhage."

The hyoid bone, which supports the tongue, was dislocated. The cause of death was strangulation.

The young victim was conclusively identified as Hae Min Lee. The missing person's case was now a homicide.

The crime scene report, dated June 10, 1999 (reports in this case often being written months after an event) reads:

> *The crime scene is found in the 4400 blk. N. Franklintown Road within Leakin Park. A body is located partially buried approximately 127 feet from the road, next to a fallen tree, within a wooded area in a shallow grave.*
>
> *A empty half pint bottle is located several feet from the remains along with a section of clothes line.*
>
> *Feathers are located on a section of the fallen tree, same are photographed and recovered.*
>
> *Six 9mm. cartridge casings along with thirteen .40 caliber cartridge casings are observed in the street and along the roadside. These casings are photographed and recovered.*
>
> *A rolled condom and wrapper are also observed along side of the road. These items are photographed and recovered.*
>
> *Several Block Buster cases are observed on the opposite side of the street, these items are photographed and recovered.*
>
> *Several tire tracks are discovered in the soil just off the roadside which is described as a parking area. These tracks are photographed and casts are made to preserve the indentations.*
>
> *After the body is disinterred, a fiber is observed under U.V. light, on the victim's outer garments [sic]. A second fiber is found after the remains are removed. This fiber is observed on top of the soil, and is illuminated under U.V. light. These fibers are recovered and are submitted into evidence at the Evidence Control Section with the proper Laboratory requests.*
>
> *On 10 February 1999 at approximately 0900 hours, an [sic] Post Mortem Examination is conducted on the victim that is disinterred from Leakin Park. The remains are that of an Asian Female approximately seventeen to twenty years of age. The examination is conducted by Doctor Aquino, Associate*

Medical Examiner and supervised by Doctor Marguerite Korrell Deputy Chief Medical Examiner.

At the conclusion of the examination, it was determined that the victim met her demise as a result of Manual Strangulation. Doctor Korrell ruled the manner of death a Homicide.

According to the crime scene narrative, written the same day by Detectives MacGillivary and Carew, the area was cordoned off, and photographs and video of the body were taken. As the medical examiner and crime lab technicians got to work, the detectives turned their attention to Sellers.

His story of how he discovered Hae's body would raise eyebrows in any event, but particularly so because of his criminal record. A history of streaking certainly makes it less likely that a man would take such pains to be discreet.

Having been to the burial site numerous times, to me the story seems unlikely. There is no path back to the site. Some have suggested that Sellers may have been back there streaking, but streaking technically requires an audience.

According to Sellers, he had downed a 22-ounce beer in a matter of minutes, and taken a longer, more winding route back to work. The natural route would have been Windsor Mill Avenue, a main thoroughfare that is not only shorter, but has more lanes and would have been nearly clear around lunchtime. Equally problematic: his home in Gwynn Oak is virtually across the street from Woodlawn High.

All of these things should have bothered the police, and initially it seems they were suspicious, because they subjected Sellers to two different polygraph tests.

It's not unheard of for the perpetrator of a murder to alert the authorities or call in a tip themselves related to the crime or the victim. But in this case it seems unlikely, given Sellers' panicked reaction and fairly innocuous criminal record, that he had anything to do with the crime. Reporting the body was, if anything, the act of a good Samaritan.

The question was not so much whether Sellers had committed the crime, but whether he had heard something that led him to look for the body. And that's precisely what the first polygraph test sought to determine.

On February 18, nine days after discovering the body, Sellers was first brought in to take a lie detector test. He was told his rights, which he waived entirely. The first time he was tested, he was asked only four questions specific to the murder.

The result was not good for Sellers. The examiner wrote that "Mr. Sellers seemed to be preoccupied with outside issues. He appeared to be nervous and time-conscious." The conclusion: "**Final Call**: Significant responses that would normally indicate deception. (**Deception Indicated**)."

<u>**Summary of case Facts:**</u>

Subject discovered a homicide victim buried in a shallow grave in a park. He denies knowing anything about her death.

<u>**Relevant Questions:**</u>

1. Are you attempting withhold any information about the death of the female you found in the park? **Ans. = No**

2. Did you do anything to that girl to cause her death? **Ans. = No**

3. Had you ever been in the company of that girl you found, before the day you found her? **Ans. = No**

4. Had you ever been to the spot where the girl was found before the day you found her? **Ans. = No**

February 18, 1999 polygraph questions.

<u>**Summary of case Facts:**</u>

Subject found a homicide victim in a local park. He denies knowing anything about her death.

<u>**Relevant Questions:**</u>

P. O. T.

1. Do you know if that girl you found died because she was stabbed with a knife? **Ans.=No**

2. Do you know if that girl you found died because she was shot? **Ans.=No**

3. Do you know if that girl you found died because she was poisoned? **Ans.=No**

4. Do you know if that girl you found died because she was choked? **Ans.=No**

5. Do you know if that girl you found died because she was hit with a baseball bat? **Ans.=No**

6. Do you know if that girl you found died because she was hit with a tire iron? **Ans.=No**

7. Do you know if that girl you found died because she was run over by a car? **Ans.=No**

February 24, 1999, polygraph questions.

Here is where the police conduct gets weird. They brought Sellers back on February 24 to take another test, but with totally different questions.

This time Sellers passed with flying colors.

Most jurisdictions in the United States stopped allowing polygraphs as evidence of truthfulness long ago, and in this instance it also seems the police had little faith in a polygraph. If they did indeed believe that these examinations would yield reliable answers to the questions on the first polygraph, common sense would dictate they would repeat the same questions on the second.

But they didn't. So then what was the point of this exercise?

The most reasonable explanation to me for the two distinctly different tests is this: the police wanted to eliminate Sellers as a suspect and dispense with him altogether. When he failed the first polygraph, they decided to give him a second one designed *to make sure* he passed, instead of further exploring why he failed on questions in the first one

After the second polygraph, Sellers was never contacted by the police again. This would be the last time he appeared in the case until he testified in the murder trial of the person the police had been eyeing even before Hae's body was found: Adnan.

In her 1969 book *On Death and Dying*, Elisabeth Kübler-Ross developed a model for understanding how people commonly cope with loss, widely known as the five stages of grief. She later clarified that the stages are not necessarily linear, but instead are the most universally expressed human responses to loss.

In tragic situations the most frequent immediate reaction is denial.

According to nearly everyone who was questioned, Adnan initially refused to believe that the body found in Leakin Park could be Hae's. He argued, between tears, that it must be another Asian girl. There was a significant Korean community in the area, after all.

On the night of February 10, 1999, news of the discovery of Hae's body spread quietly but quickly among her friends. Aisha was the first to hear when Hae's brother called her. Aisha then alerted Krista, who contacted Adnan. Adnan was home and didn't have his car that night (it was shared by his family), but when he heard the news, he ran all the way to Aisha's house.

Krista still clearly remembers the events of that night, and the following few days:

She called Adnan between 10:40 p.m. and 11:00 p.m. but at first didn't reach him, so she left him a voicemail. She called back two minutes later and he answered the phone. He sounded happy, but she knew what she was about to tell him was completely going to change his life. She told him that they had found Hae and that she was dead. Initially he seemed to be in complete shock and unable to speak. After a few minutes of silence on his end, Krista asked if he was going to be okay, then told him to come over to her place if he needed to. Adnan finally responded, asking if Aisha was home. Krista said she was, and Adnan said he was going to go over to her house instead. Krista phoned Aisha to let her know Adnan was on his way, and she asked Krista to come over as well, since she wasn't emotionally equipped to handle Adnan on her own. Krista arrived at Aisha's house around 11:30 p.m., pulling up at the same time as Stephanie McPherson, to find Adnan sitting at the kitchen table crying. When he calmed down enough to speak he said that there had to be a mistake and that Hae was still alive because her name was written on Aisha's agenda book. Krista recalls that Adnan used his cell phone to call Detective O'Shea, but the detective wasn't in. Adnan started crying again and Krista took the phone from him and spoke with the police officer to explain that they just wanted to get some information. The officer instructed the kids that they needed to call homicide in the morning—there wasn't anyone there they could talk to now.

The friends stayed at Aisha's house until about 12:45 a.m., and then Krista took Adnan with her because she didn't think it was safe for him to walk home alone that late at night. She dropped him off in the parking lot across the street from his house and he ran home from there.

By the next morning, the entire school knew that Hae was dead.

This message is from Dr. James Wilson regarding the death of one of our twelfth grade students, Hae Min Lee:

At 6:45 am this morning, we held an administrative briefing. At 7:00 am the administrative team met with the Crisis Team to discuss the action plan for our staff and students. The following statement was drafted for the teachers:

"We are saddened to learn of the death of Hae Lee, a member of the class of 1999. Hae Min Lee has been missing since January 13, 1999 and her body was found in Leakin Park, Baltimore City. At this time nothing more is known concerning the incident. Please inform the administrative team if you need assistance."

We met with our early-bird teachers at 7:10 am and again at 7:31 with our regular teachers. Teachers were asked to read the statement to their first period classes to inform the students. We have opened up areas in the building (the auditorium, health suite, guidance office, first and second floor lounges as well as administrative offices) and assigned counselors and crisis team members to those areas for persons who need assistance. We have also assigned all veteran secretaries to handle the incoming telephone calls. However, at this time we have not been contacted by the media.

We will update you on our status at 9:00 am and then again at 12 noon.

Thank you for your time.

The Magnet Program circle of friends were all at school that day, seeking comfort in the familiar and bonding over an incomprehensible loss.

Students and teachers alike approached Adnan to console him; he was dazed, still in denial, unsure of how to deal with the outpouring of sympathy. Sympathy for what? For the death of his ex-girlfriend or the death of his friend? It was all too much for him.

He went to the nurse's office, where his friend Ja'uan Gordon came to see him. Adnan was irritated with the nurse, who kept pressing him and insisting that he believe the news. Ja'uan remembers Adnan's denial, the nurse literally shaking him, and then seeing him "break down" in tears. Quivering and upset, Adnan got a pass to leave school with Ja'uan and went to the home of another Woodlawn friend, Peter Billingsley, who was on the yearbook staff along with Adnan. Hae had also been part of their yearbook team.

A number of friends were gathered at Peter's house, and Adnan retreated to the basement. After a while they found him downstairs alone in a corner, crying. Peter noted that he had been sobbing for over two hours. Krista remembers it like this:

> *Laura, Aisha, and I went to pick up lunch and took it back to Peter's house. Adnan was very quiet, kept to himself and cried a lot. Several times he went downstairs and locked himself in the bathroom. After we left Peter's house Aisha and I went to her house for the afternoon. Adnan called and stopped by to hang out for a little while. As we were watching TV the previews of the five o'clock news came on and the discovery of Hae's body was the top headline. As we watched the story you could tell by his reaction that Adnan realized that Hae really wasn't coming back. All he could do at that very moment was lay in my arms and cry.*

Adnan remembers feeling sheer disbelief. He had never seriously considered that Hae might not ever return, that she might be dead, that she might have been hurt or killed. Neither had any of their friends.

The discovery of Hae's body shocked them to the core. Krista says "February 10, 1999, was the day we were forced to become adults. We were struck with real life tragedy and lost someone we cared very deeply for. We lived more aware of the world around us and that bad people existed. As a group of friends we vowed to watch out for each other and stay in constant communication, so that none of us would just disappear again."

But there would be no waking from what Adnan wished was a bad dream; his nightmare was just beginning.

Adnan:

It was toward the end of that fourth week that Krista called me one night. She was crying as she told me she had just heard that a body had been found, and that the police believed it was Hae's. She told me she would meet me at Aisha's house, so I left home and went there. The three of us sat at the table in her parents' kitchen, and I had this strong feeling of disbelief. I even recall arguing with them about whether or not the police could've been mistaken. Afterward, I just remember us crying together, and having this overwhelming feeling of sadness, in a way that I had never felt before.

That night was almost 17 years ago; literally, half a lifetime away. And of all the horrible things I've experienced, from that day till this—nothing has ever compared to that sorrow. Beginning to realize that I would never see Hae's smile, or hear her laughter, or enjoy the warmth that she brought into our lives, ever again? I don't think I'll ever have the words to describe the grief of that moment.

Going back to that night, after leaving Aisha and Krista and going to school the next day; well, everything was pretty much a blur. I just recall going through the motions of life, school, work, etc. I remember feeling a mixture of shock and disbelief, coupled with an immeasurable amount of sadness over her loss. We began planning Hae's memorial service, and I think that is when it really hit home. That I would never again see a person that I loved so much.

It was the saddest time in my life. Each of those days kind of faded into the next. And it would only be 19 of them, until I was arrested.

The next day, Friday, February 12th, Saad took Adnan on a long drive to help clear his head. Adnan was coping, but not well. An observant Muslim home offers no outlet to express anything about a forbidden relationship, and while things have improved slightly now, in 1999 no counseling was available in Muslim communities. Approaching a religious leader about the loss of someone he wasn't even supposed to be friends with, much less date, was a no-go. And many Muslims, like those in other conservative faith communities, have lived their lives swallowing grief and processing pain on their own. In religious circles those who suffer through divorce, abuse, addiction, and loss are often encouraged to pray more and have patience, without any attention to mental health or any prospect of real healing.

Of course, Adnan was also in high school, a teenager. How many teens seek the comfort of their parents or other adults in times of crisis? They rarely do; instead they turn to friends and peers. Adnan had his friends at Woodlawn, but they did not have the same relationship and friendship with Hae as he did; they also wouldn't understand his faith perspective.

Together, Saad and Adnan headed to western Maryland, our former home and where Saad grew up. Interstate 70, whose eastern end hits Baltimore not far from Woodlawn High School, stretches in the opposite direction for nearly a hundred miles through scenic countryside, all the way to the Pennsylvania border. They drove west on I-70, crossing over the Monocacy River, before veering off onto Route 15 toward Catoctin Mountain.

The temperature was near freezing so they didn't get out of the car. Saad drove through Cunningham Falls State Park, letting Adnan sit in silence as they listened to music—hip-hop, R&B, some occasional bhangra.

They got back on the interstate and kept heading west, to Hagerstown. Right inside the town limits was a small mosque, established in the years after we had moved to Baltimore. They stopped to pray the weekly congregational Jummah prayer after listening to a sermon, and then Saad took Adnan to Rocky's Pizza, his favorite comfort food spot, for lunch.

Between hot, gooey slices of pizza they spoke about Hae and what could have happened to her. Adnan had no idea; there was no public information about how she died. All they knew was that she'd been found in Leakin Park. And they didn't even know where Leakin Park was.

In fact, most of us didn't. Many of us had never driven that way. It was an internal route to the city that we weren't even aware of, and the only part of the city my family ever went to was the Baltimore harbor, usually with guests. To get there, we simply hopped onto the interstate because it took you almost directly there. And for those who may have actually driven past that area, they never realized that it was called Leakin Park; there was no sign on Franklintown Road identifying the woods to either side as an actual park.

As they drove back they tried to reconcile themselves with Hae's death. In Islam, life and death are already decreed by God. We are each born with certain things preordained: the amount of our "rizq," or sustenance, be it food or money, and the time of our death. Even before we enter this world our days and nights are written, numbered, noted by the angels in our individual decrees of life. We must live, then, like travelers in this world, treating it like a temporary abode, until we move on to our eternal homes.

Muslims are given three days to mourn unless the deceased is their spouse. Any more than three days is considered disrespectful to God because every soul came from Him, belongs to Him, and will return rightfully to Him. We don't own each other, only God owns us.

Adnan's discussions with Saad, and later with his mosque mentor, Bilal, helped him manage what he could barely accept as reality, but he still carried a deep sadness. Yusuf recalls Adnan taking him out for dinner one night, during the last week of that month. Even as a child Yusuf knew something was wrong. His big brother was unusually somber, even as he attempted to make small talk with Yusuf, who prattled on about *Dragon Ball Z*. It was a memorable dinner for Yusuf because it was the last time he spent time alone with Adnan.

On February 11, two days after Hae's body was found, something odd happened. A "walk-in witness" showed up in the Woodlawn Stationhouse of the Baltimore City Police. The forty-one-year-old black man had seen media reports that evening that a murder victim had been found in Leakin Park, and he thought he had seen something that may have been connected to the crime. The police officer on duty called the Homicide Division and Detective Ritz arrived with a colleague to speak with him.

The man had seen a black man driving a light-colored vehicle and acting suspiciously by some concrete roadblocks on a road leading to another part of Leakin Park, about a mile from where Hae's body was found. The officers' report is sparse. It doesn't note the time of the incident, why the man was suspicious, or why the witness thought it might be connected to the murder. The police quickly dispensed with the man, concluding "investigators believe that this observance is not connected to the murder of Hae Lee." No one ever contacted him again.

That same evening the police pulled the registration records for Adnan's car. Having checked to see if he had a criminal record on February 3rd, the police seem to have considered him their prime suspect all along.

As Hae's family, friends, and community tried to cope with the horrific news, the police went into overdrive to close their case. This was not the average Baltimore murder, not a gang-bang killing, not a drive-by, not a drug crime. This also wasn't the average Baltimore victim, mostly black and poor. Hae was a bright, promising honor roll student from the suburbs. She belonged to a family and a community with a strong local business presence, and a church that rallied around them. The murder of Jada Lambert, the young black girl who was found dead seven months prior, did not get the same investigatory vigor or media coverage as Hae's case, and I don't hesitate to say that the victim's "profile" made all the difference.

In a city with a terrifying amount of violence, this case was distinct, because both the victim and their chief suspect, Adnan, were top students, popular, and came from ethnic communities that the police rarely ventured into. But mostly because the nature of the crime seemed to be a departure from anything they'd encountered before. They believed they were dealing with religiously/ethnically motivated violence, an "honor killing."

This, however, is not how honor killings operate. In honor killings, which have been documented mostly in the Middle East and the South Asian subcontinent, including Pakistan, India, and Bangladesh, and across all religions, a woman's family members (frequently men: father, brother, uncle, husband etc.) murder her for "dishonoring" the family. This dishonor can be brought about in a number of ways but is usually connected to an illicit affair, extramarital sexual activity, or marrying a person the family disapproves of. Contrary to popular belief, honor killings aren't limited to Muslim or South Asian communities. They are even found in Far Eastern cultures, including Korean culture, as documented in the memoir *Ten Thousand Sorrows: The Extraordinary Journey of a Korean War Orphan* by Elizabeth Kim. In the book, Kim recalls witnessing the honor killing of her mother by her grandfather and uncle, her mother's father and brother. She died for the crime of having a "half-breed" child out of wedlock with an American G.I.

Mandy Johnson, who would come to present herself as an expert on Muslim "culture" despite there being no evidence of her having any such credentials, met again with the detectives on February 15 and was interviewed about Hae's diary, which was still in her possession. They took the diary from her, seeking more support for their theory of the case. A theory that had been further confirmed by a mysterious call a few days prior.

On February 12, at approximately 3:19 p.m., Detective Daryl Massey of the Baltimore City Police got two calls from the same tipster.

---

12 February 1999

FROM: Detective Darryl Massey

TO: Detective Greg MacGillivary

REF: Possibly Pertaining To Hae Min Lee Investigation H99030

Sir:

On February 12, 1999, approx. 1519 Hrs., your writer received a call from an anonymous caller (Asian Male 18-21 years old) who advised investigators, should concentrate on the victim's boyfriend (Adna Ansyed A/M/17) as a suspect in the murder. The caller further advised the boyfriend has taken the victim to Leakin Park on past occasions for sexual encounter. Prior to concluding the phone interview, the caller further stated the victim broke of the relationship with her boyfriend about a week before she was reported missing.

At this point the caller terminated the conversation, simultaneously your writer activated *57 on ext. 2100. The recording informed your writer; the service was not available due to the caller not being in the service area.

On February 12, 1999, approx. 1525 Hrs., the above anonymous person again called the Homicide Unit. This time that caller remember about a year ago, the suspect informed a friend of his (Baser Ali A/M/17), if he ever hurt his girlfriend, he would drive her car into a lake. The caller stated the suspect's friend attends Centennial High School in Columbia, Maryland, and his home phone # ███████████. Again *57 was activated, the recording stated the service was not available due to the caller not being in the service area.

Respectfully,

Detective Darryl Massey

The tip was essentially a nod in Adnan's direction, with no actual information about the crime or his involvement. Beyond that, it also contained inaccurate information—Adnan and Hae never hooked up in Leakin Park, and they certainly did not break up a week prior to her disappearance; they had broken up at least a month before. Hae's car, as it turned out, was nowhere near a lake.

Still, the fact that an "anonymous Asian" male thought Adnan deserved their undivided attention supported their existing theory that he was the perp. Did "Asian" mean South Asian, and suggest that someone from Adnan's community knew something they weren't divulging? Or did it mean East Asian, and suggest someone from Hae's community or family with a hunch?

In order to find out, the police set out in search of one "Baser Ali" who turned out to be Yaser Ali, a friend of Adnan's who was also in his senior year of high school.

Detectives MacGillivary and Carew tracked down and visited Yaser a few days later, on February 15th, meeting him at Pizza Hut in Ellicott City.

Master Ali has known the victim's prior boyfriend one Adnon [sic] Syed 7034 Johnnycake Road Baltimore, Maryland M/P/17 05/21/81 for numerous years. In fact both boys attend the same Mosque "Islamic Society of Baltimore". Ali indicated that in the spring of 1998, Adnon became involved with the victim socially and apparently attended the Junior Prom together. As a result of the relationship between Adnon and Hae, Master Ali found that his friendship with Adnon began to dissolve.

Ali also indicated that during the holy month described as "Ramadan" which occurred this year from 23 December 1998 to 16 January 1999. At the conclusion of the month, a festival named "Eid" occurs on 17 January 1999, and was held at the mosque. Ali also indicated that on 17 January 1999, he arrived at the mosque at approximately 5 a.m. He eventually saw Adnon at or about 0730 hours, however, both indicated that they would meet later in the day at one of the parties scheduled. Ali stated that they actually never met up that day, as a result of missing each other between events.

Ali further indicates that Adnon eventually comes over to his house, exact date unknown, however is after the victim is found by the Police. A discussion takes place as to Adnon's knowledge of how the victim was killed and whether Adnon knew who had killed Hae Min Lee.

Master Ali was asked whether he had heard from other friends about Hae Lee's disappearance and Ali indicated that [there] were discussions about her, however, nothing pertinent to this investigation.

Master Ali was also asked that if Adnon had killed Hae Min Lee, would Adnon tell anyone? Ali indicated that he didn't think he would.

Master Ali was asked if he had called Homicide with any information concerning this event, and Ali indicated no.

Ali was then asked if Adnon had been involved, and he wanted to get rid of the car, where would he do so? Ali indicated somewhere in the woods, possibly in Centennial Lake or the Inner Harbor.

Investigation to continue.

Nothing that Yaser said connected Adnan to the crime. Whoever pointed the police in his direction did so futilely. But the police questions show their line of thinking: first, that Adnan may have told someone if he had committed the crime, and second, they still needed to find Hae's car. The anonymous tip of the 12th didn't accomplish much in the way of actual evidence, but it paved the way for investigators to narrow their suspect list down to one, Adnan, and was also a convenient excuse to not investigate anyone else.

On the same day that police visited Yaser, Adnan was pulled over for a seatbelt violation—not in itself unusual—but the real reason he was pulled over isn't known until many years later.

The police investigation continued as Hae's family and community rallied for her murder to be solved. On the 16th, Detective MacGillivary was informed by the medical examiner that none of the swabs taken from Hae's body returned any trace of spermatozoa, evidence that she had not been sexually assaulted.

The next day, February 17th, Hae's church arranged a public vigil, seen in media footage from that evening. Holding lit candles as dusk fell, local Korean Americans walked soberly, singing church songs. They would not let this young girl be forgotten. The police understood, and took the pressure seriously. So much so, they made a special request to the Maryland State Aviation Unit that day to fly over Leakin Park and Woodlawn to help locate Hae's car. The request was denied.

Another agency was willing to help with the investigation, though: the federal Drug Enforcement Administration.

The official version of events, the one presented at trial, is this: that on February 18, 1999, detectives sent a subpoena to AT&T Wireless for the cell phone records of one Adnan Syed. There was some major fact-fudging going on here, though.

Later discovered police files show that an earlier subpoena had already been sent to AT&T on February 16th, one that with odd specificity asked for the addresses of thirteen cell site locations. This will be the first time in any of the

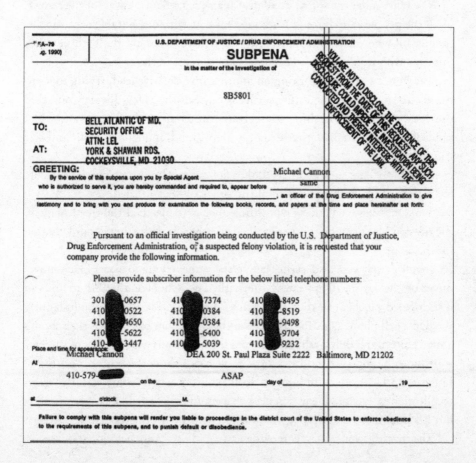

documents that cell-tower site locations come up. The next time is a February 20th subpoena that requests "a cell site directory that corresponds with the sites listed." Which means this: while the police were creating a paper trail to make it seem as if they were just beginning their investigation into Adnan in earnest, they already knew that thirteen cell towers were of interest to their case, and they even knew the exact tower sites.

How did the police get this information? There is one strong possibility. The February 18th subpoena was actually not issued by Baltimore City Police, it was issued by the DEA. Asking the DEA for assistance would not heve been all that unusual since the process of getting information took many more hoops for local law enforcement agencies to jump through than it did for federal agencies, and the DEA also had much more experience with gathering cell phone evidence. It could be that the DEA unofficially obtained the records for the police days before the subpoena was issued and never documented that fact.

The DEA subpoena wasn't even for Adnan's cell records. It was for the records of all the people called from his phone that day, with one notable exception—the person who was called more times than anyone else on the 13th: Jennifer Pusateri, who would go on to become a key witness in the case.

The police were also working on another investigative lead, trying to identify a tire tread from the crime scene. On the 16th, MacGillivary contacted the local Nissan dealership to ascertain the color of Hae's car and what kind of tires it used. The tires were Dunlop Brand, model SP 2000, and size P17565R14.

A couple of days later, February 18th, a fax was sent by an employee of Mr. Tire to Detective Ritz with a page full of tire styles.

We don't know whether or not the police ever matched the tread mark to the tires on Hae's car, or another car, because there is no further documentation for this issue.

Investigators were also, rather late in the game, trying to assess Hae's movements on the day she disappeared. They visited her school on the 18th to find out if she owned a locker (she didn't), contacted her uncle Tae Sue Kim to find out if she had a cell phone (she didn't), and on the 22nd checked in with the school's athletic director, Ralph Graham, who told them Hae was with a group of students waiting to be interviewed by a local cable news show the entire morning of January 13th—from 9:00 a.m. to 1:00 p.m. Later it becomes clear that his recollection is wrong; Hae was in class that morning as attendance records note, but his statements end up becoming intertwined with the official narrative.

The investigation was now moving at a rapid pace as police closed out leads, including picking up Sellers from work to administer the second polygraph on February 24th. Having crossed him off the list, they moved on.

On the same day, Metro Crime Stoppers of Maryland, an agency that works with law enforcement to collect crime tips and give rewards, notified the police that, as per their request, flyers had been prepared for release with a press statement notifying the public of a reward in exchange for information about the crime. This seems to indicate that the police never received any actionable leads from the anonymous February 12th tips.

Two days later, on February 26th, Ritz and MacGillivary visited Adnan at home at approximately 7:00 p.m. Adnan and his father greeted them together and offered them drinks. The mood was cordial, though serious. Adnan, along with all of Hae's friends, was now extremely worried about her and wanted to help in the investigation as much as possible. He assumed the questioning was about when he last saw Hae, or what he knew about her that might help track her down. Instead the questions were focused on their former relationship.

Adnan's father's presence made Adnan uncomfortable as he was questioned about his relationship with Hae, answering with a soft "yes" when asked if he was involved romantically with her. He told Ritz that he last saw Hae on the 13th; however, Ritz noted he "doesn't remember the events that occurred in school that day," a vague statement that could mean different things, but will eventually be held against him.

When asked if he had ever been in Hae's car, Adnan responded yes, but not on the 13th. The only thing he cared about was not upsetting his father in that moment. When questioned, he had no idea who would want to hurt Hae and had no information on possible suspects, not guessing for a second that he was their prime suspect. He should have, though. When Hae disappeared my brother Saad told him, "Hey, hopefully she's ok and turns up soon. Otherwise you know they come after the boyfriends, right?" Saad had even advised him to get a lawyer. Adnan thought he was crazy—why on earth would they consider him a suspect, and a suspect for what? He didn't give it another thought, just hoped the police would find her soon. In his naiveté Adnan wouldn't realize what was happening until the next time he was questioned by police, after they arrested him in the early hours of February 28, 1999.

After leaving Adnan's home, detectives went in search of Jennifer Pusateri, a friend of Jay Wilds and the person most called and paged from Adnan's phone on January 13th. They find her in a car, ready to drive off, and she can't (or won't) talk, saying she has to drop off dinner for her boyfriend at his

```
                              Police Department
                              Baltimore, Maryland
    CI/209                                      Case Number_____

                              INFORMATION SHEET

    Name JENNIFER LOUISE PUSATERI   Nickname JEN
    Race W  Sex F  Age 18  D.O.B. ▓▓▓▓▓
    Height 5' 4"  Weight 180  Complexion ____
    Address ▓▓▓▓▓▓▓▓▓▓▓▓▓ 21207  SS# ▓▓▓▓▓▓▓▓▓▓▓▓
    Home Phone (410)▓▓▓  Date and time of interview 2/26/99 2111
    Parent's name ▓▓▓▓▓▓▓  Address SAME
    Boy/girlfriend name NONE  Address _____
    Last School Attended UMBC  Grade FRESHMAN
    Employer HEARTLANDS  Address Rogers Ave. Ho. G
    Employers Phone 410 461-9494 Hours of employment ____
              RELATIVES IN BALTIMORE NOT LIVING WITH WITNESS

    Name_____ Relationship _____
    Address _____ Phone _____
    Name_____ Relationship _____
    Address _____ Phone _____
    Read and Write    Yes X    No _____
    Under the influence of drugs  Yes _____  No X
    If yes explain_____
    Alcohol Check One Sober X  Had Been Drinking____  Intoxicated____
    Description of clothing at time of Interview (note if bloodstained
    torn etc.) PURPLE SWEATSHIRT TAN CORDUROY
    (PANTS)
    Note any injuries_____ NA
    Meals Provided_____Date_____Time_____Date_____Time_____



    Detective MACGILL_____ Detective _____
```

workplace. Jenn will later testify that she had gone to see Jay Wilds after this encounter.

She shows up at the police station about an hour later to answer some questions. The police notes from that meeting are cryptic and make no mention of Adnan whatsoever.

The next morning, on February 27th, the police do a search of the BWI airport parking lot for Hae's car. Sergeant Lehman contacts Transit Authority at the airport and requests that "all park and ride lots be checked for the victim's auto, along with satellite parking areas."

While there is no timestamp on this search report, it appears before (and probably happened sooner than) the events described in the next document, which notes that on the same day around 1:00 p.m. Ritz and MacGillivary visit

Police notes from initial Pusateri interview, February 26, 1999.

the home of Jenn's attorney, who specializes in real estate and coincidentally lived in Ritz's neighborhood. No notes exist for this interview.

Jennifer Pusateri returns to the police station, this time with her mother and her attorney, and gives a full-length, detailed statement about how Adnan Syed killed Hae Min Lee.

Pusateri is in the station for two hours, during which she gives a confused, nonlinear account of January 13th.

While she hadn't previously mentioned Adnan, this time, after having met with Jay the night before, Adnan is now at the center of her story. Jenn says the following:

This is a taped interview is Jennifer Louise Pusateri, white female, 18 ah date of birth is ██████████ Today's date is the 27th. of February. It's approximately quarter of four in the afternoon. We're currently at 601 E. Fayette Street ah the offices of Homicide, specifically ah the Colonel's conference room. Present are ah Jennifer Pusateri's attorney, James Faley from the ah law offices of Faley and Beckley ah Miss Pusateri's mother, Althea Pusateri ah Detective Ritz and also Sergeant Lehmann.

MacGillivary: For the record could you please state your full name?

Pusateri: Jennifer Louise Pusateri.

MacGillivary: And how old are you ma'am?

Pusateri: 18.

MacGillivary: And your date of birth?

Pusateri: ██████████

MacGillivary: And where do you reside?

Pusateri: **Inaudible.**

MacGillivary: Okay. Ah Jennifer this office is currently investigating a homicide and the victim's name is Hae Min Lee. Ah she was found missing on the 13th. of January. Now what if anything can you tell me about this event?

Pusateri: Okay. On, all I heard about this event was from an individual named Jay and Jay told me around eight o'clock that evening that ah Adnar, Hae's ex-boyfriend, had killed her and ah that's, I mean as far as my day goes that day I ah got up, did my normal **inaudible**, went to work, from work I called Jay. I asked if he wanted to come to my house and hang out. He said "sure, swing by and pick him up" Um than he got back in touch with me to let me know not to come and get him that he would be at my house. Between....between twelve-thirty and one I got back to my house, between one and one-thirty Jay arrived at my house. Um Jay got there, he had Adnar's car and what I believe to be Adnar's cell phone um and he just said he was waiting for a phone call. He didn't tell me whose car he had or he didn't tell me "this is Adnars car" or "this is Adnars cell phone" or he was waiting for Adnar to call him, he just said he was waiting for a call and it was going to come around three-thirty. Um so we hung out at my house and than I guess around three-thirty, three forty-five um Jay got a call

Police notes of second Pusateri interview, February 27, 1999

- On the evening of January 13th, around eight o'clock, Jay told her Adnan strangled Hae
- Jay had come by her house during the day, between 1:00 and 1:30; he had borrowed Adnan's car (to get his girlfriend Stephanie a birthday gift) and phone, and was "waiting for a phone call."
- Jay got a call around 3:30 or 3:45 p.m. and then left her house between 3:45 and 4:15 p.m.

four-fifteen and than I left my house between four-fifteen and four-thirty to go and pick up my parents. I get to my mom's work approximately at five o'clock. We get to my dad's work approximately at five-thirty. We get home between six and six-thirty. Ah once I'm home I get some dinner maybe and I know that I'm suppose to be hanging out with Jay later on in the evening and we're going over my to my friends Chris....my friends Christy's house so we're hanging out or no so I'm hanging out at home.

Ritz: Let me stop you for a second Jen, just to go back. He comes over your house, he said he had a car with him, and you think that Adnar, he told you it was Adnar's car, had you ever seen Adnar's car before?

Pusateri: Ah yeah I seen it before at school but I couldn't tell.....I couldn't tell you what kind of car it was or

Ritz: The car that Jay had that day, describe it for me.

Pusateri: It was like a brown....like a tan color kind of tan color um

Ritz: Did it look like an older car or a new car?

Pusateri: Yeah it's probably like maybe a anywhere between a 90 and a 95 maybe and it was four doors and that's...that's all I really know about the car that he came **inaudible**.

Ritz: Do you recall whether or not he said it was Adnar's car or did it similar to the

Pusateri: Um I hadn't seen Adnar's car since I graduated from high school which would have been May and I can't remember it like....I mean if I would have **inaudible** I seen like.....since I talked to Jay since all this had happened whatever, Jay told me like last night that it was Adnar's car that he was in...that he brought to my house 'cause he wanted to know if I told you all about last night and I hadn't told you that last night and um he said well than he didn't even want....he was like "well the only reason I had his car was because I wanted" that's when I found out that he had the car to go get his girlfriend a birthday present.

Ritz: He never told you that in passing?

- She received a pager message from Jay to pick him up but the message was confusing, so she called Adnan's phone between 7:00 and 8:00 p.m. Adnan answered and told her Jay would call her when he needed to be picked up.
- Between 8:00 and 8:30 she got a call or page saying she was to pick up Jay from the Westview Mall parking lot. Jay and Adnan were waiting in a car together when she got there.

you know" and I was like "alright, what's up Boo?"
He was like "um Adnar killed Hae" and that's when I
was just like "woo, what do you mean that Adnar
killed Hae, why, what, how, when, where" you know.
Normal questions I guess you would ask.

Ritz: When you asked "why" what did he say?

Pusateri: Um, he said that Adnar said that Hae broke his heart.

Ritz: Did he say anything else?

Pusateri: No.

Ritz: When you asked him "how" what did he say?

Pusateri: He said that he strangled her.

Ritz: Did you asked him where it happened?

Pusateri: He told me um he told me...this is what he told me,
he told me that Adnar was going to, he's like "he's
going to" I was like "Jay what do we do?" I, was,
he asked, Jay asked me what we should do, he said
"you think we should go to the police now and tell
them right now" and I said "I don't know." I said
"what was your involvement, were you involved"
and he said "no", he said "Adnar showed me her body
and asked me if I...if I would help her bury him,
or bury, if I would help him bury her body" and I
said "well what did you do, did you help him, do
you know where the body is?" "No, I just took him
to some place in the city and I dropped him off.
I took him to a, then I went down, picked him up
from a different place in the city" and I don't
remember where he said they went and

Ritz: Just back track, just for a second so I can keep
up with you, when you asked him if he had any
involvement and he said "no", he said he saw the
body, did he say where he saw the body?

Pusateri: Ah I think I might have asked him, I think I him
remember saying "in the trunk of a car.' I don't
know if it was her car or Adnar's car.

Ritz: When he says he dropped him off somewhere in the
city or picked him up, did he say whether or not
he was in the **inaudible** tan vehicle or what car
he was driving or did you ask him?

- As soon as Jay got in her car, he told her that Adnan killed Hae, and he saw Hae's body in the trunk of a car, but that he had no involvement.
- Jay told her Adnan killed Hae in the parking lot of Best Buy and they had gotten rid of the "shovel or shovels" in a dumpster.
- She took Jay to the dumpsters in Westview Mall and he told her to keep an eye out while he retrieved and wiped down the shovel or shovels.

```
PAGE NINETEEN
STATEMENT OF:  Jennifer Pusateri

Ritz:        Where does Stephanie live?

Pusateri:    In inaudible Valley.  I don't know the address.

Ritz:        Do you know the exact street?

Pusateri:    I don't know the address, I don't know the street
             or

Ritz:        Do you know Stephanie's last name?

Pusateri:    Inaudible. I know her phone number.

Ritz:        What is that?

Pusateri:    ▮▮▮▮▮▮▮  At least that's what I remember inaudible
             I'm pretty sure that's it.

Ritz:        Did you physically see Stephanie?

Pusateri:    Yeah I saw, I sit in the car while Jay got out of
             the car and I saw Stephanie open the door and I
             saw him go in and give her a hug and a kiss and
             then  he  might  have  been  in  the  house  for
             approximately five to fifteen minutes.

Ritz:        When he's going up to the house does he have a
             birthday present with him?

Pusateri:    Um, I don't remember.

Ritz:        What happens after he comes out of the house?

Pusateri:    He comes out the house, gets in the car, I say
             "ready to go to Christy's house?"  He says um I
             said and we talked, we probably talked a little
             bit more about Hae and everything that happened
             and I might have asked him you know again what his
             involvement was, if he knew where the body was.
             I was like "yo, where did he bury the body.  Where
             would he have buried the body?"  And Jay said "I
             don't know where he took the body um but he used
             my shovel" or shovels.  I don't know whether it
             was one or two.  He's like "well I know where the
             shovel or shovels are" and I said "okay, so what
             do you want me to do?"  He says "will you take
             me to the shovels or shovel" and I said "sure.
             Where are the shovels or shovel" and he said "they
             are at the mall parking lot and I was like "well
             what mall" and he's like "back at Westview Mall."
             So we went back to Westview parking lot and I
```

- Jay then told her to take him to see Stephanie and the rest of the night they visited various locations.
- She did not observe Jay's clothing to be dirty, or his hands to be dirty, and did not notice any unusual behavior with Adnan.
- Jay told her that after seeing the body, he dropped Adnan off in some part of the city and picked him up later in another part of the city; there is no mention of Leakin Park.

- The following day, the 14th, it was raining, and she took Jay to the F&M dumpster so he could get rid of his clothing (though weather reports show it was not raining and emergency ice and snow conditions made most roads impossible to navigate).

And then there is this incredibly odd exchange in which Jenn responds to Detective Lehman's question of how she knows all this happened on January 13th: "Well the only reason I know that is because last night um when I was being questioned or whatever you want to call it, um ah the question asked was why Adnar [sic] called my house on the 13th, um I remember the incident that Adnar had killed Hae and I remember I had talked to Jay that day and Jay had been at my house."

Lehman then asked, "So you're saying that you're sure it's the 13th because we told you you had these telephone calls on the 13th?"

"Right," Jenn responded.

The interview wraps up a bit after 5:00 p.m. and Jenn walks out, having just essentially confessed to being an accessory after the fact.

Late that night, on February 27th, for the first time, according to official documentation, the police pick up Jay Wilds.

According to police notes, there is an unrecorded two-hour "pre-interview"

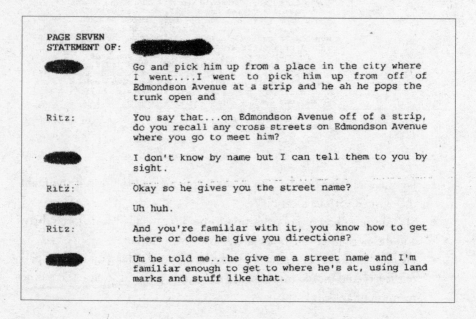

```
PAGE SEVEN
STATEMENT OF:  ▓▓▓▓▓▓▓

▓▓▓▓▓        Go and pick him up from a place in the city where
             I went....I went to pick him up from off of
             Edmondson Avenue at a strip and he ah he pops the
             trunk open and

Ritz:        You say that...on Edmondson Avenue off of a strip,
             do you recall any cross streets on Edmondson Avenue
             where you go to meet him?

▓▓▓▓▓        I don't know by name but I can tell them to you by
             sight.

Ritz:        Okay so he gives you the street name?

▓▓▓▓▓        Uh huh.

Ritz:        And you're familiar with it, you know how to get
             there or does he give you directions?

▓▓▓▓▓        Um he told me...he give me a street name and I'm
             familiar enough to get to where he's at, using land
             marks and stuff like that.
```

with Jay before the tape recorder is turned on. The taped interview lasts for hours and is filled with contradictions and internal inconsistencies. He gives this basic narrative:

- On the evening of January 12th Adnan calls and they briefly chat, making plans for the next day.
- On the 13th Adnan arrives at his home around 10:30 a.m. and they go to Westview Mall and do a little shopping together.
- He drops Adnan off at school around 12:30 p.m. and keeps his car; Adnan leaves his cell phone in the car.
- Before Jay drops him off, Adnan mentions that he is going to kill Hae that day because she broke his heart.
- Jay, unperturbed, agrees to pick Adnan up later that day from wherever he needs to be picked up from; he then goes to Jennifer Pusateri's home where he plays video games with her brother, Mark. Jenn is not home.

Ritz: When he puts her body in this shallow grave, describe to me how she is positioned?

          She's ah like her head's facing away from the road, ah like her arm's kind of like twisted behind her back and she's ah kind of leaning on her side.

PAGE SEVENTEEN
STATEMENT OF:

Ritz: Is she face up, face down?

          Face down.

Ritz: She's face down, what side is she laying on?

          Her right I think.

Ritz: Right side?

          Yeah.

- He gets a call from Adnan around 3:45 p.m. to meet him somewhere in the city.
- In his first mention of Hae's car, they leave the body and the car in the Interstate 70 Park-n-Ride close to Leakin Park and then go smoke weed together.
- He drops Adnan back off at school "when the sun was going down," around 4:30 p.m. (the sun set at 5:06 p.m. that day), for track practice.

```
                  Um one conversation he told me that he strangled
                  her, um another conversation he wanted me to
                  revisit the body with him.

Ritz:             When was that conversation?




PAGE TWENTY-SIX
STATEMENT OF:

                  Prior to her being found.

Ritz:             Let me stop you for just a second ah Jay, we'd
                  like to get into that, the tape is going to run
                  out in a minute. The time now is 2:09 A.M. on
                  Sunday, ah February 28th. We're going to terminate
                  ah stop the interview just for a second so we can
                  flip the tape over to side B
```

- He picks him back up at 6:45 p.m. and they go for a bite to eat, when a police officer calls to ask Adnan if he's seen Hae.
- Adnan panics and asks Jay for shovels. They go to Jay's house and he gets a pick and a shovel.
- They return to get Hae's car and Jay follows Adnan to Leakin Park, where he watches Adnan dig a hole as Hae's body lies on the ground.
- He notes Hae's jacket is on the ground and that Adnan throws it somewhere.
- Adnan tells him to follow him as he finds a place to park Hae's car; they end up in a lot by some row homes, where Jay says Adnan takes Hae's wallet and book bag and gets in his car with Jay.

- As Jay is driving himself home, Adnan asks him to stop at a dumpster to get rid of things—Hae's purse, wallet, book bag, and the shovel/pick.
- Jay discards his clothing in his own trash can.
- Once the tape is flipped, Jay begins describing the windshield wiper in the car being kicked and broken by Hae as she was being strangled, a detail Adnan had apparently given him.
- Adnan never told him how he got in Hae's car.

Jay goes on to mention that Adnan told "Tyad" (likely Tayyab), a Pakistani Muslim, that he had murdered someone, but did not actually specify who he murdered. Casually telling a friend about an unspecified murder you committed, it seems to Jay, is a routine thing in Pakistan. It may be that Jay got that idea from somewhere.

```
Ritz:          Other than you being with ████ that night do you
               know of any other persons that Adnar had confided
               in or bragged to that ah he killed Hae Lee?

████           No but I imagine somebody else um maybe Tyad.  I
               think he might have said something to ah...I don't
               think he told Tyad he killed Hae but he told Tyad he
               killed someone.

MacGillivary:  Tyad?
```

```
████           Oh yeah, you have to understand Tyad like for a
               lack of better choice of words, he's into that
               type of stuff, you know what I mean?

Ritz:          Into what, I don't know what you said.

████           Like murders, killing, you know.  He don't care
               I mean he talks about how it was wonderful in
               Pakistan, stuff like that.

Ritz:          Tyad is also from Pakistan and a Muselum?

████           Yeah.
```

The detectives wrap up the interview by asking Jay nicely to take them to Hae's car and he complies. The car is officially located at 2:45 a.m. on a grassy parking lot lined on all four sides by row homes on the 300 block of Edgewood Drive, less than three miles from where Hae's body was found.

The car is towed to police headquarters and at approximately 5:20 a.m. the police arrive at Adnan's home with an arrest warrant.

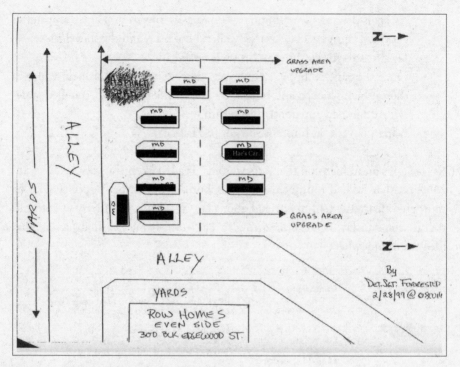

Officer sketch indicating location of Hae's car

CHAPTER 4

LIVING THE LIE

———————•———————

Love is neither disapproved by religion, nor prohibited by the law,
for every heart is in God's hands.

Ibn Hazm, "The Ring of the Dove," circa 1022

I saw it on television at my parents' house.

I sat straight up, shocked.

"Ami! Come here!"

My mother rushed in from the kitchen and stopped in her tracks.

A black-and-white photograph of Adnan with a thin, barely sprouted mustache occupied the upper right hand corner of the screen, while a news reporter casually informed us that he had been arrested in the murder of Hae Min Lee.

My mother started making calls. Yes, others had seen the news; no, no one had heard from the family. I sat stunned, my two-year-old daughter climbing around my lap.

After a few minutes of trying to figure out what had just happened, my mother grabbed her coat and told me to get up.

"We're going over there now."

Adnan's family lived just a few streets away and as we pulled up, we saw vans of camera crews parked around the house. We parked, avoided looking at the cameras, and walked up to the front door. The house was dark.

We knocked a few times, shivering in the cold and crying. After a few minutes we understood they weren't going to open the door right then. They just couldn't.

We turned to leave and were approached by reporters asking for comments on Adnan's arrest. Both my mother and I, teary and frozen, expressed our disbelief that he had anything to do with it, shaking our heads.

We went home and Saad arrived, also in shock. We did the only thing we knew how to do. We washed up and began to pray.

It would be a few days before Saad learned what happened on February 28, 1999. The police had surrounded Adnan's house and woken him at 5:30 a.m. Disoriented and confused, he was told to get up and put on some clothes. He was cuffed in his bedroom and led into the narrow hallway. His father was away at a religious retreat. His mother asked the cops repeatedly, "Why are you taking him?" as Tanveer tried to send Yusuf, who was crying and confused, into the bedroom so he wouldn't see his big brother in such terrifying circumstances.

Adnan looked at his family and tried to reassure them.

"It's ok, it must be a mistake. I'll be back."

He really believed that.

There were layers upon layers of pain for Adnan's family to deal with. This was no petty crime, no quiet case—it was the first time anyone in the community had ever been arrested, and for murder no less.

The newscasters reported over and over that the Syed's son had been arrested for killing his ex-girlfriend. Their son's private life, a life forbidden to Muslims, was known in every household. They lived within walking distance from the mosque, but now even appearing there took tremendous courage, courage they had to muster because now more than ever they needed their community.

But the community, while rallying around them, couldn't stop buzzing with the scandal. This young man, someone they considered a "good boy," had carried on an illicit relationship!

The Islamic Society of Baltimore (ISB) boasts of having the largest Muslim congregation in the state of Maryland. Over the past two decades, hundreds of Muslim families had settled around it, creating a close-knit, heavily South Asian community.

Hailing from Pakistan, India, and Bangladesh, the ISB community has managed, over time, to recreate the comforts and conveniences of back home while enjoying the security and opportunity of living in the United States. From authentic kabobs, curries, and tandoori breads sold at the mosque and many restaurants in the area, to halal grocery shops, to an Islamic school, to salons catering to South Asian women, the area is no less than a little "desi-stan." (Desi is a common term for people from Pakistan, India, Sri Lanka, Nepal, and Bangladesh.) In one short trip you can get your hands and arms henna tattooed, swing by the Islamic bookstore to grab some prayer rugs, dine on greasy parathas and chai, and hit the local cinema for the latest Bollywood movie.

Part of the preservation of their culture, as for many immigrant communities, was insisting on their cultural norms for their American-born-and-raised kids.

Basically the rules were: no dating, no alcohol, no partying, no drugs, and, for some, no opposite-gender friends.

We, meaning the kids, all knew what was really going on. Even those of us who were complete squares, like yours truly, were on the downlow grapevine. Who was dating who, who was cheating on who, who was seen drinking in the club, who got to school fully covered and yanked off jeans to reveal a miniskirt. Let's just say 90210 had nothing on 21228. But part of the game, the most important part, was making sure your parents never found out. The stricter the parents, the more elaborate the schemes to keep them in the dark.

This was a function of both trying to be respectful to the folks, and, just as important, not wanting to get your butt kicked. Looking back, there was only so much a parent could do to a teenager who was breaking all the rules, but at the time the feared Pakistani parental discipline options ranged from the infamous *chappal*, a rubber slipper and household staple that sometimes found its way to the backside of a child, to being shipped off to the motherland and betrothed to an unknown cousin eagerly awaiting his or her American visa.

These things weren't common, but they also weren't unheard of. It really depended on the gravity of the offense itself.

Living in the dorms at a prestigious college, a friend of mine fell in love her freshman year; he was her first boyfriend and first physical relationship. One weekend, while she was out with friends, her parents decided to pay her a surprise visit. The RA let them into her dorm to wait for her, where her mother, as Pakistani mothers are programmed to do, began poking around. By the time my friend returned to campus, her parents had found solid evidence of her hanky-panky. Her belongings were promptly packed and she was immediately yanked out of school and driven, sobbing and in shock, back to her hometown many hours away. A couple of years later, when she attempted to move out of the house so she could attend another university, her mother (a wonderful, loving woman) draped herself across the hood of my friend's car to block her from driving away. My friend slowly reversed out, making her mom gently slip off the front of the car, and drove away.

To people not raised by parents or in communities with strong cultural and religious traditions that make a lot of things off-limits (the "haram," a.k.a. prohibited, factor as known by Muslims), this can all sound crazy. Controlling and abusive even. But our parents were doing the best they could to save us from things they thought would hurt us. For our parents, preventing us from sinning was not about control, it was about love.

Because the trouble wasn't the sin itself, it was what that could lead to. And of all sins, the one they most worried about was getting involved in a relationship before marriage. It was love. And it was sex.

There are more than fifty words describing various kinds of love in the Arabic language, according to the famous 14th-century Muslim scholar, theologian, and jurist Ibn Qayyim al Jawziyya. From "syaghaf," love that resides painfully but silently deep in the recesses of the heart, to "ishq," an extreme and even obsessive manifestation of love with lustful connotations, to "hub," a pure, clean, unadulterated love, the sound of which appropriately rises like a sigh from the chest and ends with lips pressed tenderly together and released—the Arabs had no aversion to this affliction of the heart. But it was definitely considered an affliction.

"Love—may God exalt you!—" the frequently lovesick Ibn Hazm writes, "is in truth a baffling ailment, and its remedy is in strict accord with the degree to which it is treated; it is a delightful malady, a most desirable sickness. Whoever is free of it likes not to be immune, and whoever is struck down by it yearns not to recover."

Boy, was Ibn Hazm right.

My adolescence stands as testimony to the desirability of this ailment as I serial-crushed my way through high school, where I was the newspaper editor and photographer-at-large.

I'd run around school during and after hours, at sporting events, plays, meetings, with my trusty Nikon around my neck. I was intrepid, empowered; I got to go anywhere with my self-made press pass.

Even more importantly, I had an excuse to take pictures of every boy I crushed on, an honor I bestowed on almost every boy I went to school with for at least a few days each, sometimes simultaneously.

Once in a while I was joined in the crimson development cave by a student banished to it, forced to learn how to develop pictures to get at least partial credit from Ms. Buzzard, the photography teacher. One day it was the co-captain of the football team, Dave.

My short, plump body was literally on fire as he hovered behind me, looking over my shoulder into the pans of developer and stop fluid.

Once the prints were rinsed off and ready to be hung, Dave realized he had a chance to ask me a burning question.

"So, Rabia, what's the deal? You're pretty cute. How come you don't have a boyfriend?"

After the shock of being told for the first time in my life by a male specimen that I was not bad to look at, I got my wits together and stammered a response.

"Well. I'm Muslim. And Muslims, well . . . Muslims don't date."

The more accurate thing to say would have been, "Muslims aren't *supposed* to date." And to be clear, THIS Muslim didn't. At least not until college, when I met my future ex-husband.

You cannot lump together the cultural expectations and restrictions of all Muslim Americans or immigrant parents or communities; after all, we are one of the most diverse religious groups in the United States. Still, there are common threads, and they don't just apply to Muslims. By and large, "eastern" cultures, including "far eastern" cultures, have traditionally been highly conservative on the issues of dating, sex, and marriage.

Many such cultures traditionally skip right over the dating part and get right to marriage, with sex meant to be strictly within nuptial confines. Arranged marriages have not only been the lot of Middle Easterners and "desis," they are part of Asian culture writ large. From China to Japan, Korea, Thailand, and other parts of this region, sex segregation and arranged marriages were the custom until just a few decades ago.

For the children of immigrants in the United States and other Western nations, old ways often stick around longer than they do back in the "homeland." Parents and grandparents bring and cling to the cultural rules they were raised with, unaware that back home people have moved on, modernized, and, shockingly, changed.

A prime example of this was the time my father told me in high school that when his sisters and nieces were my age, they all wore their hair well-oiled and in two braids and I should too. He was remembering Lahore in the 1960s. We were in the 1990s, when my female relatives in Pakistan were sporting short Princess Diana cuts.

Boys, sex, and marriage were unmentionables in our house. We didn't even use the word "pregnant" because we all knew how women got that way. Well, sort of.

If Bollywood movies, our only source of romance and escapism, were to be believed, people fell head-first in love through silent but frequently exchanged glances, barely touching but breathless and bothered. If ever the "hero" reached out to try and touch his beloved, she would fake protest, blush, and turn away even as her bosom heaved. Eventually the would-be lovers would beat the odds (meaning their parents), get married, hug for the first time, and the next frame would show them happily prancing around a baby.

For most of my childhood I thought hugging was how you made babies.

This eventually was corrected when my mother reluctantly gave signed permission for me to attend a sex-ed class in fifth grade, on the condition of NEVER, EVER discussing what I learned there with anyone. Especially not my younger sister and brother. If ever there was a shock to my system, fifth-grade sex ed was it. I refused to believe for at least another three years that my parents would do any of that, and I refused to believe I'd ever do any of that for at least the next six years.

The day before my parents dropped me off at college, my mother had a little talk with me. I was going to live in a dorm against her wishes, having managed to snag enough grants and student loans to pay for it myself.

I was the first kid to go away, I knew this was not going to be easy on my parents, and a part of me didn't believe it was actually going to happen.

That's why, when I sat next to my mother, a pit grew harder and larger in my stomach as I waited for her to say something. Not believing in overt affection or anything less than a strict parent-child dynamic, my mom had never had a heart-to-heart with me before.

In her gentlest voice she said, "Look, you're going to college and will be in a mixed, co-ed setting and there may be boys who are interested in you. And that's ok. It's ok if a boy is interested in you. And it's ok if you're interested in him. After all, you have to get married at some point. So don't be scared to tell us. Come tell me if there's anyone. It's ok if you tell me. Also, better if it's a white boy. White boys will easily convert, and they don't have all the baggage of large, desi in-law families."

It was never made clear how I could entice a non-Muslim white boy to convert and marry me without actually dating one, or letting one touch me, but heck, at least I now had permission.

Except it wasn't really permission. It was a trap.

A year and change later, after I had met and fallen in love with a Pakistani international student who wanted to get married, I went running happily to my mother to break the news. It did not go well.

Just because she told me it was ok to "meet" someone, code for dating-without-touching-but-with-the-goal-of-marriage, didn't mean it was. The verbal and emotional smack-down blindsided me. How dare I be involved with a man? How dare I vocalize my desire to get married?! Where was my shame? Since when did girls talk to parents of their own marriage?! Not in 1995 they didn't, not in the Chaudry house.

But I was definitely much more old-school than the kids in our communities. By kids I mean people more than five years my junior who operated with more abandon, and started much sooner, when it came to dating.

My younger siblings were no exception. I knew this intuitively, but also because I saw little signs here and there, heard whispers and allusions to their romantic activities. But I never knew for sure.

This was another cultural rule—when you know someone is doing something they shouldn't, you look the other way.

Hiding your sins and the sins of others is not just a cultural norm, it's a religious mandate in Islam.

> Whoever fulfills the needs of his brother, Allah will fulfill his needs;
> whoever removes the troubles of his brother, Allah will remove
> one of his troubles on the Day of Judgment; and whoever covers
> up the fault of a Muslim, Allah will cover up his fault on the
> Day of Judgment.
>
> —*Prophet Muhammad (Sahih Bukhari)*

Covering the faults of another essentially boils down to not gossiping and spreading someone's business. It also means not prying, not spying, leaving people to their personal business. A sin is supposed to be strictly between the sinner and God.

There is a story about a man who came to the Prophet Muhammad (and these stories, collectively known as *hadith*, form a large part of the foundation of Islamic belief and practices) and confessed he was sleeping with a woman he wasn't married to. He felt guilty and thought he should be punished. An important early Muslim, Umar ibn Khattab, who would later become one of the Caliphs of Islam after the Prophet died, heard his confession. He said to the confessor, "Allah kept your secret, so why did not you keep your secret?"

To be clear, this applies to personal sins only. It doesn't apply to any instances in which the life, liberty, or property of another has been infringed on or damaged. Those are not just sins, they're crimes, and they have to be reported, accounted for, and the wronged person made whole.

But teenagers drinking, smoking pot, dating, sleeping around—all the things that happened in the Baltimore Muslim community (and I dare say most communities, religious and irreligious) despite parental strictness—were off the table. "Don't ask, don't tell" were, and are, the rules in South Asian communities when it comes to personal indiscretions.

The Islamic Society of Baltimore, and all the families connected with it, was no exception. Which is why part of the trauma for the community was that Adnan's personal life was cracked wide open and made public.

"How did you find out Adnan had a girlfriend?"

I had never asked Aunty Shamim this before—asking potentially embarrassing questions, prying, we didn't do this. But now, sixteen years after Adnan was arrested, it seems like enough time has passed to broach the subject.

Aunty smiles to herself and shifts, blinks rapidly, her eyes down. Even after all this time, she's not fully comfortable. But she's also not apologetic.

Dating was not permissible, not then, and not now. Not for any of her children. The first time she suspected something was when Adnan was dropped off at home by a young woman—she couldn't see her face, but could see that it was a girl, a girl who quickly drove away. She asked Adnan about her.

"Just a friend," was Adnan's response, but his mother knew something was up. Soon after she caught him up, late at night, on the phone. She heard him speaking in a low voice and knew it couldn't be with another guy, not at that hour, not in that tone. So she carefully picked up a receiver in another room and caught him red-handed.

After that came the arguments between mother and son. Adnan's father stayed out of it; he was completely unconcerned. All he knew was that Adnan was a good student, went with him to the mosque, was polite, and would soon be off to college.

Aunty is young for a grandmother. She is slight, with clear, fair skin, bright eyes, and frizzy hair that can never seem to stay within the confines of a scarf or a hair tie.

She was only sixteen when the family of Syed Rahman came around, seeking a suitable bride for him. He was forty-one, had a good life in the United States, and his father had a friend who had a niece they heard was lovely. Her name was Shamim but she didn't come from Turu, the same small village as Syed's family. Shamim lived with her parents and six sisters in Mardan, the "city of hospitality" in the Khyber Pakhtunkhwa Province. She was a student, and a bit too young to be married off just yet. But two years later her parents consented.

Aunty Shamim was eighteen when she married her forty-three-year-old husband, a man she didn't know who lived in the United States. Two weeks after the wedding in Pakistan, she found herself in Baltimore.

She was less nervous than her family about marrying a man more than twice her age and then moving halfway across the world. Her fortitude in that stressful situation is no surprise to me. Since Adnan's arrest she has been a pillar of strength, putting on an outward appearance of resolve, sometimes even cheer, when in public.

But while she was able to embrace the entrepreneurial spirit of America, opening and running her own home daycare center as she raised three boys, her cultural expectations and traditions remained relatively firm. At least when it came to dating.

Pakistan, some may be surprised to know, is much more diverse in its range of conservatism to liberalism than are most countries in the Western hemisphere. Some of this diversity is a function of local tradition, some a function of local development, and some a function of family custom.

In large cities like Lahore, Islamabad, and Karachi, you'll find young women filling universities and workplaces, hair fashionably coiffed, showing off trendy clothing. And I don't mean just now. My mother recalls being at the university in Lahore in the 1960s when some of her classmates decided to join the sexual revolution and dispense with wearing bras. At the same time my mother had decided, on her own, to start wearing a burka to cover up everything, including her face. She didn't come from a family where that was the norm. Her own mother was a college graduate at a time when not many women made it that far in education, and my "Nani" (maternal grandmother) and her sisters thought nothing of wearing sleeveless sari blouses, hair piled into beehives or bouffants. My burka'd mother, however, ran a girls' college while Nani never worked outside of the home.

It wasn't odd then, or now, to find families in the city where some women worked, others didn't get past grade school, some preferred burkas, and others skin-tight sleeveless *kurtas* (longish shirts). Out in the villages, you may find less diversity in what is socially acceptable; it usually depends on regional ethnicity and local tradition.

My parents' families are from the Punjab region, where women are stereotyped as forward and confident. I've heard this is linked to the strong agricultural tradition of the area, in which women historically worked the fields instead of staying confined to the house, or to Punjabi culture itself, which is infamous for being boisterous and unfiltered.

Adnan's family comes from a region of Pakistan that many Punjabis find as foreign as China.

Khyber Pakhtunkhwa ("KPK"), previously known as the NWFP or North-West Frontier Province, is one of four provincial regions in Pakistan. KPK is the northernmost province in the country, bordered by Afghanistan to the west and north, and by Azad Kashmir to the east. Geographically, it is one of the most stunning regions in Pakistan.

Snowcapped peaks and deep green valleys invite a lot of Pakistani tourists, honeymooners, global adventure seekers, and mountain climbers. Ancient Buddhist and Hindu ruins dot the landscape.

The Pashtuns are known to be immensely hospitable, loyal, and have a deep sense of traditional values in which the honor of family and guests is paramount. Pashtuns are also the butt of many jokes, chided for being simple-minded, with little common sense and zero street smarts. But while other Pakistanis may find their "simplicity" amusing, the Pashtun's immovable sense of family and tribal affiliation, which are both key to the Pashtun identity and sacred institutions, is duly admired. It could not have been easy for Aunty Shamim and Uncle Syed to have left their families and migrate halfway across the world, but the promise of a better life for their future family compelled them.

Adnan's parents put down roots in the Catonsville area. They had no other family in the entire country, much less in Maryland, but they had the mosque. And this would be the mosque Adnan and his brothers would be raised in; this would be the community that was their family.

Before we actually sold our house in Hagerstown and moved, my father had to start his new job in Baltimore. He rented a room down the street from the mosque in the summer of 1995. Saad was fourteen at the time and every so often he would go hang out with him.

One day during a visit, Saad was shooting hoops in the parking lot of the ISB when a gangly, smiling boy came over and introduced himself.

"Hi, I'm Adnan. Are you new around here?"

Saad was wearing a basketball camp T-shirt, which caught thirteen-year-old Adnan's interest, and they began shooting hoops. Saad explained that he lived in Hagerstown but would soon be moving to Baltimore.

Not long after, when the family shifted to Ellicott City about ten miles from the ISB, Saad gave Adnan a call as promised.

"We got together at the Security Mall and Adnan asked me, 'Ok, how much money do you have?' I told him I had $15. Adnan said, 'I have $30 so that means we have $45 together.'" Saad knew right then that this guy had a big heart.

They were both starting ninth grade that year, though Saad was a year older. A prolonged trip to Pakistan when he was in elementary school had put him back a year. But they attended different schools, and they did most of their hanging out on the weekends at the mosque. They quickly became best friends; Yusuf once remarked that Saad was more of a brother to Adnan than he or Tanveer ever were. Saad's presence in Adnan's life made a few of Adnan's other friends feel left out, though—Yaser Ali and Tayyab Hussein in particular. Yaser, a family friend since childhood, had considered himself Adnan's best friend; years later he would testify that he was edged out when Saad showed up.

Adnan and Saad weren't jocks, but sports were their primary concern. Girls had their place in conversation, but the first couple of years of their friendship neither of them dated.

"We were late-bloomers in the girls' department," Saad recalls.

It wasn't until their junior year, when they both had driver's licenses and access to cars, that the world of dating opened up. Because Saad was a year older he got his third-hand manual BMW before Adnan had a car. It wasn't unusual for Saad to park at the church across the road from Adnan's house at night, waiting for him to sneak out after his parents went to sleep so they could hit up a party.

Sleeping parents have always provided the perfect opportunity for kids to get away with their indiscretions. One of the more extreme stories I've heard is about a family of Pakistani-American brothers I know, not even Muslims mind you, who more than once served their loving parents after-dinner tea with a mild sleeping aid mixed in. The parents got the soundest sleep of their lives, waking up refreshed and clueless, while the brothers painted the town red. It was a win-win as far as those guys were concerned.

Saad and Adnan, along with other friends from the mosque, would usually stake out Indian or Pakistani parties to check out the girls. "Garba" dance parties, an incredibly festive and colorful Gujarati Hindu tradition during the season of Navratri (literally "Nine Nights"), attracted a lot of Muslim desi boys, thanks partly to the girls' traditional outfits—gorgeously decorated skirts that flared with every turn and beautiful midriff-baring, fitted blouses. During these nine nights, different avatars of the Hindu goddess Durga are worshiped by dancing in flying, concentric, increasingly fast circles around her figure, along with other rituals. This is technically about as "haram" as you can get for strictly monotheistic Muslims, just-say-no-to-idol-worship-101, but as a cultural phenomenon it is no less acceptable than carving up a tandoori-flavored Thanksgiving turkey. This is the cultural hodgepodge that kids, particularly from the South Asian subcontinent, where Muslims, Sikhs, Hindus, Christians, and Buddhists have been living together for centuries, are accustomed to. Being raised in the West adds one more dimension to an already complicated but very much culturally egalitarian identity.

Thanks to these parties and events where he met girls from around the state, Saad secretly ended up going to numerous school homecomings, but never to Woodlawn High, and Adnan never went to Saad's school either. Most of their mutual friends came from the mosque, and many of Adnan's friends annoyed the hell out of Saad.

"His problem was he was friends with EVERYBODY. I mean with guys I thought were losers, idiots, dead weights. Even guys I thought were just bad influences, like Tayyab. They'd do dumb stuff like egg houses together. Adnan was better than that, and I told him that. There were times we'd hang out all day with some of his other friends and I wouldn't even talk to any of them. I'd ask him why the heck was he giving these guys the time of day?! I guess I was kind of the snob or jerk about it. But Adnan gave everyone attention, he just couldn't say no to people. He was too nice, that was his problem."

It was partly Adnan's failure to be more selective about people that landed him where he is today. If he had followed Saad's advice, Jay Wilds, the young man who would have such an impact on Adnan's fate, could never have gotten close enough to hurt him. But then, it was his own bad habits that opened the door to Jay.

Adnan had taken up occasional pot smoking, and Jay supplied him with the weed. He had an occasional drink too. Saad hadn't crossed that threshold yet in high school. Those things were easy to stay away from.

Girls? Not so easy.

"She was Adnan's girlfriend? Adnan?? Had a girlfriend? Hae was his GIRL-FRIEND??!" I yelled in disbelief.

Saad scowled. Adnan's dating life was irrelevant.

It wasn't that the murder charge didn't strike me as monumental, it did—it shook me to my core. But it also seemed ludicrous. The cops had clearly made a mistake, and that mistake would soon be remedied.

But Adnan's reputation, now that rumors had been spreading at ISB about his recreational activities? I wasn't so sure it could be rehabilitated.

In some way, almost every child raised right in front of the community's eyes, every kid who is seen consistently at the mosque, every young boy or girl who maintains ties to their roots and religion, is a golden child. It wasn't just Adnan. It was all of us, all the boys and girls who got good grades, showed up dutifully for Sunday school, dressed and behaved properly in front of the grownups—we were all golden. Hiding what we did privately wasn't considered hypocrisy. It was considered respectful.

And though much is made of being raised in the United States, in a country and culture where the norm is often anathema to Pakistani or Muslim traditions, the truth is that every generation rebels against their elders, even those raised "back home."

One of the many lessons on decorum and parental-child relationships my father has repeated throughout our lives is this: "I never spoke back to my father. I never objected to what he said to me. I always agreed no matter what. If he forbade me from doing something, I said 'ok.' But then I did what I wanted to. I just respected him enough not to flaunt it, and to hide it. That's how you respect your elders."

This is the complicated dance of fear, respect, and love that many of us grew up with, a dance that could only be avoided by simply not disobeying your folks.

Adnan and Saad both danced and mostly got away with it—until Adnan was arrested. Then Adnan's indiscretions became a lesson between parents and kids.

"See? This is what happens when you disobey us. This is what happens when you date. This is what happens when you stop acting like a Muslim."

The aunties disguised their breathless gossip as concern and sadness.

"*Subhan Allah*, so terrible, so terrible for the family that he was doing all these things, and now the entire world knows. I can't imagine what Shamim must be going through. Should we check on her? Should we ask her if all of this is really true?"

And this was just about the dating. The pot, the alcohol, the sex, all that would come out later during the trial. It was a small mercy that these other things remained under wraps until then, giving the community enough headspace to rally together and organize for Adnan's defense.

Bilal Ahmed took the lead in organizing community support. A self-styled youth leader, Bilal was of Pakistani descent, had been raised in Saudi Arabia, and had moved to Maryland to study at the University of Maryland, Baltimore Campus, or UMBC. He was a half dozen years or so older than the kids he "mentored" at the local mosque, and as for most of the kids in the community, well, he annoyed the fuck out of us.

Bilal did himself no favors by refusing to look the other way. He strutted around campus with I'M TOO SEXY buttons on his backpack, keeping an eye on kids in the community and making sure their secrets were not kept.

One of the best-known stories of that era, a veritable legend, was a stunt Bilal pulled at an Indian and Pakistani student dance party on campus. "Ajooba" was going to be the hottest desi event that year. A party like that didn't just attract local South Asian college kids, local South Asian high school kids also planned to go—including a number of my little sister's friends.

"Everybody found out what happened, and everybody still remembers it," Rana says, giggling. Rana was one of the "Baltimore girls," a group of my sister's friends who grew up around the mosque and attended UMBC together. She was still in high school when it all went down, and so were a number of her friends who attended the party that day.

Bilal, having heard not just about the party but about the plans of some of the ISB kids to be there, showed up at the dance and planted himself outside the entrance door, a memo pad in hand. He took down the names of all the kids whose parents attended the ISB, even though many of them tried to dodge him once they realized what he was up to. One girl, the daughter of one of ISB's "pillar" families, was already inside. There was no hiding and no escape. Seated at a table, this girl saw Bilal take his position. She did the only thing she could think of. She dove under the table.

But it was too late for her, and dozens of others. At the very next Friday prayer service Bilal announced the names of kids who had been at the dance in front of a mortified congregation. Suffice it to say, it was a rough weekend for a lot of the kids. Rana remembers her father coming home from prayers and grilling her about the party. Like most of the elders, he was more irritated and angry at Bilal than he was at the kids who were exposed. A public shaming like that broke the rules of decorum and left the parents fuming.

But Adnan, again to the chagrin of Saad and others, was friends with Bilal, and Bilal, oddly, didn't "out" Adnan. In fact, he covered Adnan's exploits, agreeing to tell his parents Adnan was with him when Adnan would instead be out clubbing or with a girl. When Adnan's mother failed to get him to break up with Hae, she reached out to Bilal to help guide her son. Little did she know he was enabling Adnan. Years later, when Aunty Shamim learned that the young man she entrusted with guiding her son instead facilitated his hijinx, she was bitter and upset.

But she had other reasons to find fault with Bilal. As the person who took charge when Adnan was arrested, Bilal not only organized the community fund-raising for legal costs, he also found Adnan an attorney.

Aunty Shamim blamed Bilal for the most catastrophic decision the family would make when it came to her son's defense—hiring Cristina Gutierrez.

Adnan:

I know that there are many instances in our community where you have tension-filled households due to parents attempting to enforce conservative cultural/religious values. These strict rules would clash with the liberal society their children were exposed to. I have heard of and seen the turbulent atmosphere in homes where the parents were in a constant struggle with a rebellious teen. Witnessing this as I was growing up caused me to appreciate the calm and loving home life that my parents provided for my brothers and me.

As a child, I spent most of my free time at our local mosque. Most of us kids did. We would ride our bikes there after school and stay late into the evening. During the summer we would spend the whole day there. Prayers and religious classes only took up a fraction of our time. We usually spent most of our days and nights playing.

A large addition was being built on the property, and for several years we had access to a construction site. We would run around on the beams, climb the scaffolding, and other things. One summer, we stole a bunch of scrap wood, some two-by-fours, a hammer and nails, and we built a bridge across the creek. It was about ten feet long, with a handrail and three-feet-tall support poles we had sunk into the creek bed. My childhood was full of happy days playing with my friends at the mosque.

Once we all began entering our teenage years, around the end of middle school and the beginning of high school, things began to change. Many of us started dating and going to parties. We also began experimenting with marijuana and alcohol. These were things typical of almost any kid at that age. For us, however, it was different because of the conservative nature of our families. We were doing things that our parents did not approve of, and now a different and new dynamic came into play.

For some of our friends, life became very stressful. Those with parents who were very strict ended up in extremely difficult situations as they tried to do the things that normal kids did. Their households would become very chaotic as the parents struggled to enforce a strict code of behavior. The friend would rebel, and it would create a very turbulent home life. The sad irony is that it would usually cause the teen to engage in the most reckless behavior of all of us, like drug and alcohol abuse and failing classes. It seemed as if the parents' attempts to clamp down seemed only to instigate more harmful behavior. Perhaps it was the notion of "I know I'm gonna get in big trouble, so I may as well make it worthwhile." Whatever the case, I have had friends who grew up in these very strict households, only to end up in a bad way. Witnessing these sad outcomes always caused me to be thankful that I was never in that situation with my family.

I was very fortunate to have very supportive and loving parents. They were never the type to be strict with us in general. They raised my brothers and me with the religious and cultural values they believed in. More importantly, they taught us that we were free to make our own choices, but that we always had to be prepared to take responsibility for our actions.

They did both have individual aspects of life they were strict about. For my father it was school. He was someone whose education had earned for him an opportunity to raise himself out of poverty. Owing to that, he never failed to instill in us the importance of doing well in school. Our maintaining high grades was the number-one priority, for him.

For my mother it was the subject of social interaction. She was more in tune with the problems facing young people. Substance abuse was one of her major concerns, as she had seen several other teens fall victim to it. To her, staying out late and going to parties was the gateway to all of that.

From a religious standpoint, my mother was also against dating. Our religion has very strict rules about that, essentially that it was not allowed. It was never something that caused her to give us ultimatums, or threaten to kick us out of the house. It was just that she expressed her disapproval and let it be known that she did not want us to have girlfriends.

It didn't stop me; however, it did cause me to be very mindful of my behavior. Or rather, work extra hard not to get caught. It wasn't so much that I was worried about getting in trouble; mainly, it was that I wanted to be respectful to my parents, in a way. I was going to do the things that I wanted, but it was also important to me that I never make them unhappy. I never wanted to disappoint them.

So as high school began, I did my best to hide the things that I did. I secretly bought a pager, so no girl would have to call the house to get in touch with me. I would wait for my parents to go bed before I went out at night on the weekends. I always made sure my clothes would never smell of perfume, or marijuana, when I returned home.

At the same time, I worked very hard to achieve the things that would make my parents proud of me. I got good grades in school, I did volunteer work, and I always had some type of job. I did whatever I could to help around the house. I've always had a great deal of love and respect for my parents. Not just because of how hard they worked to provide a good life for us, but also because of the contrast between their parenting styles and that of others. Seeing the stressful situations of my other friends' home lives caused me to have a greater appreciation for my own.

I'll be honest, I hate hearing/reading that portion of my adolescence being described as a "double life." To me, that phrase implies a negative connotation associated with hypocrisy. It brings to mind someone who calls people to do one thing, but does the opposite in secret. And that is something I never did. I only wanted to live my life the way other kids did, but I also realized that in order to protect my parents from hurt and disappointment, I had to hide things from them. I didn't hide anything to protect some "righteous" persona I had cultivated . . .

From a religious perspective, my friends and I didn't really feel like it was a big deal. It seemed that we all kind of had the same idea; we would have a good time, do good in school, grow up, get married, and then become more serious about our faith. There really was not a whole lot of self-doubt, or soul-searching. In a way, we felt that being Muslim was more about loving our people than about adhering to the conservative tenets of our faith. Which, to an adult, may seem far-fetched. But to a teenager it made perfect sense. We were all pretty much doing the same thing, and none of us viewed ourselves as being bad Muslims.

By the time Hae and I began dating I had a relatively scandal-free career. Having never been in a relationship, I never had a reason to go on capers every single day. I could hang out on the weekends with girls and go to parties, but during the week it was pretty much just school or work. Being in a relationship, however, had me talking on the phone with Hae each night, wanting to spend every evening with her after school, going on dates, and so on. I was having to evade suspicion every day. Pretty soon it was impossible not to get caught.

The first time my mother caught me talking to Hae on the phone was the morning after our Junior Prom. We were talking about how much fun we had the night before and all of a sudden I heard my mother's voice cut in, "Hey, I just want you to know that Adnan has many other girlfriends, and you're not the only one." I was stunned and speechless to hear her voice interrupt our conversation with no warning.

Hae and I were both well experienced in the need to have secret conversations on the phone, as she had a similar home life. We both knew that if you heard a "click" someone had picked up a phone. We would usually just hang up at that point, as we would have no way of knowing whose home it was in. We would then page each other when the coast was clear. But in this case, there was no "click." My mother's voice had just broken into our conversation. I would find out later that she had unplugged the phone jack from the wall outlet. Next she removed the handset from the cradle, and then plugged the jack back in. That way there was no "click" from the handset disconnecting from the cradle.

As far as what she actually said, well, I couldn't help but laugh at her creativity. Even now, all these years later, I still laugh about it. My mother told me she had thought of it on the fly, and she just wanted to say something that would make the girl not want to talk to me anymore. It was actually very funny.

Later that day my mother had a long talk with me about it. I denied everything, of course, and told her Hae and I were just friends. I don't think my mother believed me, but she left it alone. Throughout the rest of our relationship Hae and I both experienced those same types of situations. Her mom had issues with us dating as well. There were never any huge blowups, however, or ultimatums or threats. Both our mothers eventually became upset, and I think that's what weighed on us the most.

Once it became clear that we were continuing to see each other, it caused friction between us and our mothers. And it was not something we could hide from them. Eventually, Hae decided that it wasn't really worth the stress it seemed to be causing them, and us. So that was when she first decided to call off our relationship. And each subsequent breakup was for essentially the same reason.

To be honest, I really don't have any regrets from those days. Dating Hae was an amazing experience, and I wouldn't change it for anything. She became someone I cared for deeply, and I cherish the times we spent together, both as girlfriend/boyfriend and as friends. I treasure the memories I have of her.

I'm grateful for all the friends I had, and I can't help but smile as I think of all the crazy and silly things we did. As a Muslim, I know I did things that were not compatible with Islamic rules. But I feel that all of those experiences combined to give me a broader perspective on life, and I believe that perspective allows me to have a deeper appreciation for my faith. I'm fairly certain that most of us who had similar adolescent experiences probably would say the same thing.

CHAPTER 5

MURDER IN THE FIRST

————·————

The burden of proof is on the proponent
and the oath is incumbent on the one who denies
Ahmed ibn al-Husayn al-Bayhaqi, Book of the Great Sunnah

After the police picked up Adnan, he was put in the back of a Baltimore City Police cruiser, driven to the police station, and his car was impounded and towed away. He recalls one of the officers in the car teasing him, telling him he was so pretty he was going to get fucked frequently where he was headed. He was talking smack and Adnan knew it, but he didn't understand why the officer was being so mean to him. The female officer driving the car was polite though, telling him that he was being taken for questioning, a small kindness he still remembers.

He was taken into an interrogation room and cuffed to the wall, then read his rights. He agreed to answer the detectives' questions without an attorney, thinking this would soon be over.

POLICE DEPARTMENT CITY OF BALTIMORE				
ROSECUTION REPORT ORM 67\9				
FENDANTS NAME (LAST, FIRST, MIDDLE) SYED, ADNAN MASUD	COMPL. NO. 88-5801	SEX M	RACE I	DOB ▮▮▮▮
CHARGES FIRST DEGREE MURDER	ARREST NO. 98-0000	DATE OCCURRED 09 FEB 1999		

Prosecution report of charges of first degree murder against Adnan Syed

Detectives Ritz and MacGillivary tried a variety of tactics to get Adnan to talk, from showing empathy ("Hey, I know how you feel, my ex-wife makes me mad too"), to getting tough ("We know what you did and we're going to prove it by finding your boots, process your car, finding your red gloves"). Then they told him that they knew he and Jay did it.

Adnan responded that he had no idea what they were talking about. Red gloves? He and Jay did it? He was completely baffled. As he sat there cuffed inside the homicide unit he was thinking about his school work. It was Sunday morning, and he had an annotated bibliography due the next day. How long was this all going to take, he wondered.

The detectives left the room after questioning him for a bit, then returned with the Metro Crime Stoppers flyer, sliding it across the table toward him. Adnan leaned forward, looking at it, then looked at them. He still didn't understand what they were implying. They told him to look at the flyer, look at Hae, take some time, and then tell them what happened. They then left him to be alone with Hae's picture.

After a bit they returned and placed a document on top of the flyer. It was the charging document, stating that Adnan Syed was arrested for the first-degree, premeditated murder of Hae Min Lee.

This was the point at which Adnan, thinking back to the years of *Matlock* he had watched, asked for a lawyer. What he didn't know was that even before his interrogation was over, a lawyer was already at the police station, trying to stop the questioning and see his juvenile client.

Attorney Doug Colbert, a professor at the University of Maryland School of Law, had been retained within an hour of Adnan's arrest. He was contacted by Bilal Ahmed, who had been called by Tanveer as soon as Adnan was taken away. For many years Colbert was the senior trial attorney in the Criminal Defense Division of the NYC Legal Aid Society and had spent much of his career writing and speaking on defendant rights. Before joining the Legal Aid Society, Colbert taught the criminal justice clinic at Hofstra Law, where one of his students was an eager and sharp young man by the name of Chris Flohr. Upon graduating, Flohr also joined the Legal Aid Society, where he litigated trials for every kind of felony. But Flohr eventually left New York and moved to Baltimore in 1998, and when Adnan was arrested he was the legal director of a program focusing on bail reform in Baltimore City. Colbert tapped him to help assist with Adnan's case.

Adnan had waived his rights to an attorney at 7:55 a.m., but by 7:10 a.m. the police had already known Adnan was represented and had been advised to stop the interrogation. And yet they didn't. They continued their questioning of a minor, preventing his attorney from being present, refusing to let Adnan's parents see him, and also refusing, despite the attorney's request, to record the interrogation.

Finally, after attempting all morning to gain access to his client, attorney Doug Colbert faxed a frustrated letter to Detective Marvin Sydnor at 1:34 p.m.

> *Dear Detective Sydnor,*
>
> *I represent 17 year-old Mr. Adnan Syed, whom I understand you have had in police custody concerning a pending homicide investigation since approximately 6 a.m. this morning. I write to reiterate my numerous requests that I have made this morning to permit me to speak to my client immediately and that you cease any questioning in my absence. [. . .]*
>
> *Despite my repeated requests, Detective Sydnor refused to tell Mr. Syed that his attorneys were present and declined to cease questioning. I also asked Detective Sydnor to videotape the interview and questioning of Mr. Syed, but the Detective refused by saying that I 'wouldn't want to tell you how to defend someone in court.' Finally I asked Detective Sydnor to permit Mr. Syed's mother and father to see their son immediately. Detective Sydnor again declined my request. [. . .]*
>
> *We repeat our request to see our client, Mr. Syed, immediately upon receipt of this letter.*

The letter and their repeated attempts failed. Having held Adnan for six hours of interrogation, the police did not record or videotape any of it and did not inform Adnan about his attorneys until it was over. Only a few lines of notes were produced, notes pertaining to the reading of Miranda rights and Adnan's waiver of his right to having an attorney present during questioning.

According to Adnan, after he had asked for an attorney, he didn't speak to the police again and the interview wrapped up. But one of the last things he remembers Ritz saying to him, after he asked when he could go home because he had school work to do, was, "Adnan, you're not going home."

After a long booking process Adnan was given one five-minute phone call. He spoke to Tanveer, telling him he had been charged with Hae's murder, and then he asked for his mom.

Adnan:

> Subsequent to my interrogation at the police station, I was transported to the Central Booking Intake Facility. I was fingerprinted, photographed, and also

given a basic health screening. I was next brought before a court commissioner, who informed me that because I was charged with First-Degree murder, I would be placed on a "No-bail" status. He further explained that because of this status, I would immediately be remanded into the custody of the Baltimore City Detention Center until trial. I actually remember the exact words he spoke; he was reading them off a piece of paper. He ended up with, "until trial, or such time as the Court orders your release."

This entire process lasted several hours, as between each step there was a period of time which I spent waiting in various holding cells. Once the booking process was complete, I was permitted to make one phone call. I was directed to a chair that was adjacent to a desk with a phone on it, and informed that I had five minutes. I dialed the number for my home, and after a few rings, my older brother answered. Initially, I couldn't respond to his "Hello? Hello?" because I had no idea what to say. Eventually, I said to him, "Tanveer, hey, it's me." I told him that I had been taken to the police station, and that they had charged me with Hae's murder. I didn't know at the time, but by then I believe there was news coverage, and my family was already aware. I explained to him that I was in the Booking Facility, and that I was being transferred to the City Detention Center. He asked how I was doing, and if I was alright? Hearing the worry and fear in his voice, I did my best to assure him that I was fine, and surely this whole thing must be a huge mistake, and that it would probably be straightened out soon.

By then, the officer informed me I had only one minute left. I asked my brother, "Is Mom there?" and he passed the phone to her. I heard her say, very softly, "Adnan . . ." and immediately I could tell that she had been crying. It was the first time throughout the whole ordeal that I felt my resolve begin to crack. I struggled to keep my voice steady, as I conveyed to her that I was alright, and that this would all end soon. I asked her how Yusuf was doing, and she told me that he had been very upset, but that he had gone to sleep. I only had a few seconds left, and I reassured her once again that I was well, and that she shouldn't worry. I promised I would call home again as soon as I could. I was relieved to hear a measure of calmness in her voice as we said our good-byes.

I was next taken to a shower area, and strip-searched. There was a faucet which dispensed anti-bacterial soap, and I was instructed to wash my entire body with it. An officer stood there and watched to make sure I complied with that order. I was handed a green jumpsuit, and given a brown bag which contained breakfast. In it was an 8 oz. carton of milk, two boiled-eggs, four slices of bread, and an apple. After I was finished eating, I was handcuffed and escorted to the Detention Center, which was linked to the Booking Facility by a series of long corridors.

I was taken to the juvenile wing, and from that point on, it was just a matter of waiting. I would spend the next several months reading a lot of novels, playing basketball, and exercising. I learned a lot of table-top games, such as chess, Scrabble, various card games, etc. We'd have an opportunity to make phone calls once a day or so, during our recreation time. There was a television in the rec. hall area, and we could also take showers during that time. Sporadically, there were disturbances, fights, etc., and we would be placed on lock-down. We would be confined to our cells, and this could last a day, several days, or even weeks, depending on the nature of the disturbance. We were also allowed to submit requests to the law library. I would order legal materials, trying to understand the trial process. It was very difficult; I had no idea what to request as I had no clear understanding of what I was going through, legally.

Adnan tried to maintain a calm demeanor with his family. But when he called Bilal he wasn't able to control his emotions.

At a grand jury proceeding on March 22, 1999, Bilal testified about the call saying Adnan was "hysterical," and "he was crying a lot so—and it was hard for me understand from his conversation was that he was—I mean, he was devastated. He's like denying it. I didn't do it."

It's not surprising that Adnan called Bilal and let his emotions loose. Bilal was his mentor.

Adnan now describes Bilal as a real-life Fagin from Oliver Twist: encouraging kids' corruption while protecting his own reputation, feigning self-righteousness to cover misdeeds. Adnan and the other kids knew things about Bilal that the rest of us didn't. But upon his arrest, Adnan knew Bilal was the guy who could help his family cope.

And he did. It was Bilal who recommended Colbert to the family the morning Adnan was arrested, and now he was organizing meetings at the mosque to raise money and get ready for the bail hearing, which was what the attorneys told him to do.

The first bail hearing was set for March 1, 1999, when Adnan appeared via video conference in the Baltimore City District Court. His attorneys requested that bail be set at $25,000, but it was denied thanks to an error on Adnan's charging documents: his birth date.

DISTRICT COURT OF MARYLAND FOR Baltimore City
Located at 1400 E. North Avenue, Baltimore, MD 21213   Case No.: 005B00351587

STATE OF MARYLAND   VS   **SYED, ADNAN**
                                              JOHNNYCAKE ROAD
                                              BALTIMORE, MD   21207
                                    CC#:998B5801   SID:
                                    Local ID: DL#:
                                    Race:4   Sex:M   Ht:6'1"   Wt:160   Hair: Eyes:
                                    DOB:05/21/1980   Phone(H):   Phone(W):

Charge | Statute | Arrest   Charge | Statute | Arrest
MURDER-FIRST DEGREE | 27407 |

ARREST WARRANT ON CHARGING DOCUMENT - Warrant No. D990187155
STATE OF MARYLAND, Baltimore City
TO ANY PEACE OFFICER, Greetings:
    YOU ARE ORDERED to arrest and bring before a judicial officer the above-named Defendant as soon as
practicable and without unnecessary delay. If a judicial officer is not readily available, this Warrant shall
authorize the prisoner's detention until compliance is had with Rule 4-212 and the arresting officer is authorized
and required to comply with Rule 4-212.
    IF THE DEFENDANT IS NOT IN CUSTODY FOR ANOTHER OFFENSE,
Initial appearance is to be held in county in which Warrant was issued.
    IF THE DEFENDANT IS IN CUSTODY FOR ANOTHER OFFENSE, this Warrant is to be lodged as a
detainer for the continued detention of the Defendant for the offense charged in the charging document.
When the Defendant is served with a copy of the charging document and Warrant, the Defendant shall be taken
before a judicial officer of the District Court.

Date: 02/28/1999 Time: 04:43 AM   Judge/Commissioner: _____   ID: 1243
Given to: **BALTIMORE CITY POLICE-NORTHEASTERN**

Adnan's birthday is May 21, 1981. But his arrest warrant, the document before the judge, incorrectly noted his date of birth as 1980. In fact, this mistake remains on his criminal record to this day.

In 1999 the death penalty still existed in the State of Maryland, but not for minor defendants. However, this judge, seeing the arrest warrant, incorrectly assumed Adnan was an adult and twice referred to the case as a capital case, thus not eligible for bail.

On March 16, Colbert and Flohr filed a Writ of Habeas Corpus with the circuit court, a legal mechanism by which to challenge the imprisonment of a defendant. A hearing on the writ was held shortly thereafter, on March 31.

In the week before the bail hearing, the community scrambled to both raise funds and collect character letters of support for Adnan from people with whom he had grown up, worshipped, and gone to school. About one hundred such letters were submitted to the court, and buses were arranged from the mosque to the court early on the day of the hearing. Nearly a hundred people filed into the courtroom and hallways outside the courthouse.

"I'd never seen anything like it," says Doug Colbert. A number of community members, all doctors, offered their homes as bail collateral.

They expected Adnan, a kid with no record, well-loved and supported by a community spanning professionals, religious leaders, and peers, would be viewed by the judge favorably. And he might have, if prosecutor Vicki Wash hadn't made an argument that left us all stunned.

Before a room full of Muslim citizens she said to the court, "Your Honor, the fact that the defendant has strong support from the community, that *is* what makes him unique in this case. He is unique because he has limitless resources; he has the resources of this entire community here. Investigation reveals that he can tag resources from Pakistan as well. It's our position, Your Honor, that if you issue bail, then you are issuing him a passport under these circumstances to flee the country. [. . . T]here is a pattern in the United States of America where young Pakistani males have been jilted, have committed murder, and have fled to Pakistan, and we have been unable to extradite them back. [. . .] We have information from our investigation that the defendant *has* an uncle in Pakistan, and he has indicated that he can make people disappear."

That was the first time that the community got an inkling of what was really going on: the police went after Adnan because he was Muslim and Pakistani. If they, upstanding citizens, could be indicted by this prosecutor in one broad sweep, then it was clear that the core of the police's theory hinged on Adnan's religion and ethnicity. No one expected—least of all Adnan's attorneys—to hear such an argument. But Wash didn't make that argument up on the fly. She had prepared for it, having spoken with a legal advisor at the Department of Justice (DOJ) and, just a few days prior, having honed in on mosque members and a friend of Adnan's to ask questions about Islam. Defense notes indicate that three days prior, "Detectives Ritz and MacGillivary along with Vicki Wash made a 7:30pm visit to the residence of a Hindu friend of Adnan's and asked questions about Islam."

Many points affirm that Adnan was targeted because of his religion and ethnicity. This is one of them. There is no other explanation for a prosecutor, who could easily argue against bail based on the heinous nature of the crime, based on premeditation, or based on witness statements, to research and prepare an argument connected with his ethnic background, which for them was basically interchangeable with his religious affiliation. This, of course, doesn't even address the fact that Adnan isn't, and never has been, a Pakistani citizen. He is an American citizen, born and raised in the United States.

The following day, bail was denied.

Wash's arguments inflamed Adnan's attorneys, who reached out to the DOJ legal counsel she had consulted, and wrote a letter of complaint to the State's Attorney.

In arguing that Mr. Syed presents a risk of flight, Assistant State Attorney Vicki Wash relied upon improper and erroneous assertions concerning Mr. Syed's nationality, ethnicity, ancestry, and religion. Ms. Wash also referred to the national origin and religion of Mr. Syed's parents and made a similar references to the Baltimore community that supports Mr. Syed's pretrial release. [. . . I]n my opinion, Ms. Wash's presentation was wholly outside the boundaries of proper argument.

Colbert had also contacted the legal advisor from the State Department, Harry Marshall, whom Wash had cited in making the argument that there was a "pattern" of Pakistani men killing their partners and then fleeing the country. Marshall reached out to Wash to correct her, and she subsequently wrote a letter of apology to the judge, stating that there was no such pattern. In fact, there was exactly one case in Chicago in which a Pakistani man was charged with murder. The victim was known to the defendant and an element of "treachery/deceit" was involved. Even Wash's apology was deeply insulting. In essence she explained to the judge that because, in a murder case in another state a Pakistani defendant had used treachery and deceit, she assumed Adnan would as well. This is textbook biased or bigoted behavior.

In any case, Wash's correction and apology didn't matter anymore. Adnan wasn't getting bail, and no matter how many times the issue was raised in the future, it was denied. Ritz was right, Adnan wasn't going home.

After the bail kerfuffle Colbert and Flohr realized that this case was going to require some major fire power, an aggressive attorney with much greater experience than they had. They advised Bilal Ahmed, who was acting as a liaison between the community, family, and attorneys, and then began searching for another attorney. One came to mind immediately, a legend in the criminal defense world—Cristina Gutierrez.

Gutierrez was already involved peripherally in the case. She had been hired to represent two witnesses from the community who were called to testify at the grand jury proceedings: my brother Saad Chaudry and Bilal Ahmed.

My parents were terrified, like many parents of Adnan's friends. After hearing Wash's arguments at the bail hearing, they were convinced the State was going to try to rope in as many of their young boys as possible.

"Don't go, just don't go," my mother said when Saad's subpoena came.

"He can't do that, it's against the law. He has to go, he has to have a lawyer, and then he'll be just fine," I said, trying to reassure both my parents and myself.

Both Saad and Bilal testified between March 22 and April 7 but did so only after Gutierrez had attempted to quash the State's subpoena calling them—a routine move by defense counsel. When that didn't fly, she advised them that while they would have to testify, they should, between every question, reaffirm their privileges and confer with Gutierrez before answering. It resulted in testimony that, though lacking in substance, was high in drama and difficult to follow. It wouldn't be the last time Gutierrez left a jury with a bad taste in their mouth.

Bilal Ahmed and Saad were both asked whether Adnan had confided in them about the murder.

The prosecutor asked Bilal, "Did you ever have a conversation with Adnan Syed prior to January 13th about murdering Hay [sic] Min Lee, about his intentions to murder Hay Min Lee?"

Bilal answered, "No, I didn't."

Likewise, Saad was asked whether Adnan ever denied involvement in the crime, and Saad responded that Adnan indicated he had no idea who did it. The prosecutor challenged him, "So you're saying that his response to your question of I have no idea who did this is the same as saying he denied any involvement in the crime?"

Saad, who recalled being confused, said, "Yes."

Both not only maintained that Adnan had never indicated that he was in any way involved with Hae's disappearance or murder, they also testified to how Adnan reacted to the news of her death and his arrest.

"He was crying and he informed me . . . that she had died . . . he was upset and crying," testified Ahmed.

Ahmed's testimony was much more substantive than Saad's. He was questioned for days about his role at the mosque, his relationship as a mentor to Adnan, what Islam had to say about dating, sex, and marriage, and repeatedly, Adnan's relationship with Hae and his involvement, if any, with the murder.

While Ahmed didn't provide anything that could be used against Adnan, he did mention something very important: on the evening of January 13, 1999, he specifically recalled seeing Adnan at the mosque. In fact, he looked over Adnan's notes to help him prepare to lead prayers the following day.

Suddenly, Ahmed posed a potential problem for the State—he could derail Jay's story about where Adnan was the night Hae disappeared. The suspicion of the State extended to Adnan's Muslim friends, though.

This explains why, shortly thereafter, on April 13, 1999, the Baltimore City Police subpoenaed Bilal's phone records. They were looking for some way to shut this guy down.

Not all the grand jury testimony was made available to the defense. Other than the detectives, the only witness for the State, at least the only one disclosed, was Jennifer Pusateri. Jay Wilds was not called.

On April 14, 1999, Adnan was indicted for the murder of Hae Min Lee.

Adnan:

We had visits once a week, and that's what I looked forward to the most. Only two adults were allowed, so my mother would always come accompanied by either my father or older brother. The visiting room contained a u-shaped table, with clear plexiglass separating the inmates from the visitors. It was a non-contact visit, and we had to speak through a mesh grill. In the beginning of our first visit, my parents seemed very tense and upset. As we talked, however, they began to calm down. I told them about the things I had eaten, and about something funny I had read.

As I saw their change in demeanor, I felt relieved. The thing that worried me the most was thinking about how hard this was on my family. How they must have been hurting, and the helplessness they were feeling. I came to understand that they were very concerned about my well-being; scared that perhaps I was experiencing some emotional and/or physical harm. I made a decision at that point, determining that no matter what happened regarding my case, I would do my best to remain positive when it came to my family. I would exercise and stay in good shape, so they would see me healthy when they would visit. And during every phone conversation, I would always try to have something positive to talk about. I realized that if I could not affect anything else, I would try to ensure that my parents had no reason to worry about my physical and mental health, because they would always see me in a good state of mind.

It would require a good deal of effort, though. Some days were harder than others. During one attorney visit, my lawyer handed me an envelope, telling me it had arrived at my parent's home the previous day. It was an acceptance letter from one of the colleges I had applied to. There was also my 18th birthday, which occurred about two and half months after my arrest. There was our high school commencement day, where I was scheduled to have graduated. And at the end of that summer, there was what would have been the first day of college. Every few weeks, it seemed that a moment would come where I would realize I had planned to be somewhere else.

There was one day in particular. Several weeks after I was arrested, there was the Eid festival. It would normally be a time of joy & celebration in our household, but now it was a moment of incredible sadness. It was particularly difficult for Yusuf, as we would always make it especially fun for him, with presents, candy, cake, etc . . . I worried a great deal about how all of this was affecting him, as he was so young. My parents would refrain from telling me, but I constantly questioned my older brother about how Yusuf was doing. Finally, one day Tanveer broke down during a phone conversation and admitted to me that Yusuf was no longer attending school. He was being bullied by his classmates to the point where he would come home crying, begging not to be sent back to school the next day . . . To learn of what my little brother was experiencing brought about an immeasurable amount of sadness. It made the hardships of what I was experiencing pale in comparison, and there was a great deal of frustration as I felt helpless to do anything about it.

As Adnan waited in jail, his family and mosque friends would often visit him, but he hadn't heard much from his classmates. He had no idea why or what was going on but thought it best, at the advice of counsel, not to initiate contact; for all he knew, that might make people uncomfortable. In addition, he could only make collect calls, expensive calls, and he didn't want to burden or pressure people to take them. But he did hear from one student, someone he wasn't even close friends with.

Asia McClain.

Asia was a beautiful girl who used to date one of Adnan's friends, Justin Adger. Adnan knew her casually through Justin, but she wasn't part of the Magnet Program so they weren't close. Plus, she and Justin had broken up and she was dating someone else now, someone who didn't go to Woodlawn.

Sometime in the first few weeks of being locked up Adnan received two letters from Asia, back-to-back. The letters are dated March 1 and March 2, right after his arrest, but there is no record of when he actually received them. It might have taken up to a month or more, according to Flohr, for Adnan to receive them since he was moved a few times.

Asia's first letter describes visiting Adnan's family on the night he was arrested, and details her recollection of seeing Adnan on the afternoon that Hae disappeared.

The second letter reiterates her having seen him and discusses some of the school gossip about Adnan.

Asia's letters jogged Adnan's memory. Until then he had simply recalled that Jay had his car that day and he had hung out at school until track practice at it's late.

I just came from your house an hour ago.   March 1, 1999

Dear Adnan, (hope I sp. it right)

I know that you can't visiters, so I decided to write you a letter. I'm not sure if you remember talking to me in the library on Jan. 13th, but I remembered chatting with you. ~~was~~ Throughout you're actions that day I have reason to believe in your innocense. I went to your family's house and discussed your "calm" manner towards them. I also called the Woodlawn Public Library and found that they have a survailance system inside the building. Depending on the amount of time you spend in the library that afternoon, it might help in your defence. I really would appreciate it if you would contact me between 1:00pm - 1pm or 8:45pm → until... My number is ████████████. More importantly I'm trying to reach your lawyer to schedule a possible meeting with the three of us. We aren't really close friends, but I want you to look into my eyes and tell me of your innocense. If I ever find otherwise I will hunt you down and wip your ass, ok friend. //

EXHIBIT
4

3:30 p.m. But now he remembered seeing Asia, and the conversation they had had, and later teasing Justin about seeing her new boyfriend with her.

These letters were vital. Adnan thought about contacting Asia but then decided it would be better if his attorney did so—he didn't want to do anything that could be misconstrued, like talking to an important witness.

At that point they were still trying to choose an attorney.

Cristina Gutierrez came highly recommended by both Colbert and Flohr. After

Adnon Syed   #992005477
301 East Eager Street
Baltimore, MD. 21202

Dear Adnon,

How is everything? I know that we haven't been best friends in the past, however I believe in your innocence. I know that central booking is probably not the best place to make friends, so I'll attempt to be the best friend possible. I hope that nobody has attempted to harm you (not that they will). Just remember that if someone says something to you, that their just f**king with your emotions. I know that my first letter was probably a little harsh, but I just wanted you to know where I stode in this entire issue (on the centerline). I don't know you very well, however I didn't know Hae very well. The information that I know about you being in the library could helpful, unimportant or unhelpful to your case. I've been think a few things lately, that I wanted to ask you:

1. Why haven't you told anyone about talking to me in the library? Did you think it was unimportant, you didn't think that I would remember? Or did you just totally forget yourself?

2. How long did you stay in the library that day? Your family will probably try to obtain the library's surveillance tape.

3. Where exactly did you do and go that day? What is the <u>so-called evidence</u> that my statement is up against? And who are these WITNESSES?

Anyway, everything in school is somewhat the same. The ignorant (and some underclassmen) think that you're guilty, while others (mostly those that know you) think you're innocent. I talked to Emron today, he looked like crap. He's upset, most of your "CRUCHES" are. We love you, I guess that inside I know that you're innocent too. It's just that the so-called evidence looks very negative. However I'm positive that

March 2, 1999

asking around, and then being represented by her at the grand jury, Bilal Ahmed agreed—Gutierrez would be an effective, aggressive, take-no-prisoners advocate.

Gutierrez went to visit Adnan in prison on April 16, and on April 18 she was hired by his parents for the legal fee of $50,000.

Having overcome a relatively minor 1971 shoplifting conviction that created major issues in her admission to the bar, Cristina Gutierrez was licensed to practice everything will work out in favor of the truth. The main thing that I'm worried about is that the real killers are probably somewhere laughing at the police and the news, that makes me sick!! I hope this letter and the ones that follow ease you days a little. I guess if I didn't believe in your innocence, that I wouldn't write to you . ☺

The other day (Monday) We (some of Mr. Parker's class) were talking about it and Mrs. Shab over-heard us; she said, "Don't you think the police have considered everything, they wouldn't just lock him up unless they had "REAL" evidence." We just looked at her, then continued our conversations. Mr. Parker seems un-opinionated, yet he seemed happy when I told him that I spoke to you family about the matter (I told him) Your brothers are nice, I don't think I met your mother, I think I met you dad; does he have a big gray beard. They gave me and Justin soda and cake. There was a whole bunch of people at you house, I didn't know who they were. I also didn't know that Muslims take their shoes off in the house…thank God they didn't make me take mine off, my stinky feet probably would have knocked everyone out cold.

 I over-heard Will and Anthony talking about you, they don't think you did "IT" either. I guess most people don't. Justin's mom is worried about you too. She gave me your home number, when Justin was in school. Classes are boring, that's one benefit to being "there", no school!!

They issued a school newsletter on the issue, so everyone is probably aware. It didn't say your name, but between that, gossip and the news, your name is known. I'm sorry this had to happen to you. Look at the bright side when you come back, won't nobody f**k with you and at least you'll know who your real friends and new friends should be. Also, you're the most popular guy in school. Shoot…you might get prom king.

You'll be happy to know that the gossip is dead for your associates, it's starting to get old. Your real friends are concentrated on you and your defense. I want you to know that I'm missing the instructions of Mrs. Ogle's CIP class, writing this letter.

March 2, 1999

It's weird, since I realized that I saw you in the public library that day, you've been on my mind. The conversation that we had, has been on my mind. Everything was cool that day, maybe if I would have stayed with you or something this entire situation could have been avoided. Did you cut school that day? Someone told me that you cut school to play video games at someone's house. Is that what you told the police? This entire case puzzles me, you see I have an analytical mind. I want to be a criminal psychologist for the FBI one day. I don't understand how it took the police three weeks to find Hae's car, if it was found in the same park. I don't understand how you would even know about Leakin Park or how the police expect you to follow Hae in your car, kill her and take her

car to Leakin Park, dig a grave and find you way back home. As well how come you
don't have any markings on your body from Hae's struggle. I know that if I was her, I
would have struggled. I guess that's where the
SO-CALLED witnesses. White girl Stacie just mentioned that she thinks you did it.
Something about your fibers on Hae's body...something like that (evidence). I don't
mean to make you upset talking about it...if I am. I just thought that maybe you should
know. Anyway I have to go to third period. I'll write you again. Maybe tomorrow.

Hope this letter brightens your day... Your Friend,

Asia R. McClain

P.S: Your brother said that he going to tell you to maybe call me, it's not necessary,
save the phone call for your family. You could attempt to write back though. So I can
tell everyone how you're doing (and so I'll know too).

Asia R. McClain

Apparently a whole bunch of girl were crying for you at the jail...Big Playa Playa
(ha ha ha he he he).

March 2, 1999

law on October 26, 1982, three years after graduating from law school. By this
time she was already a well-known Baltimore activist. In 1973 she had traveled
to Cuba and joined the Venceremos Brigade, a group of young American activists who challenged U.S. policy toward Cuba by showing solidarity with Cuban
laborers. Her fighting spirit clearly spilled over into her legal work.

A *Baltimore Sun* article notes that she was considered one of the best attorneys in her office, trying more cases than anyone else and rarely taking a plea
for clients. A colleague called her the most tenacious lawyer he'd ever seen and
said, "You push her, you better be ready to kill."

After leaving the Public Defender's office in 1986, she joined forces
with a nationally known criminal defense attorney, Billy Murphy. Together
they commandeered the most feared and aggressive criminal defense firm in
Baltimore.

Gutierrez litigated fiercely for her clients, getting acquittals in numerous high-
profile cases, including a 1991 murder case in which the client had made incriminating remarks to the police. Her tenacity led to a victory before the Supreme

Court in a 1990 landmark case, in which she became the first Hispanic American woman of record to argue a case before the highest court in the land. Her victory in this case, *Maryland v. Craig,* is still cited in evidence textbooks as setting the precedent for a defendant's right to confront the witnesses against him.

In January 1995 she parted ways with Murphy in a move that left the Baltimore legal community a bit stunned.

A January 17, 1995 *Baltimore Sun* piece reported that "Flamboyant criminal defense lawyers William H. 'Billy' Murphy Jr. and M. Cristina Gutierrez have parted ways after years of sharing controversy and high-profile clients. The long-rumored professional split became official yesterday, when receptionists began answering the phone 'Murphy and Associates' at the partners' Calvert Street office, and Ms. Gutierrez completed the task of moving into the downtown firm of Redmond, Burgin & Cruz, where she will have a limited affiliation. Ms. Gutierrez, a divorced mother of two, called the breakup 'amicable' and said that she was hoping to better control her workload and spend more time with her family."

The split was anything but planned, however, and Gutierrez later admits this to the court in an appeal case for her client John Merzbacher. Explaining why she failed to convey a plea deal to him, Gutierrez states "On January 15, without planning whatsoever, I was forced to move my law office, literally overnight. And that created a great burden on me. Also in January I was in the middle of hearings in front of Judge Ferris, an administrative law judge in Anne Arundel County in the case against Laurie Cook. Those hearings took well over 200 hours and had been started about the second week of December."

Looking back now, Murphy recalls that shortly after the split Gutierrez's personality began to change "dramatically."

"She became really hostile towards people she had known for years," says Murphy. She alienated colleagues and friends over the next few years, losing many of her allies. Many of them were aware that these changes were probably due to her failing health.

"She was going through evidently very, very serious mental decline as a result of her numerous other illnesses. She was on dialysis, she had kidney problems, I think she had problems with diabetes, so these things evidently changed her mental state to such a degree that her ability to attend to her practice sharply declined . . . this was not the Cristina of old," Murphy said in an interview with journalist and attorney Seema Iyer.

In 1999, by the time she was hired to defend Adnan, the effects of her multiple illnesses had long impaired her work in ways that in many cases would not be discovered for a few more years. Unaware of this, the community placed Adnan's life in her hands.

In the next two months, both the police and defense conducted a flurry of interviews.

The day after the arrest, and the day of the first bail hearing, my brother Saad and Krista Meyers, both friends of Adnan's, were interviewed by the BCPD. According to Saad, he was harassed and threatened by the detectives to tell them what he knew about the crime, or face being charged too. Saad wasn't intimidated, he says; he was on the verge of telling them to "get the fuck out of here."

Krista was interviewed about Adnan and Hae's relationship but little was gleaned by the police that could be used against Adnan, except for one thing: "Krista Myers stated that on 13 January 1999, 1st period Photography Adnan had a conversation with Hae Min Lee. Adnan was requesting a ride home from Lee."

This wasn't the first time in the investigation that the police heard that Adnan had asked for a ride. In Officer Adcock's very first interview with Adnan, the day Hae disappeared, Adnan told him he was supposed to get a ride from her but she got tired of waiting and left. But when Adnan was questioned by the police at home in front of his father, he said no, he did not ask for a ride at all.

The ride issue cropped up yet again, though, when the police interviewed Becky Walker, a friend and classmate of both Hae and Adnan. Becky was interviewed by the State's Attorney and detectives in April, when she also recalls that she had heard, but not witnessed, that Adnan had asked Hae for a ride after school to his car, but then at the end of the day she told him she wouldn't be able to take him.

Police notes from Becky's April 9, 1999, interview state, "Heard about it at lunch. Hae said she could—there would be no problem. At end of school—I saw them. She said 'Oh no, I can't take you, I have something else to do.' She didn't say what else."

The problem was that Adnan completely denied the ride. But then, if a ride was part of his plan to kill Hae, it would be utterly nonsensical of him to ask for it repeatedly in front of others.

The notes from the same April 9 interview say that Becky also said that "defendant always in victim's car. Almost every day he would go to back (parking lot) and she would drive him around front so he could go to track practice."

Earlier, on March 26, Debbie had said to the police, "Um he would either be in the car after school when she went to bring the car around the front and go with her to bring the car around front. Sometimes he would go and he wouldn't come back um, that's only when er, after school at that time he would be in the car with her."

Whether or not he asked for a ride, at the end of the day, if Becky is to be believed, Hae told him no. And Aisha also told Krista Meyers that later in the day Hae had told Adnan that something came up, and she couldn't give him the ride anyway.

If a ride was part of Adnan's premeditated plan to murder Hae, Jay Wilds and Jenn Pusateri certainly didn't know about it during their initial interviews. Jay point-blank told the police "no" when asked if Adnan mentioned how he got in Hae's car, and Jenn likewise said in her February 27 interview that Jay "didn't know where her car was or how Adnar [sic] got to Best Buy or how um he got into Hae's car, if he did it in Hae's car or whether he did it in Hae's car."

Between the time Adnan was arrested and April 29, detectives conducted nearly fifty interviews with Adnan's friends and teachers at Woodlawn, friends

Adnan's
Relationship w/ Hae:
        both very loving, both very faithful, loved to tease each other and make jokes, publicly affectionate yet very respectful, never fought around anyone, had little disagreements sometimes but always worked them out by talking, neither one ever tried to hurt the other, if one was hurt both were hurt (a lot of empathy), if one did something to upset the other an apology was always made & problem resolved, both would do anything for the other, if Hae wanted space @ a certain time Adnan said okay no questions asked (King's Dominion), both were happy in relationship but both knew it wouldn't last forever, very supportive of each other,

From Becky Walker's journal after Adnan was arrested

outside of school (mosque friends and Nisha Tanna), and friends of Jay Wilds. They visited the school repeatedly, and assured the students and staff that they had the right guy, that there was solid evidence against Adnan.

Asia mentions this in her second letter when she recalls Hope Schab interrupting a student conversation to say, "Don't you think the police have considered everything, they wouldn't just lock him up unless they had 'REAL' evidence."

The substance of nearly all the police interviews was to establish what kind of relationship Adnan and Hae had, what challenges with family and religion they faced, how he reacted when they broke up, and how he reacted when she was found dead.

It was a hunt for any behavior that was suspicious, any inkling that would confirm their foregone conclusion: that he was an obsessed, heartbroken, angry young Muslim man who couldn't take the end of the romance lightly, who thought he had some Islamic duty to kill Hae, and whose community would accept his behavior.

Woodlawn friends and teachers weren't able to offer much more than banalities, many of them in fact affirming that Adnan and Hae had a good relationship, that there was never any violence between them, that even after breaking up they were friends. But they did all report that their relationship suffered because of family and his faith.

Debbie Warren was the only one who reported that Adnan was possessive, but initially her suspicion was clearly on Don, as evidenced by her belief that he had perhaps "hidden" Hae and her surreptitious e-mail message to him that led to their seven-hour phone call.

Debbie had reached out to Don before Hae's body was found. It's worth noting that in the interviews Don gave to Baltimore County Police and the investigator Mandy Johnson, he doesn't mention the possibility of Adnan's involvement in Hae's disappearance. It may have been that early on he didn't realize that she had truly disappeared, assuming she had gone to California, but later, when it became clear that something was very wrong he began to think Adnan was involved and told Debbie so. The seven-hour phone conversation is a little harder to explain—especially in light of an undated police note that reads: "None of Hae girlfriends like new boyfr. New boyfriend assaulted Debbie."

The only new boyfriend Hae had was Don. But nowhere else in any of the files is this assault by Don explained.

Because the police didn't begin interviewing most of Hae's classmates and teachers until long after she disappeared, and after Adnan's arrest, the statements they give end up conflicting on a few points, one major one in particular—when Hae actually left school.

Becky recalls seeing Hae leaving school immediately after dismissal, around 2:20 p.m., when she tells Adnan she can't give him a ride. But about a month earlier, Debbie told Detective O'Shea she saw Hae leaving close to 3:00 p.m., saying she was going to see Don at the mall, though Debbie didn't actually see her leave school.

Inez Butler, the school athletic trainer, backs up Becky's recollection in a police interview when she says Hae pulled up to her concession stand in the bus loop to grab Andy Capp Hot Fries and apple juice. According to Butler in a March 23 interview, this happened around 2:30 p.m. the day Hae disappeared.

The police only get two statements about where Adnan was around the end of and after school that day. The first is from Debbie, who recalls seeing him at the guidance counselor's office picking up a letter of recommendation around 2:45 p.m., dressed and ready for track practice. The second is from Coach Michael Sye, Adnan's track coach, who says in his March 23 police interview, "Ms. Graham lets them go from study hall, they change, come to track. I usually arrive around 3:30. From what I remember he was there on time, left on time."

The police weren't able to get information that would tie Adnan to the crime from anyone at Woodlawn, but they did think there was another set of people who might be able to tie Adnan to the crime.

Of Adnan's Muslim friends who were questioned (including Nisha because they couldn't distinguish between Muslim and Hindu), all were asked if he had told them anything about the murder—but none of his non-Muslim school friends were asked that.

Of particular interest to the police was Yaser Ali, the same person thought to have been referenced in the February 12, 1999 anonymous tip. Yaser, an old family and childhood friend of Adnan's, had grown apart from him in the last couple of years. He knew Adnan was dating but was disappointed by the fact that he was having sex. Though he didn't attend Woodlawn High, Yaser knew Hae, had met her at a party. He also knew Jay, whom he saw at a party in late January, but Yaser also had gone to school with him for a couple of years in the past.

The interview notes, taken on April 8, seem to suggest Yaser had already spoken to Detective MacGillivary once before, though no record exists. He also mentioned that he had been contacted by Andrew Davis, a private investigator working for Adnan's attorney.

A couple of things Yaser said put holes in the cops' case: first, that Adnan had been looking for a cell phone for months, contradicting the idea that he had gotten it specifically for the murder, and second, he denied everything attributed to him in the anonymous call.

Though he didn't have any knowledge of the crime, the police were able to get this information from him:

KNOWS ABOUT PROBLEMS BETWEEN ▲ AND VICTIM
BELIEVED ▲ HAD SOMETHING TO DO WITH DEATH (GOT FEELING AT THE TIME)

KNOWN ▲ SINCE 11 TO 12. KNOWS FAMILY VEHICLES. SUGGESTED ---
TANVEER'S INVOLVEMENT.

Inexplicably, in the same notes is a handwritten section that says: "Tanveer—older brother, student @ Towson State, pretty straight guy."

How Yaser would both state that Tanveer is a "straight guy" and at the same time imply he had some involvement with Hae's death is hard to reconcile. It didn't seem that the police took it seriously, though, since there's no evidence that they investigated Tanveer at all.

The police struck out with Yaser, but they tried hard to find someone in the Muslim community that Adnan may have confessed to or confided in. The implication is striking: Muslims were the kind of people who would quietly accept and cover for the murder of a young girl—much as Wash was implying at the bail hearing.

The suspicion of the Muslim community was so deep that after local Pakistani activist Alfreda Gill visited the school with Adnan's father to collect Adnan's school work to deliver to him in jail, a school official took down her license plate number and immediately informed the police of this suspicious character. That one act of kindness on Gill's part earned her the prize of having her phone records subpoenaed by the police on March 24, 1999, five days after the visit. In fact, the list of people who had their phone records subpoenaed is exclusively Muslim: Gill, Bilal Ahmed, Adnan, and my brother Saad. Jay Wilds' and Jenn Pusateri's phone records are not subpoenaed, and neither are the records of the people Jay called on Adnan's phone on January 13: Phil Mendez and Patrick Furlow.

Even the kinds of questions posed by jurors in the grand jury to Saad and Bilal Ahmed indicate that they were well aware of the State's theory of the case—that this was a religiously sanctioned murder. Not having the full transcript of

these confidential proceedings, we can only imagine what the opening statement by Wash must have been like to produce questions with such suspicious
and disturbing pretexts.

Among them:

"In the Islamic community, suppose a young adult goes to an adult that he
respects, a mentor, and confesses the same thing, that he has committed a terrible crime . . . is there a particular course of action that is dictated by the Islamic
faith for that mentor? Would he be required to notify the civilian authorities?"

"I have one more question. You stated before in your community you have
no punishment for dating per se. Is there in the Koran a punishment for dating
or marrying outside of the Islamic faith?"

Ahmed was also asked about his immigration status and command of English and why he hired an attorney. Clearly, the jury was suspicious of him as
someone who might be keeping a confession by Adnan secret.

The line of questioning about Islamic punishments for dating and sex are
still confounding to me. Is it the State's theory that these punishments are
meant for the person who a Muslim is dating, which seems the implication, given
the allegation that the community would hide or support Adnan's killing of Hae?
Or that Adnan risked some terrible religious punishment for dating Hae, and
when he was dumped he was angry that he risked it all for nothing? Regardless, it
wasn't just Adnan being indicted at this grand jury proceeding, it wasn't just
him being investigated and prosecuted. His faith, his ethnicity, even his
community—they were all on trial.

It would be up to Gutierrez to defend us all.

Gutierrez met with the community group that had formed at the mosque to help
organize Adnan's defense twice that summer as she prepared for the trial. Each
time, in response to the many questions about the likelihood of success, she emphasized one thing: it was the State's burden to prove Adnan did it. And from
what she knew there was little evidence to support the charges. As long as she
was able to poke enough holes in the case, she'd win. It was about reasonable
doubt, after all.

Saad spent almost an entire week with Gutierrez when she was representing
him and Bilal for the grand jury proceedings, and he would repeatedly press her
on how to go about Adnan's defense.

"I would tell her, hey Adnan was seeing other girls, you need to call them,
and are you going to get the DNA tested, and he was definitely at the mosque
that night so you gotta find others who saw him, and what about video cameras,

maybe he was on video somewhere like at the school or mosque," Saad said, exasperated.

Gutierrez listened but her response was the same: it's not our burden to prove anything. Stop worrying.

Before she was hired, Colbert and Flohr had already begun doing what attorneys should—building a defense for their client.

Defense Private Investigator Andrew Davis first entered the scene on March 4, 1999. He met with Flohr and Adnan a few days after Adnan's arrest. The first order of business in this case was obvious: establish where Adnan was after school on the day Hae disappeared. There are no notes of Davis's interview with Adnan, but the very same day he went to meet Coach Sye, an indication that Adnan must have told him he was at track practice that day. Unfortunately, there is no definitive confirmation by Sye that he was definitely at track on the 13th, but he did say that Adnan was at track the majority of the time. He medaled in track, and would have gotten a varsity letter if he hadn't been arrested, according to Sye.

Most importantly, the notes say "3:30–4:30-5:00," indicating that track began at 3:30 and ended between 4:30 and 5:00 p.m.

About a week later, on March 10, Davis interviews Jay's boss, a woman only ever identified as "Sis," who tells him that Jay was hired around January 24 and was supposed to begin training the very next day. But he didn't show up from the 25th through the 27th of the month. His first actual training day ended up being January 31. Sis told Davis that Jay would usually get rides to work, not having his own car, and gave him a rundown of his working hours through February and March.

Sis noted that the police had come by several times to speak with Jay and she eventually asked him if it was in connection with the "girl found in the park." He said yes. He told her that he knew who killed Hae, stating that "no one thinks he did it but he did kill her."

That same day Davis also interviewed one of Adnan's closest friends and fellow Magnet Program student, Stephanie McPherson. Stephanie was so close to Adnan that it may have been a point of discomfort for her boyfriend, Jay Wilds.

Stephanie was another overachiever—smart, driven, athletic, and headed for a bright academic future. Her boyfriend, on the other hand, was not who her parents had in mind for her. Jay was in many ways from the wrong side of the tracks. Stephanie came from a solid middle-class home and had parents who demanded excellence from, and for, their daughter. The future they envisioned for her didn't have someone like Jay in it, and he was painfully aware of that. But Stephanie loved him and they dated throughout high school.

Adnan and Stephanie had been classmates and friends since middle school and had an ongoing flirtation that never got further than that. Adnan considered Stephanie to be one of his closest friends, but things changed a bit when he began dating Hae—Stephanie didn't completely approve.

Still, they continued to hang out, darlings of the other students who had named them junior prom king and queen the prior spring.

Now, however, a wall had come down. Stephanie had not reached out to Adnan or his family since his arrest, though other students like Asia had visited his home. According to other students, she went on emotional lockdown, refusing to talk to anyone about anything related to the case.

She did, however, speak to PI Davis twice. The first time was at her home in the presence of her parents. In this interview Stephanie notes that Adnan "is one of my best friends." She had known him since grade school, but she had only met Hae during their freshman year in high school. She had found Adnan and Hae's relationship "odd" because she found Hae to be shallow, but also odd because of Adnan's religious beliefs. She said that in November or December of 1998 Hae became strange because she had a new boyfriend and that Adnan "was said to be upset because he didn't see it coming." She said while Adnan wanted to meet Don to size him up, he was happy that they had broken up because now he didn't feel guilty talking to other girls and hanging out with his friends. She remembered when Adnan got his cell phone and said they spoke nearly every night on the phone.

On the day that Hae went missing Stephanie recalled getting a birthday gift from Adnan, a stuffed reindeer, and that Hae was very quiet at lunch. Nothing else unusual happened that day, and she left school at around 2:15 p.m., arriving home at 2:55 and then returning for a basketball game around 3:30 or 3:45 p.m.

The day Hae's body was found, on February 9, she said she spoke to Adnan on the phone and then he came over to her house along with a number of other friends. Hae's brother called them and confirmed that Hae had been found, and Adnan immediately said they should call the detective because he didn't believe it. As Adnan was crying, they attempted to contact O'Shea and ended up leaving him a message.

Stephanie told Davis that there was no talk in school at all about Adnan being involved in Hae's death until he was arrested, but that her boyfriend Jay told her he had personal knowledge of Adnan's culpability and that he'd also told her that Adnan had threatened Stephanie as well. Stephanie also stated that she "did not believe that Adnan would ever threaten her but she believed her boyfriend of many years, Jay, was an honest person."

Stephanie doesn't report anything unusual in this interview, other than the threat Jay says Adnan made toward her, and one other thing—that while she spoke to Jay late on the night of January 13, she didn't actually see him that day. This contradicts both Jay and Jenn, who say they went to Stephanie's house that night so Jay could wish her a happy birthday. As for the threat, it seems clearly false to me: Stephanie knew nothing of Adnan's connection to the murder or his alleged threat until after he was arrested, meaning until after Adnan couldn't reach or harm her anyway. If the threat were real, why would Jay allow Stephanie to hang out with Adnan and speak to this alleged murderer on the phone every single night? The threat Jay brings up after Adnan's arrest seemed to be a mechanism to keep them from communicating ever again.

The very next day, on March 11, 1999, a memorial service was held at Woodlawn High School for Hae. Adnan had a hand in organizing the event (it was his responsibility to purchase a tree to plant in Hae's name as well as draft a speech to give) but he missed it because of his arrest.

The memorial was held in the school gymnasium, and Davis showed up to try and get some interviews with students. The only one he was able to connect with was Stephanie, whom he had just spoken to the night before. This time she added a detail she hadn't mentioned before: between 4:15 and 5:30 p.m. on January 13, she had called Adnan on his cell while waiting for her basketball game to start, and Jay was with him at the time.

The night before the memorial, when Davis had been interviewing Stephanie, Jay showed up at the house, knowing Adnan's PI was going to be there. Her parents had turned him away but he was told to return later. Undoubtedly their conversation was about Adnan and Jay's involvement in the case, and the importance of Jay being placed with Adnan that late afternoon. Maybe Stephanie thought she would be helping her boyfriend with this additional detail, or maybe Jay asked her to say it. But not only does Jay never mention such a phone call in any of his statements, past or future, according to Coach Sye, Adnan was most likely at track practice at that time.

This invites the conclusion that Stephanie is willing to do what it takes to protect Jay from the defense investigation, but she isn't willing to lie to the police for him. If she had, she certainly would have been a prosecution witness as someone who could corroborate Jay's story. But Stephanie—the only person in the story who is so close to both of these young men—never again makes an appearance in the case after her interviews with Davis and the police.

Stephanie may have had her boyfriend's back but Adnan, one of her best friends, is on his own now. He's the only one who can prove where he was after school on January 13, 1999.

CHAPTER 6

WITNESS FOR THE PROSECUTION

—————•—————

The Prophet said thrice,
"Should I inform you about the greatest of the great sins?"
They said, "Yes, O Allah's Apostle!"
He said, "To join others in worship with Allah and to be undutiful
to one's parents."
The Prophet then sat up after he had been reclining and said,
"And I warn you against giving false witness,
and he kept on saying that warning till we thought he would not stop."
Sahih ul Bukhari, book 52, hadith 18

As Adnan waited in prison for the trial, my family and I did the only thing we knew how to do—we tried to keep his morale up. Adnan did the same thing with us, never once discussing details of the case or the tremendous stress he was under. We all acted like this was a temporary thing.

Adnan would tell funny stories of people he met on the inside, to distract us. He was terrified. But he never let any of us know. All around, it was a carefully orchestrated dance to avoid more pain than anyone could bear.

It wasn't always easy for him to hide his feelings, though. Once in a while, the pain would jump off the pages of his letters. When he received his high school diploma in a ceremony at the prison, his sadness was clear in a letter he wrote to me:

6/21/1999

Dear Rabia,
Asalaamulaykum. How is everything w/ u and ur family? Fine, I hope.
It hasn't been hot the past week or so, and the temperature in here has been

pretty nice. Sometimes it gets kinda chilly, but I'd rather have it be cooler than hotter. Hopefully, it'll last 4 awhile.

I received my diploma on the 11th. It was kinda nice, it was during the function held for the end of the school year. It was nice, they called my name, and I went on stage and received it, + shook the hand of the school principal. A lot of people clapped + cheered, so it made memorable. It's weird though, cause there were a lot of cameras flashing, and a lot were for the PR dept. they have in here. I was really happy that my parents were there though. I know it meant a lot to them for me to receive my diploma. I guess it's a memorable event for every parent. Honestly though, it didn't mean so much to me as it would've if all this stuff hadn't happened. I mean, I really appreciate the trouble the teachers went to get my diploma, and I'm grateful that my parents were there, but to me it really was just a piece of paper. (actually, an italicized jacketed certificate). I guess while some people would look at it + say this is 12 years worth of work; I think that my mind is 12 years worth of work (actually 18). In the beginning, I used to think, man, they took my graduation day away from me. But now, it's like, all those years are shown in my head, not on a piece of paper, and they can never be taken away from me. I'm really glad my parents were there, though.

You know what, I've developed a liking for crossword puzzles. Not w/ clues, but the word searches. I don't know if you could send me a book, but maybe if you just sent the pages, do you think u could find some for me? Not little kid ones, but sometimes u can find them in little kid magazines, or they probably sell crossword puzzle books. If you get the chance, do you think you could send me some. I don't think they would fit in a small envelope. So maybe you could send them in a 8"x11" envelope. I think they're called manilla envelopes. I go through them pretty fast, so as many as you could send I would really appreciate it. Not the kind w/ clues, though, cause it's really frustrating if you can't figure them out, and there is no answer key.

I hope your exams went well, and so is everything else. Take care, give Sunnah a hug for me.

—Adnan Sayed

As we all feigned ignorance about the enormity of the situation, Adnan and his defense team were busy trying to nail down the seminal questions: where was Adnan (and how could they prove it) from after school on January 13, 1999, until he went to the mosque for Ramadan prayers that night, and why would Jay implicate him in Hae's murder?

Gutierrez's files show that Adnan was grappling with these issues but initially seemed to have a decent grasp of exactly what happened during the day. Not all of his attorney visits are documented, but there are numerous notes in Gutierrez's handwriting that show Adnan had discussed Asia.

One note reads in part: "Asia and boyfriend saw him in library 2:15-3:15. Went to library often. 3:30 practice started."

The notes confirm that Adnan remembers seeing Asia and her boyfriend at the library and also reflect something else that becomes very important at trial: that track practice began at 3:30 p.m., as Coach Sye indicated to detectives and PI Davis earlier. So Adnan would have had to get dressed in time to be there by 3:30. This narrows the window of opportunity for the crime to have been committed by Adnan.

The notes are undated, but we know from prison visitor logs that Gutierrez met with Adnan on May 28, June 5, June 26, and July 10. The latest they could have been written was July 10, months before the defense or Adnan know anything about Jay's timeline, who puts track practice later.

Asia comes up again in these notes, dated July 13, 1999, taken by Gutierrez's law clerk during a visit with Adnan:

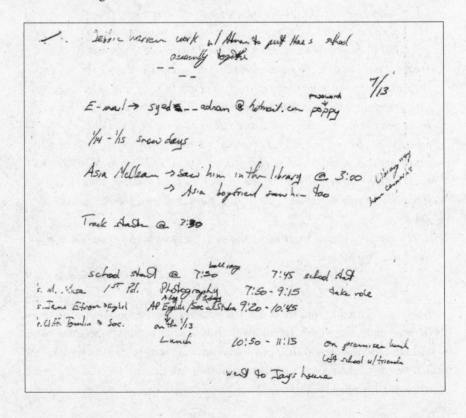

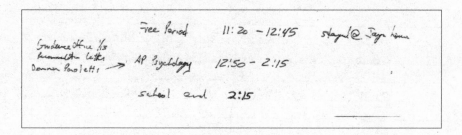

Adnan's schedule for January 13, 1999, is clearly laid out, including the time he spent at Jay's house. Most importantly, though, is the notation about Asia McClain: "saw him in the library @ 3:00, Asia boyfriend saw him too; Library may have cameras."

Again, at this point neither Adnan nor Gutierrez know the State's theory of the case—they have no idea what Jay has said about when Hae was killed. But they do know she disappeared sometime between school and when Adnan got the phone call from Officer Adcock around 6:00 p.m. that day. So independent of any knowledge of when Hae was killed, Adnan has already established a firm alibi for that exact time.

About a month later, on August 21, a law clerk takes more notes during a visit with Adnan that reiterate his recollection: "States he believes he attended track practice on that day because he remembers informing his coach that he had to lead prayers on Thursday." He also recalls that when Hae's brother called on the evening of January 13, he was with Jay in his car, recalling "reaching over Jay to get the cell phone from the glove compartment."

He also provided a handwritten account of his recollection of the school day.

There is a marked difference in these notes and the ones from July—there is no mention of Asia. By this time, having given Gutierrez Asia's letters and repeatedly asking her to speak with her, Adnan has given up on Asia. Gutierrez told him that she had checked with Asia, but Asia had her dates wrong; she hadn't seen Adnan on January 13 after all.

Adnan was confused, he was sure it must have been that day because he also remembered the following two days of school being closed, the days right after Hae went missing. Asia's letters had jogged his memory; he remembered teasing his friend Justin Adger, Asia's ex-boyfriend, about seeing her with her new man. And he was certain this happened right before the big storm in January that shut everything down for a couple of days.

He could have called Asia himself. He didn't, though, because Gutierrez had strictly warned him against talking to too many people, kids at the school in particular. It's not clear why, but she may have worried about his calls and mail being monitored or that he could be accused of influencing potential witnesses.

There were two important time frames he had to account for: the hour or so between school and track practice, and the time between track practice and the night prayers at the mosque. He was sure that he was there the night of the 13th because he had to lead prayers the next day. Gutierrez had spoken to a few people in the community who also remembered that Adnan led prayers on January 14, including the president of the mosque, Maqbool Patel, and his son Saad Patel. It's considered an honor for a young man to get to lead prayers for the first time, and it was a meaningful day for Adnan, his family, and others in the community.

Adnan didn't think he had to worry about the evening anyway; everyone knew Hae went missing right after school. That was the most important time to account for, and he wasn't able to do it. He had no alibi. It was in those days, as he spent time with other inmates who filled his head and heart with fear that beating such serious charges was nearly impossible, that he began thinking about the possibility of a plea deal. Asia was gone, he had no alibi, he had no idea what evidence the State had against him, or what was in Jay's statement to the police. He had spent time with Jay during the morning when he dropped off the car, and after track practice when they grabbed some food and smoked some weed. If he had no way to prove that's all they did, Jay could say whatever he wanted. It would be his word against Adnan's.

After all, Jay had Adnan's car that day. It was Stephanie's birthday and Adnan let Jay borrow the car to make a mall run for a present. It wasn't the only reason he gave him the car, though; Jay got him weed. He didn't particularly like Jay and wasn't friends with him, but he was, simply put, useful. He had to hang out with Jay every so often anyway, because of Stephanie, so he might as well get something out of it. Jay had connections none of Adnan's other friends had, to get cheap pot. Jay also did a little dealing, and if Adnan let him borrow the car (and sometimes money), he might get a bit of a kickback, or at the very least, free weed.

Jay also had Adnan's phone on the 13th.

Adnan couldn't take the cell phone to school so he left it in the glove compartment on January 13th, and it was with Jay all day, just like his car was. Jay could have used his phone, and his car, in any way while he was at school; he might even have gotten to Hae that way, which explained why he was framing Adnan for the murder. Adnan had no idea where Hae went after she left school, but she had his cell phone number. What if she had called it and connected with Jay instead? What if she met up with him and he killed her?

But why would Jay hurt Hae? Adnan had one theory, though even he didn't really believe it.

Jay had been cheating on Stephanie. Jay had told him about another girl he was seeing, his "booty call," while Stephanie was at school or basketball. He had one regular girl he would hook up with, but there were other random girls too. During an assembly in school about a year prior, Stephanie had told Adnan she was going to swing by Jay's house, and he had talked her out of it. He knew Jay had one of his girls over, the girls he called "ghetto white girls."

Adnan didn't understand it, because Jay was crazy about Stephanie. He couldn't imagine his life without her. Would he kill someone who threatened that prospect? That's what Adnan worried about. Because he had made the mistake of telling Hae that Jay was sleeping around, and she was livid. She'd told him that she'd confront Jay about it, that Stephanie needed to know. But Adnan begged her not to. He knew it would wreck Stephanie's heart. He figured that next year Stephanie and Jay would break up anyway, once she went away to college.

Adnan, said Hae, was thinking like a guy. It wasn't fair to Stephanie, but Hae agreed not to say anything. She and Stephanie weren't that close, and she realized that being the one to break such news could backfire—Jay could deny it and then Stephanie would hate her and Adnan.

But what if Hae changed her mind? What if she inadvertently connected with Jay using Adnan's phone and just couldn't hold it in?

This thought plagued Adnan.

That's why, in Gutierrez's undated notes from her visit with Adnan, it says at the top, in reference to Stephanie, "Jay—if anyone ever tried to get between her & I, I'd kill him."

But of course, Adnan had no proof. The state refused to turn over Jay's statements. All Adnan knew was that up until around 8:00 p.m., when he was at the mosque for prayers, he had no one to vouch for him. In a nutshell, things weren't looking great for Adnan.

Still, said some of the jailhouse F. Lee Baileys, the State almost always offers a plea deal. Especially to someone like him, who had a clean record and was a juvenile. The State was going hard but if all they had was a witness and no other evidence, they probably also knew their case wasn't rock solid.

So Adnan asked Gutierrez, as the trial date of October 14, 1999, approached, whether the prosecutor had offered a plea deal. She said, categorically, no. They had said nothing.

Well, then, could she approach them and ask if they'd consider it?

She said she would.

Adnan never told any of us that he did this—he knew that everyone, the family and community, would be in an uproar. None of us could fathom the idea that he would or should spend twenty, ten, or any years at all in prison for a crime he didn't commit. But none of us were in his shoes. He knew that if he didn't win at trial, he would spend the rest of his life in prison.

"A couple decades, man, and you'll still get out young. You still got your life. That, or you die in here," was the message he was getting from other inmates.

He waited anxiously for her answer, thinking the State would definitely make an offer. He'd figure out how to deal with the rest of us, how to explain it to his family and friends, later.

But he never had to because when Gutierrez came back to him she repeated what she said before. There was no offer on the table, the State said no.

If there was ever a time to worry, this was it. If the State wasn't interested in a deal, it could only mean one thing: they had the evidence to put him away forever.

Baltimore City Police were indeed doing their best to gather evidence against Adnan. On March 9, 1999, the cops executed a search warrant on Adnan's car.

Every loose item was retrieved from his car, including the trunk lining, to be tested for traces of blood, hair, or other DNA sources linking him to the crime. Samples of soil and leaves were also taken—presumably to match with soil and leaves from Leakin Park.

The police had already taken vacuum samples of soil from different parts of his car on the day they seized it, the same day they recovered Hae's car. All items from Hae's car were also collected and catalogued: a $10 checking withdrawal receipt dated 1/10/99, a credit card receipt from a gas station, a woman's school ring with no stone in it, Almay hand lotion and Mystic perfume spray from her purse, a plastic hanger, a red Big Gulp cup, a red ink pen, a blue ink pen, banana flavored lip balm, a package of maxi-pads, three stuffed animals including a Tweety Bird, a pair of black socks, a "happy birthday" paper crown, a size 7 pin-striped miniskirt, Nike cleats, a card with pictures of currants, a paystub for Adnan Syed dated 11/13/98, a folded note made out to "Don," a pack of index cards, six pictures of flowers, a thank-you card made out to the Lee family, a medium cotton T-shirt with short sleeves, a multi-county map with a pages 33 and 34 missing, a striped short-sleeved shirt with possible blood on it, a vehicle registration and insurance, a Baltimore Zoo map, a dried rose and baby's breath in a wrapper, a mango drink, an empty apple drink box, black dress heels, an empty gift box, a hockey stick, a gold heart charm with attached $119.95 price tag, a University of Maryland admissions card, and her East-pack blue book bag with miscellaneous items including a copy of *Othello*, a senior portrait order form, various photographs, and a high school agenda with Don's name written all over the first page.

A hair sample taken from the front right floor between the seat and the door and seventeen vacuum samples were also taken from Hae's car.

The prints found in Hae's car were compared to Jay's and Adnan's, and while there wasn't a single match for Jay, Adnan's prints appeared three times in her car: a partial palm print on the rear cover of the map book, on an insurance card in her glove compartment, and on floral paper wrapped around the dried rose and baby's breath.

Considering the fact that Adnan had been in Hae's car dozens of times, his prints should have been everywhere. The fact that they were not seems to suggest the car had been wiped down for prints when it was dumped, but the person who wiped it down didn't think to wipe down less obvious things—like paper.

Sixteen other prints found in the car were run through a database with no hits. Two of those appeared on the car's rearview mirror. These prints were compared against Adnan's, Jay's, Hae's, and a criminal database, with no luck, but prints were never taken from Don or Hae's family members.

According to State disclosures, "about 40" hairs were recovered from Hae's body and clothing. The majority were Hae's but two were not. Those two also didn't match Adnan's. Three hairs recovered from Hae's car weren't tested at all.

The soil samples taken from Adnan's and Hae's cars, and Adnan's home, clothing, and shoes, were all compared against soil samples from Leakin Park. Given Jay's narrative, having trudged through Leakin Park in the dark, dug a grave, and gotten back in both cars with dirty shovels and shoes, some dirt or soil from the park should have been present in the cars or on Adnan's clothing and shoes. But nothing matched. There was no soil from Leakin Park anywhere to be found.

A T-shirt found in Hae's car, which turned out to be her brother's, appeared to have a small amount of blood on it. Testing showed the blood matched Hae's and no one else.

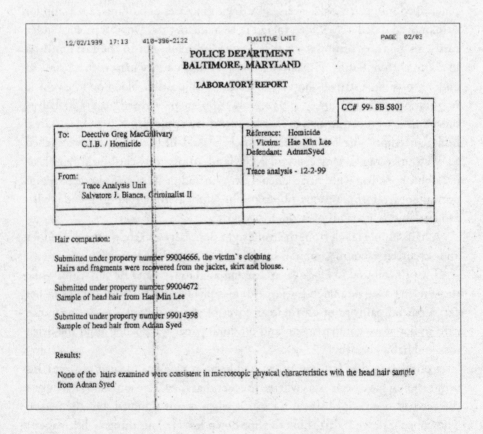

12/02/1999 17:13   410-396-2122   FUGITIVE UNIT   PAGE 82/83

POLICE DEPARTMENT
BALTIMORE, MARYLAND

LABORATORY REPORT

CC# 99- 8B 5801

To: Deective Greg MacGillivary   Reference: Homicide
      C.I.B. / Homicide   Victim: Hae Min Lee
                                          Defendant: AdnanSyed

                                          Trace analysis - 12-2-99

From:
      Trace Analysis Unit
      Salvatore J. Bianca, Criminalist II

Hair comparison:

Submitted under property number 99004666, the victim's clothing
Hairs and fragments were recovered from the jacket, skirt and blouse.

Submitted under property number 99004672
Sample of head hair from Hae Min Lee

Submitted under property number 99014398
Sample of head hair from Adnan Syed

Results:

None of the hairs examined were consistent in microscopic physical characteristics with the head hair sample
from Adnan Syed

The clothing Hae was wearing was examined for spermatozoa, but the lab found nothing. And then there were the swabs taken from Hae's body. The lab report indicates six of them were not analyzed, a very odd move considering that these items, listed in the lab report, consist of nearly every potential source of perp DNA from Hae's body: the vaginal, anal, and oral swabs, pubic hair sample and combings. Similarly, a brandy bottle retrieved from the crime scene had skin cells on it that were never tested for DNA, and neither was a thin, white rope recovered from within inches of the body.

Fingernail clippings tested were returned with results that read "nothing of evidentiary value was detected."

The lack of sperm is not as telling as it may seem, though. To be clear, examining clothing for semen is not the same as running a DNA analysis. According to the autopsy, along with Hae's clothing, the oral, vaginal and anal swabs were tested for spermatozoa and returned negative results. But there are two glaring issues here: first, sperm is not the only source of DNA. The medical examiner was only looking for signs of rape or sexual activity by seeking sperm traces. Second, they were using a common phosphate enzyme test to check for the presence of sperm—a test that can only detect sperm within roughly a hundred hours of sexual activity; if Hae had been raped or otherwise had sexual activity on the day she disappeared, this particular test would be useless to determine it.

At the end of the day, other than the partial palm print on the map book, a book Adnan had used many times while in Hae's car, the State found no physical evidence tying him to the crime scene or her body. Or, for that matter, tying Jay to any of it either. And for some reason, the State put a hold on the DNA testing.

During the police's search of Adnan's home, executed on March 20, they retrieved his clothing and shoes, the boots they believed he had worn while committing the crime. But they also turned his room upside-down looking for any other evidence of his plans to murder Hae. In doing so, they came across a psychology textbook on Adnan's bookshelf crammed with cards and notes from Hae, and pictures of them together. It was his secret stash of relationship memorabilia. In that stash was a note from four months prior, the note written by Hae to Adnan right after she broke up with him because of the homecoming dance fiasco.

Back in November, the note had lingered in his binder, and he showed it to Hae's best friend, Aisha Pittman, during health class one day when they were discussing pregnancy. On the back of Hae's note they began writing notes back and forth to each other, messing around about whether Hae was pregnant. Aisha was friends with both of them, and there was no hiding anything from her.

The police didn't care much about the banter. What caught their eye were the words written in Adnan's handwriting across the top of his exchange with Aisha.

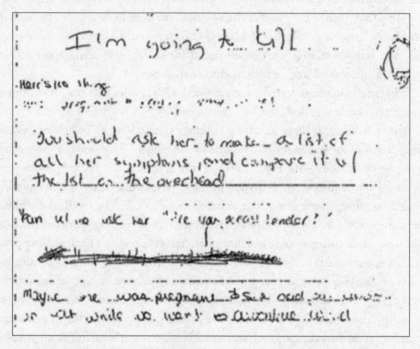

Note traded between Aisha Pittman and Adnan in November 1988, admitted to evidence at trial

An ambiguous line written on a four-month-old note and no forensic proof does not a conviction make, so the State was spending a considerable amount of time making sure their key evidence was not only solid, but solidly tied down. That evidence was their star witness, Jay.

Since his first recorded police interview on February 28, 1999, hours before Adnan's arrest, Jay had given three more interviews on the record.

Jay's second interview was at 6:00 p.m. on March 15, at the Baltimore City Homicide office, and this third interview happened three days later, on March 18, complete with a "ride-along" where the police took Jay out to recreate the events of January 13. The fourth interview was conducted on April 13, 1999, but no record of that interview exists anywhere in police or defense files. The only indication it even took place is a short memo noting it.

While the first interview already had internal inconsistencies, the second and third added layers and layers of confusion and contradiction.

In the second interview, Jay now said he knew how Adnan killed Hae, telling MacGillivary: "He tell me that ah, he's going to do it in her car. Um, he said to me that he was going to ah, tell her his car was broken down and ah, ask for a ride. And that was, and that was it, that."

The story of Adnan asking for a ride comes, notably, after the police have heard this from Krista Meyers on February 29, a couple of weeks earlier. Neither Jay nor Jenn knew, when questioned earlier, how Adnan got hold of Hae to kill her.

This time Jay also said that during a previously unmentioned store run with Jenn as he awaited Adnan's call, he told her that Adnan was planning on killing Hae that day. Jenn had said no such thing, maintaining that she didn't know any of this until that night when she picked up Jay. But then, the first time Jay had spoken to police, he had told them that he didn't know of Adnan's plans until the day it all went down. In the first interview Jay said he went to the Westview Mall to buy Stephanie's gift; in the second he said he went to Security Mall, both located in the suburbs of the city.

Hundreds of small inconsistencies like this pepper Jay's interviews, and a few big ones stand out, for example, where it was that Adnan showed him Hae's body. In the first interview, the "trunk pop" to reveal Hae's body happens on Edmonson Avenue. In the second interview it happens at Best Buy. By the third interview Adnan has killed Hae in Patapsco Park but he doesn't show Jay the body. The trip to Patapsco Park also jumps around, at 2:15 p.m. in one interview, at 4:30 p.m. in another. In the first interview he is at Jenn's home, which she confirmed, when Adnan's "come and get me call" comes in. By the third interview he is driving home when the call comes.

In the first interview, only Adnan buries Hae. In the second, they both do. In the first interview, Jay disposes of his clothing in the trash cans at his own house; in the second he gets rid of them at the F&M store dumpster.

In the second interview Jay visits the apartment of a girl named Kristina Vinson three times on January 13; in his first interview he doesn't visit her at all.

Whether and where Adnan smokes pot, where they get the pot, if and where they eat, who Jay visits during the day on the 13th, all of these details change with each interview, and sometimes within the same interview. Jay describes Adnan removing Hae's items from her car and putting them in his car in two different locations in the second interview: at both the I-70 Park-n-Ride and at Edmonson Avenue.

One consistency between the first and second interviews, an important one given the way the State's case is going to go, is that the call Adnan made to "come and get me" came to Jay around or after 3:30 p.m., and that he didn't leave Jenn's house until around 3:45 p.m.

Another consistency is the constant referrals to cell phone calls, their timing, his location during the calls, and the content of the calls. The calls to Adnan's cell phone, which Jay had all day, are unmovable. Their records are fixed and they must be dealt with; Jay's statements have to work with and around them. And to the best of his ability, he seems to do that. Over and over he's asked about different calls, and two undated documents titled "Jay's Chronology" and "Cell Phone Chronology," found together in police files with notes from his March 18 police meeting, seem to indicate that they worked with him to get his stories to match the record.

The cell phone records solve one of the State's big problems—most of the varied, and changing, details of Jay's statements are unverifiable. Jay's testimony and corresponding cell phone records will become the basis of the State's case at trial, in particular a 3:32 p.m. call to Nisha Tanna (the girl Adnan had met at the New Year's Eve party) and the 7:09 and 7:16 p.m. incoming calls. But first they have to make sure they can get Jay to the trial.

Throughout his interviews Jay has, repeatedly, implicated himself as an accessory to a very serious crime. He knows he needs an attorney but can't afford a private one, so he does the next best thing—he contacts the Baltimore public defender's office asking for a lawyer. He hits a wall, though—he doesn't qualify for a public defender because he hasn't been charged. And he continues to be in that limbo, implicated but not charged, until September 7, 1999.

On that day, prosecutor Kevin Urick finally charged Jay as an accessory after the fact to first-degree murder. But Jay did not need to worry. The charges were not just filed nearly concurrently with a plea deal he was being offered, but also at the same time that he finally got an attorney, albeit in a highly irregular manner.

Attorney Anne Benaroya had recently entered private practice after seven years as an assistant public defender in Baltimore, Maryland. In September of 1999 she was working with a boutique criminal law practice and was occasionally asked by prosecutors to speak with indigent defendants. On that particular day she had a jury trial against Urick that ended sooner than expected. As they wrapped up Urick asked her to speak to a young man who needed an attorney. She was qualified to be a court-appointed pro-bono attorney, so she agreed.

Jay was being offered a plea deal, right then and there. Upon speaking with Jay she realized that he was already "loaded with prior statements to BPD," in her words, and that the plea was a foregone conclusion. If he didn't take the plea, Urick implied that the case could be tried in mostly white Baltimore County where a defendant like Jay wouldn't fare so well. Benaroya realized that, having tangoed this long with BPD, Jay was actually lucky he was getting a deal at all. Urick didn't have to offer him anything; he could just subpoena him based on

Jay's Chronology

1. Approximately 1 hour after call, Adnan at Rich Avenue
2. Security Square Mall shopping
3. Adnan back to school for 1ˢᵗ period after lunch
4. Jay to Jennifer's, ▮▮▮▮▮ Avenue. Several trips to store and back
5. Jay gets two (maybe 3) calls on cell phone from Adnan, one to see if phone is on and one to say he's leaving school.
6. Waits for "come get me" call but leaves before it comes in. Goes to Jeffs @ ▮▮▮▮▮ Road but Jeff not home. Jay then heads for home to ▮▮▮ Avenue. Jay at Bardswell and Craigmont when Adnan calls, "Meet me at Best Buys"
7. They leave Best Buys following each other to Rt. 70 Park and Ride where Honda with Hae's body in trunk is left and both leave in Honda. (Adnan moves stuff??from front of Nissan to trunk)
8. Travel south on Cooks Lane towards Edmondson while unsuccessfully calling ▮▮▮▮▮ Road, Patrick, for grass connect.
9. Head for NWD to cop grass via Rt. 40, Johnnycake, Ingleside, Forest Park to Norfolk and Granada where connect 2 dimes grass. Talked to girl ??? while driving past Forest Park golf course.
10. Then to "cliffs" to smoke dope via Cooks Lane, Old Edmondson, Ingleside, Frederick to Hilltop and dead end at "cliffs".
11. Smoke dope at "cliffs", sun going down.
12. Leave "cliffs" to take Adnan back to school for alibi track practice. Adnan talks to his mother @ being late because of track practice.
13. Jay travels via Beltway to "Christie and Jeffs" @ ▮▮▮▮▮ near Wilkens Avenue & Maiden Choice Lane, arriving @ 5:20 or 5:30. Smokes some dope and then Adnan calls "Come get me!"
14. Jay back to Woodlawn High via Beltway gets Adnan outside gym, thinks "Will" was with Adnan. Jay thinks about 6 PM.
15. Both now back to Christy and Jeffs via Ingleside, Frederick, Paradise and Maiden Choice. While there Adnan gets 3 incomings, 2 from Hae's family (one maybe a misdial by Hae's family) and then call from Police
16. Adnan then asks Jay to help get rid of body. They drive to Jay's house, get shovels, then to Park and Ride where Adnan gets into Nissan telling Jay to wait at McDonalds on Security. Jay thinks it's @ 20 minutes before Adnan shows.
17. Jay in Honda then follows Adnan in Nissan to Rolling to Dogwood to Holyfield to Johnnycake back to Woodlawn. Maybe around 7PM now. Then to Dogwood to Kernan to Security to Forest Park to Franklintown to burial site.
18. After arguing they leave and park Nissan in front of 4651 Briarcliff and both in Honda back to burial site to dig grave. Snow on ground but melting.
19. While in woods digging 2 incoming, one from Jennifer and one unknown. Leave to go back to Briarcliff for Nissan and body. Jay doesn't go back but waits at Briarcliff.
20. 10-15 minutes later, Adnan back to Briarcliff, "Help me!"
21. Both back to grave, finish covering body.
22. Back to Briarcliff and get Hae's car. Jay in Honda follows Jay in Nissan to 300 S.

MPIA 15 459 1383

Edgewood where Nissan dumped. Jay says it seemed like Adnan knew where he was going.
23. Back to Westview Mall via Edmondson Avenue where Hae's things and shovels dumped at dumpsters behind Mall
24. Jay remembers Adnan taking him home, Jennifer states she meets both of them in front of Westview Mall where she picks up Jay and sees Adnan.

Cell Phone Chronology 12/13 January 1999

Call#	T/P# Dialed:	Listed to:	Time Dialed:	Duration:	Cell site location:
34	410-602-2544	Hae Lee	12:01AM	0:02	201 N. Charles St. (C)
33	420-602-5244	Hae Lee	12:35AM	1:24	824 Dorchester Catons(A)
			(10 HOUR AND 10 MINUTE LAPSE)		
32	410-███-8495	Jay	10:45AM	0:28	1500 Woodlawn Dr. (A)
31	410-███-2609	Jennifer	12:07PM	0:21	Rts. 29 & I-70 (A)
30	410-███-2609	Jennifer	12:41PM	1:29	714 Poplar Grove St. (A)
29	Incoming	N/A	12:43PM	0:24	714 Poplar Grove St. (A)
			(1 hour and 53 minute lapse)		
28	Incoming	N/A	2:36PM	0:05	1500 Woodlawn Dr. (C)
27	Incoming	N/A	3:15PM	0:20	1500 Woodlawn Dr. (C)
26	410-███-2609	Jennifer	3:21PM	0:42	1500 Woodlawn Dr. (C)
25	301-███-0657	M.Nisha	3:32PM	2:22	1500 Woodlawn Dr. (C)
24	301-███-8485	Unknown	3:48PM	1:25	1500 Woodlawn Dr. (A)
23	410-███-4650	D.Furlow	3:59PM	0:25	1500 Woodlawn Dr. (A)
22	410-███-2609	Jennifer	4:12PM	0:28	2121 Windsor Grdn Ln.(A)
21	Incoming	N/A	4:27PM	2:56	824 Dorchester Catons. (C)
20	Incoming	N/A	4:58PM	0:19	824 Dorchester Catons. (C)
19	Incoming	N/A	5:14PM	1:07	WB443??????
18	443-███-9023	Adnan Cellph	5:14PM	1:07	BLTM2??????
17	410-███-9704	Krista	5:38PM	0:02	501 N. Athol Ave. (C)
16	Incoming	N/A	6:07PM	0:56	UMBC Campus (A)
15	Incoming	N/A	6:09PM	0:53	3600 Georgetown Rd. (C)
14	Incoming	N/A	6:24PM	4:15	3600 Georgetown Rd. (C)
13	410-███-7374	Yassar Cellph	6:59PM	0:27	1500 Woodlawn Dr. (A)
12	410-███-0384	Jennifer Pgr.	7:00PM	0:23	1500 Woodlawn Dr. (A)
11	Incoming	N/A	7:09PM	0:33	2121 Windsor Grdn. Ln. (B)
10	Incoming	N/A	7:16PM	0:32	2121 Windsor Grdn. Ln. (B)
09	410-███-0384	Jennifer Pgr.	8:04PM	0:32	501 N. Athol Ave. (A)
08	410-███-0384	Jennifer Pgr.	8:05PM	0:13	501 N. Athol Ave. (C)
07	301-███-0657	M.Nisha	9:01PM	1:24	1500 Woodlawn Dr. (C)
06	410-███-9704	Krista	9:03PM	5:28	1500 Woodlawn Dr. (C)
05	410-███-9704	Krista	9:10PM	8:41	1500 Woodlawn Dr. (C)
04	301-███-0657	M.Nisha	9:57PM	0:24	1500 Woodlawn Dr. (C)
03	410-███-7374	Yassar Cellph	10:02PM	0:06	2040 Powers Ln. Catons. (B)
02	410-███-9498	Saad Chaudry	10:29PM	0:18	1500 Woodlawn Dr. (C)
01	410-███-9232	Maria Rogers	10:30PM	1:44	1500 Woodlawn Dr. (C)

his existing statements. Of course, an uncooperative witness can do plenty of damage at trial.

The plea was the bargaining chip used to make sure Jay testified as needed, with the threat of imprisonment hanging over his head, but to enter a plea Jay needed to have an attorney. Urick couldn't parade him before a judge without legal representation. Lucky for Urick, and Jay, Benaroya had the heart of a public defender and couldn't say no. But at that point Jay hadn't been arraigned yet, so Benaroya asked the court to proceed with the arraignment in order to enter her appearance as his attorney as well as to enter his plea.

The parties then immediately entered a plea before the court, with Jay pleading guilty to one count of accessory after the fact to the murder of Hae Min Lee.

According to the plea, as long as Jay cooperated by continuing to "tell the truth," the State would recommend a five-year sentence with all but two years suspended. However, when Jay is finally sentenced the following year, this is not the sentence he gets.

With Jay's testimony secure, the State now has to deal with Gutierrez and her barrage of discovery requests. While the State ostensibly has an "open file" policy that would allow defense counsel to have full access to prosecution files, Gutierrez was forced to file demand after demand to get information about the charges.

As of September 1999 the only information given to the defense is what was contained in the indictments and warrants from months ago:

> On 09 February 1999, at approximately 2pm., the Baltimore City Police Department responded to the 4400 block N. Franklintown Road, for a body that had been discovered by a passerby. Members of the Armed Services Medical Examiners Office responded and disinterred the remains. A post mortem examination [ruled the] manner of death a homicide. Subsequently, the victim was identified as Hae Min Lee . . . On 27 February 1999, your Affiant along with Detective William F. Ritz had the occasion to interview a witness to this offense at the offices of homicide. This witness indicated that on 13 January 1999, the witness, met Adnan Syed at Edmondson and Franklintown Road in Syed's auto. Syed, who was driving the victim's auto, opened the victim's trunk and showed the witness the victim's body, which had been strangled. This witness, then follows Syed in Syed's auto, Syed driving the victim's auto, to Leakin Park, where Syed buries the victim in a shallow grave. Subsequently, this witness then follows Syed, who is still driving the victim's auto, to a location where Syed parks the victim's automobile. Syed then gets into his car and drives the witness to a location in Baltimore county where the digging tools are discarded in a dumpster.

Gutierrez had been attempting since May to compel full discovery on the details of the case, including repeated filings for the autopsy report and Jay's statements. At one point she contacted the medical examiner's office herself to get the autopsy report only to be told that they'd been instructed by the prosecution not to provide it to her.

Although Gutierrez already knew the identity of the State's witness because the police had told Adnan who it was during his interrogation, the State filed a motion with the court to bar discovery of the witness's ID. In response to Gutierrez's request in June for "[a] copy of any statements made by Jay Wilds as an unindicted co-conspirator or codefendant," the prosecution replied that "[t]here is no unindicted co-conspirator or co-defendant." Technically, the State was right—they hadn't yet charged Jay.

It is not until about a month before the trial is scheduled, on September 3, that the State discloses it has Adnan's cell records and intends to introduce them at trial as business records.

On the same day that Jay pleads guilty to accessory after the fact, Gutierrez files a motion to compel further discovery with the court, asserting that the defense hadn't been given enough information to raise an alibi defense.

> Moreover, the State has identified, only upon inquest by this Court, that Ms. Lee was murdered sometime in the afternoon of January 13, 1999, but the State has contended it cannot establish the time of death with any further precision. Jay Wilds, according to the State, met Adnan Syed directly after the murder at a prearranged time and location and was present and assisted in the burial of Ms. Lee's body in Leakin Park. While the State has "paraphrased" Mr. Wilds' statements for various purposes, the State has not "paraphrased" or revealed any information regarding the actual time(s) Mr. Wilds alleges this activity occurred.

Gutierrez has no idea at this point that Jay will testify that the burial took place long after school was out, because the indictment reads as if the burial happened right after Hae was killed.

On September 24 the State discloses that it will introduce a witness from AT&T wireless, implying the witness will be a "documents representative"— someone who can authenticate the records, but not someone who will testify to the calls in a substantive way. They follow this up on October 8 with a disclosure that the State will call an AT&T expert witness at trial, someone prosecutor Kathleen Murphy and a Baltimore detective took a ride with that day to test cell tower locations. Jay joined them. The cell expert, whose name they disclose the following day, is Abe Waranowitz, a radio frequency ("RF") engineer with AT&T.

They also disclose a summary of Waranowitz's oral report. The summary is not accompanied by any written results but is Murphy's account of the expert's oral reportings to her. The ambiguity results in a frantic letter by Gutierrez two days later to AT&T attempting to get the information alluded to in the State's disclosure, namely maps with cell tower sites. This is the first the defense has heard the State will be offering any evidence related to cell tower site locations, and the trial is scheduled for three days later, on October 14.

A motion by Gutierrez to "continue," that is, delay the trial, is granted by the judge on October 14, and at that point she still doesn't have a single statement made by Jay, any statements by Jenn, or cell tower location information or maps.

But the day before the new trial date of December 8, Waranowitz faxes Gutierrez a list of the relevant cell tower sites, two maps he prepared, and a spreadsheet of cell tower frequencies, all of which still add up to less than meaningless documentation, given that Gutierrez has no idea what the significance of any of it is.

And just like that, with barely anything to go on, Adnan and his defense team go to trial.

The first-degree murder trial of the *State v. Adnan Syed* began on December 8, 1999, in the Baltimore City Circuit Court with the Honorable Judge Williams Quarles presiding.

I wasn't there. It was a weekday, of course, a Wednesday, and my law school semester was fast coming to a close. Final exams were around the corner.

I spoke to Adnan frequently in the weeks leading up to the trial. He was nervous but trusted Gutierrez. I had yet to meet her, but I had heard all about her and done my share of Internet sleuthing. She had an incredible reputation and, according to Adnan, had offered him a lot of attention and kindness in the past eight months. He could sense that she felt protective of him and it reassured him. She told him, repeatedly, that the State had nothing. The forensic disclosures they had made so far indicated that neither the blood on the T-shirt found in Hae's car, or the hairs they tested, matched Adnan. They had nothing but Jay.

It wasn't until the first day of trial, when evidentiary and preliminary motions took place, that the State finally turned over Jay's police statements from February 28 and March 15, after repeated motions by Gutierrez. Nothing about his March 18 or April 13 meetings was disclosed. The State still didn't turn over Jenn's statements, or those of any other witnesses, and challenged Gutierrez's request for Jay's statements by arguing (1) there was nothing exculpatory in them and (2) he was a witness and not a co-defendant.

```
DEC-07-1999  13:00                                                    P.02/09



Site   Site Name              ADDRESS                                            Lat       Lon
L608   WRBS Radio             3600 GEORGETOWN RD. BALT.                          39.25528   -76.6753
L651   Social Security Bldg   1500 WOODLAWN DR. WOODLAWN                         39.30806   -76.74
L653   Edmonson Ave           300 NOTTINGHAM RD.                                 39.28556   -76.6986
L654   BC RI40 WT             824 DORCHESTER RD.CATONSVILLE                      39.28639   -76.7339
L655   UMBC                   Walker Rd.-off WILKENS RD. UMBC CAMPUS CATONSVILLE  39.26083   -76.7133
L689   Bernard Mason          2121 WINDSOR GARDEN LN.                            39.31111   -76.7008
L698   Catonsville tower      2040 POWERS LN. CATONSVILLE                        39.28861   -76.7606
```

Cell tower location information faxed to Gutierrez.

Gutierrez understood—probably after sitting through the grand jury examination of Bilal, and hearing from Saad and others that the police were asking about religion—that Islam and Adnan's ethnicity were the foundation of the State's argument toward motive. And she wanted the court to be aware and take into consideration any jury bias that could taint the proceedings as a result.

Prior to voire dire, in which the jury was selected, Gutierrez says to the judge that "there have been particularly in print, but also in TV and radio media non-stop for the last eight weeks or so since the coup in Pakistan, news events regarding that coup and the political implications for peace in that area and others and specifically related to this country." Judge Quarles asks her if she is "going for . . . basically, Arab, Islamic bias?" She says yes.

The judge assures her that he will attempt to elicit any such bias from the jury pool and then asks this follow-up, "I understand the importance of Islam in the case, does her [Hae's] Catholicism or lack thereof play any part in the case?"

Even before opening arguments, the court is already aware that Adnan's religion plays a role in this case, though it's not clear how this information is known, since charging documents have no such information. Either the judge has in hand the bail hearing transcript, or the grand jury testimony, or has simply heard it through the legal grapevine. Regardless, it is now publicly known that this is not a run-of-the-mill dating violence case.

Jury selection begins on the 8th and runs into the next day, when both the State and defense also give their opening statements. This is the first time Gutierrez and Adnan get to hear exactly what the State will be alleging in the particulars of the crime. The State lays out its case:

[Jay] gets a page to meet the Defendant at Best Buy. He meets the Defendant there. The Defendant has Hae Min Lee's car and says look I did it, pops the

trunk, there's the body of Hae Lee. At that point Jay Wilds is totally shocked and stays in a state of shock. [. . .] You're going to see another exhibit which is a map of cell sites and how they correspond to the City, and you're going to see. [. . .] That both of those calls were made from the [Leakin] Park cell site. And you're going to hear how the body was buried and recovered from [Leakin] Park.

It is a short, methodical, precise opening. Gutierrez, however, opens with a long, rambling (and sometimes inaccurate) lecture on Pakistanis and Islam:

[Adnan] happens to have been born of Pakistani extraction. His parents are American citizens by choice. For those of you—you may or may not know some of the history of Pakistan, which is a country that was formed in the Arab world in the tip of the land mass called Asia. (Indiscernible) is in the northwest corner of what was once India. [. . .] And Pakistan was formed because, within India, hundreds of years of settlements from Hindus and Moslems could not get along and subsequently Pakistan broke off. [. . . A]t some point, many Pakistanis—the bulk of whom were Moslem—many of them came to this country to seek peace and economic opportunity. [. . .] They brought with them their religion. [. . .] And they brought their customs and way of life. [. . .] And they formed communities as Moslems and as Pakistanis. [. . .] On the rest of the world, Islam is a major religious force for people in many different countries—Arabic, Asian—but all over the world Moslems live. It is a mono- phystic (phonetically) meaning they believe in a single god and they believe in a way of life. [. . .] They operate on a different calendar year. [. . .] which doesn't recognize—other than as a dividing point—the birth of Christ that one the basis of most Christian calendars. And in the Islamic calendar, which runs ap- proximately 12 months—but on a different system—there is one month that the Islamic calendar use as a sacred month of renewal and discipline, and a call to the faithful Islamic to come together and do certain things to remind them of the discipline of their faith [. . .] in addition to the house of worship where the faithful of Islam gather—and particularly during Ramadan—five times a day to pray according to the book of their religion—the [Koran]—to pray and open their souls and their hearts to the discipline of the words of Mohammed. [. . .] The hope of the mosque in building the school is to prevent the impact on their children in what they view as the outside world, and every year they add a grade so that there is a fundamental Islamic school system where they can keep their children away from the evilness of a world that they interact with but they know does violence (inaudible). That is a world that Adnan Syed came from.

*And that friction certainly caused him friction. Now Adnan—and you will
learn this from everyone—his friends, from the teacher, from the friends of Hae
Lee herself. Adnan was a young man who was liked by everyone. He was a
leader. He was a scholar. He was an athlete. [. . .] And he viewed himself [. . .] as a strict, fundamental Moslem, as a good Moslem.*

In many ways, spending so much time speaking about Islam and Pakistan,
Gutierrez has not only confused a jury that probably had little knowledge and is
now getting all sorts of conflated, unconnected facts thrown at them, but she is
also confirming the role of Islam in the case and "otherizing" Adnan far better
than even the State can do. Not to mention that much of her opening is unrelated and irrelevant to the crime itself and has little discernible organization. Her
best bet was to open with the facts of January 13, 1999, tell the jury her witnesses will show Adnan was at school when the State says Hae was killed, and
emphasize that the State's case is based on bias and bigotry. Instead, she inadvertently legitimizes their theory.

Gutierrez goes on for fourteen transcribed pages before the judge asks her
how long she'll be. She responds that she needs another fifteen, twenty minutes.
Half an hour later, it takes a five-minute warning by Quarles to finally shut her
down.

The next day, the State begins to put on its witnesses, starting with Hae's
brother, Young Lee.

Lee testifies to the events of January 13, including the phone calls he made,
Adnan's and his sister's relationship, and the T-shirt with bloodstains found in
Hae's car. Lee states that the shirt is a rag she kept to clean up around the car.
Using Lee's testimony as a foundation, the State enters Adnan's phone rec-
ords, a prom picture of Hae, and her diary into evidence and ends their ex-
amination. Gutierrez does a short cross-examination in which she asks about
Lee's knowledge of Hae's new boyfriend, Don, and ends by asking if Hae hid
her relationship with Adnan from her parents. Lee responds, "She did."

The State's next witness is Nisha Tanna, whom Adnan had met nearly a year
prior at a New Year's Eve party on December 31, 1998. Nisha was asked specifically about a call placed to her phone from Adnan's cell on January 13. The
call was made at 3:32 p.m. and lasted two minutes and twenty-two seconds. But
before showing her the call records, Urick asks her about the one time she ever
spoke to Jay Wilds.

Nisha testifies, in response to whether she was sure she spoke to Jay on January 13, "It's a little hard to recall but I remember Jay invited [Adnan] over to a

video store that he worked at and he basically, well Adnan walked in with the cell phone and then he said, like he told me to speak with Jay and I was like okay, because Jay wanted to say hi, so I said hi to Jay and that's all I really recall."

On cross Gutierrez has Nisha reaffirm that she isn't sure what date she spoke to Jay and that it happened at a video store.

Nisha's testimony adds one more piece of the narrative puzzle of the State's case—by using that cell phone call, they are going to corroborate that Adnan and Jay were together that afternoon.

The rest of this first day of testimony includes Officer Scott Adcock, who testifies about his investigation the day Hae went missing, and then Sergeant Kevin Forrester, who testifies to the condition of the windshield wiper/selector switch in Hae's car when it was found. Forrester had taken a video of the car on March 16, 1999, to show that the windshield wiper was hanging limp from the steering column. He also testifies to where the car was found, pointing it out on a map for Urick.

Gutierrez has exactly one question for the sergeant: "Detective Sergeant, the person who directed you to where the car was found was Jay Wilds?" Forrester responds yes.

Salvatore Bianca, a criminalist in the trace labs unit of the Baltimore City Police, testifies next. Bianca had tested the T-shirt found in the car and under Urick's direct examination, admits that it is possible that it is not just blood but also mucous staining the shirt. He testifies that the blood on the shirt comes from Hae and no one else and that two fibers found on her body did not come from her clothing.

On cross Gutierrez elicits from Bianca that there was no semen found on any of the samples he took, and also that the comparisons done of the blood stains were limited to two suspects: Adnan and Jay. As Gutierrez tries to establish that testing was unduly delayed, Urick responds that the defense was on notice of the samples and could have requested testing themselves but didn't. This doesn't sit well with Gutierrez, who mutters her disapproval out of the judge's hearing range.

Prosecutor Kathleen Murphy hears it though, and raises an objection: "Judge, I'm going to object to defense counsel calling my co-counsel an asshole at the trial table that she did just a moment ago."

The last witness called that day is Romano Thomas, assistant supervisor of the Mobile Crime Lab Unit of the BPD. Thomas had been part of the team that responded to both the burial site and the location where the car was recovered, and he testifies as to how evidence was collected from both crime scenes. In particular Thomas testifies about how the fingerprints and palm print were collected from the floral paper, insurance card, and map book. He also testifies about the note found in Hae's car, in her handwriting and addressed to Don that he reads for the jury, "Hey cutie sorry I can't stay I have to go to a wrestling match at Randallstown High, but I promise to page you as soon as I get home. K? Till then take care and drive safely. Always, Hae. PS, the interview went well and I promise to tape it so you can see me as many and as often as you want."

Gutierrez has no questions on cross and the day's proceedings end. The next day further testimony is presented about the fingerprints by Sharon Talmadge from the latent print unit of the BPD. Talmadge essentially affirms Thomas's testimony but adds one very important fact: that sixteen of the fingerprints taken from Hae's car returned negative results. They didn't match Hae, Jay, or Adnan, or anyone in their database.

Gutierrez, on cross, makes the point that Talmadge was only given two suspect prints from which to compare the recovered prints, and wasn't even provided the prints of Alonzo Sellers, the neighborhood streaker. Showing the myopic focus of the investigation is her goal.

"Did there come a time when the fingerprints and the palm prints of a person by the name of Alonzo Sellers were submitted to you?"

"No, they were not."

"And did you, Ms. Talmadge, put any restrictions on the police department as to how many names—of how many suspects they could submit evidence against which you were to compare any evidence that you could recover?"

"No."

"If they had submitted to you a list of ten names would you have conducted the very same thorough analysis that you did as you've described to us today?"

"Yes."

"If they had submitted twenty names, would you have done the same thing?"

"Yes."

Day three of the trial opens with testimony by Emmanuel Obot, a crime lab technician with BPD, who was present during the search of Adnan's home. Obot identifies a picture of the book pulled from Adnan's room that held the cards, letters, and pictures of and from Hae, including the note with the "I'm going to kill" line written across the top. Gutierrez makes an attempt to imply on cross that the book, out of an entire bookshelf, was specifically pointed out by Ritz to investigate, trying to raise suspicion about the fortunate coincidence of this discovery.

Detective O'Shea next takes the stand and testifies, most significantly, about the ride that Adnan was supposed to have gotten from Hae after school but then denied when later interviewed. Gutierrez does a solid cross-examination then, raising the facts that Hae was seen by someone other than Adnan at school at 3:00 p.m., that Adnan was likely at track practice, and that Adnan himself had asked to meet with O'Shea to answer questions willingly.

The State then calls witnesses connected to Woodlawn High—the principal Lynette Woodley, nurse Sharon Watts, athletic trainer Inez Butler, and students Krista Meyers and Debbie Warren.

Woodley testifies to events on the night of the homecoming dance when Adnan's parents showed up at school. She states that she saw his parents talking to Hae and intervened, telling her to return to the dance, and that she later asked her if she really wanted to be involved in a relationship where it was creating family problems.

Watts gives more testimony that raises questions about Adnan and the context of his relationship with Hae. She recounts the day it was announced in school that Hae had been found murdered.

"He appeared shocked. His eyes were big. He was mute. He wasn't talking. He wasn't crying. He was just absolutely stone still . . . As soon as I touched Adnan and started to walk him into the health suite the look changed. The eyes weren't so big. His posture wasn't so erect. He walked easily. He didn't need any leading . . . And just with that alone, his supposedly catatonic appearance changed . . . My opinion was that this was a very contrived emotion—very, very rehearsed—very insincere."

Gutierrez doesn't do much to counter this assessment other than draw Watts to testify that she hadn't seen Adnan and Hae together other than once, and that she had no experience with Adnan—she had never examined him before. On redirect, Urick asks one question: "What is a pathological liar?" Guterriez objects, and the court sustains the objection.

Krista Meyers and Debbie Warren primarily testify about Adnan and Hae's relationship, the impact of the family pressure on it, how they both took their eventual breakup, and how Adnan reacted at the news of Hae's death. Urick has Krista identify the writing on the "I'm going to kill" note as Adnan's without actually reading it out loud in order to enter it into evidence—he's going to "publish" it with another witness. Urick also asks her about the conversation she had with Adnan the morning of the 13th and she responds, "I recall him mentioning . . . that Hae was supposed to pick him—pick up his car that after-noon from school because he didn't have it for whatever reason. Either because it was in the shop or his brother had it, I'm not sure which."

Gutierrez does nothing to address this potential ride but has Krista testify about the fact that Hae and Adnan were still close after breaking up, still friends, and that likewise Adnan and Stephanie McPherson were also very close friends.

Having established Debbie as a friend of Hae's who knew about the problems of their relationship, Urick has Debbie read a series of passages from Hae's diary in which she discusses her concerns about Adnan's religion, doubts about their future, and about falling for someone new, Don. Debbie is also asked to read for the jury the exchange between Adnan and Aisha Pittman on the back of Hae's note to him, and she concludes her testimony in dramatic fashion by reading the words "I'm going to kill." Gutierrez continuously objects to all of it, from the diary passages to the note, and her objections are continuously overruled.

On cross, Gutierrez gets to the most important point she needs to elicit from Debbie, that she told detectives she saw Adnan in school by the guidance coun-selor's office around 2:45 p.m. on January 13.

Gutierrez reads from Debbie's police statement: " 'And I'm positive just about then I saw Adnan that day before he went to practice. I spoke to him and a couple other kids. And then that was very short—that wasn't a long period of time that we did that.' And then probably about 2:45 you left. Do you remem-ber telling them (police) that?"

"Yes."

One last important witness takes the stand on this day: Donald Clinedinst.

Don testifies to having seen Adnan before he and Hae began dating because Adnan would occasionally swing by the store, and after they began dating, he saw him one more time. Hae had a small accident in the snow and called Ad-nan to take a look at her car, an incident Hae writes about in her diary. A dis-crepancy here, though, is that she indicates this happened in December, before she and Don began dating, and he testifies it happened after they began dating, which would have to have been in January.

Urick offers Don's employment records into evidence through his testimony, helping to establish that he was at work until 6:00 p.m. on the day Hae dis-appeared.

Gutierrez asks Don to describe Adnan and his relationship with Hae after they broke up—that they were still friends, and there was no hostility.

The next day, Tuesday, December 14, the State calls more witnesses to testify about the forensics, including the medical examiner, Dr. Margarita Korrell, who testifies about the autopsy and manner of death. She offers evidence that led her to conclude Hae was strangled in a homicide: eye hemorrhaging and a broken hyoid bone. She also testifies about the condition of the body and how it conforms to the theory that Hae was killed on January 13, 1999. The State then brings up evidence that shows Hae was not just strangled, but that she was hit viciously beforehand, asking the doctor to refer to the portion of her report that refers to bruises on Hae's head.

Dr. Korrell explains, "These are bruises that are in the right occipital and right temporalis muscle . . . (T)hey are under the skin, subfilial is on the surface of the bone and into the muscle of the right temple. And they only occur when the heart is still pumping."

Gutierrez is able, on cross, to get the pathologist to admit that there is no way to pinpoint the time of death. She also gets her to admit that there was no sign of external bleeding on the body. Lastly, under cross Korrell testifies that there was no sign of semen in any of the swabs taken from Hae's body.

Next on the stand is Melissa Stangroom, a forensic chemist with the Maryland State Police Crime Lab. Stangroom was in charge of the DNA testing on the bloodstained shirt. Her conclusion after testing was that while Adnan and Jay could be ruled out as the source of the blood, Hae could not. This allowed for the possibility of other suspects. Gutierrez pounced on this, asking Stangroom about how many samples she was asked to compare the blood to—only three, making a point to show how narrow the State's investigation was.

The prosecution also calls Woodlawn French teacher Hope Schab, who quickly establishes herself as someone deeply suspicious of Adnan's behavior. She testifies about a time when Adnan was waiting for Hae in her classroom and Hae called the room phone, pretending to be a teacher, and asked Schab not to tell him where she was because they had a fight. She also testifies that she has been coordinating questioning with teachers and students, and indeed was even investigating Adnan herself, because Detective O'Shea had asked her to. She was asking around about his sex life, and Adnan asked her to put a stop to it, saying, "Are you asking questions about me, because, you know, my parents don't know everything that goes on in my life, and I would appreciate it if you would, you know, not ask questions about me."

The State then calls Yaser Ali, Adnan's friend of many years who also attended his mosque. Yaser's number shows up twice on Adnan's cell phone on January 13, but Urick also wants him to testify about the do's and don'ts of being a Muslim. Gutierrez isn't having it, objecting that this teenager is no expert on Islam, and the judge calls them both to the bench to make their points.

Urick argues that Yaser's testimony regarding the requirements of Islam are important because, "This defendant was leading a double life. He was leading one life that his parents' religion wanted him to lead. He was leading a hidden or illicit life that caused him to lie to many people to create different personas, different fronts for different people."

Gutierrez renews her objection, saying that nothing Urick was exploring with this witness had any relevance to the day the murder was committed.

The judge sides with Gutierrez, stating, "I have some difficulty in exploring any witness's religious beliefs sort of generally . . . I think we raise needless due process considerations if you're going to do generally an exploration of his adherence to his religious beliefs," and telling Urick that he will have made his point if he gets to whether Adnan and Hae's relationship was frowned upon in Islam.

Having been duly guided, Urick returns to examine Yaser further about what Islam has to say about dating and premarital sex.

Gutierrez is successful on cross in getting Yaser to testify that this "double-life" angle Urick is getting at actually applies to all the young Muslim men at the mosque who are dating. She ends with a long line of questioning on Ramadan, the involvement of Muslims at the mosque in this month, and the honor of leading prayers.

The last witness to testify before the State's key witness is a young woman named Kristina (Christina in trial documents) Vinson.

Adnan does not really know Vinson except as a friend of Jay and Jenn. But her testimony is about to place him with Jay in her house at a crucial time on January 13, right before he is supposed to have buried Hae around 7:00 p.m. It's the first time he's going to hear this part of the State's case, and he's perplexed because while he remembers once having swung by her apartment with Jay, he is almost certain it wasn't on that night. But he could be wrong—after breaking his fast that night he had gotten high and, in all honesty, what happened after smoking pot wasn't exactly clear for him.

Vinson, however, recalls January 13 as the night that Jay showed up with someone she had never met before at her apartment between 5:30 and 6:00 p.m. while she was home with her boyfriend, Jeff Johnson. She had been at a conference all day and had gotten home shortly before they arrived.

She says that Adnan was out of it, high as a kite, didn't say a word, just came in and slumped over on some pillows on the floor. She tried to make small talk with Jay, whom she knew through Jenn, and he told her that they were coming from a video store and were waiting to be picked up. The conversation got confused, she said, so she dropped it. At some point, Adnan apparently popped up and asked, "How do you get rid of a high?" and she told him he had to wait it out.

She describes a call to Adnan's cell phone then, and his responses along the lines of "What am I going to do? They're going to come talk to me," shortly after which he jumped up and just walked out of her apartment. Jay, she says, is a bit taken aback, but then gets up and follows him, leaving behind his hat and cigarettes.

Jay returned later that night, she testifies, this time with Jenn, around 9:30 or 10:00, and they were "acting really funny, really strange." But no amount of questioning got her any answers about what was going on, so she dropped it.

An important part of Vinson's testimony is how she helps the State create a visual timeline of events for the jury. A large, blown-up map in the courtroom becomes the guide and, along with Adnan's cell records, helps the State pinpoint which call corresponds to Vinson's story, and which cell tower site on the map corresponds to her house. Everything fits.

On cross, Gutierrez points out that Vinson first became aware of the crime when she took her good friend Jenn Pusateri to the police station on March 9, 1999. On that same day she had also given statements to the police, which differed a bit from her testimony. Gutierrez asks her about the discrepancy, noting that Vinson had earlier told detectives that Jay and Adnan had arrived at her home between 5:15 and 6:00 p.m. and stayed 35 to 45 minutes. She begins to question her about the description she gave the police about Adnan being Indian or mixed-race, but misses something crucial—that in her police interview she describes Adnan as five feet seven. Adnan, however, was around six feet tall at the time of his arrest. She does point out that Jay never introduced Adnan to her, implying that she may not know if it was Adnan or not—though at this point Vinson has already identified Adnan in the courtroom.

After an exhaustive, repetitive cross, going over Vinson's testimony and all manner of collateral subjects like Vinson's favorite television show, Judge Quarles finally says, "In an effort to finish this millennium, Ms. Gutierrez, can we get back to the points at issue in this case?"

Jay Wilds is sworn in on the afternoon of December 14, the fifth day of the trial. Urick wants to get one thing out of the way immediately, the plea agreement. He asks Jay, in his own words, to describe it. And Jay does, in a single sentence: "The plea was just that, basically a sentence cap that I can only be sentenced to the maximum—sentencing for my part as long as I told the truth and nothing but the truth."

Urick quickly gets Jay to the night of January 12, when Adnan first got his cell phone and, according to the State's theory, called Jay to set up Hae's murder.

But instead of telling the jury what the State said he would, in response to Urick's question regarding what Adnan told him when he called him on the night of the 12th, Jay responds, "He just asked me would I like to join him. He asked me—asked me what I'd been doing. The next day was my girlfriend's birthday, the 13th. Her birthday follows mine. I told him I was going to the mall and shop and he told me he'd give me a lift."

He goes on to testify that they later went to the mall, where Adnan called Hae "that bitch" and said he was going to kill her, but that Jay "didn't take in the text of the conversation for what it was." He says Adnan then said, "If I let you hold my car, can you pick me up later?"

This is in contradiction to his previous police statements where he stated that Adnan called him the night before to request his help in the crime, having planned this all out before, premeditated.

Jay says he has Adnan's car until Adnan calls him to come to Best Buy, where he shows him Hae in the trunk of her car. He describes not being able to see her face, because she's facedown, but knowing it was her anyway. He says she's not wearing shoes, and he notes that she is "kind of blue."

How Jay manages to see her skin color when she is fully clothed, wearing pantyhose, and lying facedown is a question I wish Gutierrez had asked, but she didn't.

Jay describes leaving the car at the I-70 Park-n-Ride and then going to pick up weed at his friend Patrick's house. Gone from the story is Patapsco Park. He says he then leaves Adnan at school for track practice and goes to Vinson's house, a visit she never described in her testimony. After a bit he goes back to pick up Adnan and then again returns to Vinson's home. He describes a series of calls to Adnan's phone that Vinson, again, never testified to.

He says Adnan received a call from Hae's parents, then another call, again, maybe from her family, then a third call from a police officer.

With more such inconsistencies, Jay continues his narration of their trek to Leakin Park where he helped dig a grave and bury Hae. During the digging, he says, a call came in to Adnan's phone. He answered and said, "he's busy," and hung up.

He describes a complicated dance of the cars where he and Adnan go back and forth, up and down a hilly road that intersects Franklintown Road. First they both park at the top of the hill. Then Adnan takes Hae's car with her body down by the burial site as Jay waits in Adnan's car at the top of the road. A while later, he says, Adnan returns with her empty car and orders Jay to come back to the burial site, where Hae is lying facedown, to help him cover her up.

Jay moves through the timeline, describing ditching Hae's car in a parking lot between a bunch of houses, and then Adnan dumping some of her things in a dumpster, and finally Jenn picking him up in front of the Westview Mall, or his house—he can't recall anymore.

Urick then calls his attention to the cell records, pointing to different incoming and outgoing calls, trying to match Jay's recollection with Jenn's and Nisha's.

Knowing his prior statements have all kinds of contradictions, Urick attempts to stave off Gutierrez by broaching the subject head-on. He asks Jay why he changed his story about where Adnan popped the trunk and showed him the body from Edmonson Avenue to Best Buy.

Jay responds, "Really there was no reason. I just felt more comfortable if the cops had returned me to a place I feel comfortable in."

While the answer is a bit cryptic, it seems to be suggesting that Jay changed his statement because initially the police had told him to make the trunk pop at Edmonson. Urick, of course, doesn't follow that up for any clarification.

Urick then asks why Jay didn't mention meeting up with Jenn or saying anything to her in his first statement when he did in his second statement.

Jay states, "I didn't want her to have to be questioned by the police."

He seems to be forgetting that according to the State's official version of events, the police only came to him after Jenn had already given them a detailed statement, with a lawyer present, regarding her involvement.

Nonetheless, Jay manages a number of convoluted responses as to why he followed Adnan's orders (scared he would be turned in for dealing weed and because Adnan threatened Stephanie) and the State finally rests.

Instead of beginning her cross-examination, Gutierrez asks for an overnight recess to review Jay's statements and taped interviews. In doing so she loses a valuable opportunity to immediately press Jay on these responses.

On December 15, the last day of the trial, Gutierrez cross-examines Jay.

One of her first punches misses completely when she asks if, on January 13, Jay was already working at the porn video shop and he responds in the affirmative. That's completely untrue, however, and Gutierrez has the interview of Jay's employer Sis noting that he didn't start working there until the very end of the month. But she moves on, missing the chance to show that the call Nisha Tanna remembers in all likelihood didn't happen until a few weeks after Hae disappeared.

She spends a considerable amount of time painting a picture of the social order at Woodlawn, and how Jay wasn't part of the group of gifted and talented students that his girlfriend, Adnan, and Hae were part of—the Magnet Program. She then spends as much time drawing out the fact that Jay was, for much of the past few years, a drug dealer, pointing out that while Stephanie is now at college, Jay isn't. Gutierrez's strategy seems to be to show Jay's character and his motive for wanting to frame Adnan—out of jealousy for the kind of lives Magnet School kids were going to lead versus the kind of life Jay had.

She notes that Jay is always borrowing other people's cars, getting him to admit that he borrowed cars from his friends Laura Strata, Jenn Pusateri, and Chris Baskerville as well as his girlfriend Stephanie.

Gutierrez's cross is long, and exhausting. She repeatedly goes over many of the same things, Jay's drug dealing specifically, until the judge can't take it anymore and says, "Ms. Gutierrez, I'm trying to get this finished again by Christmas. You've used an hour. Perhaps we can be more pointed in the cross-examination. It might be helpful to all of us."

Gutierrez continues unfazed, though. She jumps from when Jay met with detectives, to how many people he dealt drugs to, to how and when he learned Hae's body was found. Every so often Jay would say something incredibly odd, for example, when Gutierrez asked if he knew that Hae's body had been discovered inside Leakin Park when he was interviewed by police on February 28.

Jay answers, "That's where it turned out to be, yes."

Jay's cross-examination goes on for another few hours before Gutierrez finally rests and the State starts to redirect. They are just getting started when an astonishing exchange takes place. Urick attempts to present State's Exhibit 31, cell phone records for January 12–14, to the jury. Judge Quarles asks Gutierrez if she has seen the records and she says no.

Urick counters, saying she has seen it and that it was entered into evidence by stipulation, meaning by the consent of both parties.

Gutierrez again says she has not seen the exhibit Urick is referring to, even when the judge also reminds her she agreed to the exhibit being entered into evidence.

The judge then calls both attorneys to the bench to figure out what is going on. Gutierrez had stipulated to Exhibit 31, meaning she did not challenge its admission. She absolutely knew about the records, yet here she was telling the court that she hadn't seen them.

Judge Quarles admonishes her, saying, "Ms. Gutierrez, if you are going to stand there and lie to the jury about something you agreed to come in, I'm not going to permit you to do that."

Gutierrez gets belligerent.

---

7   THE COURT: That was a lie. You told a lie.
8 I'm not going to permit you to do that.
9   MS. GUTIERREZ: That's not a lie, Judge, and I
10 resent the implication.
11   THE COURT: It's a lie because it was by
12 agreement.
13   MS. GUTIERREZ: By agreement doesn't mean that
14 I have seen it, and so it is not a lie.
15   THE COURT: I assume --
16   MS. GUTIERREZ: And so I resent that
17 implication.
18   THE COURT: I assume -- I assume that you
19 didn't agree -- that you've seen what you agreed --
20   MS. GUTIERREZ: I agreed to the admission of
21 cell phone records because I did not care.
22   THE COURT: (Inaudible.)
23   MS. GUTIERREZ: I had not looked at them. I
24 had not seen it. It is not a lie.

It is impossible to understand how an attorney with decades of criminal defense experience (1) stipulated to the admission of documents she had not looked at and (2) could tell a judge with a straight face that she stipulated to admitting documents without looking at them because she "did not care."

Gutierrez explains to the court that the documents "didn't concern me on any other date," getting louder as the judge asks her twice to "please be quiet."

She responds, "It's very hard to be quiet when a court is accusing me of lying."

The white noise machine is on the entire time to prevent the court from hearing this exchange, but it didn't work all that well.

Jay's redirect continues as Urick asks him about the significance of Best Buy to Adnan and Hae's relationship—Jay responds that according to Adnan, they had sex there. Urick then tries to establish the importance of the map book in Hae's car, which had a page torn from it, the page that happened to include Leakin Park. He asks Jay if he knows, as Adnan is driving Hae's car and he is following, how Adnan is navigating. Jay says no.

Gutierrez gets a chance at recross and takes Jay back to this issue, asking Jay about following Adnan all around the city before finally making it to Leakin Park. Jay agrees that this is indeed what happened. Gutierrez lands her point that the long, uncertain route Adnan took there must show he hadn't decided on the location beforehand.

Jay is finally released from the stand, even though Urick wants to re-redirect, but is cut off by the judge.

Dr. William Rodriguez of the Armed Forces Institute of Pathology is next called to testify about examining the burial site.

He describes the location and condition of Hae's body as follows:

We observed initially that the body was placed in a position near a very large log or tree that had been downed. It was in very close proximity to this and that the body was partially covered with dirt. It was very shallow. However there were three components of the body that were partially exposed; that being some portions of the hair, a portion of the hip, and a foot and knee area. And in examining those, it was obvious that these had been exposed as a result of post-mortem animal activity; that is, animals coming to feed or that are attracted to the remains, and through their activity, they basically had teased out the hair from underneath the ground and also had uncovered dirt and removed it from areas that covered portions of the body.

He describes small scratch marks and mud prints of small animals that had uncovered portions of the body. This would seem to contradict the autopsy report that shows no evidence of animal activity on her body, which is also a bit of a mystery, given that in most such circumstances, soft fleshy parts of a body so exposed (such as the ears, fingers, nose) are often quickly nibbled on by foraging animals.

Rodriguez then explains how the body was disinterred, carefully, using small trowels and brushes, and discovering two fluorescent fibers—one orange, on top of the body, and another bright blue, underneath the body.

Urick asks whether the condition of Hae's body was consistent with her having been killed on January 13, 1999. Rodriguez says yes.

On cross, Rodriguez is asked by Gutierrez about the condition of the park itself and the ease or difficulty of reaching the burial site, agreeing with her when she says the terrain is hard to get through to take a body and that there was no path, other than the ones the officers ended up creating, leading from the road to the body.

Gutierrez is attempting here to show the unlikelihood of Sellers traipsing back to the burial site to take a leak, and she's done a good job.

As she's wrapping up her cross, she notices a juror is trying to say something to the judge and calls the clerk's attention to it. Rodriguez finishes his testimony and they take a short break.

Once court reconvenes, Gutierrez tells the judge that she has just been told that their exchange, in which she was called a liar by the judge, was heard over the white noise machine by colleagues Chris Flohr and Doug Colbert as well as others. She moves for a mistrial based on the fact that the court has attacked the credibility of Adnan's attorney.

Judge Quarles already knows what happened, because the juror who was trying to get his attention sent him a note, reading, "In view of the fact that you've determined that Ms. Gutierrez is a liar, will she be removed? Will we start over?"

The judge immediately grants Gutierrez's motion for a mistrial, and Adnan's trial for first-degree murder ends on the sixth day.

Doug Colbert was still deeply invested in the case even though he no longer represented Adnan. On the afternoon of December 15, after the heated exchange between Gutierrez and the judge, he had to leave. But he returned as soon as he could, only to find the proceedings had abruptly ended.

Colbert later submitted an affidavit to assist with yet another attempt to grant Adnan bail as he awaited a new trial, now scheduled for January 21, 2000. In it he states that as the jury filed out he spoke to most of them and they advised that had the trial resumed, they would have acquitted Adnan based on the State's case so far. Colbert notes Adnan's stellar record and inexperience with the criminal justice system and that his life could be "needlessly destroyed by wrongful incarceration or conviction." He cites the hardship Adnan is experiencing while incarcerated and requests the court grant Adnan's bail as he awaits trial.

But like the past three applications, this too was denied.

Adnan would remain incarcerated pending another trial, which, thankfully, would begin soon.

Though denied bail, at least the defense, Adnan, and his family now knew this: despite many rambling moments by Gutierrez, and not yet having even put on the defense case, jurors were still likely to acquit. Maybe all this time Gutierrez had been right—it was the State's job to prove their case, and they couldn't. The evidence they presented would not pass the "beyond a reasonable doubt" standard.

But Adnan was still worried, and considering a plea deal. He knew the State hadn't yet presented its full case when the mistrial was called, and he saw how effective they were in using the only real evidence in the case, the cell phone records, in corroborating Jay's timeline. He worried about whether another jury would find Nisha's testimony about the cell phone call damning, and if the State would return with an even stronger presentation. After all, it wasn't just the defense that got a preview at the first trial, the State also got to do a trial run with Jay Wilds.

Adnan sat through Jay's testimony mostly stunned. None of it was true, but he had to sit there and listen to the lies, conscious of the eyes and attention of the courtroom of people behind him. He pretended to scribble on a legal pad, trying to hide his mortification.

Now he'd have to do it all over again.

Adnan asked Gutierrez again to ask the State if they were offering a plea, and again she returned with a negative.

So he waited, trusting Gutierrez would be even better prepared for the next go.

The second trial was presided over by the Honorable Wanda Heard of the Baltimore Circuit Court. It began in earnest with opening statements on January 27, 2000.

This time Urick had learned his lesson. The jurors had told him his witness wasn't credible. Urick was going to turn Jay's lack of credibility on its head.

His opening struck an entirely new tone, but he didn't forget to set up Adnan as the slighted young Muslim man.

"This relationship caused problems. The defendant is of Pakistani background, he's a Muslim. In Islamic culture, people do not date before marriage and they definitely do not have premarital sex. Their family is a very structured event. They're not supposed to date. They're only supposed to marry and engage in activities after they marry. So he was breaking the cultural expectation of his family and religion to date Ms. Lee."

He goes on to read passages from her diary that drive home the message that religion was the issue here, focusing on an entry Hae wrote when Adnan had accompanied his father to the Islamic conference in Dallas.

Then he went into the whole explanation of the purpose of the trip to Dallas. He told me that his religion means life to him and he hates it when he sees someone purposely going against it. He tried to remain a faithful Muslim all his life, but he fell in love with me which is a great sin. But he told me that there is no way he'll ever leave me because he can't imagine life without me. Then he said one day he would have to choose between me and his religion. [. . .] He said that I shouldn't feel like I'm pulling him away from his religion but hello, that's exactly what I'm doing. I don't know how we'll live through all this. But this is bad.

But Urick still has to account for Jay, the star witness that the first jury didn't believe.

Urick develops a masterful strategy to counter Jay's inherent credibility problems. He tells the jury that Jay comes from an impoverished, broken home, that he deals weed, that he worked in a porn shop. "He doesn't have a lot of money for clothes to dress well," Urick says. "So you may not like Jay Wilds. There may be things about him that you do not like, but remember, ask yourself when you hear these things, what was it about this individual that made him susceptible to being used and manipulated by this defendant." He repeats this again a few minutes later, "You may not like all of this, but every time you hear about this ask yourself, what is it about this individual that allowed this defendant to use him in such a crass and manipulative way."

And poof, like magic, the very thing that makes Jay incredible, unbelievable, unlikeable, is what will endear him to the jury because the story now is this: Adnan picked Jay specifically because he KNEW no one would believe a weed dealer with poor character. Adnan picked Jay because he calculated that if Jay came forward, no one would believe him. Now all of Jay's inconsistencies and lies will work for the prosecution, and the majority black urban Baltimore city jury will look at Jay and understand where he is coming from.

This is all new. It is a brilliant, manipulative stroke of genius.

While Urick's opening is much longer and more dramatic than in the first trial, he's still no match for Gutierrez.

She begins by setting the stage in a manner that could not have helped Adnan at all.

"Young, star-crossed lovers, of different races, from different countries, from different families, from different religions, from one side of the street to the other, from one set of answers straight to another, throughout history populated our collective human history. The younger they are the more tragic it is."

The sad irony in all of this is that for both Adnan and Hae, it was a typical high school romance—passionate, lusty, dramatic, and short-lived. Like most teenagers, they were madly in love when they were madly in love, and almost just like that they were ready to be madly in love with someone else.

The framing of their very normal teen romance as a breathless Romeo-Juliet saga by both the State and defense turned it into a Shakespearean tragedy. In reality, it was no more serious than any other high school romance.

Gutierrez also does Adnan no favors by highlighting his religion and ethnicity again, alienating him from the jury. Instead of presenting him like a typical teen, she turns him into something unrecognizable to a panel of people who could never, having heard this, be a jury of his peers.

> *His ancestry on both his mother's and father's side, whom you will get to know and identify, is of Pakistan. They are Pakistani. And they came to this country before he was born or thought of in hope of a better life from their native land, like generation after generation of immigrants. [. . .] Pakistan is, depending on your viewpoint, an Arab country, a Mideastern country, a Near Eastern country, a Far Eastern Asian country. Pakistan was a country that was formed out of the bloodbath that was India right after India gained its independence from Great Britian. It was a bloody revolution. And one of the distinctions between Pakistan and India were the deep divisions of culture. Pakistan is predominantly a Muslim country. Muslim is the common definition to term those who hold Islam as the core of their fundamental belief system.*

Gutierrez's opening stretches for nearly forty transcript pages, delving in and out of religion, tradition, witness accounts, crime scene information, high school anecdotes, until she concludes to the jury, "I give you Adnan Syed in your charge."

Then begins an eighteen-day march of State witnesses, many of whom testified in the first trial: Forrester, Obot, Lee, Schab, Rodriguez, Tanna, Meyers, Adcock, O'Shea, Thomas, Talmadge, Bianca, Clinedinst, Long, Watts, Ali, Korrell, Woodley, Butler, Vinson, Warren, and of course, Wilds, who is much more polished both in his presentation and testimony, even though it stretches over the course of five long, grueling days.

But there are new State witnesses too: Aisha Pittman, Detective MacGillivary, Jennifer Pusateri, and Abraham Waranowitz

On January 28, 2000, Aisha provides much of the same kind of testimony Warren and Meyers did in the previous trial, about Hae and Adnan's relationship,

Aisha is also asked to read the "I'm going to kill" note to the jury and testifies that she last saw Hae when school was dismissed at 2:15 p.m. talking to Adnan in psychology class.

Gutierrez does a long cross-examination, covering Aisha's knowledge of Hae and Adnan's relationship, the homecoming dance incident, and the religious issues, but ending with Aisha testifying to the fact that despite everything Hae and Adnan remained friends until the day she disappeared.

Perhaps the most vital witness for the State, second to Jay, is Abe Waranowitz, the AT&T RF engineer, who takes the stand on February 8, 2000, to explain how cell towers in different locations pick up cell signals—testimony the State uses to create an entire route on a map following the towers that had pinged from Adnan's phone on January 13, 1999.

Much like the medical testimony, in which the prosecution asked the pathologist if the condition of Hae's body was *consistent* with the theory that she was killed and buried the same day she disappeared, Urick gets Waranowitz to testify that the towers pinged are consistent with Jay's testimony—that it is within the realm of possibility for the phone to have been where Jay says it was. What Gutierrez fails to do, though Waranowitz explains that each tower has a range and being pinged could mean being anywhere in that range, is plot an entirely new route that is still consistent with the tower pings. Hundreds of routes and locations could have been plotted that still would have been consistent with the pinged towers. Gutierrez does point out the difference in the type of phone used by Adnan and the type of phone used for Waranowitz's drive test, and grills him on billing issues.

Despite the hours of circular, repetitive cross-examination of Waranowitz, the State's theory sticks, loud and clear. Their witness says Adnan was burying Hae in Leakin Park around 7:00 p.m., and two calls that come in at 7:09 and 7:16 ping the tower that covers the park. As far as the prosecution is concerned, they have corroborated Jay's story scientifically.

Then the State presents another witness to support Jay's story: Jenn Pusateri. She didn't get a chance to testify in the first trial, but her testimony is now fairly consistent with her police statements. On January 13, 1999, she came home from work and saw Jay hanging out there; he left after getting a call around 3:30 or 3:45 p.m. (a point Jay also still maintains in his testimony while simultaneously asserting the "come and get me call" from Adnan is the one that appears on his bill at 2:36 p.m.); and that evening she returned a page from Adnan's phone around 7:00, at which point someone picked up the phone and told her Jay was busy and he'd call her back. Jay paged her about an hour later to pick him up at the Westview Mall, and as noted in her police statements, she took him to the dumpster to wipe down the shovel (or shovels).

Gutierrez crosses Pusateri aggressively and for hours, questioning her repeatedly about every police interaction and about her relationship with Jay, implying they are more than just friends. Pusateri's cross runs into the following day, again going over every movement since the moment the police first approached her on February 26, 1999.

Once in a while Gutierrez lands a punch, such as when she asks Jenn, "Another thing that Jay had told you was that he didn't know where the body was?"

Jenn answers, "Right."

"That he had been asked by Adnan to help bury the body, right?"

"Right."

"But that he had adamantly refused to do so?"

"Right."

"And according to him as to what he told you, he didn't have any involvement, right?"

"Right."

"Right, he just drove Adnan around and picked him up and dropped him off at different places but that he had nothing to do with killing her or burying her, right?"

"Right."

"He didn't assist Adnan other than to drive him around, right?"

"Right."

"But that he had no knowledge of what happened to Hae before it happened, right?"

"Right."

There are many, many inconsistencies between Jay's and Jenn's testimony, just as there were in their police statements. But hours and hours of testimony can dull anyone's senses, especially a juror's. Unless they are paying very close attention or taking notes, many times what is left with them is an overall impression. While this exchange is jarring, it is a small snippet of hours of testimony. It may be that by the time she ended, the jury simply lost sight of the significance of what Jenn was saying here.

Another witness who did not appear at the first trial, or rather didn't get the chance to testify, is Detective MacGillivary, who took the stand on February 17, 2000. His direct examination covers the timeline of the investigation, focusing primarily on Pusateri's initial statements and how that led the police to Jay. MacGillivary recounts Jay's initial statement and his taking the police to Hae's car in the early morning hours of February 28, 1999. The detective, cognizant that the multiple, contradictory Jay statements are now in the hands of the defense, attempts to bring some clarity as to why. He states that after the first interview, he received Adnan's cell phone records and returned to question Jay because his initial statements weren't consistent with the records. Together, armed with the records, they ironed out the wrinkles.

Of course this makes little sense because, according to the State's narrative, the police initially approached Jenn because her number appeared multiple times on Adnan's records for January 13. The police certainly had those records before Jay's second interview, and even before his first one.

Gutierrez's cross focuses on the crime scene, asking MacGillivary to describe the area where Hae was found.

The detective says, about the burial spot, "[I]t was a natural depression the tree was laying over . . . [I]t was a natural gully there and the tree was lying across the gully. So on the far right side you could actually walk right over the tree. However, on the section closest to the stream, you could not."

This characterization of the body's location—in a natural, shallow depression according to MacGillivary—seems to contradict Jay's statements that he and Adnan had dug the shallow grave.

Gutierrez spends a considerable time examining him about the terrain, about the visibility of the body, about the viability of reaching the burial site easily—all in an effort to show that Sellers' story was highly unlikely. Which leads her into exhaustive questioning about the police investigation of Sellers.

MacGillivary also testifies at length in response to questions about his interviews with Jay, Jenn, and Adnan, questions that are repeated so often that the court finally has to say, after yet another objection raised by Urick, "Sustained and please move on . . . I mean we've been over this fifteen different ways, counsel."

This will not be the last time the court has to ask Gutierrez to keep moving. While Gutierrez was long-winded in the first trial, her questioning still moved forward. Now, a couple of months later, something has changed. She seems to get stuck in a vicious loop, repeating questions incessantly.

I wasn't able to attend most of the second trial because of law school and work. But the few times I did I noticed this speech pattern, dismayed. More than once I saw jurors nodding off as Gutierrez droned on and on. I could barely follow what she was getting at; I could only imagine how the jurors, who had to sit there for days and weeks, were processing any of it.

It was only worse with Jay's cross-examination, which went on for days and in which Gutierrez repeatedly got aggressive, sarcastic, and confrontational with him while Jay remained the image of coolness, not once responding rudely, and consistently calling Gutierrez "ma'am." Gutierrez was losing points not just for failing to ask pointed, limited, purposeful, and clear questions, but also for her demeanor, something I had come to know a little bit about now.

Before the start of this second trial I had accompanied Aunty Shamim and Uncle to Gutierrez's office to discuss the case and finances. They felt intimidated by her and asked me to come along, thinking she'd be less aggressive with a law student. They were wrong. If anything Gutierrez took my questions, which I had prepared together with Adnan's parents and community members, as a challenge—a challenge from a stupid law student to a legal legend. The meeting was disastrous, with her informing us that she didn't have to answer any of our questions, but we did have to pay her big legal bills.

We left more terrified than before.

At the second trial this extremely confrontational part of her emerges every so often, and it could not have made a good impression on the jury. It comes to a head when she explodes in the courtroom upon learning something she hadn't known before: that Urick had arranged the meeting between Jay and Anne Benaroya, who then became his attorney.

Gutierrez gets loud, outraged, and animated over how Urick provided Jay with an attorney for the plea proceeding—the transcripts of which she is never given—without having disclosed this to the defense beforehand. She makes repeated, exasperated referrals to "the attorney that the prosecution provided" in her questions to Jay. The entire time he maintains his composure, until the judge finally excuses him so Gutierrez and Urick can battle out a Brady motion that Gutierrez heatedly raises.

Gutierrez says, "Judge, at this time I would make a number of motions. The first would be that I would ask at this time to be forwarded an opportunity to question Mr. Wilds concerning whatever assistance Mr. Urick made in him obtaining his lawyer and to do so questioning outside the presence of the jury and outside of Mr. Urick's presence. [. . .] I believe it would have been absolutely improper for all kinds of reasons for Mr. Urick who assist in getting a lawyer outside of going to a Court and asking for the appointment of a lawyer or going to the Public Defender's office and assisting in getting a person about to be charged with a crime a lawyer under normal circumstances. [. . .] Ms. Benaroya was insistent on the Court knowing that Friday, six days ago, is a benefit to a witness connected to his plea bargain and as such is a benefit that we were clearly entitled to know. If that's not Brady, there's nothing that's Brady. Judge, this is an absolute and complete surprise. I will confess to you I've thought this for a long time but never, ever once did I ever think that they would say it, that I would ever be able to prove it."

Like nearly all the motions she raises, Gutierrez loses this one too, though she doggedly pursues the issue with Jay for days of testimony, exhausting him, onlookers, and the court.

After nearly five weeks, the State rests its case against Adnan.

On February 22, 2000, the defense introduces its first witness, private investigator Andrew Davis. Davis is questioned about a $1.71 charge on Hae's ATM card at a Baltimore City Crown gas station on January 13, 1999. Gutierrez asks if he was able to track down records of what Hae purchased and he reports that he was unable to do so.

No one involved seems to realize, however, that the bank records show that the purchase in the amount of $1.71 was actually made two days prior, on the 11th, but showed up as a completed transaction on the 13th.

Gutierrez next calls the city surveyor Phillip Buddemeyer to the stand. Buddemeyer accompanied the police and crime lab team to the burial site on February 9, 1999. He testifies briefly, noting that the body was 127 feet from the road and he had difficulty seeing it because it was "95% buried" in what looked like a place that had been long undisturbed.

Gutierrez next calls Alonzo Sellers. Definitely a hostile witness, Sellers is belligerent and quite unhappy to be there because it meant taking time off of work.

Nearly the entire direct examination of Sellers is tense and unfriendly; he often refuses to speak up, prompting Judge Heard to frequently ask him to sit forward, speak into the microphone, and repeat what he said. Like Pusateri and Vinson, at times Sellers is directly hostile to Gutierrez. He doesn't prove helpful to her case with ambiguous answers and a tone that sometimes reflects how ridiculous he thinks her questions are.

At some points, Gutierrez may deserve that disdain as she repeatedly takes him through an extraordinarily long line of questions on roads, locations, and routes from his house to work, often confusing him and onlookers.

Gutierrez calls into question the route Sellers chose to take on his way back to work when he pulled over to take a leak in Leakin Park, and the premise of his trip that day. After an hour or so of wrangling over why he would need a plane when he worked in maintenance at a large, well-appointed college, the judge decides to call it a day.

The next morning Gutierrez goes right back to the plane but then finally leads Sellers to describe how he found Hae's body, with dozens of questions about every step he took to get there.

```
2        Q    Okay.  But to get to Liberty Road from your

3   house, sir, don't you.have to cross Windsor Mill Road?

4        A    Yes, you cross that.

5        Q    Okay.  And --

6        A    That's Gwynns Falls -- Gwynn Oak.

7        Q    -- you also have to --

8             THE COURT:  I'm sorry, you what?

9             THE WITNESS:  That's Gwynn Oak Avenue.

10            BY MS. GUTIERREZ:

11       Q    Okay, Gwynn Oak Avenue.  And then from Gwynn Oak,

12  you have to get to --

13       A    Liberty.

14       Q    -- Liberty, is that right?

15       A    Right.

16       Q    And then from Liberty Road, you've go to get all

17  the way down to North Avenue, is that correct?

18       A    No, Gwynns Falls.

19       Q    Gwynns Falls Parkway?

20       A    Um-hum.

21       Q    And from there, you have to get to North Avenue,

22  do you not?

23       A    No.

24       Q    Or you have to get close to it, don't you?

25       A    No.  To Walbrook Avenue.
```

121

She manages to make some solid points, including that the police never fingerprinted Sellers or asked for hair or blood samples, that they never asked him to produce the plane he said he needed, and that indeed the first time he spoke to police he never mentioned the plane at all.

But she also drops a few balls. In one place she mentions briefly that Sellers had trouble returning with the police to where the body was later that day, that he couldn't find the place. Sellers mumbles "uh-huh" and she moves on instead of exploring why he couldn't remember where he found a body just a few hours prior. She also doesn't ask him to point out on a map where he parked, the route he took to the body, or where the body was found.

She does try hard, however, to bring in Sellers' prior convictions on public indecency. But the judge isn't buying it because in order to bring in the conviction, Gutierrez would have to get Sellers to say something about going that far into the woods in order to avoid exposing himself. Instead, he says he wanted privacy for urination—an important difference as far as the court is concerned.

What ensues is a lengthy discussion between Gutierrez and Judge Heard about penises, exposure, and urination. At one point the judge asks Gutierrez to keep her voice down as she loudly says that "indecent exposure, which involves the exposure of his penis . . .". After a robust debate, the judge disallows it. She also disallows admission of Sellers' polygraph tests.

The State asks Sellers a few questions related to his work, all of which are met with objections that are sustained, and like that, Sellers is off the stand.

Gutierrez, now in the second day of the defense, calls Coach Sye.

Sye testifies that Adnan joined the indoor track team in 1999 after the coach saw him running sprints for football practice.

Gutierrez asks him about practice policy during Ramadan, and Sye responds that as long as Adnan came to practice, he didn't actually have to run while he was fasting. He was expected to be there daily, and, according to Sye, he was. Sye also testifies that Adnan was a good athlete and good student, and got along with everyone.

But while Gutierrez may have gotten him to say that Adnan was at track even during Ramadan, she fails to catch two important things: (1) She fails to get Sye to testify to what he had said to investigators earlier, that he believed Adnan was at track because he notices if someone is not there, and (2) Sye told investigators the prior year that track began at 3:30 p.m. but now testified at trial that it started at four o'clock. If Gutierrez could have made Sye confirm his earlier statements, it would have challenged Jay's timeline directly.

Rebecca (Becky) Walker is next on the stand and Gutierrez asks her, as a mutual friend of Adnan and Hae, to describe both the trajectory and nature of their relationship. Becky testifies to their being a generally affectionate couple but experiencing issues because of family and cultural differences. Gutierrez asks her about the homecoming dance incident, to which Becky responds that while Hae knew Adnan's parents had shown up and was upset about it, Hae had not indicated that his parents actually spoke to her, confirming Aunty Shamim's recollection, but different from some of the rumors at the school.

Gutierrez tries to introduce testimony that Hae's family was also opposed to the relationship. This is reflected in her dairy and already admitted into evidence, though only a few passages have been read to the jury, but the prosecution objects. The judge sustains their objection.

Becky does testify that after the breakup Adnan and Hae were "very good friends" and that they both "still cared very much about each other." She describes her interviews with police about Adnan, after his arrest, and telling them that he had been deeply upset when Hae disappeared.

Becky had written several journal entries regarding Adnan, Hae, their relationship, his character, and behavior after Hae disappeared, which Gutierrez also tries to get into evidence. She is repeatedly challenged by the State and asks to approach the judge to make her case.

Gutierrez argues, "Our belief and part of our defense is to establish that, notwithstanding the existence of other evidence that might have challenged what they sought, they willfully ignore evidence of Adnan's good character, evidence of information that went against their view of what their relationship was when it broke up, what reason it was for, and how they acted toward each other, all of which information would have disproved their theory."

While accurate in her assessment of what the police actually did, Gutierrez has chosen a much more complex defense by trying to undermine the premise of the police investigation rather than presenting a coherent defense of Adnan—which would have entailed simply establishing where he was on the afternoon of January 13.

Gutierrez next presents Adnan's father, who begins by testifying to his ethnic background and his story of immigration to the United States. Gutierrez asks him about his citizenship, and the citizenship of his children, she asks him to point out his sons in the courtroom, and then she asks him questions about his religion.

It is a fairly linear and coherent line of questioning meant to get the jury to an understanding of Ramadan—from daily prayer obligations, to fasting, to Islamic months, to the month of fasting that happened to be during January of 1999.

Gutierrez then asks him about the day Adnan led prayers, a very proud day for his father. Uncle indicates that it was Thursday, January 14, the day after Hae went missing, and that Adnan had spent a number of days beforehand practicing. He doesn't know specifically where he practiced or how, but he knows it took him that much time to prepare. He remembers the 14th distinctly because it was one of "the happiest occasions of my life."

Gutierrez then gets into dating and religion, and Uncle testifies that while Muslims are not allowed to date, they can have opposite-sex friends, as long as the interactions are innocent. He explains that Adnan had told him about Hae and that when something like this happened, elders would counsel the kids to do what's right.

Gutierrez asks him when he learned of Adnan dating Hae, "Did you ask him to leave your home?"

Uncle says, "No. That would not resolve the problem."

"Okay. And did you take away his car?"

"No, we didn't."

"Did you beat him?"

"No."

"Did you inflict any other physical punishment?"

"Nothing, no."

"Or the loss of any other privilege?"

"No."

"Why not?"

"Because I believe if he is treated otherwise it would influence him better than punishing him like that."

Uncle makes two important points for the defense: first, that Adnan, who had gotten the cell phone through Bilal with his parents' permission, had worked through the month of December to save up for the phone, challenging the idea that he had gotten it as part of a murder plan. But more importantly, Uncle testifies that every night of Ramadan, around 7:30 to 8:00 p.m., Adnan went to the mosque with him. Every single night.

If Gutierrez had honed in on this—that Adnan never missed the evening prayer during Ramadan—she might have been able to convey to the jury the improbability of Adnan coming straight to the mosque from the dark, muddy woods.

The next day, February 24, 2000, Gutierrez calls Detective Ritz to the stand and walks him through the interviews police conducted with Adnan during their investigation. But what she really wants is to introduce an internal police memo written by Detective Massey about the two anonymous phone calls that the cops received nearly a year ago. She had tried to serve Massey with a subpoena but he evaded it. Since the memo was written by him, and because the caller was anonymous, she couldn't establish a basis to enter the memo into evidence. And that hurt her defense strategy.

Urick objects to the inclusion of the memo into evidence, and the judge sustains it but does agree to help Gutierrez find and serve Massey.

Gutierrez asks Ritz about the steps the police took after getting the memo, specifically having him testify that before the anonymous calls on February 12, 1999, Adnan had not been considered a suspect.

On cross, Urick makes an interesting move. Having first objected to the introduction of the memo, he now asks that it be published to the jury and has Ritz read it out loud on the stand. Urick probably hopes Massey is now off the hook and can't be examined by Gutierrez.

A lengthy direct, cross, redirect, and re-cross of Ritz then ensues about inconsistencies in Jay's statements, particularly about why he lied about the initial trunk-pop location. Jay had said that he was afraid there were cameras at Best Buy and "I'm associated with it." Ritz attempts to explain Jay's convoluted statement.

"One of the inconsistencies that we clarified was the location where they first saw the body of Hae Min Lee. He originally told me and Detective MacGillivary it was on Edmonson Avenue. In his follow-up statement, he said the first time that he saw the body and described it in great detail was on the parking lot of Best Buy out in Security Boulevard area. He stated the reason that he did not—wasn't truthful with us at the beginning was that he thought they had surveillance cameras on the outside of the building and didn't want to get caught or involved in it. He knew the defendant would get caught eventually and he didn't want to get involved in it. He was trying to disassociate himself from the parking lot in that regards."

Gutierrez bears down hard on this statement, though, trying to get Ritz to admit that Jay's only admitted "involvement" at Best Buy was a brief look at the body in the trunk of the car.

Ritz doesn't fold, though, and after one last round of redirect, Gutierrez lets him off the stand.

Gutierrez next puts on a series of character witnesses: my brother Saad, Adnan's friend and classmate Saad Patel, Saad's father and president of the mosque, Maqbool Patel, and school guidance counselor Bettye Stuckey.

Gutierrez asks Saad if he was present when Adnan led prayers on January 14. Saad was not, but had heard about it. He didn't see Adnan during the week as much because of his own sports commitments.

She asks him about dating and sex, and its prohibitions in Islam, which he acknowledges, and then says that he did know about Hae and had met her once. Saad testifies about Adnan's demeanor when he broke up with Hae.

"He was pretty laid back. He just told me that they broke up, and I wasn't too surprised," he testifies.

"Why was that?"

"Because Adnan was showing interest in other girls."

Another important thing Saad testifies to is the function of Adnan's cell phone, because he had one just like it. Gutierrez has him explain how numbers are stored in it, how it can scroll and automatically dial a number that's been saved on speed dial or in the phone log—seemingly obvious things in 2016 but in 1999, to a jury of many older people, still a mystery. They spend a good amount of time explaining how easy it is to dial a number already in the phone, attempting to infer that the call to Nisha Tanna was made inadvertently by whoever had the phone, and not by Adnan.

When Urick gets his turn on cross, he takes Saad right back to the basics of the State's theory—that this murder had a religious component, asking him "you testified that premarital sex is generally not accepted within Islam, isn't that correct?"

The next witness, Saad Patel, testifies that he attends school with Adnan, believes him to be a good friend, a good athlete, and a good student. He knew Adnan was dating and he knew he was having sex. The exchange between Gutierrez and Patel suggests a level of confusion over how the Muslim community operates that is rather astonishing—a level of confusion that Gutierrez knows the State is banking on.

She asks him, "As a result of your finding out that information [that Adnan was dating Hae], did you report Adnan to anyone?"

"Did I—excuse me?"

"Did you report him to anyone?"

"No, I didn't."

"For dating against the Muslim religion?"

"No. I didn't tell no one."

"Or for having sex with a woman to whom he was not married?"

"No, didn't report that to anyone."

"Is there any procedure for you, as a Muslim, to report that kind of activity?"

"There is no procedure."

Gutierrez knows this is what the prosecution is getting at: that dating is so anathema and alien to the Muslim community, that Muslims are so weird about it, that it would be considered a serious enough offense to have very serious consequences. And she knows the jury might be buying it.

Gutierrez asks Patel the same question she asked Adnan's father—whether leading prayers in Ramadan would require Adnan to practice beforehand. She knows that Bilal Ahmed had testified at the grand jury that the day before leading prayers, Adnan had revised his notes with him.

The trouble she is having behind the scenes, however, is that she can't find Bilal anywhere, though she needs him to testify.

Patel ends his testimony by noting that while he can't remember every specific night from a year before, he was at the mosque on most nights in Ramadan, and on most of those nights Adnan was there as well.

The elder Patel, the president of the mosque, testifies once again about the rituals of Ramadan and what an honor it is to lead prayers. He recalls specifically being present when Adnan led prayers on January 14.

Gutierrez then presents her very last witness, Adnan's guidance counselor.

Woodlawn High School

1801 Woodlawn Drive, Baltimore, MD 21207

RECOMMENDATION FOR
ADNAN SYED

As a student in our challenging Magnet Program for Pre-Engineering and Student Conducted Research, Adnan Syed has had many rich educational experiences, not only in the classroom but also in the community, serving as a tutor for elementary school students and working on research projects with mentors in mathematical and scientific fields. Whatever his assignment, Adnan strives for excellence at all times. His teachers remark that he is a bright, conscientious, and hard working student who approaches his studies with sobriety. He accepts criticism well and works to improve any area under consideration. His classroom contributions, verbal and written, reveal an analytical mind and a highly perceptive young man.

Although his coursework is paramount to him, Adnan has found time to participate in a number of activities, at school and in the community, that require time and dedication and reflect his special interests. An avid member of our MESA Team, he participated in building a solar vehicle that won sixth place in national competition in Topeka, Kansas last spring. Furthermore, he works diligently on projects sponsored by the National Honor Society, such as food and clothes drives and on various committees for the Multi-Cultural Club. In the community he is an effective youth coordinator for Islamic functions at his mosque. He also volunteers at the local Woodlawn Fire Department where he has EMT mentors from whom he is learning new and useful skills.

Adnan enjoys an excellent rapport with his peers and teachers who represent a diversified, cultural background. His warm, friendly manner linked with his genuine interest in the welfare of others have been definite assets in establishing his interpersonal relationships.

·This is a fine young man whose academic record, fine character, and strong commitment to his educational goals make him an excellent candidate for admission to the University of Maryland: College Park.

Sincerely,

Bettye M. Stuckey

Bettye M. Stuckey, Chairperson
Guidance & Counseling Office
(410) 887-1311

01/13/99

BMS:alj

Bettye Stuckey testifies having known Adnan since his junior year and that she came to know him well in his senior year when she coordinated the Advanced Placement programs and testing, which he took part in.

Adnan would swing by and chat with her when he had free time. Based on her interactions with him and his academic record, she had written him a letter of recommendation for college. The letter was dated January 13, 1999.

Gutierrez hands Stuckey the letter and asks her to identify it, then enters it into evidence and asks her to read it out loud.

Then, without having presented a single expert witness or establishing where Adnan was after school the day Hae disappeared, Gutierrez rests her case.

The next day, Friday, February 26, 2000, the State and defense both present closing arguments.

And, unlike during much of the trial, the courtroom is packed.

The day begins with attorneys from both sides arguing their points with the judge on jury instructions, including whether or not to call Jay's plea a guilty plea. Gutierrez argues against it, but again loses the argument.

We wait as Adnan sits at the defense table, looking earnest in a tie and glasses. Finally the jury is brought in.

Judge Heard instructs them not to take into account that Adnan has not testified, that it can't be held against him. We all thought, as most people do, that an innocent person should speak up in their defense, and Adnan also wanted to testify. But Gutierrez wouldn't allow it. Some lawyers make it a hard-and-fast rule never to allow a defendant to testify, while others feel like the right client should take the stand. I believe it could only have helped for Adnan to have testified.

Judge Heard then instructs them on Jay's testimony, saying, "The defendant cannot be convicted solely on the uncorroborated testimony of an accomplice—however, only slight corroboration is required."

In hindsight, this instruction opened wide the door to a conviction, given the cell phone evidence that was presented to back up Jay's testimony.

After noting objections by Gutierrez on some of the jury instructions, the judge asks for the State to present its closing arguments.

Kathleen Murphy begins.

"'How can she treat me like this?' The words of this Defendant to Jay Wilds regarding Hae Lee, as if she deserved to die. 'No one treats me like this.' What does that mean? What exactly did Hae Lee do to him? She fell in love with him. When you read these diary entries, you'll sense the joy and the excitement that she had about her relationship with this Defendant. . . . And then, as people do, Hey [sic] Lee met someone else, Don Kleindas [sic]. And at that point, it became readily apparent to everyone, including the Defendant, she wasn't coming back. It happens all the time. So why then did he tell Jay Wilds 'No one treats me like this'? What is it that this Defendant saw on January 13th when he looked at Hey Lee? He saw the hours they spent talking on the phone in hushed voices so their parents couldn't hear. He saw all the things they did together. He saw a woman who made him do things he never thought about doing before. He saw the poems that he wrote. He saw him give her a flower in class, in front of the whole class. He saw that they openly discussed marriage and that this was known to their friends, and even their 5 teachers. He saw his parents standing at the window of the Homecoming Dance. He saw his mother raise her voice at Hey Lee in front of his classmates. 'Look what you're doing to our family.' He saw the pain in his mother's face because she knew they were together. He saw Hey Lee falling in love with someone else and he saw himself, in the end, standing there with nothing to show for it but a guilty conscience and a pack of lies in which he cloaked himself. That is what he saw on January 13th. That is what he saw when he put his hands around her neck and squeezed, literally, the life from her. He felt strong, almost superhuman. He felt the little bone in her throat pop and still he continued to hold her there 10 seconds, long seconds, and it was done. So ended the life of Hae Min Lee, a beautiful young woman, a scholar, an athlete, a friend, a daughter, a sister."

It is an impassioned, moving, and deeply emotive closing argument. She goes on to name the evidence, Jay's testimony, the cell tower pings. She reminds them of how Adnan deceived Hae by saying his car had broken down and he needed a ride, and that Hae gave him one because that's the kind of girl she was.

She describes Hae's excitement as reflected in her diary, her new romance, her zeal for life, her plans for college, all snuffed out.

She talks about premeditation, and how Adnan planned it, getting a cell phone the day before, giving it to Jay, telling him to wait for his call.

And she talks about why Adnan chose Jay of all people for this job. Of all his friends, he chose the one he barely knew, the one who didn't belong to his inner circle, to help him cover up a murder. And like Urick did in his opening, she transforms Jay from an inconsistent, incredulous liar to a victim, used because of his lowly socioeconomic status by a manipulative, smart, pretty-boy.

Murphy closes:

"Hey [sic] Lee wrote in her diary May 11th, 1998, 'When I look into his eyes, know that he loves me. I really love him.' And again, September 8th, 1999, Hey Lee writes in her diary. 'I don't know what I would do without him. He is the sweetest person I have ever met. When life is hard, all I have to do is look into his eyes. Then it'll all be better.' Imagine the disbelief and the terror when she looked into those eyes on January 13th, those same eyes that she writes so politely about in her diary, with one purpose: to kill her."

It is impossible not to wince and feel a deep sense of pain at the closing. The courtroom is pin-drop silent.

After a brief recess, the court reconvenes for Gutierrez to present her closing statement, but before she does, she raises an important issue with the court: Murphy twice referred to the guilt of "someone who didn't take the stand" in her closing remarks. These are, according to Gutierrez, "outrageous" and prejudicial comments. She asks the court to reinstruct the jury that they cannot hold Adnan's not testifying against him.

The court says it already did so.

Gutierrez then asks that her law clerk be able to sit at the defense table to hold up notes for her—a clear sign that something is very wrong.

Throughout the second trial there were many moments when it seemed Gutierrez was confused and rambling. But nothing has prepared us for the closing, which begins like this:

As you've become aware in the six weeks—this is the only time that you will hear from me. And as I sit down, they get to get up again and say whatever they can to rebut—the Judge talked in instructions this morning about the kind of criminal justice system we have. It is unlike any other system in the world. In many places not in this city, not in this state, not in this country.

The minute that Detectives MacGillivary and Ritz made the decision back on the 28th of February to arrest the presumed innocent teenager that would have been it—no one going back to question why did you make that decision.

Gutierrez's closing was like a storm of hundreds of different points that should have connected, but instead were thrown randomly in no certain order. Separately each point makes sense, there is a purpose to it, but she has no ability to connect them into a story and is barely coherent.

He is sure that nobody else ever, whoever they are, were ever sat in a chair, at a table, in a courtroom like this and asked and put to test as a defendant in the murder of [Hae Min] Lee. Not even—unusual circumstances. Donald Klein- das [sic] was her current boyfriend. He was—as to his whereabouts on the 12th. Ms. Murphy dares to ask you to speculate as to whether or not [Hae Min] Lee spent the night at his house in Harford County the night before, but they didn't even ask him that. [. . . T]hey never asked him anything, never asked to account for his whereabouts, the last time he saw her—a map of West Baltimore, and West Baltimore—it doesn't take rocket science to know that the Crown station that allows people to use ATMs, not credit cards, as they suggested, but ATMs to make purchases, but only if they come inside, that is located—isn't on the way to any part of Harford County.

She tries desperately to make it clear that the police fixated on one suspect without conducting a thorough investigation, by ignoring important evidence. But her point gets lost in the jumble. Other times she loses a sentence, or changes subjects in the middle of a sentence. Something is happening, she is losing the ability to form sentences right in front of our eyes.

Alonzo Sellers will never be charged. He's never even been asked, never went down—was there another anonymous call, if there was evidence that shifted it to them, he knew it was already there because on the 26th, which is Friday, remember—that's how they got to Jen Pusitari [sic]. Something turned them toward Adnan Syed and, once turned, they never turned away.

It was nothing short of distressing to listen to her ramble. I was alarmed, horrified.

We're not here to decide if he was a good Muslim. Islam is not the only reli- gion in the world that forbids dating and certainly isn't the only religion in the world that says no sex before marriage. And it certainly—parents who exercise their right—I'm a Catholic not because I chose it. I was born in Catholicism, my parents chose it. If you're a Methodist, it is likely that's how you got there. They're no different in many ways. They're no different—so that—Ms. Murphy made much of Inez Butler, a very dedicated teacher and molder [sic] of human lives—Ms. Butler on the stand described in detail—except Ms. Butler back then on the 24th—25th of January, less than two weeks from when she was first asked by the Baltimore County Police detective involved in this—she said then that she knew [Hae] wasn't. Now—correction this. But then when asked about the closest point in time, she says—[Hae] wasn't coming back.

I keep looking at the jury's expressions. Some have looks of studied boredom while others sit with scrunched foreheads, trying to figure out what Gutierrez is trying to convey.

Judge Heard eventually has to stop her.

```
6              THE COURT:  Ms. Gutierrez, you have a minute to
7    wind up.
8              MS. GUTIERREZ:  Thank you, Judge.
9              I have to sit down now -- say what I wish to
0    say -- but when you took this charge, you took -- I hope
1    what I've said has been helpful to you.  If it's not, it is
2    up to you as a juror to answer those questions.
3              He is charged on the word of -- only you can send
4    him home.
```

"I hope what I've said has been helpful to you. . . . [O]nly you can send him home."

This was not the closing argument of a nationally renowned criminal defense attorney. The closing was a disaster. The Judge should have been as alarmed as the rest of us and stopped her, realizing she was not able to defend her client at this point.

Instead, the court grants the State thirty minutes to rebut, and this time Urick takes a turn.

He makes a measured argument for the importance of circumstantial evidence and lays out, in this case, how much circumstantial evidence there is, and how to draw reasonable inferences from it.

He draws a conclusion about the hair evidence that is not at all what expert Bianca testified to, stating that Adnan was not excluded from the hair analysis but that there weren't enough characteristics to be able to determine there was a match. Gutierrez objects, saying "That was not Bianca's testimony," but the judge lets it go.

He points to the fact that Adnan's name is misspelled in the phone company's bill—spelled as "Adrian," implying this was done deliberately to cover for the murder he was planning. He talks about the "I'm going to kill" note and the fact that Adnan is a trained EMT, training not for the purpose of saving lives, but for the purpose of learning how to kill someone.

He proffers that Jay's testimony about being in Leakin Park at 7:00 p.m. and the cell phone tower pings in the park at that time "mesh," coming together as overwhelming evidence.

At the very end, Urick picks up a dummy head, holding it with his hands wrapped around the neck as he paces the courtroom and says,

"It took 15 seconds, by the way, to kill Hey Men [sic] Lee. Have you ever thought about how much you can think about in 15 seconds? And the person who did this had a lot to think about because this was an intentional, deliberate killing."

I feel shock and disgust, and just like that it is over.

Adnan sits with his back to us, his head straight. I wonder where his eyes were when Urick was demonstrating the fifteen seconds it took to strangle Hae. I look around at others, at my aunt sitting with a prayer book from which she has not looked up the entire time, at Adnan's mother sitting stone-like.

Judge Heard dismisses the jurors, letting them go for lunch and instructing that they return afterward to begin deliberations.

Adnan gets up, stretching slightly and looking back at us as he is cuffed to be led out. He gives the room a weary smile. He is exhausted; he hasn't slept in a few days. The pressure of the trial has begun to get to him. His days have been extremely long; he has had to get up and be ready hours before every day of the trial, sitting in waiting rooms with other defendants for hours, sitting in the hard wooden chair in the courtroom for hours. He is stiff, achy, tired.

But after the jury is released for lunch and deliberations all the tension from his body and mind melt away. He is taken to his holding cell and finally, after numerous slumberless nights, almost immediately falls into a sweet, deep sleep.

We also feel collective relief, after weeks of prayer and anxiety, that the result is now in God's hands. There is nothing more to do. It is a Friday afternoon and we assume we will not be hearing from the jury until next week, or maybe the week after. The trial lasted almost six weeks. There was a tremendous amount of testimony, confusing documents, and dozens of exhibits to review.

We bustle out of the courthouse. It is a crisp day, sunny and cloudless but cold. We split up, some people heading home, others looking for food. I want to walk a bit; my legs sore from the wooden benches. After a few slow circles around the block I call my mother, who wants to know how the closing went.

We speak for about half an hour. She tells me all the prayers she's been reciting during the day and lets me know what to recite now that it is time for a decision. I listen obediently but am mentally checked out because of stress and hunger.

Finally I get off the phone and go inside a Subway, glad to be out of the cold. I am still eating when I get a call from Adnan's mother. The jury has reached a verdict and we have to return to the courthouse. I can't believe my ears; only a couple of hours have passed.

There is no way a jury could have reached a guilty verdict this quickly in a murder-one case with only circumstantial evidence. No responsible jury could do that, and no court could accept it. Even in cases with physical evidence tying a defendant to a crime, juries take days to deliberate, knowing their responsibility, knowing this decision is permanent.

I am almost giddy with excitement as I quickly take a last few bites and head back to the courthouse.

Many of the others have returned too, including my brother, Tanveer, Aunty Shamim, friends, aunties and uncles from the mosque. We take our seats.

Adnan comes back in, shackled but looking more refreshed. His blissful sleep had been interrupted when he was told the jury had a verdict. He is bewildered but also feels a rush of hope, as we all do.

We rise as Judge Heard comes in, and then the jury.

```
3            THE CLERK: Madam Foreperson, please stand.

4            Madam Foreperson, as to the case of State of

5     Maryland versus Adnan Syed, Cases No. 199103042, 43, 46, as

6     to Case No. 199103042, question 1 as to Count 1, charge of

7     first degree murder of Hey Men Lee, how do you find the

8     Defendant Adnan Syed, not guilty or guilty?
```

```
9              THE FOREPERSON:  Guilty.

10             THE CLERK:  Case No. 199103043, question 3 as to

11   Count 1, charge of kidnapping by fraudulently carrying

12   Hey Men Lee within the State, how do you find the Defendant

13   Adnan Syed, not guilty or guilty?

14             THE FOREPERSON:  Guilty.

15             THE CLERK:  As to Case No. 199103045, question

16   no. 4 as to Count 1, charge of robbery of Hey Men Lee, how

17   do you find the Defendant Adnan Syed, not guilty or guilty?

18             THE FOREPERSON:  Guilty.

19             THE CLERK:  Case No. 199103046, question no. 5,

20   as to the charge of false imprisonment by deception of

21   Hey Men Lee, how do you find the Defendant Adnan Syed, not

22   guilty or guilty?

23             THE FOREPERSON:  Guilty.
```

CHAPTER 7

LIFE PLUS THIRTY

Avoid legal punishments as far as possible,
and if there are any doubts in the case then use them,
for it is better for a judge to err towards leniency than towards
punishment.

Prophet Muhammad, Sunan al Tirmidhi

Adnan was convicted on Friday, February 25, 2000, of first-degree murder, kidnapping, robbery, and false imprisonment. After the jury had passed their verdict, we shuffled out of the courtroom and I ended up in the elevator with Aunty Shamim and Gutierrez. It was tense and silent. No one said a word until the doors opened. Before exiting Gutierrez said, "I'll need $50,000 for the appeal," and walked away, leaving us stunned.

On Monday, February 28, three days later, I visited Gutierrez's office with Tanveer and Adnan's mother. Until this time I had not just taken a back seat, I hadn't even really been involved in Adnan's defense. Busy with my studies, I had just been there for moral support, trusting that this very expensive, experienced lawyer had it all under control. But I could no longer stay on the periphery, I had to figure out how to fix what had just happened. So as loathe as I was to see Gutierrez, I went along. It would be the last time I ever saw or spoke to her.

I left Gutierrez's office disgusted with her, but not only because of the way she treated Adnan's family, or her incessant demands for more money, or her lack of humility at having lost this case. But also because by this time I'd had a

MEMORANDUM

TO: COMMITTEE FOR ADNAN SYED

FROM: Rabia Chaudry

DATE: March 1, 2000

RE: Meeting with Christina Gutierrez

On Monday, February 28, Mrs. Shamim Rahman, Tanvir Syed, and I held a meeting with Ms. Gutierrez to address concerns of the community and the family. Initially, Ms. Gutierrez was very hostile, to the point of being harsh and simply rude. On numerous occasions she threatened to leave the meeting and questioned my right to be involved. Many times she tried to answer the questions with a "yes" or "no" without giving explanations and when furthered pushed to explain her answer, she refused to do so. When I pointed out she had a duty to satisfy her clients, she said she had no duty to me. At one point I raised the issue that perhaps she had been speaking over the jury's head at an intelligence level they couldn't grasp, and she became extremely contemptuous. She attacked and mocked my understanding of the system, and basically blamed the family and the community for the verdict. It was her reasoning, as well as her partners, that had they been paid for a jury expert and for the jury to be bused to the scene of the crime, the result would have been difference. There are a number of responses to that issue: first, the firm had asked for $5000 for a jury expert, which was paid to them. However, instead of using the money for the expert, they put it towards their balance and then asked for more money. This may be an unethical practice that can be reported to the Bar Association. The second point is that the prosecution didn't use a jury expert, they used their common sense. What good are Ms. Gutierrez's years of experience if she still can't select a jury on her own? The third point is that I believe, as do most others, that it was Ms. Gutierrez's presentation of the case, and not so much the jury, that caused the result. Ms. Gutierrez is a good attorney, no doubt about that, she has a complete grasp of the law. In this instance she just didn't consider her audience, the jury, and spoke in language that they simply didn't understand.

Nevertheless, after much argumentation, Ms. Gutierrez did answer many of the questions, which I will outline below.

WHAT WE CAN DO AS A COMMUNITY:

- I asked whether we should hold a demonstration, and Ms. Gutierrez agreed but said we should do it closer to sentencing; We were hoping if we did it before the hearing for a new trial, it might affect the judge's decision. I don't know why Ms. Gutierrez wants to wait since she often refused to explain her answers and especially since she repeatedly said the sentence would be life no matter what we did. If that is the case, then why demonstrate before the sentencing? Just for media effect perhaps.

- We asked about doing independent investigation such as trying to speak with people involved in the case and put some pressure on them: for example, if we spoke with Jennifer or Stephanie, Jay's girlfriend, maybe they would buckle under pressure or guilt or maybe with an offer of award money they might tell the real story. After all, since we all ██████ Jay is ██████ murderer, the lives of Jen and Stephanie might be at risk if they know things about him and he is walking around a free man. Ms. Gutierrez was very adverse to this idea, although she said she couldn't stop us, she said she certainly wouldn't rely on any information our community gathered through investigating. But again, do we care if she relies? If we have enough evidence, we could take it to the Attorney General or a judge to reopen the case.

- Ms. Gutierrez didn't want us to contact the media because she is having discussions with her colleagues as to the best approach to the media and how to utilize them. I am not sure when she will make a decision as to the media, however she again said she can't stop us from doing anything. Adnan's mother informed me she had an acquaintance who was friends with two reporters for the Baltimore Sun. This could prove to be an important tool if we are able to convince them to cover the story in depth. I was also hoping to get copies of the transcript to send to shows like Dateline and 20/20, etc. but the transcript won't be available for at least a month, if not longer. Last night Dateline did cover the story of a man wrongfully convicted and awaiting appeal. I think they might be interested in this story for a number of reasons: the convicted is a Muslim, he was only 17 at the time of the arrest, and all the evidence points to someone that the D.A. has struck a deal with.

- The above points have to be discussed by the community or committee before deciding how to proceed on these matters. I suggest we get a legal advisor, since Ms. Gutierrez may not be 100% reliable at this point, to consult with as to whether Adnan's case will be helped or hurt by contacting the media, investigating on our own, or having a demonstration.

WHAT WILL HAPPEN NEXT:

- First a motion for new trial will be filed. This must be done within 10 days of the verdict. The same judge who sat in trial will hear this motion at a hearing, the date for which has to be set. The judge will not consider 'issues of fact', in other words what the jury believed to have happened or what the prosecutor or Ms. Gutierrez says took place. The judge will only be concerned with 'issues of law'. Such issues include all the rulings the judge made during trial, for example if Ms. Gutierrez objected to something and the judge overruled, the judge may reconsider that overruling and reverse. Another example is that Ms. Gutierrez wanted to admit Jay's attorney's testimony but the judge didn't allow it, saying that it didn't affect Adnan's case. This time she may think it was a mistake to exclude the testimony and reverse because it was a legal error. Ms. Gutierrez does not have much hope for this motion because basically we're asking for a judge to overrule her own previous rulings. Such motions are rarely granted.

- If the motion is granted, Inshallah, there will be a new trial. This trial will wipe the slate clean and a new jury will be selected, etc. If the motion is denied, Adnan will be sentenced on April 5. Before sentencing anyone is allowed to address the court. That means family and friends will be allowed to speak to the judge in open court and submit letters on behalf of Adnan that pertain to his character, his clean record, anything that might help reduce his sentence. Adnan himself can also speak. Ms. Gutierrez is adamantly against anyone addressing the court, for no ascertainable reason. We had a heated discussion about this and she concluded "it makes no difference what anyone says, he's going to get life". Well, I know that if it can't help, it certainly can't hurt. Besides, Maryland has no mandatory sentencing, meaning the judge has the discretion to sentence as she pleases within a range of allowable sentences. Since this is true, I think if the family asked the court for leniency, it just might work. Ms. Gutierrez refuses to be involved if anyone wants to address the court. I personally think that she is wrong, if for no other reason other than to satisfy the family. After all, they have voices too, which have yet to be heard. They have every right to address the person that will decide their son's fate.

- After sentencing, Adnan will be sent to another facility. He wants to go to Patuxent because that facility is known for giving inmates somewhat more freedom than others and there he will be able to get involved in many activities, even take Arabic classes.

- At appeal it is generally suggested a different attorney is used rather than the trial attorney. This was even suggested by Ms. Gutierrez herself. There are a number of advantages to this and many firms specialize in only criminal appeal.

- The appeal process will be very time consuming. It will begin with transcribing the videos into a transcript. Once the transcript is prepared, the attorney and staff have to go through it very thoroughly to locate every instance of objection and occasion where the judge made a legal decision or finding. For each of those instances, an argument must be crafted. This process might take around a year. After that, briefs will be submitted by both sides to the Court of Special Appeals in Annapolis, MD. This court is a panel of three judges who will consider the briefs and then probably ask for oral arguments by both parties. The judges will again only consider the same thing considered at the hearing for motion – matters of law, not of fact. If they find one single issue they think the judge decided incorrectly and that prejudiced the case against Adnan, they will reverse. There is no time limit to how long they must take to decide. They could take days, weeks, and even years. Once decided, they will issue an 'opinion' – the opinion does not have to be unanimous, it can be a majority.

- If the appellate court reverses, again we start at square one with a new trial. If they affirm the lower court decision, there is another level of appeal with the Court of Appeals of Maryland. Again, that court will consider the same factors.

- As regards sentencing, the usual sentence for first-degree murder is life in prison. This means different things. Counties differ in the length of time inmates actually spend in prison. For example in Allegany county the average length of time spent by inmates with this sentence is 21 years whereas in Baltimore City it is 50 years. A time for parole is also set and is determined by the parole board.

FINANCES:
- To begin with, Ms. Gutierrez gave a copy of the original contract and details of the billing and balance to us. From those papers, it seems so far $ 90,800 has been paid. There is a question of another $5000 which Mr. Bilal Ahmed was supposed to have paid but was not noted. This would bring the total to $95,800.
- Ms. Gutierrez asserts there is a balance of $57,292.83 remaining.
- Ms. Gutierrez further demands the balance be paid before she will pursue the appeal. She will go through with the hearing and sentencing, but not the appeal.
- In addition she expects the appeal will cost another $50,000 plus expenses.
- This will bring the total to over $200,000 not considering the cost of a new trial
- We should consult other attorneys because it has come to my attention that this firm is overcharging, especially when the original contract stipulates a fee of $50,000 plus $10,000 expenses.

This generally covers the important issues for consideration in the future. I will write another memo detailing concerns about the facts of the case within a day or so. If anyone has any ideas or concerns that I missed, feel free to contact me at (703) 578-3326 or email me at rabiaanwar@hotmail.com or rabia@lawyer.com .

Asalamalaikum

Rabia Chaudry

March 2000 memo written by Rabia to mosque committee.

conversation with Adnan that made me suspicious of what, if anything, she had done to prepare for his defense.

Adnan and I remember that time completely differently. My memory is that, having taken a couple of hours to gather myself after the verdict, I went to visit him where he was being held for the duration of the trial, at the Baltimore City Detention Center (BCDC). I remember a plastic or mesh divider, which meant you had to stand to see each other and talk.

Adnan remembers that he called me the weekend after the verdict.

Either way, we talked.

"The prosecutor's closing remarks," I said to him, "they were all about the twenty-one minutes after school that day. They said Hae was dead by 2:36 p.m. Where WERE you, Adnan, how could you guys not figure out where you were for that little bit of time?!"

Adnan began explaining, beginning a conversation we had never had before.

In the year of his incarceration, as he awaited trial, I had never probed him about the facts of the case. I knew that calls were recorded, and that he might be prohibited by his attorney, but I also didn't want to talk about serious things. He was a kid, a seventeen-year-old kid. When he called or we visited we kept things light, caught up on what was going on with family, on TV, joked around, teasing him about getting a break from school.

But now I had to figure out what had just gone wrong.

"So what happened? How was Gutierrez not able to find out where you were for just half an hour that day?"

By the time Adnan had been arrested, he explained, almost six weeks had passed since Hae disappeared. The police questioned him and he told them what he remembered: he was at school all day, though he had gone to give Jay his car and then come back after lunch. He stayed at school the entire time because he had track practice, and then Jay picked him up, and they went out so he could get some food and break his fast.

At 2:36 he was still at school, he had never left. He had until 3:30 to get to track practice, so he usually hung out with friends, went to the library to check e-mails, did some schoolwork, or would sometimes pop over to his house to change and come back. But that day he didn't because he didn't have a car.

"Do you remember specifically where you were right after school?" I asked.

Adnan explained that at first he wasn't sure, but then soon after he was arrested he received two letters from a classmate, a girl named Asia McClain.

Asia, he said, had a really clear memory of seeing him at the public library, where he often hung out along with other Woodlawn kids. She remembered talking to him as she waited for her boyfriend to pick her up. The letters jogged his memory; he had a clear recollection of running into her and even speaking to her boyfriend when he showed up.

"So why wasn't she at the trial?"

He had given the letters to Gutierrez and over the course of the past year, before the trial started, asked her and her law clerks a few times about Asia. At some point Gutierrez told him she had contacted Asia, and Asia didn't have her dates right—she had seen Adnan a different day, not on January 13th.

After that Adnan dropped it; he never wrote Asia back because of Gutierrez's instructions, and never asked anyone else to contact her.

It must have been my skepticism and distaste for Gutierrez, the way she treated the family, her erratic performance in court, that made me want to check Asia out myself.

"Do you have copies of her letters?"

Adnan said yes.

"Ok, send them to me as soon as possible."

A couple of weeks later I got the letters.

Either one of the letters or the envelope had Asia's grandparents' phone number—she apparently lived with them at the time she wrote the letters. I called and spoke with someone but was told Asia was away at college and would be around on the weekend.

What happened next is another example of the fallibility of human memory. I recall speaking with Asia and arranging to meet her, but she recalls me showing up at her house. Saad was definitely with me, but today Asia doesn't recall him being there.

Nonetheless, we met on March 25, 2000. I remember I simply asked her what she recalled of January 13, 1999. She recounted much of what she had said in the letters, her memory still sharp about that day for a number of reasons— her boyfriend got mad she was talking to Adnan, there was a big storm that night, and school was closed the next two days. She was sure that her boyfriend and his friend would probably remember the incident.

I asked her why, if she remembered it so vividly, did Gutierrez say she had her day wrong. She blinked at me. She didn't know who Gutierrez was.

Adnan's attorney, the lawyer who contacted you, I pressed.

Asia shook her head.

"No one contacted me."

I thought I heard her wrong and asked her to repeat that.

"No one, not a lawyer, not his family, not Adnan, not the police, NO ONE contacted me after I sent those letters."

I have felt a lot of anger over this case, but certain moments of absolute rage stand out. This was one of them. Gutierrez had not only utterly failed to do what a first-year law student would have done immediately—contact an alibi witness— she had also lied to Adnan about it.

I felt panic. I had no idea how to handle the situation or what could be done now. I was just wrapping up my second year in law school in Virginia and didn't know how the criminal process actually worked, much less worked in Maryland. But I figured I should at least, *at least*, get it in writing that no one had ever contacted Asia. To me, a failure this big should be remedied by a court of law; there had to be some mechanism.

I pulled out a yellow legal pad, wrote the word "Affidavit" across the top, and handed it to Asia to write down what she had just told me. I asked her if her boyfriend and his friend would be willing to talk to me and give me affidavits too, but she hesitated. She asked me not to contact them just yet, but assured me, if her affidavit got the case reopened and Adnan's lawyer summoned them to court, they would definitely come. I didn't want to push the issue so I said ok, let's just get this affidavit down for now.

It was a Saturday, banks were closed, and we didn't have smart phones to track down the closest notary back in those days. Saad remembered a check-cashing place across from Security Mall, right next to the Best Buy, and he was pretty sure they had a notary.

We drove to this little square building covered in bright signage. It cost a few bucks, we paid, Asia notarized the affidavit, and then we dropped her off back at her house.

I immediately went to Adnan's parents' house with the affidavit and discussed it with them. We had no idea what to do. Aunty called Gutierrez's office and left a message, but it was a weekend so there was no response. She had gone to visit Adnan a few weeks prior to discuss appeal options, but since then no one had heard from her.

It just so happened that Adnan called his parents while I was with them and I told him what I had just learned—that Asia had never been contacted. He sounded perplexed at first, and then incredulous when the monumental nature of what I was saying sunk in.

"She's filing a motion for a new trial, Rabia," he said. "We have to get her to include this."

We tried in vain to reach Gutierrez, but she wouldn't return our calls. So I told Adnan to write her a letter and I drafted one on behalf of his parents to send along with the affidavit.

We waited after the letters were sent but still heard nothing. Frantic that the clock was ticking and she was clearly done with Adnan, we knew we had to do something. I felt strongly that she needed to be fired, but Adnan's parents weren't so sure. They feared her and thought if they fired her she would sue them—she had continued to harass them for money, threatening to take their house away.

After a long discussion with the family and some of the community members, it was decided that Gutierrez had to go. I drafted a letter for the family to Gutierrez, firing her, and then we sent one to Judge Wanda Heard.

Nothing came of our frantic flailings to get Asia included in the motion as a supplement. The sentencing was postponed, however, and Judge Heard accepted Adnan's request to dismiss Gutierrez. Adnan now had to get a public defender to represent him at the sentencing.

The sentencing was scheduled for June 6, 2000, at which time the judge would also rule on the motion for a new trial filed by Gutierrez.

We already knew what was coming but it was hard to internalize. A part of everyone hoped against hope that the judge would show some leniency, take into account Adnan's age and clean record.

Dear Christina,

I'm writing you to voice my concern about the motion for new trial that you have filed on my behalf. I don't believe it presents anything that would convince Judge Heard to grant a new trial. I understand that areas previously covered and ruled upon by the Judge are included in this motion; however I don't think they are compelling. I believe that this motion should instead request an overruling of the verdict due to new evidence; information that bears a direct relevance to my case.

I have previously told you of the recollections of Asia McClain & 2 of her friends on 1-13-99, the day the state alleges I committed this crime. These 3 individuals remember being with me in the Public Library after school, between 2:20 and 2:45 p.m., the same block of time the state alleged that I killed Hae. These 3 people discredit the states theory, however they were never presented to the court.

I believe this new information would have affected the outcome of my trial. I'm asking that you change this motion to include this new evidence. I know you've refused my request before, but I'm asking you to please reconsider. Theres only a few days left until Apr. 5th, when this motion will be argued. This is my last chance before I get sentenced, and I'm asking that we please not waste it with a motion that we know will not accomplish anything.

Sincerely,
Adnan M. Syed

Adnan had prepared remarks expressing grief for Hae's family but maintaining his innocence. The public defender, Charles Dorsey, who had met with him only briefly, advised him not to do so.

"Show remorse for what you did," he said.

Adnan said he couldn't; he didn't do anything.

"Fine then," Dorsey said, "you're fucking yourself."

Hae's mother began by giving an impassioned plea to the court through an interpreter:

Mr. and Mrs. Syed Rahman
7034 Johnnycake Road
Baltimore, Maryland 21207

Christina Gutierrez
Redmond & Gutierrez, P.A.
1301 Fidelity Building
210 North Charles Street
Baltimore, Maryland 21201

March 30, 2000

Dear Ms. Gutierrez,

We would like for you to include in the motion for new trial the newly discovered evidence provided by Ms. Asia McClain. We are aware that under Maryland laws, the evidence is considered newly discovered only when it is indeed newly discovered. We feel, however, that Asia's information falls into a gray area because in fact no body contacted her for her story, and that until now her story was undiscovered. Attached please find a copy of an affidavit signed and sworn to by Ms. Asia McClain. According to her, the other two eyewitness alibis are also willing to submit affidavits.

Furthermore, for sentencing we would like to have mitigating witnesses address the court. Please contact us to arrange for this.

Thank you,

Mr. and Mrs. Syed Rahman

"I'm the mother of Hae Min Lee. In Korean proverb there is a saying that parents die, they bury in the ground, but when children die, they bury in their hearts. . . . [O]ur daughter, my daughter, our daughter was so precious to us and everybody surrounding us . . . [H]er hope and aspiration was my hope and aspiration, and her dream was my dream, and she always wanted to be a good person in her life as her society . . . I would like to forgive Adnan Syed, but as of now, I just don't know how to do that, and I just cannot do that right now. When I die, my daughter will die with me. As long as I live, my daughter is buried in my heart . . ."

Urick followed the statement, focusing on the potential Adnan had in his life. That he came from a good family, had religious instruction, medical training, but used his "skills that he had as a paramedic and used them to kill." He said

RE: State of MD v. Adnan Syed, Case No. 199103042-46

VIA : HAND DELIVERY

Honorable Wanda Keyes Heard, Judge
Circuit Court for Baltimore City

Dear Judge Heard,

We are writing on behalf of our son, Adnan Syed, who is incarcerated at the Baltimore City Detention Center. He is unable to send the court a letter quickly due to his circumstances; however, he has mailed the court a letter which will take a day or two to receive. Adnan is scheduled to appear before the court on Wednesday, April 5th for a hearing on Motion for New Trial and to be sentenced. We are respectfully requesting that the hearing and sentencing be postponed due to the fact that Adnan's attorney, Ms. Christina Gutierrez, has been discharged from the case.

For the past two weeks Adnan has been trying to get in touch with Ms. Gutierrez. She has not spoken to him on the phone, nor come to see him. He waited patiently day after day hoping she would come to help prepare for sentencing. Contrary to what Adnan and his family and friends want, Ms. Gutierrez refuses to schedule mitigating witnesses for sentencing. In addition, Adnan has repeatedly asked for the Motion for New Trial to be amended, but Ms. Gutierrez will not consider it or even explain why she won't. These issues, along with many others that came up during Ms. Gutierrez's representation of Adnan, are the reason Ms. Gutierrez has been dismissed.

Because Adnan has been incarcerated for a year, he has been completely dependent on Ms. Gutierrez. Adnan has been trying to get in touch with her, calling every day for her, in order to tell her that she is being discharged so that he can apply for a public defender. At the same time, the public defender's office has informed us that Adnan cannot apply for a public defender until Ms. Gutierrez puts it in writing that she relinquishes all ties with Adnan. Adnan's hands have been tied because Ms. Gutierrez will not contact him, nor can he apply for a public defender until Ms. Gutierrez gives him written documentation that she is no longer representing him. At this point, it is critical a postponement be granted to ensure Adnan receive competent representation.

The attorney-client relationship has been irreparably destroyed due to Ms. Gutierrez's actions. Adnan is not prepared at all for sentencing and he strenuously objects to her continued representation. He is hoping a public defender will help him prepare and also help schedule mitigating witnesses. We implore you to take into consideration these circumstances and grant us a postponement.

Respectfully,

Mr. & Mrs. Syed Masudur Rahman

cc: Christina Gutierrez
Assistant State's Attorney Kevin Urick
Office of the Public Defender for Baltimore City

that during Ramadan, a holy time, instead of following religious practices, Adnan planned to kill Hae. He argued that there were no mitigating factors, that Adnan committed a "deliberate adult act that was reprehensible." He recommended the maximum sentence.

Dorsey then began, and much to Adnan's horror, threw him and his innocence under the bus.

"Your Honor, my client was 16 at this, when this happened, in a relationship and in love . . . my client comes from a quality family of quality religion. He made a bad decision, and I ask this Honorable Court to have mercy on him, consider possibly a sentence within the guidelines that would give this young man an opportunity to somehow make up for his mistake in his life."

Dorsey then turned to Adnan and asked if he had anything to say to the judge.

Adnan, showing remarkable composure for an eighteen-year-old facing the rest of his life in prison and having just been screwed over by two attorneys, said, "Since the beginning I have maintained my innocence, and I don't know why people have said the things they have said that I have done or that they have done. I understand that I've been through a trial, and I've been found guilty by a jury, and I accept that. Not because I agree with what they did. I respectfully disagree with their judgment; however, I accept it and there's nothing at this point that I can do except to be sentenced and to go on with the next step, which is to file my appeal.

"I have maintained my innocence since the beginning and to my family and to those who have believed in me since the beginning, I would just like them to know that it is for a reason. I can only ask for the mercy of the court in sentencing me, and I can only remain strong in my faith and hope that one day I shall have another chance in court.

"I'm just sorry for all the pain that this has caused everyone."

Despite Adnan's claims of innocence, and our prayers, Judge Wanda Heard showed no leniency, no mercy, no compassion. Her cruel words, as she sentenced Adnan, were like a knife to the hearts of all who loved him, all of us there.

"This wasn't a crime of passion. The evidence, as I recall it to be and the jury found by its first degree conviction, meant premeditated with malice afore-thought, as we say in the law. That means you thought about it. The evidence was, there was a plan, and you used that intellect. You used that physical strength. You used that charismatic ability of yours that made you the president or the—what was it, the king or prince of your prom? You used that to manipulate people. And even today, I think you continue to manipulate even those that love you, as you did to the victim. You manipulated her to go with you to her death."

We were reeling from the sentence. It was not just life and not just life with thirty years concurrent. It was life plus thirty years to run consecutively. My parents later asked me, what does life mean? Twenty years? Twenty-five years? In Pakistan that was what life meant.

I explained to them that in the State of Maryland, life meant until you died.

After Adnan was convicted and sentenced, the ISB community quietly faded away. His family stopped talking about him with others. They didn't know how to explain the case or conviction, and were going through so much internally that they didn't have the additional strength to deal with the community. People in the community didn't know what to say either; how do you console the parents or siblings of a convicted killer? They whispered among themselves but otherwise stopped mentioning him at all.

The only exception was my mother, who unabashedly took up for Adnan, fought with anyone who had anything negative to say about him, never stopped talking about him with Aunty Shamim, and prayed for him with the intensity of a thousand burning suns.

I watched, over the years, my mother stay up many nights saying special prayers for him, fingering her prayer beads 120,000 times, reciting the prayer of the Prophet Jonah when he was trapped in the belly of the whale.

She collected the pits of dates, sacks and sacks of them, and commandeered groups of women to gather and say a prayer on each pit, counting tens of thousands in a number of hours.

She vowed to read the *Quran*, in its entirety, dozens of times, to send blessings Adnan's way, and she did. She copied and clipped prayers out of booklets and pamphlets to send to Adnan, ordering him to follow the prayer instructions exactly to make sure they worked.

And most importantly, about a year after his conviction, she went all the way to Mecca and prayed there for him during a pilgrimage. She told us she prayed more for him than she did for any of her children, more than anyone she has prayed for in her life.

While there, she had a dream.

Dreams, you see, are not just overworked imaginings of a tired, dozing mind in Islam. They are doors to the spiritual realm, found in scriptural parables, remnants of prophesy. If you are spiritually pure, of good and kind character, and sincere, your dreams have meaning.

My mother dreamt that she saw Adnan emerge from an underground chamber after having been held captive there for a long time. He was shining, she said, he looked "brand new" even though he had aged. He blinked, looking around, smiling slightly. My mother had a good feeling about the dream; she said it meant he would be exonerated and freed from incarceration. She also said he looked like he was in his mid-to-late thirties.

At the time she told us this, Adnan was around nineteen years old. Instead

Dear Rabia 6-14-00

It's plwl - How are you doing? How is Saira & Amir doing? I hope everyone is well. Tell Saira I said Happy (very) Belated Birthday. I had asked Tanveer on May 20th to send me a B-day card for her, but it's now June 14th and I still haven't got it. Did you guys have a big birthday party for her? I always look at the picture of her and Yusuf, and it always makes me smile. I always pray that Inshallah maybe I'll be home for their weddings. (If Yusuf ever gets married ☺)

I've been here for about a week now, it's okay, I guess. It's airconditioned, so it's never hot. In fact, sometimes @ night it gets pretty chilly. I'm on the 6th floor, and one whole wall is a window, so I can see the skyline of Balto. City. It's actually a pretty nice view, + I can easily tell the times of Salaat by looking at the sky. It's weird, cause they got me bunking w/ a dude who only has 2 years on his sentence. He's a pretty cool guy though, he used to live in Randallstown and go to Woodlawn, so we can talk @ some of the same places/people. He's 22, so its not like he's some old, crazy guy. (I've seen a lot of them) I think they made a procedural error putting me in here, though. Normally they don't put people w/ a lot of time w/ someone who has a little bit of time, cause anything can happen. A lot of people have that attitude "What have I got to lose?" Not me, though. I've always felt that my situation doesn't determine who I am, I do. A lot of people don't think like that, though.

I'm glad the sentencing is over though. Man, it seemed like everything that could go wrong did. That night, (5th June) I still hadn't heard anything from Dorsey, so I had decided what I was going to say. I was gonna be simple, that I didn't kill Hae, this court has made a mistake, and I'm gonna continue to fight this, cause I know I'm innocent. Anyway, in the morning at the courthouse, Dorsey comes to see me. He asks to

Letter from Adnan written after sentencing

of feeling uplifted, I got angry. Muslims believe that dreams come true once they're told to others. We don't relay bad dreams, she shouldn't have told us about it.

"No," my mother said, "it was a good dream. You just don't know."

I guess I didn't.

hear what I've prepared, and I tell him. He says that I shouldn't say any of it, that it would just make the judge angrier. He tells me that I should just talk @ myself. I tell him that the judge already knows @ me, but and that I want to say what I've prepared. His exact words were "Well, you're just gonna f--- yourself over with the judge." I'm already nervous as heck, imagine what it's like for me to hear that.

Later we go into the courtroom, and another surprise: Hae's mom wants to speak. I hear what she's saying, and I can feel her pain, but at the same time I'm thinkin' my mom's going thru almost the exact same thing. Where's her chance to speak out? Where's her justice? Then she says that she wishes that my punishment would be the same as Hae's, and it didn't hit me at first, but then I realized she just asked for me to die. All the while, everyone's starting to look at me like I'm not even human, and I'm thinkin' can this get any worse?

Alhamdulillah, this genius Dorsey gets up and says some things. I don't remember exactly, but than I hear him say "He made a mistake...it was a crime of passion." I was completely stunned, and I turned to him and felt like hitting him w/a chair or something. With those few words he took the only thing I had left, my innocence. Suddenly, he's done and the judge asks me if I have anything to say. All I can think is, "Oh my God, can I possibly say anything that won't make it worse." After Hae's mom, my lawyer, and the way everyone was looking at me, I didn't know what to do/say. On one hand, I was remembering what I had planned to say. On the other hand, I was thinkin' about Dorsey's warning/advice, and on the 3rd hand I'm thinkin maybe I should just apologize for everything even though I had nothing to do with it. So I did me, I said a little bit of everything. I'm not sure exactly what I said, but I know I maintained innocence, asked for the courts mercy, and apologized for all the pain that's been caused.
(the last 2 things I had told myself I'd never do)

After being sentenced, Adnan was moved from the Baltimore City Detention Center to the Maryland House of Corrections in Jessup, Maryland, a prison notorious for its violence. The blessing here, though, was that he could have been moved hours away, making it hard for his loved ones to visit. Jessup was only about twenty minutes from his parents' home, with fairly generous visitation hours and enough corruption to give the inmates more freedoms than regulations otherwise allowed.

There was a tremendous amount for Adnan to process: being in a new prison, with new inmates, knowing this would likely be his entire life, and

Afterwards, the judge promptly rips into me, which was yet another shock. I was totally unprepared for things she said, and to tell you the truth, my anger kept me from breaking down in tears. What kept me going was thinkin' "Who the heck do these people think they are?" To conceal the truth behind their badges and law degrees I know, that those people knew that, either I didn't kill her or that there was definitely not enough evidence to convict & sentence me. But they still went ahead and did it for the sake of public opinion & personal reasons. That's alright though cause I read an ayat in the Quran that talks @ how Allah puts all of us through hardships, but we Muslims are the only ones who can call upon him. They don't have that. And mashallah there is a grievous chastisement for all the pain they are causing.

I was glad when it was over, cause it was horrible. There was something nice, though. Mr. Gilmore, the officer who sat thru my trial and was there @ sentencing, he also was pretty upset @ what the judge said. When we left, he asked me if I was surprised @ the sentence, and I said no, cause I thought it would've been worse. What said to me was "Don't worry, she just doesn't know." This lifted my spirits, and I thought after a while that it was from Allah. A lot of people have had words of encouragement for me, and it's all a testimony to the comfort Allah provides us when we go thru hardships. Truly the signs are there, we just have to open our eyes.

Well, nothing much going on 'round here. I haven't met any "real" Muslims, jest a lot of people who know @ Islam and have a lot of likewise. Nobody's prayed w/me, though. That's the true acid test of a Muslim, whether or not they keep their Salaat. It's different to miss it and make it up or to

struggling to figure out what the hell had happened. He still tried to keep things light for us on the outside, and his letters were mixed, full of jokes with moments of sadness and infrequent glimmers of his emotional turmoil.

Shortly after writing this letter he wrote me again, saying he had decided to reach out to Stephanie. He would send her a short note to see if she responded. If she didn't, he would send a longer letter, a plea to her based on their years-long friendship, to tell him anything, anything that could help him. He would keep trying.

She never responded.

Adnan's family was preparing, financially and otherwise, to hire an attorney (just not make it at all. Inshallah this Friday I'm attending my 1st Jumah service, I'll meet some ~~more~~ brothers there.

In this facility you can't get visits (unless you've been here for) and the phone calls are once (1) a day, and they only last 5 min! (60 days) Inshallah I shouldn't be here for long, though. It's different for everybody. Some 1-3 weeks some 1-2 months. It only takes a week to classify you (bloodwork, physical exam etc.), but you have to wait for bedspace to open up. I'm not sure ~~to~~ exactly how long it'll take though. Inshallah, it should be better wherever I go to.

I've been reading this book by Ahmed Deedat. called "What is His Name". It talks about different peoples around the world, and how no matter what they call God, usually the belief in his Oneness is the same. Even in religions where they have minor Gods, there's ultimately one who is in charge. It's a pretty interesting book. Ahmed Deedat is hilarious in some of his arguments, but he always gets the pt. across.

Other than that, I've just been prayin' a lot. For my family for your family, for all Muslims everywhere who are struggling, I pray a lot for guidance, cause I just don't know what the future has in store. ~~cause~~ I hope everyone is doing well, give them my salaams, and I'll write to you again soon. Take care.

Love, Adnan

—I wrote on the next page some legal things. I've asked my brother to check up on some things, but he's really not that reliable where I'm concerned. ~~So~~ I asked Saad to help, do you think you could too? It's really not too much, and I'd be very grateful.

to file a direct appeal to his conviction. That would take time, years even. In the meantime he had to just get by in a place where he encountered people and situations he never could have imagined.

Adnan's family suffered greatly, each of them falling to pieces in their own way.

Yusuf was in elementary school, nine years old, when Adnan was arrested. When he was convicted he was ten. He had seen the police take his brother away in cuffs, he saw the story all over the news, he heard it in the hallways at school. But his parents did their best to shelter him, not taking him to the trial, not discussing it in front of him.

6-14-00

*I have 3 options
① file for Application afor Review of Sentence
 - a panel of 3 judges will review my sentence, and they
 can reduce, increase, or leave it the same
 must be done w/in 30 days of sentence
② motion for Modification/Reduction of Sentence
 - it'll be considered by the judge who sentenced me
 who can reduce it or leave it the same. this must be done
 w/in 90 days sentence special
③ appeal to Court of ~~special~~ Appeals
 w/in 30 days of sentence

* ~~~~ the Post Sentence Assistance Unit @ the
office of Public Defender can assist me in filling out forms for these
things, but I would need to know what those say has done. I can't get
in touch w/him, do you think you can. ~~~~~~~~~~~~ if
necessary, (he can't get in touch on the phone) maybe he could go down
to the office of P.D. (on Calvert St.) and see him personally, & just
ask him what he's done so far, and for copies of any papers
he's filed or filled out on my behalf? I know I have to do
at least one of these ↑(3) things, but I need to know what he's
done 1st. What you & I said, I don't know who else to ask
for help. ~~~~~~~ I just need to find out soon, cause it's
already been 8 days ~~~~~~. If you could tell my
mom, then when I talk to her I ask/find out. I know you guys are
real busy, and I'm very grateful for all everything you're both done for
me.

love, A

But the day Adnan was convicted, his mother and Tanveer came home and told him. The three of them went to tell their father, who was in his bedroom, in bed, together.

Adnan's father has largely been missing from the story, but not because he was missing from their lives. Uncle, more than two decades older than his wife, simply couldn't bear to see what was happening to his son.

Adnan is his father's spitting image, just a foot and half taller and twice as broad. When Adnan was born, his father, who told the story to my mother, had wanted to name him "Qurat-ul-Ain," a beautiful Arabic name that means "coolness of the eyes"; it is a blessing found commonly among Muslims upon the birth of a child; we say "may this baby be the coolness of your eyes," meaning may the child bring you joy and contentment. He had a dream, though, in which

Dear Rabia,   ~Assalamoalaikum!   10-16-00

    This is a funny joke I just thought of today:

Knock-Knock.

Who's there?

Aminah.

Aminah who?

Aminah I really messed up situation!

          (hehehehehehe☺)

    This is just one of several jokes I've thought of that pertain to Indo-Paks. Inshallah you can look forward to seeing more in the future!!

    I know you probably spend hours reading off of paper like this (legalpads), sorry to make you spend some more, but you wouldn't believe how far away my regular 8½ × 11" pad is from this chair I'm sitting in. Please excuse my laziness. I was actually writing down some thought I had @ my case. You know what? For some reason Stephanie McPherson keeps coming to my mind. I seriously believe that she either knows something, or can shed some light onto something also. I already trust her a lot of ?'s, but you know of the situation between us. I've actually been planning something w/my friend Krista @ how to initiate contact w/her, but Krista doesn't really like her. They kept in contact over the summer (in the beginning) but they haven't talked to each other since. She said she's going try to "reopen" the lines of communication, and who knows what'll happen?

    There's a couple of things I need to talk to Krista @, so she can ask Stephanie in a roundabout way. I don't feel comfortable telling her over the phone or in a letter, so I put her on my visiting list. Actually, there is a couple of girls (whom I attended school w/) as well as Stephanie who wanted to come visit, but I just made up some excuse or another. I could just imagine my man coming to see me one day, and she's told I'm already having a visit and you can imagine the rest.

بسم الله الرحمن الرحيم   9.25.01

السلام عليكم ورحمة الله؟

Dear Saad,

What's up dawg? Is every thing cool w/ u? Things are kinda crazy over here. Somebody got stabbed pretty badly on Sun, and he ended up dying. The last time somebody was killed (last Jan.), the warden said that if anybody else got killed, he would lock the jail down indefinitely. Last time it was 3 weeks, I don't know how long it'll be this time....

When we get locked down, we just stay in our cells. We don't come out except to take showers. We don't go outside for anything, not working out or to eat. I don't think we get to make phone calls either, but I don't know @ visits.....

It's cool, though, cause lately I haven't been studying enough lately. I've been busying myself w/ other stuff, but now I've got more free time. That's kinda the feeling w/ majority of us Muslims, that when we get locked down, it's Allah's way of showing us we need to spend more time studying Quran and Hadith, etc. I funny, cause after we open back up, all of us are a lot more on point (Islamic) for a couple weeks! But then it goes back 2 normal.....

I'll probably start writing to people. Not just Muslims, but some non-Muslims. It's really weird, I've been kinda feelin' too sorry for my self and bein' reactive instead of proactive.

he was told to name the baby "Adnan" after an ancestor of the Prophet Muhammad. Adnan means "one who abides or settles in an area," who has characteristics of stability and fortitude.

If their firstborn Tanveer was his mother's favorite, Adnan was the apple of his father's eye. He took great pride in his second-born son, in the fact that they had similar upbeat natures, that Adnan was talented, kind-natured, and hard working. Yusuf, a chubby boy with a curly head of hair, was pretty enough to be a girl when he was born and was everyone's darling.

Adnan's arrest emotionally debilitated his father, who was already approaching retirement age at sixty-three. He went to visit his son but could not bear to see him in a court of law, to see him being brought in and out of the room in shackles. Over time he became increasingly frail, and today, at eighty years old with a white wizened beard, he looks like a slight, small Father Time.

On the day the verdict was rendered, Uncle didn't leave his bed. When his wife and sons came to him, he sat up, looking at them expectantly. They broke the news to him and he didn't say a word. His eyes, Yusuf remembers, went wide.

"Something in him died right then," Yusuf says.

Something died in all of them. There were no second chances after the conviction, they knew what was going to happen at the sentencing.

Tanveer, who was so close to his mom he often took her out for dinner and took her to events, began withdrawing from the family. He spent less and less time at home until one day he just disappeared. For years they weren't sure where he was, though once in a while he would call the house to tell them he was ok, but he never told them where he was.

If the loss of Adnan was heartbreaking, the loss of their eldest, who should have been shouldering the tremendous collective family burden, was perhaps harder. They knew where Adnan was; Tanveer, they felt, had abandoned them.

Adnan's mother, father, and brothers all grieved in different ways. While Uncle turned slowly into a hermit, and Tanveer simply vanished, Aunty did her best to keep up a chipper exterior. She continued to run her home-based daycare center, and would sometimes show up at parties or prayer gatherings or the mosque. I had watched her sit through a verdict and sentencing no mother could reasonably bear, stoically. She would smile at Adnan, reassuring him that she was ok, and he would do the same.

But at home, at night in particular, she would come undone. Yusuf recalls too many nights to count when he found his mother weeping alone in the dark. Some nights, he said, "she totally checked out."

She would tell him to leave the lights on so Adnan and Tanveer wouldn't have to return in the dark. Or she would tell him that when Adnan and Tanveer got home, to tell them to turn the lights off before going to bed.

If her older sons were physically gone, her youngest son was emotionally lost to her. A mere child when his brother was sentenced for murder, he was regularly approached by a fifth-grade girl named Latoya whose older sister attended Woodlawn High. She would taunt him mercilessly, saying the entire high school thought Adnan was a killer. He wasn't safe at the mosque either, where he'd be approached by kids asking nonchalantly, "Hey did your brother do it?" or teasing him, "We all know he's guilty." Once Yusuf warned a kid that he had five seconds to run before he would get pummeled.

A number of kids got pummeled by Yusuf, who ended up moving from school, to school, to school.

He left his elementary school during fifth grade because, along with becoming sullen and depressed, uninterested in school work, he had become belligerent and quick to anger. Toward the end of sixth grade this anger got him kicked out of the next school he attended, Al Huda, a private Islamic institution about twenty-five miles away.

He remembers how much he missed Tanveer in those days. Thinking back on it, he is full of both sadness and rage at his big brother. There were days, he said, he would call Tanveer twenty times with no response. On other occasions Tanveer would promise to come pick him up and take him to the movies and he would wait two, three, four hours for him, right by the phone, and Tanveer wouldn't show.

Tanveer dropped out of college with a year remaining; his parents had no idea where he was working or what he was doing. Yusuf says they thought maybe he had become a junkie. Once, after Uncle tried repeatedly to go see him, Tanveer capitulated and gave him his address so his father could see where he was living.

It was snowing that day, and Uncle spent much of his time wandering around in the cold, asking people to help him find the address. The address didn't exist, Tanveer had made it up.

A few years after he was imprisoned, Adnan, frustrated with Tanveer's lack of responsibility, had a talk with him. He urged him to finish college, to get his degree, to take care of his parents and little brother. He told him that it was his job to be there for him. According to Yusuf, that was the last time Tanveer ever visited him.

The anger Yusuf has toward Tanveer is palpable and relentless.

"It's not just about me, it's about my parents. They needed him. Our mom needed him."

What about Adnan, I asked him.

"Adnan," he said, "was the one who kept it together the most. He was selfless, he never let us feel like he was sad or upset. We'd go visit Adnan at the prison and leave laughing. Who leaves a prison laughing? That's because he worked so hard to keep our spirits up."

Yusuf attended two more schools, first a rough local one close to Woodlawn called Southwest Academy where many of the students came from broken families. Yusuf said he could relate to them, as lots of them had screwed-up home lives and he didn't feel out of place there like he did at the Islamic school.

Next, he went to a private Christian high school but was asked to leave after a year. He was fifteen and his family was running out of options.

They then decided to send him to a madrassah in Karachi, Pakistan, where he would study and memorize the *Quran* for the next three years.

The madrassah was a boys-only institution, with many students from around the world. Someone had recommended the school to his parents, and a friend of Yusuf's was already studying there. It would be hard for him to leave his mother. In their loneliness they only had each other, but he knew it was the right thing to do.

The curriculum was all in Urdu and Arabic, languages Yusuf didn't know. The school had a dark, seedy side with drug and alcohol abuse, and even sexual abuse of younger kids by older students. He managed to steer clear of all of that and in his more than three years there, he also met a lot of wonderful young men who became like brothers to him. At the end of his time there he had memorized the *Quran*, but upon returning to the United States he wanted nothing to do with religion anymore.

Yusuf had suffered from depression since his early teens, but he went into a black depressive spiral after coming back home. All of his former friends had forgotten him, and he missed the friends he had back in Pakistan. The only exception was a young man named Hasan, who would check in on him every so often, pick him up to go grab something to eat, go see a movie. No one else called him, ever.

He was eighteen and had no idea what to do. Once, out of sheer angst, he slammed his head into a dresser mirror, splitting open his head and passing out. Other times he went online to search for ways to commit suicide but out of fear of going to Hell forever, desisted.

"It was the only thing that stopped me from doing it," he said.

Eventually he took his GED, passing after the second time, and joined a community college. From there he went on to Towson University where he began feeling suicidal again. A close friend of the family, Dr. Atique Rahman, reached out to him, and they then spent many hours together. He was prescribed antidepressants, which, he says, turned him back into a human being.

All this time, as every man in the family was breaking into bits, in the center of the storm was Aunty Shamim.

There were times when, unable to keep the pain from spilling into ugliness, Uncle would tell her it was her fault that Adnan was gone, her fault that all her sons were gone. And most of those times she believed him, even when he later said he didn't mean it.

Aunty, says Yusuf, suffered the most. "She had to deal with my crazy ass, her husband was depressed, one son left her, her other son was in prison and she had to be there for him, for all of us. She was there for everyone. Like there were five of her. But no one was really there for her. The biggest regret I have is that I wasn't there for her."

Adnan's family wasn't the only one going through turmoil. My marriage was bad, deeply damaging to me emotionally, for many reasons.

I also didn't have a job in 1999, which made things difficult. My husband gave me a tight allowance for groceries but that was it. I was on my own for other expenses, including the expense of calls from the prison.

The cost of collect calls for inmates, which many prisons utilize, are a disgrace and a crime in and of themselves. The charges associated with them were not routine calling charges, they were exorbitant. At the end of the month, having spoken to Adnan six or seven times, I would end up with hundreds of dollars of additional billing. This added up for me and for my parents, and there were months when my ex told me that I had to tell Adnan to stop calling. But I could not.

I kept drawing money from my student loans to help cover costs, to send him things, to every so often put small amounts into his commissary. About a year after his arrest, I had begun an internship at a local immigration law firm. I had been offered an internship at the public defender's office in D.C., but declined. The hours were too difficult to manage with a young child and family obligations. I have always regretted that decision because I wonder how much better positioned I would have been to help Adnan if I had taken it.

It was a strained existence. The core of my world was my daughter, and I tried to distract myself by staying busy, but as time went on my misery increased. I was desperately lonely and sad, felt unvalued and indeed loathed. After five years, the marriage unraveled dramatically one night, when circumstances forced me to leave with nothing but a suitcase and my ancient computer. I was devastated, but I was finally free; the only problem was I had to leave without my daughter.

I was broken, broke, bewildered. My marriage had ended both spectacularly and at the same time with barely a bang. One day I was married and the next I was on my own.

I moved in with my parents as I prepared to fight for custody of my daughter. Her father was ten steps ahead of me. The week before I left his house he had gone to Child Protective Services (CPS) and filed a complaint against me, alleging that I gave my daughter drugs.

I found this out when I went to file a custody petition for her and the judge told me, to my astonishment, that CPS would have to conduct a full investigation taking a number of months to investigate the allegations. I stammered to the judge that I had never touched drugs in my life. It didn't matter; once a complaint was filed it had to be investigated for the welfare of the child.

In hindsight, as painful as it was to be separated from my only child, in those few months I gained back some confidence. I began going to the gym, found some contract work, began studying for the bar again, and began focusing on the appeal that Adnan was about to file.

As concerned as he was about his appeal, Adnan was even more concerned about me. I remember the first time I told him that I was now separated, that I had moved in with my parents, and that I didn't have my daughter. He was silent for a while and then full of grief at the news.

He told me he couldn't imagine what I was going through and I recalled thinking, as I held the phone, that this boy is serving a life sentence in prison and he is telling ME that he can't imagine my pain? I was floored by his compassion. Floored. I took courage from him. If he felt his situation was manageable, who was I to complain?

I got myself together and managed to outmaneuver my ex in the custody proceedings. I had been cleared, after extensive interviews with friends, family, and colleagues, of the CPS charges and our permanent custody hearing was approaching. I wanted the judge to see the family that my daughter would be living with if I didn't get custody. The people whose immigration status was questionable, the chain smoker, the compulsive gambler. So I marched into the family court and subpoenaed every last one of them a few days before the hearing.

1.15.02

السلام عليكم

Dear Rabia,

What's going on, man? Not much over here. I just came back from
the law library, and the case i had ordered has not come in. They have this
central facility where they keep all the law journal/periodicals and you
have to fill out a form to get a copy of a case. It's cool, cause they send
you the entire reported opinion, and that can run to like, 30 pages. It's free,
but sometimes it takes long as hell for it to come. I'm not in any particular
rush, so it's cool....

So what's going on with your legal situation? It's so many people
I now know who have pending cases, that it's not uncommon to ask someone when
greeting them "what's going on in court?" i never imagined i'd be asking you...
Alhamdhulillah, i was real glad to hear they dropped the assault charge, the
prosecutor, that is. I don't think there is any such thing as a 'small victory'
when dealing with these courts. Did you tell me that the child protective services were doing an investigation? if so, how is that going? i can't imagine
what they'd be investigating, but inshallah they'll be done real soon. I hope
inshallah that throughout all of this, you maintain your composure and always
garner your strength from the fact that it's all bs...and that Allah knows
the truth, and surely He will always do what's best for us.

Yo, to be honest, i really get sad when i think about you. not
just your situation, but how you deal with it. i mean of course, i don't think
there really is a "right" way to deal with it. and whenever i talk to you
you're always alright, but i just hope you're not like that all the time. i
hope you get a chance to really let loose, honestly talk about how you feel.
i hope you have a close friend who you can share your pain with, someone who
doesn't make you feel that you're burdening them with your problems. you don't
have to be a superwoman all the time.... just when you're putting up with lilly.
lord knows i can't.....

it wasn't until i started praying that i really got a grip of things.
after i heard the jury say guilty, i knew i was getting at least a life sentence.
it's mandatory in maryland. for the next couple of days, i was like a zombie.
i was doing things but my mind wasn't there. then finally one night i decided
to pray, for real. not that fake salaat that i'd been doing all my life, or
the half-a## kind i'd been doing in here, but the real deal. a real wudhu,
sitting in the place of prayer to clear my mind and get mentally ready. and
then just put everything on the table. how i feel; my anger at being locked
up for something He knows i didn't do, my frustration in not being able to
really help myself, anxiety about not knowing what's gonna happen next, and
deep down inside the fear that i might never go home. that my name would never
be cleared, that my little brother would always have a brother in prison for
murder, that my mother might never be able to live down all the women who talk
about her son who's locked up. anything i could think of, i said it as if Allah
ws right there. and no bullsh##, as soon as i was done i did feel different.
not so much better, or that it was gonna be over soon, but that no matter what
happened i'd be able to get through it, cause i know Allah will always help
me. and that even though it may not be what i want, He knows that it's best
for me, and that gives me comfort. there is an arabic word "sakina" it means
something like tranquility, complete soundness of mind, peace. it can't really
be translated into english, only if a person experiences it can they know what
it truly means. i asked my father about it, and he told me one time in his
life he feels he experienced it. He said he'd had a very hectic day at work,
and on his way home he got stuck in a traffic jam. Even though it was very

cold outside, he pulled over to make Asr salat. he pulled into the shoulder, and made salat under a tree. he told me that from the moment he said Allahu Akbar, all his fatigue went away, the cold went away, and he felt as if he was in a garden. he said their were really sweet smells in the air, and that he lost all track of time. he told me that by the time he was done, almost 30 minutes had passed. now, imagine 30 minutes in salaat, and than add to it cars rushing by at 60 mph. and this was like 20 years ago, before abu started losing it. i didn't feel the exact same thing, but it was something similiar, and it really changed my whole outlook on things, for the better.

i hope inshallah i said something that can help you out. you've done so much for me and my family, i wish there was more i could do for you. i always keep you in my dua's, and i'm not talking about that fake desi crap... plus, i do think you got it worse than me, so i pray more for you. quantitatively, i got it, but it's to my benefit. it's too much happening to me for me to worry about 5 years from now. i'm too busy looking out for my young pakistani a** to worry too much about anything else. strangely, as much of it that goes on in here, alhamdhulillah i haven't been bothered yet... maybe i'm losing my sex appeal.... i don't know....

anyway, take care man, and inshallah i'll see talk to you soon....

p.s. how come you never come see a nigga no more? you nor saad. if u see him, tell him i'm glad someone stole his car, he should never have put 3 t.v's in a honda accord. it's just plain tacky...

p.s.s i hope you like the picture, don't show it to anybody i know cause i'd be extremely embarassed. i hope it made you laugh!!!

Love, your lil' bro.

Letter written by Adnan after he learned of my separation

Within a few hours of being served, they called and said I could have her. They weren't going to contest custody anymore.

Those eight months until I got my daughter, and the moment that phone call came, truly turned my backbone into steel. Going forward I would become a single working parent, one of the hardest jobs in the world, but I wasn't afraid anymore. If I could handle the thugs that were my ex-in-laws, I could handle anything.

I had my daughter and my freedom and was ready to start my life over.

At the same time, Adnan and his family were ready to fight for a new trial.

Adnan had strong legal issues and he had something else on his side—the very public disbarment of Cristina Gutierrez the year before. In June of 2001, facing record-breaking client complaints, Gutierrez agreed to stop practicing law. For someone who had lived her life and career fighting every step of the way, her concession was uncharacteristic, but telling.

That was the first that any of us realized what had been going on with her during Adnan's trial. She had been sick and overworked, neglecting and hurting dozens of clients including Adnan. Her disbarment was no secret in the legal community and when Adnan's appeal would be filed, the court would certainly notice that he had been represented by someone who was unfit to represent anyone.

The family had begun preparing for an appeal, a direct appeal where technical issues from the trial could be challenged. New evidence, like Asia's affidavit, could not be raised in direct appeal; it could only be raised in post-conviction relief (PCR), on which Adnan wanted to hold off.

He was surrounded by hundreds of fellow inmates, all giving him the best legal and strategic advice they could muster. They advised him to give the direct appeal a shot before going straight for PCR; better two bites of the apple than one.

Attorney Warren Brown, well known in Baltimore's legal community, was hired after some consultation with community members. Brown filed an appeal with the Court of Special Appeals (COSA) of Maryland based on three issues, two of which were objections to the admission of Hae's diary and her breakup letter by Judge Heard.

But the main issue raised was Jay's plea deal and the circumstances surrounding it: that the State had committed prosecutorial misconduct, violated Brady, and violated Adnan's due process when it suppressed favorable material evidence of a side agreement with Jay, and that the trial court committed reversible error in prohibiting Adnan from presenting this evidence to the jury.

Adnan sent me his lawyer's brief and I thought, as an inexperienced law graduate, that it made very sound arguments. I felt hopeful and told Adnan so.

The brief was filed with the court on February 27, 2002, and not long after, oral arguments were held. Adnan was deeply worried about how things would go. All this time he had never spoken with Brown. Brown had never taken his collect calls and never visited him. An associate in the firm was handling Adnan's case, and he had no idea how this person would do.

5/6/02

Asalaamualaykum. Bismillah'irrahman ir'raheem
What's up sis? Not much over here. I got the states brief (answer to mine). I don't know what to make of it. They don't seem to be denying that they withheld the evidence (1st pt. of Brady), but they're arguing that 1. The information was before the court/judge in other ways [and] 2. That it wasn't that important anyway. I've read some Stork Briefs (responses) before, and

this one seemed like they put quite a bit of work in it. They cited a lot of civil cases, which of course the case law still apply to criminal but nonetheless I still think it's pretty weird. Allah knows best . . .

Inshallah I'll send you a copy as soon as I can. The copying machine here has been down, on & off. So Inshallah as soon as I can.

Eh, I talked to my pops, and he said he'd call Uncle Patel. The Oral Argument is scheduled for June 3, 2002 in the Court of Special Appeals. I don't know exactly how that works; if I'm there or not, but I think I heard somewhere that each side only gets 5–20 mins. My dad said he'd go, but that he wouldn't know what's going on. I wanted to ask you if you could go? You know more @ law then anyone else, and could follow what's going on. My a#hole lawyer probably won't even tell me what happened, he'd probably just say wait for the decision!

Man, I really need you Rabia. I got to know how he rebuts their arguments and what he says. I can always get the transcript, but they won't be ready till months later. I also need to know what the state throws in the game, cause if the judges affirm my conviction, their opinions will essentially mirror the states arguments. That way, I'll have a head start on my writ of Cert to the higher court.

If you can, Inshallah, I'm gonna try to get the info @ the hearing from Brown, & have my father contact him for it. His #'s 410.576–3900. If you call him, he may/may not give you the info./Or he might just be the jacka$$ he is and refuse to talk 2 u.

Eh, I know you're really busy, w/ your custody hearing & your bar & job-hunting. If you got some prior commitment/too busy, it's cool. I know you'd do it 4 me if you could . . .

Inshallah let me know when you get a chance. Take care.

Love,
Adnan

Adnan knew life was a bit crazy for me then as a single working mom, but he requested that I attend the hearing, one of the few times he's ever really asked me for anything.

He didn't have to worry, I wasn't going to miss this for anything.

That morning, Aunty Shamim and I were the only people to attend the oral arguments before a panel of three judges. Adnan's attorney did a good job. I thought she was prepared, professional, and courteous to the family. But winning a direct appeal is a near impossibility; the odds are completely against the defendant.

A year later, on March 19, 2003, COSA denied the appeal, upholding every ruling of Judge Heard's in relation to Jay's plea, discovery of the plea, and the admission of the documents at issue.

No one was surprised. Adnan least of all. He had now been in prison for four years and knew enough stories of the cases of other inmates, denials of even stronger appellate issues, that he was expecting to be denied. As such, he had already begun mentally preparing for the next step: submitting a Petition for Writ of Certiorari, also referred to as a writ of cert.

This petition is granted on even rarer occasions; in essence it is an appeal to the highest court in Maryland, the Court of Appeals. Adnan had seen this coming and, knowing both the extreme unlikelihood of winning and the cost associated with another appeal, decided to draft the petition himself.

He sent it to me to review, as if I knew anything about Maryland law, but I looked it over anyway for grammar, style, structure; he had written a better petition than many attorneys I knew.

Adnan had little time, so in accordance with court rules he filed an original and seven copies within fifteen days of COSA's ruling. The Court of Appeals took little time to return their answer: on June 25, 2003, they denied the petition.

There was only one shot left now, post-conviction relief. Adnan, however, wasn't quite ready.

I think it was the first real fight I ever had with Adnan. Gutierrez had not only been disbarred but she had died from a heart attack after being ill with multiple sclerosis. We had Asia's letters and affidavit. Why couldn't we move on the PCR immediately? It was the end of 2004, and his last appeal had been denied almost eighteen months prior. But Adnan wasn't having it. He had been burned too badly. And despite trying to get recourse for what Gutierrez had done to him, he got nowhere with the Attorney Grievance Commission and the Client Protection Fund. They had both denied him relief, with the Grievance Commission directing him to the Fund to file a claim, and the Fund stating that while Gutierrez had consented to be disbarred, she "did not admit to any theft of monies" so they couldn't help him. They told him he had a malpractice problem and his only recourse was probably to sue her estate.

It was one more truly low moment for Adnan and his loved ones. He had been failed over and over again, by every part of the system that should have protected him. He knew he had one last chance and was willing to wait as long as he had to, to make sure all of his bases were covered.

My sense of urgency, the desperation of his family, all of it paled in comparison to his very astute grasp of reality. This last time, it had to be done exactly right.

I knew there was no arguing. Adnan had to handle his business the best way he thought, though I worried that he was influenced by his fellow inmates. I also realized he was full of fear. As long as the PCR was out there, he had hope. If he filed early and then lost, it was over.

I decided to back off, and also backed down on something else I had been bugging him about for years—going to the media. On that issue he also told me no, it wasn't the right time, though at moments he faltered and gave me a "maybe."

I understood his concern, though. Asia was our ace, an alibi witness the State had no idea existed. Going to the media before the PCR meant giving them all the time in the world to come up with a way to discredit her or otherwise interfere with her. That certainly wasn't worth it.

All we could do now was wait, wait until he felt ready.

I was wandering through the bazaar in a large, annual Islamic convention, holding a cardboard box with a hole on top, a stack of flyers under my arm. Every so often I would approach whoever made the mistake of making eye contact with me, hand them a flyer, and begin telling them about Adnan, hoping to get a few dollars out of them before they cut me off.

I was raising money for his PCR appeal—though not imminent, it was going to happen at some point. After a few days of intermittent begging, I managed to raise $178. But I also managed to hand out hundreds of flyers with Adnan's address on them, asking people to write and support him, the address where they could mail checks to help with legal fees, and my own personal e-mail address in case they had any questions.

One of the people who got a hold of this flyer reached out to me. His name was Irfan Aziz, a twenty-three-year-old from Toronto who happened to be at the convention. Irfan had recently returned from England where he'd finished an "aalim" program in Islamic scholarship. He was now getting accredited as a chaplain. I was impressed. He e-mailed to ask about whether

بسم الله الرحمن الرحيم

November 28, 2004

السلام عليكم ورحمة الله

Dear Rabia,

I pray that everything is well w/you & Sanna, Inshallah. I received your letters these past 2 weeks. Jazakallah Khayr for contacting
the lawyer Christopher Flohr. I had responded to his original letter,
briefly thanking him for taking the time to write. Additionally, I informed him that I decided not to pursue this "Brain Fingerprinting"
avenue, mainly because it was not admissible in court. (I had heard @
it 1½ yrs. ago, and had already researched it) However, I had not mentioned much else, because I wasn't sure of his agenda. (Chalk that up
to my jailhouse paranoia) Alhamdhulillah, hearing @ your conversations
with him leads me to believe he may be genuinely concerned. Inshallah,
something good may come of it...

I'm afraid I must apolgize to you, Rabia, for giving you the impression that I was intent on filing my own State Post Conviction Petition. I can't recall what it is I may have said to have given you that
impression; however, I can assure you that it couldn't be farther from
the truth. I believe that submitting my Petition 'Pro-se' would be extremely stupid. Almost as much as a man who breaks his leg, and after
reading a Surgeon's Manual, proceeds to perform surgery upon himself.
I know that I filed my own Writ of Certiorari, but that was really quite
simple. It was just re-arguing my Direct Appeal to a Higher Court. It
was really just a formality, because probably 99.9% of Writs of Certiorari are denied.(at least those involving 1st Deg. Murders) It was
really more of a morale booster than anything, because it was the culmination of 5-months of research. Not just case-law, but the format of
writing a Petition, as far as the language, borders, etc. The reason
why I said I must apologize is because I know how frustrating it is
when I hear brothers in here (that I care @) say that they are submitting their own Petitions. I believe in a lot of cases, it is out of ar-
rogance, and it's ridiculous. I mean, that's what the professionals are
for. And as far as actually litigating in Court; man, after this experience, I wouldn't even defend myself in Traffic Court...

In response to your question @ what/why I want to wait for, the
answer is I don't want to; I have to. Similiar to a rape victim's determination to never again walk in a dark alley; I will never again
walk into a courtroom and not know what the hell is going on. Never a-
gain. And the only way I can insure that, Inshallah, is by learning
as much law as I possibly can.

he should try and raise some funds for Adnan or organize his friends to write
letters to him and I thought it was a great idea. I said sure and thanked him
profusely.

In 2003, I was living with my five-year-old daughter back in Virginia and
working at the General Counsel's Office of the U.S. Department of Health and
Human Services in D.C. Things had smoothed out for me and I was starting to
enjoy life again.

At twenty-eight, I was free and loving it.

Every so often I would connect with Irfan online. At some point I mentioned
my daughter, taking him by surprise. When he asked me about my husband I

The pros of taking the time to file:

-getting a better understanding of the case and the law

-the possibility that a "smoking gun" appears, either through investigation or someone coming forth. While it may not be something
as solid as"I know who did it, and heres the tape to prove it." it
would bolster the hell out of any argument I present, Inshallah.

-easier for my family to accumulate the $$$ required.

-Patience never hurt anything, Ishallah that'll apply here.

The cons of taking the time to file:

-lose any chance of review at the federal level. but i already
explained my view of the time and $$$ constraints, so that's really
not an issue.

- a helpful witness (like Asia McClaine) could die, recant, refuse
to come to Court

The Unknowns of taking the timeto file: (*meaning, I'm not sure of*
its effect/ pro or con)

~~- a helpful witness (like Asia McClaine) could die, recant, refuse
to testify~~

- Chrisitina G. dying. Whether that has an effect upon my Ineffective
assistance of COunsel claims. I just learned that it's possible
for the Judge to procedurally default my claims if she is not there
to testify as to her reasons for doing/not doing something. And
even if he doesn't literally procedurally default me, he could do
it just as well by saying "Since she's not here to respond, Ill
just assume it was a "trial tactic".

(I call these 2 Unknowns because I don't know how they will play
out)

So that's basically my plan, in brevity. Inshallah, i will explain it
to you more indepth in coming letters, but I have to cut this short because my mind is exhausted.

So I take @ 9 yrs. to research my case & the law, and then I hire
a lawyer and share my research with him, and then obviously see what he/
she comes up with. It doesn't matter how long they need,1-2 yrs. because
we can always submit a Petition to be amended, and postpone. Ishallah.

told him I was divorced. Not long after that he asked if I was interested in getting remarried.

"No," I said unequivocally.

He had some friends, he said, in case I was interested.

Thanks, but no thanks.

A few months later he finally got around to saying what he had been wanting to say—what did I think of him? Would I consider him for marriage?

Now, to be clear, all this time we only chatted online infrequently. I didn't
even remember what he looked like. When he proposed over instant message I
was exasperated. Was this his agenda all this time?

I shut the door to his romantic aspirations in 2003 but still kept in touch and once, when he was visiting the area to lead a prayer service, I finally got to meet him properly. He was, I grudgingly and internally admitted, pretty good looking.

But still, I wasn't ready to be married.

Adnan, on the other hand, totally was.

Kandra is tall, mocha-skinned, and beautiful, exceedingly sweet and gentle, with a radiant smile and warmth you can feel even in her voice. A native of Indianapolis, she's lived in North Carolina for over two decades now.

She's in the insurance industry, highly educated, a consummate professional.

The first time she ever laid eyes on Adnan she was at the Jessup prison, visiting a friend in Maryland who had a loved one at the prison. The friend had asked Kandra to tag along, which she reluctantly did.

The Maryland House of Corrections in Jessup had an extraordinarily bad reputation—for violence, corruption, and extreme laxity. Inmates were able to "earn" the freedom to do things, albeit not officially, which they wouldn't ordinarily be allowed elsewhere. Visitation was also fairly relaxed and didn't require you to be on a predetermined list to pop in and see someone.

As Kandra sat in the visitation room, slightly bored, a tall, broad-shouldered, bearded man entered. His eyes went directly to a small woman with a head scarf who was smiling up at him as he walked her way.

Aunty Shamim was there to visit her son.

Kandra, now completely distracted, was thinking, "Hello, this man is gorgeous. Just gorgeous!"

"I'm not a stalker," Kandra says to me, "I'm very shy, and old-fashioned when it comes to relationships. I don't approach men, I'm not that person."

She reached over to her friend and whispered, "Isn't he cute?"

The man they were visiting heard it and turned around to see who she was talking about.

"I know him! We call him *Saaaeeed*."

"Do you want to talk to him?" the friend asked.

Kandra squirmed. She did want to talk to him, but this was all just too weird. She knew there were women who got involved with incarcerated men, but she never envisioned herself to be one of them.

But there was something about this man that compelled her to say ok, yes, I'd like to speak to him. At the time she wasn't looking for a relationship; she was busy in her studies in nutrition and health care administration along with her twin sister. But in that moment she stopped acting like herself.

Her interest in Adnan didn't go unnoticed. Aunty Shamim saw this strange woman staring at her son and glared at her. The situation was tense, and Kandra certainly wasn't going to make it worse by asking to be introduced right then and there.

She left but only after giving her number to the man they were visiting to pass along to Adnan if he was interested in talking.

It turned out Aunty Shamim wasn't the only one who noticed her.

A couple of days later, before she left Maryland, she got a call from Adnan.

"He was just sweet," she remembers. His radar had picked up the beautiful woman with the big smile sitting in his periphery. Even in prison, he was deeply aware of not disrespecting his mother. Kandra and he connected immediately and spoke for a couple of hours, sharing their backgrounds.

"I laughed a lot," Kandra says. "He's got a great sense of humor and just makes you feel like you've known each other a long time."

Even though she was still in Maryland, she didn't swing by the prison to see him before leaving. She wasn't ready to do that and she wasn't quite sure what she was getting into; instead she returned to North Carolina.

It was the fall of 2008, and for those first few months they spoke incessantly over the phone, connecting daily, multiple times a day. The rapport was instant, and they quickly grew attached to each other. Even in prison she wasn't the first woman he had "spoken" to. But this woman was different.

Prison is not exactly a conducive environment for love—those inmates who have a partner, a romantic relationship, a spouse on the outside who stick by them are very, very lucky. Many relationships die off after a person gets locked up. But the moral support and hope you get from someone who cares about and loves you gives you a reason to dream about a future outside bars. In all these years Adnan had not met anyone who made him feel like he did now.

He told her, "I've never had feelings like this since I've been locked up. I don't know what I'm feeling." Kandra really did "like" him and cared about him but wasn't head over heels. He was funny, sweet, attentive, smart, handsome, but he was also serving a life term for murder that he said he was innocent of. She believed he was innocent. But how would they ever actually have a future together? And how on earth do you tell your family about a relationship like this?

For Adnan there was little caution, and the feelings came much faster. "This was the second time I fell in love in my life," he says.

They still hadn't spent any time together in person, but she was planning on making a trip up to Maryland to see him soon. Adnan began to worry a bit. He knew where this was going, but he couldn't quite go there. Over the years his juvenile posturing about Islam had turned into a serious commitment. He knew he couldn't, or wouldn't, be physically close to Kandra unless they were married.

A few times a year the prison held "family days" when inmates, family, and friends openly mingled either in the yard or inside a large gymnasium. I'd been to a couple of the events and it was actually quite wonderful. There were no cages, no barriers. Inmates were in charge of the festivities, barbecuing, playing a live band. Everyone hung out as if they were at an actual picnic. Lots of things changed hands on these occasions. Once, when I went with Saad and our sister, he had a new pair of sneakers on for Adnan. We sat at picnic-style tables and as we casually chatted, they traded shoes under the table.

Family day was coming up and Kandra was going to be there, and while neither of them expected any physical intimacy, not to that extent, Adnan at least wanted the chance to hug her, hold her, kiss her. But he not only wanted to do what was right by his religion, he also wanted to do what was right by her.

She was struggling in some ways back then; her finances weren't strong, and she had run out of money to finish her degree. Adnan wanted to take care of her and he wanted a relationship that gave her the right to expect to be cared for.

He asked if she would marry him in an Islamic ceremony, a "nikkah."

"The ceremony would be real, a legitimate marriage in Islam," she said, "but just not on paper."

She felt how conflicted he was, that he wanted a romantic relationship with this woman but his faith was preventing it. After thinking about it she agreed. After all, it was a verbal ceremony with two witnesses, nothing legal. It would put him at ease and not be any kind of a burden on her.

He began discussing a dowry with her.

"A dowry?" she asked, perplexed.

Yes, he explained. In Islam a man must give a woman a dowry, the "mahr," when they marry, as a gift, and for some, as a form of financial protection. The dowry was an obligation, the nikkah wasn't complete without it. He wasn't just posturing, he was doing this for real, as real as it got in his religion.

"What did Adnan give you?" I asked.

"Ten thousand dollars," she responded.

I balked.

How the hell did Adnan have ten thousand dollars? I laughed, joking with Kandra.

It turned out that by working small hustles, like making photocopies, trading items, getting other inmates things they needed like medicine, books, and other "contraband" over the past eight years, he had managed to save up quite a stash. There was an elaborate system set up with the inmates in which they managed to get prepaid Visa cards to send to the outside world, and Adnan managed to send Kandra her dowry before she arrived for the ceremony.

Kandra first met Adnan formally on the same day they got Islamically married, sometime in the winter of 2008. It took a total of five minutes, with another inmate officiating and two others standing witness.

I had to ask.

"Did you have a chance to . . . er . . . be close after the marriage?"

"No. We never consummated the marriage."

There were some rules about physical touching during family day, as guards stood in the perimeters. No prolonged hugging, no kissing, no funny business. Despite the rules, funny business was routine. With the right incentives there were always guards willing to look the other way as a couple would find a corner, or duck under a table, for a quickie. Some were so brazen that they would have sex while sitting openly—the woman having come prepared in an easy-access skirt, she would sit in her partner's lap, often at the table where others were eating, for a few minutes until the deed was done. Kandra filled me in.

"Are you telling me people are shagging on family day?"

"Yes." Kandra laughed. "All over the place they're shagging. The guards know what's going on."

But she wasn't raised like that, she was shy and she wasn't going to be doing any public shagging, married or not. Adnan was fine with it. "He knows me, he knows I'm a private person, he never pressured me," she said.

Adnan tried to get a private room arranged for them but wasn't able to. Barring that, it was not going to happen. And it never did.

She went home, now a duly married woman, and Adnan finally felt like he had the freedom to speak to her affectionately, intimately. He constantly sent her gifts, mostly thanks to Saad.

"Yeah, any time he needed flowers or candy or gifts sent, he'd ask me. I helped out with her smaller bills sometimes, and would do the travel arrangements for her. He's my boy. Of course I'd do that for his wife," Saad said.

When Adnan told me he had gotten married I was shocked but genuinely happy. I could hear the levity in his voice and I knew what it meant to find someone he could dream of having a life with.

He wanted me to talk to Kandra. She was interested in Islam and he wanted to foster that interest, though whether or not she became Muslim wasn't paramount. He asked me to answer any questions she had, give her any support she would need. He also asked me to talk to his mother—he had broken the news to his family and, forever the traditional Pakistani mother, Aunty Shamim wasn't happy that he made the decision independently. Marriage, where we're from, is a family affair.

I spoke to Kandra and she was lovely. I could see why Adnan had fallen for her. She had tried visiting a mosque and didn't feel comfortable because she didn't know anyone there. I, admittedly, did not encourage her to go again unless she could go with someone. I didn't want her feeling like an outsider and frankly, I knew too many converts who had left Islam thanks to the judgment and dysfunction of other Muslims. She didn't need to be around us en masse just yet.

Adnan wanted his family to get to know her, so his father and Yusuf spoke to her a number of times.

"They were very nice and friendly, really welcoming," she recalls.

But Aunty Shamim wouldn't speak with her. I tried to work on that.

"Aunty. Come on. There is no reason to object to this, he is *allowed* to marry who he wants to in Islam, and he can marry a Christian woman, and you know it." But I got nowhere. She just repeated, "It's not fair, he can't make a decision like that without asking." It was the first time she seemed truly hurt.

Kandra visited Adnan four more times before he was abruptly moved in 2009 from Jessup, which was shut down and eventually demolished, to the North Branch Correctional Institute (NBCI) in Cumberland, Maryland.

After his move to this supermax facility, an institution of legendary security housing the most violent criminals in Maryland, and hours away from Baltimore, she never saw him again.

"He's done more for me than any person I've ever been with. He took care of me. He made sure if I needed money for anything I got it. He had flowers and chocolates sent to me all the time. He made sure my travel was paid for, my rental car, my hotel, the best hotels, when I went to visit. He had it together, he knew what he was doing. But once he was moved, everything changed. He changed. For the first time I heard him depressed."

I could tell too. He wrote to me on June 20, 2009.

Dear Rabia,

I pray that everything is well w/you + Arfan [sic] and the girls, inshaAllah. I have been transferred to the Cumberland area. Everyone who is maximum security status was transferred to this region over the past two years. I was part of the last load, mashaAllah. The rules are stricter up here . . . but . . . it's not that big of a deal. It's a 2 ½ hour drive from Baltimore, so it's kinda far away.

Alhamdulillah other than that, everythings pretty much ok. My mother's still beefin about my marriage, but not so hard as before. InshaAllah, she'll come around. My wife is alright . . . our relationship is long-distance to begin with. She's been helping me out a lot, doing some computer searches and making copies for me. We don't get a chance to talk as much because I'm using the regular phones now, but we write everyday. . . .

I'll be honest, I'm very nervous about this appeal. I've spent all these years researching & praying. I really hope Allah will grant it. I'm so anxious about this, cause I've been waiting so long . . . all these years I've been waiting for this. This Post Conviction Petition was the event I was working towards. And it was steadily coming closer, I had it to look forward to this past year. It seems like this incarceration has finally started to wear me down. My heart feels so heavy. Having this life sentence, I feel like there's no light at the end of this tunnel. And that's what I need; some light. Even if I don't go home now, if they were to cut my time. I have 10 ½ years in, with a good record and no past criminal history. If I could get a sentence that would get me an expiration date, it would change my whole perspective.

Kandra and Adnan remained married only for a short while longer, until Adnan told her it was better if they ended it, though they could always remain friends. He was hitting rock-bottom in Cumberland. In Jessup he had an active life with some semblance of normalcy. He had an extraordinary level of freedom, working in different parts of the prison, having an excellent relationship with the staff and guards. Once, while he was assisting the prison librarian, she asked him to go drop off some books in her car. She handed him her keys and he walked out to the lot where her car stood. He was outside the prison, free and clear, in the employee parking lot. If he had wanted, he could have gotten in her car and driven away.

Instead, he put the books in her trunk, turned around, and went back to his imprisonment.

He had a cell phone at Jessup for a number of years, thanks to an elaborate scheme in which one of the maintenance workers would bring in a few phones at a time inside the cavity of a drill handle and leave the designated drill in a shop for inmates to retrieve. The doors of their cells were solid, so guards couldn't see inmates speaking on their phones. Some of them knew but looked the other way, not wanting to come down hard on those they had developed friendships with, to the extent they could be called friendships.

The freedom and hope he felt at Jessup all faded at NBCI. Gone were all his relationships, his gigs, his routine, his friends, his community. There were no more family days, no more mingling with his loved ones. Here he was on level ten, state-of-the-art, supermax lockdown. He was surrounded by crewcut white guards who didn't give the inmates, mostly men of color, the same kind of leeway the mostly black guards at Jessup gave.

And he was far, so far from his family. His visiting hours were shrunk, his phone access cut to a fraction.

Kandra sensed the change in him, a despondency that he hadn't ever shown before. There was another reason for the despondency, though: it was high time to hire an attorney for the PCR, but there was no money for it.

7/14/09

Dear Rabia,

Asalaamualaykum wa'rahmatullah wa'barakatuhu [peace, mercy, and blessings of God be upon you].

. . . I got the message from my mom, and I tried to call you, but I guess it got your machine. Right now, there really isn't a set phone schedule, but inshaAllah it may improve soon. I don't know when's the next time I can call, but I think I can catch you soon, inshaAllah.

You know one of the 3 law firms I mentioned was the one Christopher Flohr recommended, Larry Nathan. You + him both contacted that firm back in 2004. I just received a letter last week after I had sent him the # of pages my transcripts were, and asking his fee. He wrote back and mentioned that you both had contacted him regarding my case in 2004. Anyway this guy said that the review fee (because I have so many documents) would be $30,000! And that wouldn't include the separate fee of litigation. Bair wanted $20,000 for the review fee, and I think the firm of Byer Warnken is just as much as Nathan if not more. In fact, he sent me a booklet, in it are his prices. He charges $15,000 for 2 issues and $8,000 for each additional issue. That's his litigation fee. I'm pretty sure his review fee would be between $20,000-$30,000. Allah knows best but I think they are financially out of the question.

You know I was completely blind-sided by the "review fee." Everyone I spoke to and read about, all the info I compiled. I realize now was about the litigation fee. And you know what sucks? My transcripts are full of crap. It is 6300 pages of nothing, with a little bit of substance. . . . It's frustrating, cause that's what is driving the price up so much. . . .

I think I found this one lawyer, his name is Justin Brown. He was the point man at Larry Nathan's firm, specializing in Post-Conviction Petitions. About 2 months ago he started his own firm. I know 2 guys who have dealt with him—their appeals are still pending. They spoke highly of him, and they felt that he was very thorough in his research and preparation. One thing he said was that when he started his own firm, he would charge less because he wouldn't have as much overhead as the bigger firms. He responded to my initial request with a questionnaire which I mailed back last week. . . . The thing is that, at trial and my appeal, we had big firms and look where that got me, mashaAllah. They treated me like a case #, and I truly feel it was all about $$ to them. Maybe I need a lawyer that believes in my innocence. . . .

I really hope now is my time, it's just been getting to me. I just want some Daylight, inshaAllah.

Adnan had heard from other inmates about a number of attorneys who specialized in PCR petitions. Some were big names and came with big fees. He knew he had to hire someone who was very, very good at this (often measured by how much they charged) because it was his last shot.

He had spent the last five years studying the law, poring through his case files and keeping up on recent Maryland court decisions. He already had a good sense of what issues would be most important.

He sent me a list of attorneys he was interested in so I could check them out. He was particularly curious about one who had just recently started his own law firm, breaking away from a larger firm.

C. Justin Brown was based in Baltimore, and Adnan asked if I would be willing to meet with him at some point. I said sure. At this time I was no longer living in the area; in 2006 I had remarried and moved to Connecticut.

Irfan had turned out to be rather persistent. It took a few years before I felt ready to get remarried and when I did I told him, "Look, I know you're young, but I'm not that young and if you want to get married, it's now or never. I don't know how your family is going to take an older, divorced, single mother (the perfect trifecta to give any potential Pakistani mother-in-law heart palpitations) and if anyone in your family, or my family, objects to this, I'm out. You have thirty days to give me your answer."

I was thirty-one, my daughter was eight, I had been alone for four years, and I had no time to waste.

Within the month he had spoken to his parents and within another month two vans crammed full of his family, extended and nuclear, arrived from Toronto. They brought sweets, roses, and an engagement ring.

On December 9, 2005, I married Irfan in Toronto, with my daughter present (unthinkable in Pakistani culture), and together we moved to Hartford, Connecticut, where he began a master's degree in Christian-Muslim Relations at the Hartford Seminary.

It was a relief to start a new life in a new place, though it meant leaving behind my immigration practice in Virginia. I didn't mind, and was energized by the interfaith community that surrounded the seminary.

As my new husband studied, I got busy setting up my immigration law practice and also immediately got involved in a local nonprofit focused on charity and interfaith outreach, the Muslim Coalition of Connecticut (MCCT).

In the years leading up to 2009, when we began preparing for the post-conviction appeal, my life had been transformed by that move and by the political landscape of America. After 9/11, anti-Muslim sentiment grew each year, and counterterror policies steadily encroached on our civil liberties. The widespread surveillance of mosques and Muslim student associations by local and federal agencies was common knowledge.

I found myself representing about a dozen immigrants who were being leaned on by federal law enforcement to become informants inside their mosques; this was not happening in response to any imminent threats, instead it was a sweeping fishing expedition in Muslim communities nationwide. My clients were being backed into a corner through extreme coercion; if they didn't cooperate they were threatened with deportation or having their immigration cases denied.

Publicly, I worked through the MCCT to better relations between local communities and law enforcement. The fact that this work was being undermined by troubling surveillance and infiltration policies—coupled with news of horribly bigoted anti-Muslim training in the FBI, Pentagon, and local jurisdictions—was deeply frustrating. But it also created an opportunity for change, which I began to think about while, from hundreds of miles away, keeping an eye on the upcoming PCR.

On a trip to Baltimore I went to meet Justin; Saad joined me. Justin was enthusiastic, polite, and smart. He had not only read through Adnan's court filings but had actually traveled hours to meet him, and he believed Adnan was innocent. I'd already done some research and knew he was a former war reporter in Bosnia during the horrendous ethnic cleansing in the early 1990s. I liked that he had been exposed to a world outside of the law, because many lawyers I knew became cynical and jaded over their years practicing in silos, and that he also presumably had experience with Muslim communities.

I had a good feeling about Justin, and I had a good feeling about our issues. After all, we had Asia in the bag. I told Adnan over the phone that I liked the guy, and Adnan did too, so after some fee negotiation, Justin Brown was hired to represent Adnan in his PCR petition with the Circuit Court of Baltimore.

The first order of business was to find Asia McClain. She no longer lived in the Baltimore area but Justin had a private investigator on the case, and she located Asia on the other side of the country.

Justin had already attempted to reach her by letter to let her know we were looking to speak to her about her 1999 letters and 2000 affidavit, but he had heard nothing back. So his PI eventually went to her home. A man answered the door, and the PI explained who she was and asked him to pass along her card to Asia. When she didn't hear back, she tried again. This time the same man told her to leave them alone, and Justin never heard from Asia.

This was terrible, literally the worst thing that could happen after all these years. Why was Asia stonewalling us? We desperately needed her for the PCR; otherwise all we had were those three documents and my testimony about what she had told me, which didn't count for much as hearsay. Adnan had waited so many years for this, and we had all banked on the moment when Asia could finally testify for him. There were a lot of tears, prayers, and shock as we realized that we had lost Asia, the most vital aspect of this appeal.

Justin had to make a strategic decision. He could definitely subpoena her and force her to come all the way to Baltimore to testify. But she could end up being a hostile witness, he said, hostile meaning hurtful to the case. Adnan remembered her as a really nice girl, but he didn't know her that well, and many years had passed since. Anything was possible if we forced her to testify.

Justin conferred with Adnan and decided it was best to move forward with the letters and affidavit and not call Asia. The documents alone sufficed, he believed, to prove that Gutierrez failed in a basic duty to call an alibi witness, prima facie ineffective assistance of counsel. And he was raising another strong legal issue: Gutierrez had failed, despite Adnan twice asking her, to approach the State to see if they would offer a plea deal.

There was strong legal precedent in Adnan's favor on this; numerous courts had ruled that when a client asked, his or her attorney must at least find out if the State would negotiate a plea. It doesn't matter if the client, upon being offered, would have said no. It also doesn't matter if clients maintained their innocence; there is no dearth of literature on innocent people taking plea deals, and even innocent people expressing remorse before a parole board. The system incentivizes this convoluted and unjust dynamic, where nearly 95 percent of criminal cases are pled out.

To prove to the court that Adnan had indeed asked Gutierrez for a plea, Justin submitted Adnan to a polygraph test, which he passed.

On May 28, 2010, Justin filed the petition for post-conviction relief with the Baltimore City Circuit Court, just making the ten-year deadline. It would be more than two years, with multiple continuances and motions, until the hearing date was scheduled.

We had a wonderful life and community in Connecticut but after five years we needed to move. Irfan had immense trouble finding work in chaplaincy, at least work that could sustain a family, and had begun working in IT consulting. But all of the consulting jobs he got were far from home. After trying for three years, we finally had a beautiful baby girl, bringing my beautiful daughter count to two. Since the little one was born, I was only working part-time and juggling taking care of the house, the girls, my work, and my activism, all while Irfan was working out of town.

After six years in Connecticut, during which time I barely saw Adnan, I moved back to Maryland in August of 2011, roughly a year before the PCR hearing.

Once back, I began transitioning out of legal practice and into national security work. My experiences—making me aware of law enforcement coercing immigrant clients into unconscionable situations, even coercing Imams to spy on their congregations—weighed heavily on my heart. I spent my first year back in the D.C. area studying national security policy, with a particular focus on a framework the White House called "CVE," or Countering Violent Extremism. The idea behind CVE was to engage and include the Muslim community on issues of violent extremism and create a space outside of counterterror operations for prevention of recruitment by terrorists, particularly online. The problem was that CVE totally ignored the greatest extremist threat to the homeland as articulated by the FBI itself: homegrown, right-wing, sovereign-citizen militia groups.

In January of 2012 I founded the Safe Nation Collaborative, a firm focused on training law enforcement on how to work with Muslim communities respect-fully and providing accurate information about Islam and Muslims. We (myself and a team of trainers) also delivered community trainings on violent extrem-ism, because this was an issue we couldn't and shouldn't ignore even though it's a miniscule problem among American Muslims. More importantly for them, extremist recruiters target our kids in particular, online, while parents have no idea what's going on.

As the hearing date approached in October 2012, Justin told me I would have to testify about how I got the affidavit from Asia. I wasn't too worried. My cre-dentials and credibility were strong, I had already worked with hundreds of law enforcement officers and even conducted an FBI training, I was a Truman Na-tional Security Fellow, and my legal career was unblemished. I felt confident the court would believe my testimony.

Adnan was also going to testify, but as luck would have it, he suddenly found himself in a bit of a bind once the hearing dates were finalized.

7/13/12

Dear Justin,
Please thank Melissa for faxing the letter to the prison about the postpone-ment. I received my copy as well.

I'm writing you because I have a problem with the Oct. court dates. I don't know if you remember but about 18 months ago I had asked you to write a letter to the prison regarding my foot injury. I had not received any medical attention at the time, but upon receipt of your letter I was evaluated. Subsequently it was determined that I would need surgery. But as it was not life threatening I was placed on the medical waiting list. I'm constantly in a lot of pain, I don't take the painkillers they prescribe because of the adverse side effects. I don't want to destroy my liver just so my foot feels better. I've been waiting 18 months now . . .

Anyway about a week ago, I found out my surgery is scheduled for the same day as the first hearing in Oct. This presents 2 problems:

#1 if I miss the surgery (due to court) I immediately go back to the bot-tom of the list. They do not stagger patients. So I would have to wait another 18-24 months.

#2 The only reason I know my surgery date is because a nurse was nice enough to tell me. The problem w/that is that inmates aren't supposed to know their surgery dates in case someone plans an ingenius you-know-what. The great irony of that policy is I know my court date months in advance, and it's

the exact same trip/method. Leave Cumberland → Hagerstown layover →
Jessup. Whenever I go to court, half the guys on the bus are medical trips . . .
The point is that you/I couldn't try to reschedule [. . .] because their first con-
cern would be, "Whoa, how did inmate Syed know about his surgery date??"

[. . .] I've given this a lot of thought, cause I know you have a very busy
schedule and you have witnesses lined up to testify, etc for what its worth. I
was gonna tough it out. But it is a very painful injury & in the end I'd
rather wait a few more months for another court date than to wait another
15–24 months for another surgery date.

If you could get a postponement w/out telling the Judge about the sur-
gery, could you please do it? [. . .] But if you can't get a postponement, or if
you feel it'll be detrimental to the case, then it is what it is, and I'll just have
to tough it out.

The hearing date wasn't postponed, though, and Adnan just had to forgo
his surgery. Justin still had to put Adnan on the stand, in spite of his condition, to testify about Gutierrez's failure to take action after telling her about
both Asia and the plea. I was a little worried; he had never testified before, he
was in pain, and I heard Kathleen Murphy, the same prosecutor from the first
trial, was going to be arguing for the State in the PCR—she would fight hard
to keep her conviction. It turned out Adnan was not the one I needed to worry
about.

The first day of the hearing a small group of us—Aunty Shamim, Yusuf,
Saad, Irfan, a few community friends, and myself—arrived at the courthouse.

A mild-looking and mild-mannered judge, Martin Welch, presided.

Adnan shuffled in, constrained in five-point shackles. Having never seen him
like this, I choked up. We were all a bit taken aback.

Justin had let me know that I'd be called as a witness that day, and I said ok,
I had all my prayers in order and was ready. But first he called Kevin Urick.

He questioned Urick about the plea deal, who testified that he had never been
approached by Gutierrez about a plea. What we didn't expect was that he would
bring up Asia.

We were surprised to hear that Asia had called Urick, and then shocked at
what she had to say to him.

Urick testified, "She was concerned, because she was being asked questions
about an affidavit she had written back at the time of the trial. She told me she
had only written it because she was getting pressure from the family. And basically wrote it to please them and get them off her back."

Adnan:

Although I experienced a great deal of worry and frustration when I was arrested, I expected that everything would work out. I thought people would see I had no reason to kill Hae, and certainly there could be no evidence to say I did. I had complete faith that I would never be held responsible for a crime I did not commit. But by the end of that year, the exact opposite happened. It seemed everyone thought I had reason to kill Hae, and that there was hard evidence to prove I did.

To be convicted and sentenced to prison for Hae's murder was one thing. But it was even worse to feel that the whole world believed I was a liar and a manipulative person. Because I did not kill Hae; there was nothing for me to feel bad about. I was angry and sad, but there was no internal conflict taking place. To be accused of being an evil person, however, was a whole other thing. Because I did lie to my parents about different things. And while I never manipulated my parents into giving me money or material things, I did manipulate them into thinking I was not messing around with girls and stuff which I was not supposed to do. So with Hae's murder, I had no culpability; but as far as the State saying I was a bad person? Well, maybe they were right . . . It was a really tough time for me, emotionally.

When I arrived at prison, I decided that I was going to try and better myself; specifically, strive to become a better Muslim. And you know Islam has some pretty strict tenets, if you take it literally. No cursing, listening to music, watching TV, taking pictures, dealing with the opposite sex, etc. For several months, I did my best to adhere to what I thought was right. And I felt as if I was making some progress, but I was also a bit miserable at the same time. I still had a desire to do certain things, and I had never been a very disciplined person. So I began veering back and forth; it was a real struggle. I would do good for a couple of days, but then fall back into old habits. It became an emotional roller-coaster I could not handle. So I decided to just give up. I told myself that I was who I was, and that I did not possess the fortitude necessary to better myself.

There was only one issue of contention that I could resolve in my life. And that was the desire I have to never be accused of being a liar and manipulative again. I knew I had lied to my parents about things. But on the other hand, it was never with evil intentions. And I never really had a reason to lie to other people. Sure, my friends' parents didn't know we were doing things, but I never attempted to make it seem as if I was someone that I was not. So I did not really know how to avoid being perceived as manipulative when I felt like I was not ever being manipulative in the first place. I came to the conclusion that the only way I could protect myself from ever being accused of being manipulative again was if I never interacted with people from the outside world. I mean people from the street, school, the mosque, etc. Because if I never wrote or called anyone, then no one could ever accuse me of having evil intentions. So that was the deal I made with myself. I decided I would not write to or call anyone except my parent's home or Rabia and Saad and their family. It was a brutally simple understanding; no one could ever accuse me of ulterior motives for an interaction, if there never was any interaction. So I stuck to that for all these years. I decided to just live in prison, and that would be enough. I would mind my own business, not request anything from anybody. Initially, I worried how I would deal with someone reaching out to me; however, that turned out to be an unnecessary concern.

After coming to terms with that, next I had to figure out what to do with my life. I saw a lot of people who had succumbed to substance-abuse, joined gangs, and engaged in very self-destructive behavior. Looking back, I realize how easily I could have ended up going down one of those paths. I was extremely fortunate, however, to meet some people who helped me. They saw a scared and lonely teenager, and instead of trying to take advantage of me, they embraced me and helped me deal with the hardest time of my life. They stopped me from going down the terrible road most people in here end up on. My values come from my mother and father, but the man that I am today (or at least try to be) is thanks to them. They refused to allow me to be miserable and give up on trying to better myself.

The thing which troubled me the most was that I felt everyone thought I was an evil person. It bothered me because I tried to be a good person growing up. Did my best to treat people with respect, and be there for others. It really caused me to question myself, and it was very difficult to deal with. I read a lot, and I came to realize a good Muslim is someone who has good character. And it was something I could work on and achieve. I decided to dedicate myself to improving my character, and becoming a better person, the best that I could be. Not for anyone else, but for me. Maybe I could not prove I did not kill Hae, and maybe I would spend the rest of my life in prison. But at least I could prove I was not a bad person. Not to anyone else, but to myself. I know this all probably sounds ridiculous, but it was the only thing I had to grab ahold of. So that was how I began living my life in prison.

I read any books I could find about becoming a better person. Self-help books, religious books, just about anything I could find. And it turned out to be way more complicated than I had anticipated. I would have long conversations with individuals that I had come to respect, but I never really attained the blueprint for how to better myself. But as I closely observed the people I looked up to, I began to notice the things that I respected about them. And I decided to incorporate those same characteristics into myself. One guy was someone who always greeted people first, and with a smile. And when you talked to him, he always gave you his full attention, no matter who you were. Another guy would always have the same positive demeanor, day in and day out. Another guy would always lift weights in the yard; rain, snow, or sunshine, he'd go out and exercise. One guy was never able to be baited into an argument. Even if someone was rude to him, he'd still maintain his composure and continue speaking in a calm manner. One guy seemed to know something about everything. I asked how he knew so much, and he answered very simple, "I read the paper." He meant the newspaper, so I started reading the newspaper every single day. I mean, I could go on and on. At the same time, I witnessed the negative consequences people experienced as a result of reckless living. They served as a cautionary tale, in a way.

So ever since then, I have just tried to better myself and treat others well. Whether I interacted with guards, inmates, staff, anybody; I tried to always exhibit a positive and upright character. It was not easy, and can still be difficult at times. But it was very beneficial for me, emotionally. I began to have confidence in myself again; I felt like I had my dignity back. I did not feel like a piece of trash the world threw away anymore.

And it turned out to be my saving grace. As I look back now, I realize there were only 3 things I wanted after I was convicted: to stay close to my family, prove my innocence, and try to be accepted as a genuine person again. I have been blessed to stay close to my family (physically in Jessup), and I have been able to find a sense of self in prison. People in here know me as a stand-up guy. Guards, inmates, staff; people I have been around for almost 17 years and who have seen me every day, recognize me as someone whose word can be trusted. I try to help people if I can, and I never throw it in anyone's face. If someone confides in me, I never break that trust. I try to always be respectful to anyone, and I make sure to be a voice of calm in potentially volatile situations. I try to maintain the ties of friendship with the people I care about, and try to be considerate to strangers.

I guess what I am trying to say is that I was able to find the peace of mind in prison that I lost at my trial. I have lived my life entirely within these walls, not dealing with the outside world. I was able to become someone people trust, and it was not based on any falsehood or manipulation. The one thing about prison that I really appreciate so much is that you really get to see who someone is. When you are around someone 24/7, 365 days a year, you get to see exactly who they are, and how they feel about you. I appreciated that so much because when I was home, I thought people cared about me. But I would come to find out they did not. And I am not saying anyone had to care about me; it was a naïve assumption on my part . . . So in prison, people see exactly who I am, and treat me accordingly. To have the reputation that I have over all these years is because I earned it . . .

People (guards, inmates, staff) express sentiments like that to me. They share with me stories about their children, families, personal things. They may be asking for advice; not because I have any particular knowledge on these subjects but because they trust I will keep their confidence. And this takes place over years. It humbles me and inspires me to be better, because I owe it to the people who feel that way about me. And I owe it to God, who helped me get to a point in my life where I no longer wonder if people think I am evil, or just some horrible person. The people in here know I am not a liar or manipulative because they have been around me for almost 17 years, and I have never exhibited those characteristics.

I have also worked hard at becoming a spiritual person. Not religious; my dad is the most religious person I know. He follows Islamic laws in a very disciplined manner. He is strict with himself, but not with others. That is one of the reasons why I respect him so much. So many people are only as religious as the number of opportunities they get to look down/chastise others. Or be harsh with others. My dad has never been like that. He has always been very kind and compassionate with others, never chastising them. I am more like my mother. She is a spiritual person, but not so much religious. She has her morals & principals, but she also has a lot of fun. She has a strong belief that we are not perfect, but if you treat people well, God will love you. And that if good comes your way, it is from Him. And that if you experience hardships, that may be a means to draw nearer to Him.

So my dad is the type that prays all the time, whereas my mom prays when she needs something. But to her, her worship is the way she treats people and tries to help others. I try to incorporate the things from them I can, and I feel as if I have arrived at a place of understanding the balance. And I can bear witness that since I have been incarcerated, God has protected me from harm and blessed me with so many good things. I feel

He's always protected me because He knows I am innocent. And I believe I earn His blessings through trying to be a good person. I am not saying that I earn all the good things in my life, or even that I earn any of them. I am just saying that I believe that if I do good, I receive good. And if I do bad, then I receive bad. I think if you ask anyone of any religion, they would pretty much say something similar. And they may have experienced the same thing. I do not know if this makes sense, but I can share with you something that may illustrate my point.

As Muslims, we are not supposed to have relationships outside of marriage. So when I arrived at prison, I decided that I was going to try and honor that particular tenet. It was fairly easy at first, because I did not communicate with anyone from outside. But I soon came to learn that living in prison does not preclude someone from having a relationship with a woman. Whether it was a woman working in the prison or from outside, I have seen many relationships occur. There are pen-pal websites, friends of friends, etc. I had several opportunities where I could have chosen to pursue something with a woman, but I always declined. I did my best to abide by that particular tenet of my faith. And then one day, I met Kandra. She had initiated contact with me, and I explained to her that as a Muslim man, I cannot have a relationship with a woman unless there is an intent to consider marriage. To my surprise, she expressed a shared view. We spent time becoming acquainted with each other, and then we decided to get married. We had an amazing relationship and we still care about each other a great deal, and are very close years later. She is such a beautiful and compassionate woman. To me, I feel that I respected the tenets of my faith, and God blessed me with a wonderful experience.

As far as my case, I just studied my transcript and would go to the library and read legal books. It was very hard, but I did my best. And I never really could find anything that proved my innocence. But I was confident that as long as I persisted in trying to better myself & researching my case, God would bless me with something beneficial for my appeal.

As you know, I waited 10 years to file my post-conviction petition. In Maryland, State law provides a 10-year time limit to file it, beginning from the day of sentencing. As I was sentenced June 3, 2000, I had until June 3, 2010 to file this appeal. It was filed on May 29, 2010, 4 days before the expiration date. I had my Direct Appeal, which was denied in 2003. As a matter of procedure, I could have filed my Post then, but I did not. Well, it is not that simple. My family had exhausted their savings on my trial. So there was no money to hire a lawyer. I wrote to several appellate attorneys in

Baltimore City, and each price quoted was between $20-$50,000 just to read my entire case file. Obviously, I did not have any money. And the Public Defender's office does not handle Post-convictions, they only were obligated to handle Direct Appeals. Rabia and Saad would tell me to write the mosque and ask people, but I would have rather died than do that. I never wanted to ask anyone for money. When I was arrested, I was asked to write a letter to the mosque. And I did. But other than that, I never called anyone or wrote anyone asking for anything. Even when I was a kid, I never liked asking for something. I would do it myself, or just do without. And after my trial, I never asked anyone for anything, because I did not want to be accused of manipulating anybody. My parents even offered to sell their house but I told them no.

When I told Rabia & Saad I was not going to ask anyone for anything, that was the first time we got into an argument. I explained that on one hand, if God wanted me to go home, I just had a trial and an appeal. Those did not work out, so it was probably not meant to be for me to go home at that time. I told Rabia I wanted to learn my own case and the law applying to it. I did not want to be completely unaware in court. I never wanted to feel that way ever again. And I wanted to trust in God that He would send me help when it was meant to be . . . Rabia told me I should re-examine the situation because I was making the wrong decision. But that was what I truly believed, and at the end of the day it was my decision, and my life. I was the one sitting in here. This was not a one-time conversation; it took place over years. I tried really hard to convey my gratitude to both Rabia and Saad for standing by me, while at the same time trying to express my reasons for waiting. I know they were coming from a place of love, but how do you handle people thinking you are not fighting for your life, when you are actually fighting for it every single day, the only way that you know . . . I prayed about that decision, and it was not as if I made a decision to wait the entire 10 years, day for day. I was just waiting for something to happen.

But nothing really happened for all those years, and the 10th year was approaching. I researched and researched, but was unable to find anything which proved I was innocent. It was coming close to the expiration date, and I really started to become nervous. Other than the Asia McClain alibi issue, I had not really discovered anything significant in my case. And in the last few months of 2009, I grew really worried. I had never communicated with Asia, not once since I had been arrested. We had no way of knowing where she was, or if she would ever come to court. Or even if she remembered anything from so many years ago.

Anyway, you know how the post went. Even though it was denied, I was still at peace. Upset for my family's sake because I knew it hurt them, and for myself too. But I had peace, as I reflected on how God had taken care of me. He provided me with an opportunity, and I had to be grateful for that. I was able to testify on the witness stand in court, and was finally able to say I did not kill Hae. And if no one believed me, it did not matter. I just wanted to say it. I had a lawyer who was sincere and treated my family in a genuine way. And I was grateful for that. I do not know if Rabia remembers, but we spoke on the phone around the time I got the denial, and she asked me how I was feeling? She was concerned I may have been having a really difficult time, emotionally. But I was not, and I could try to explain why.

So all these years later, my best chance at getting my conviction overturned failed, and I realized I might never make it home. But I had 2 out of 3 things I wanted from the day after my conviction. I was still close with my family, and I had achieved some semblance of being a good person. I do not mean with the outside world. I mean in my world, in here. No one could ever take away all the work I had put in over the past 15 years. All the people in here who care about me (and whom I care about); I am still the same person to them. I can be trusted without betraying that trust, and depended upon. No one in prison has ever accused me of being manipulative or a liar, and that meant everything to me. Maybe more than anything else. And no one from the outside could accuse me of trying to manipulate them because I never dealt with anyone from the outside world anymore. I had made that deal with myself when I was a teenager, and I kept it for all these years. I never asked anyone for anything. To be honest, I never even asked Rabia. Rabia has always cared about me and supported me more than anyone other than my parents. If you re-read every letter that I wrote her, you'd be unable to find anywhere where I'm asking her to advocate for me. It was always just me letting Rabia know I was okay, like religious stuff and funny prison stories, or things like that. I just never wanted her to worry about me.

It used to drive Rabia crazy, and she even cussed me out several times. She had a lot of ideas for the media, reaching out to people, lawyers, etc. But I would always say no. I did not want Rabia to worry about me, or to have to take time away from her own family. She would leave it alone for a while, but inevitably it would come back up, and I would say no. I just wanted to wait for God. I prayed He would not just leave me in here, and as I reflected on all the situations I had witnessed in prison, I always felt His Love and Mercy. But I did not know how to convey that to her. It would really upset Rabia, and it hurt me to understand the negative impact my decisions were having on her. But I felt as if I had no other choice but to wait.

A lot of it was that I did not want to put myself at the mercy of the world. Maybe it sounds crazy, but I could never describe the pain of how it felt to believe that everyone thought I was a murderer. And not just of anyone, but the murderer of one of my closest friends. Someone who loved and trusted me. I never wanted to revisit that. Because when people say I am a manipulative, lying murderer, they are not just saying that I killed Hae. They are saying that I left her body lying in the dirt like garbage, and went about my life as if it was nothing. As if she was nothing. That I made her mother and family's life a living hell for all those weeks they did not know where she was. And that I did not even care that her death would destroy their lives. They are saying I destroy people's lives . . .

I just never wanted to go back to any of that. And without any way to prove my innocence, I was just content to live in prison. Minding my own business; I did not want anything from the outside world. I only wanted to be left alone. I would always work on my case, going to the library and continuing to keep up on cases that were overturned and see if any legal precedents applied to mine. We filed the Leave to Appeal, and I researched how I could try to get one of my issues into federal court. I was just doing my best to be grateful for what I had, and not worry about the things I did not have . . .

And at least I had the peace of mind that I did everything I could. I stayed out of trouble in prison, educated myself to the law & my case to where I could help my lawyer. And I had prayed and tried really hard to become a better person. One of the worst things for me at trial was to feel helpless. I did not know what to do, or understand what was going on. But this time (at my Post), I was able to advocate for myself, in a way. I was able to come to a firm understanding with my attorney, and I spoke up for myself in court. So at the end of the day, I could at least look back and say I did everything I could, and I was grateful for that. For whatever else lay ahead, it would be what it would be. I accepted that, and it gave me peace. And I had some contentment with the circumstances of my life.

CHAPTER 8

SARAH KOENIG

———————•———————

And verily, with hardship, comes ease.

Holy Quran 94:6

If there was tremendous hope in the years leading up to the post-conviction appeal, the aftermath of the hearing brought a sense of depression bordering on desperation. A state prosecutor had testified that we had pressured our alibi witness, an absent witness at that, into making statements. What judge would take our word that a witness who refused to show up had written her more-than-decade-old affidavit in good faith?

It was one of the few times in over a decade that I heard a hint of despondency in Adnan's voice. I think on some level we all knew that the chances of winning the appeal were slim to none, and the prospect of him living the remainder of his years in a supermax facility far from his family were high.

One night about a year after the hearing, in October of 2013, as we still awaited a decision from the court, I flipped through the new shows on Netflix. It was late, the dishes were done, my husband had already retired for the night, and my girls were peacefully conked out. But I couldn't sleep.

I lay on my sofa, feeling restless, when a familiar name caught my eye as I ran through the titles: *West of Memphis*.

It was a new documentary, the most recent of four about a case that had long haunted me, and haunted much of the country. In 1994, three teenagers in West Memphis, Arkansas, were tried for the murders of three young boys a year prior.

Damien Echols, Jessie Misskelley Jr., and Jason Baldwin were all convicted, with Echols receiving the death sentence. Misskelley was sentenced to life plus twenty years and Baldwin was sentenced to life imprisonment.

The crime was shocking, gruesome. On May 3, 1993, three eight-year-old boys disappeared. The three friends, Michael Moore, Steve Branch, and Christopher Byers, had last been seen riding their bikes in the neighborhood. But as darkness fell and their parents began to look for them, they were nowhere to be found. Three days later, after an extensive police search, their small bodies were discovered naked, mutilated, and bound in a nearby creek.

At the time, in the early 1990s, the country was gripped by the fear of occultism and satanism. There was no daytime talk show host who had not covered the topic, and across the nation law enforcement agencies were being trained in the rise of crimes that might be tied to occultist rituals, such as human and animal sacrifice. In the eyes of the local police, this terrible tragedy immediately had the hallmarks of ritual or cult murder.

The impetus for the focus on a satanic angle came from the confused statements of a local child during a May 6, 1993, interview. The boy had accompanied his mother, Vicki Hutcheson, to the police station, where she was going to be interviewed in connection with the case. The attention of the police turned from mother to son when he began offering information about the case, saying the victims had been killed by Spanish-speaking satanists, though he could not pick out Echols, Misskelley, or Baldwin from photographs.

Armed with the conviction that this crime was tied to satanism—much like in Adnan's case where the police were convinced the crime was tied to his religion and culture—the police early on focused in on Echols, who was known to be involved in the occult, kept pentagram-inscripted artifacts, and was also familiar to law enforcement for previous petty crimes. The fact that Echols came from an impoverished family and was diagnosed with severe mental illness, including hallucinations and delusions, which led to months spent earlier in a psychiatric hospital, did not factor into the investigation or mitigate the results of a polygraph that indicated deception.

Misskelley, age sixteen at the time, was questioned exhaustively for nearly twelve hours, though less than two of those hours were actually videotaped by the police. In that time, he confessed to the murders and the involvement of Echols and Baldwin. He would later recant that confession, saying he was exhausted, threatened, and manipulated by the police, and also did not understand the entire interrogation, but the Arkansas Supreme Court would uphold the confession as voluntary, despite the fact that Misskelley had a demonstrated IQ of 72, only three points above the range of mild mental retardation.

From Oprah to Geraldo, the media was breathless and giddy, focused on how occultism led to this tragedy, terrifying the parents of kids who liked heavy metal music and wore smudged black eyeliner to match their brooding dispositions.

A precursor to the media circus that the O. J. Simpson murder trial would become later that year, the West Memphis Three trials were no less of a news frenzy.

But subsequent appeals gave enough time for the release of documentaries in 1996 and 2000, and the publication of the book *Devil's Knot* in 2002. The publicity, which cast doubt on the convictions, spurred a national movement to exonerate the three young men.

Over the following decade the case would be publicly dismantled. Hutcheson recanted her testimony, citing police coercion that forced her to lie or face losing custody of her son; juror misconduct came to light; and most compelling, DNA testing on a hair found in the shoelace used to tie up little Stevie Branch's feet came back negative for all three defendants. Instead, it matched Stevie's stepfather, Terry Hobbs, whose whereabouts were unaccounted for in the hours the boys went missing.

The defense team strategically made the DNA findings public and laid the groundwork to move for a new trial. After the same trial judge refused to re-open the case, it moved to the Arkansas Supreme Court.

Finally, in November 2010 the Arkansas Supreme Court granted all three defendants new trials based on the DNA testing results and juror misconduct. But the State opted not to retry the case, and instead offered Alford pleas to Echols, Baldwin, and Misskelley.

In August 2011 the three were released, having accepted the plea—a convoluted legal construction that requires them to accept guilt for the crime, but also maintain their innocence. Three young men lost eighteen years of their lives, but as far as the State is concerned, the case is closed. The investigation into the brutal murder of three little boys will not be reopened, and the culprit will remain free.

In 2012, the documentary *West of Memphis* was released, chronicling the eighteen-year-long battle of these three young men.

Over the years, as appeals came and went, every so often I'd float the idea to Adnan of taking the case to a journalist. I pointed out that numerous wrongful convictions were revisited and reopened when public scrutiny came to bear on the State. But time and time again, often after arguing, we made the calculation to wait until the post-conviction, when Asia could be presented along with a claim of ineffective assistance of counsel.

That night, when the documentary ended, I made an executive, unilateral decision. I was going to find a journalist to investigate the case. And I wasn't going to ask anyone's permission. Adnan's resignation was increasing and I didn't want him to make a decision to spare his family public scrutiny at the expense of an independent investigation of the murder.

I rolled off of the sofa and took my place at the laptop on the dining room table. It was very late at night, but this couldn't wait any longer. I had to move on my impulse immediately and find the right person for the job.

Imagine a gritty, worn-down crime reporter. A seasoned, cynical, smart-ass skeptic with a face full of worry lines and a trash bin full of liquor bottles. A journalist who cut his or her teeth on the streets of Baltimore, someone who knew all the snitches, the dirty cops, the tough judges. Who had sources and street cred. Who knew how to dig up skeletons buried deep and long ago. Most importantly, a local.

Such a reporter maybe only exists in John Grisham novels, but that's who I had in mind. It was not remotely close to the one I found.

That night I began looking for a reporter who had actually covered the murder or Adnan's trial in 1999. The very first person I came across was Sarah Koenig.

Her name wasn't familiar, but she had written a piece for the *Baltimore Sun* in June of 2001 on the disbarment of Gutierrez in the face of overwhelming client complaints.

I thought about it for a second. It wasn't the kind of coverage I was looking for, but if this woman recalled writing about a lawyer who had botched many cases, maybe she'd be interested in one of those cases.

So I crossed my fingers, said a little prayer, and began my Internet hunt, hoping Sarah was still at the *Baltimore Sun*. She was not.

She was now a producer at *This American Life*, a radio show that I was vaguely familiar with. I couldn't remember if I had actually listened to any of their shows, but I knew they played on public radio.

At that point I really hesitated. A radio producer? And not even for local shows? But I went ahead and shot her an e-mail anyway, and within a day I heard back from her.

I was careful to write to Sarah from my New America Foundation e-mail account. After all, I wanted her to know I wasn't some kook with a conspiracy theory.

Rabia Chaudry <chaudry@newamerica.org>   8/12/13
to Elise ▾

Can you please pass this message on to Ms. Koenig:

Dear Ms. Koenig,

In 2001 you covered a number of stories for the Baltimore Sun related to the disbarment of attorney Christina Gutierrez. Of the many client complaints that lead to her disbarment, one was missing, that of Adnan Syed. Adnan was Christina's client and, as an 18 year old, facing murder charges. Adnan was found guilty and has been serving a life sentence since 1999.

Since that time I have been peripherally involved in his case, through many appeals, and now his final state appeal. Over the years we have gathered enough evidence to show that Christina willfully lost Adnan's case and that serious prosecutorial misconduct occurred, indicating the police and DA's office knew that Adnan was innocent but were best positioned to get a conviction against him.

This is a matter that can and should have serious repercussions against both the DA's office and police. This story needs to be told. I was hoping you have contacts with investigative reporters at the Sun, or that you would be interested in taking a look at this.

I appreciate any help or guidance. I assure you, I'm not a quack. I'm an attorney doing national security work, but this case has haunted me since law school. I look forward to hearing from you,

Rabia Chaudry
Fellow, National Security Studies Program
New America Foundation

After exchanging many e-mails and a couple of phone calls, we met about ten days later in Baltimore. I wanted to show her not just the documents I held but also the area surrounding the case, so we decided to meet at my little one-room space across the street from Woodlawn High. There was another reason to meet there—to possibly facilitate a meeting between Sarah and Adnan's family.

That was the tricky part, though. I hadn't asked Adnan, his attorney, or his family for permission to take the case to the media.

My plan was to forge ahead and ask for forgiveness afterward. I'd get their blessing once I knew Sarah was going to take the story. For now, I had to focus on making my case to Sarah, and I looped in Saad in order to do so.

Saad and I waited in my little office, where I mostly kept client files of cases I was closing out as I wrapped up my legal practice, visiting a few times a month to check mail and messages.

On my desk was a battered, water-damaged cardboard box. I had kept this box with me for the past fourteen years. In it were two sadly beat-up folders. One contained letters, dozens of letters Adnan had written over the years. The other contained a selection of documents from Adnan's extensive case files that I thought showed something was deeply wrong with his conviction. I had pulled them years before from the rest of his files, which had been passed around to various appellate lawyers and now rested in the basement of his parents' home.

The front doorbell played a jingle and then came a tentative "Hello, Rabia?"

I walked out of the room and into the main office reception area to greet Sarah, with Saad close behind me.

I had no idea that Sarah Koenig was a big deal, in a nationally known, award-winning-big-deal kind of way. And nothing about her unassuming appearance, or demeanor, would suggest it either. She was tall and lanky, looking every part the seasoned, pavement-pounding reporter in an informal green cotton blouse, loose woven pants, and a network of black bags slung across her shoulders. Without makeup, her wavy hair on the verge of rebellion, she looked like she was serious about her work without taking herself too seriously. She entered with a broad smile, cautiously friendly, but also slightly awkward as she fumbled with the microphone she held.

I invited her back into my room and we got settled in. She wanted us to start at the beginning. So we did.

I gave her a short summary of the case, of who Adnan was, of our belief in his innocence, and our disbelief in the State's primary evidence, their dodgy eye witness. Saad chimed in about his friendship with Adnan, their girlfriends and dating habits, and what it was like to be the first-generation kid of immigrant parents. All the while Sarah asked questions and continued taping.

Then I began pulling out the documents, apologizing for their condition. Even some of the individual pages themselves were damaged from having been in the trunk of my car for years.

I showed her a copy of Alonzo Sellers' polygraph tests, the police report taken from the man who said his daughter was told by Ernest Carter, Jay's friend, that he had seen a body in the trunk of a car, a vast spreadsheet created to keep track of the details of Jay's changing police statements, and most importantly, the letters and affidavit from Asia.

After doing my best to convince her that there was a real story here, a wrongful conviction, I broke the news—that I hadn't yet told (or asked) Adnan about any of this.

But I told her I would, and in the meantime, to help her decide whether to proceed or not, that she should write to Adnan and ask him to add her to his visitor list.

My plan, however, was to get to him before she did. And to do that, I needed his mom on my side.

I was nervous; I knew this could go badly. Aunty Shamim might be really upset that I betrayed their trust and contacted a journalist without asking permission, and she could refuse to cooperate because she didn't have the emotional wherewithal to deal with reopening old wounds so publicly.

Either way, I knew I had to be honest about it.

"Adnan never wanted me to go to the media because he thought it would really hurt you. He thinks the community has gone quiet about the issue and if it's brought back up in the media it will be hard on you and Yusuf. That's why he's been hoping that the post-conviction appeal would give him relief and we could avoid the media altogether. But Aunty, the appeal is not going to work."

Aunty looked confused.

"What do you mean, Adnan doesn't want me to be hurt?"

I explained it all again and she started crying.

"I don't care about anything, about the community or what people will say, the only thing that matters is getting him home. Yes, please, let's do this. I want to talk to the reporter too."

It took less than five minutes to get her permission. Now it was time to write to Adnan and tell him all about Sarah Koenig.

November 25, 2013

Dear Ms. Koenig,

I hope this finds you well. Thank you for finding the time to respond to my letter. I definitely understand that you must be very busy with your work, and I just want to express how grateful my family and I am for your efforts in trying to shed some new light on my case. Rabia always used to say that a fresh pair of eyes may uncover something that we have overlooked or discover something that may be crucial. And regardless of the outcome, just the fact that you have taken time to read through the voluminous paperwork involved really means the world to us. I don't think we can thank you enough.

I received your letter on the 19th and I submitted your name (the same day) to be placed on my visiting list. I received the approval today [. . .]

On another note, I really appreciate what you wrote in your letter about deciding to work on the story. I understand that until something that truly exonerates me is uncovered, no one other than me (and the person who really killed Hae) will ever know that I am innocent. And I'm grateful that you wrote that you trust me, and I place that in a very high regard. [. . .]

I've been trying to recall any aspects of the case that could use some explanation. I've thought of a few things, and if it is alright with you, I wanted to take some time to explain who Jay Wilds was to me, and why I lent him my car that day.

In order to understand my relationship with Jay Wilds, I have to first explain my relationship with Stephanie McPherson (who was Jay's girlfriend at the time). Stephanie and I met in 6th or 7th grade. We were really sweet on each other, and became good friends. By the end of 8th grade, we had officially became boyfriend and girlfriend. We would hug and kiss in school, write each other love notes etc. I would go to her house and play basketball, and we would make out and stuff in her basement. As you would imagine 2 8th-graders would. This was in 1995.

That summer, we didn't really see much of each other. She went to some basketball camps, and me and some of my buddies had got some fake I.D.'s. So we started going to clubs, where I was meeting other girls. So we kinda lost touch, until the first day of 9th grade. We talked about our summer vacations, and it was cool. We just decided to be friends, and we were the best of friends up until the day I was arrested. We were kinda more than friends, like she would sit in my lap, and we world sorta make out (I'm talking about in class). We would talk on the phone a lot, and I would still go to her house sometimes. Anyway, in the 9th grade she started dating Jay. Now, I had known Jay in middle school. He was one grade ahead of me. I used to ride bikes and smoke marijuana with some of my friends, and Jay was like a mutual friend. So he wasn't my friend per se, but he was friends with some of my friends. So that was the extent of our relationship up until he and Stephanie started dating (in the 9th grade—1996).

So, throughout high school, Stephanie and I grew closer. Once we got our driver's licenses, we would go out together on like, double dates. Sometimes during the evening, usually Jay and I would go smoke some weed. I got to know him a little better, along with Stephanie talking about him to me over the phone.

[. . .] So now, fast forward to January 13, 1999. That is the day when Hae disappeared. That is also Stephanie's birthday. About 10am in the morning, I left school that day to go to Jay's house, to see if he had bought her a birthday present. He said no, so I told him he could drop me off at school and use my car to go to the mall and buy her one. I had already gave her a birthday present in class that morning. I left my cell phone in the car, cause back then you could get suspended from school if you had a beeper or a cell phone on you. So I finished the school day, went to the library after school, and then went to track practice. Afterwards Jay came and picked me up. By this time it was dark, so it had to be around 5:00pm.

Looking back, I always knew that Jay was jealous of my relationship with Stephanie. He would ask me things (when we were smoking weed) like, "Man, would you tell me if you were screwing Steph?" and "She talks to you on the phone more than me." Particularly around that time period. Stephanie had told me she was gonna break up with Jay when she went off to college. Jay told me, and asked me if I knew about it. I told him that I did, and he wasn't too happy about that. At our prom (in '98) I was the prom king and Stephanie was the prom queen. We had a dance together in the middle of everyone, and had our pictures taken for the yearbook. I had bought two copies of the yearbook and gave one to Stephanie, and she told me Jay caught an attitude when she showed it to him.

Prior to my dating Hae, quite a few people in school thought Stephanie and I were involved. Some knew she was dating Jay and still would say that. We had a social studies class each day, and for the first five minutes of class (before the bell rung), she would sit in my lap and we'd be joking and laughing with our friends. We would hug and kiss each other, and in a more-than-friends type of way. This was in my senior year, up until I was arrested. If she didn't have any money, I would buy her lunch and we'd sit together. Things like that.

My reason for mentioning all this to you, Mrs. Koenig, is that I think it's pretty relevant. I shared all of this with Ms. Gutierrez, in much more detail. She told me she tried to arrange a meeting with Stephanie and a P.I. but Stephanie's family (and she) refused to talk. So none of it was mentioned at trial. A few years after I was sentenced, a friend of mine named Krista Meyers (now Krista Remmers) struck up a conversation with Stephanie via e-mail, it was like an online chat, I think. She asked Stephanie why she turned on me and Stephanie's reply was: He was my best friend, but I never heard from him after he was arrested, so all this stuff must be true.

Which brings me to my next point. When I was initially arrested, each lawyer I came into contact with stressed vehemently "Do not talk to anyone about your case." They told me that my phone calls were being recorded, my letters were being screened, etc. And so I didn't. Some people would write me asking me if I committed the crime, but I never wrote back. And over the years, I would come to find out that a lot of people took that as a sign of guilt. [. . .] Now, don't get me wrong. My family and Rabia's family on one side, and the whole world on the other, and they are more than enough support for me . . . But I think a person may look and wonder how could so many people who knew me come to believe I could commit this crime. And I think my lack of denial/communication played a good-sized part in that.

Krista was someone who was really in my corner. She knew Hae and Stephanie, and was a really amazing friend, both before and after I was arrested. She visited me in Jessup several times, but as the years went by, we fell out of touch. Not in a bad way, but just as life goes on. I have no idea if she still believes I'm innocent or not, but I have a feeling that either way, she wouldn't mind speaking with you. [. . .]

Sorry for this to be so long. Other than at trial, I've never really talked to anyone about these things. I've certainly never talked to anyone in-depth about Hae and I. I did not know how it would go over with you. I tried to talk to Justin Brown about it and he immediately cut me off and said that none of that mattered at this stage. [. . .] In my heart, I always wonder if things would've turned out differently if the jury had heard me speak about Hae and our relationship/friendship. But I guess that's just wishful thinking . . . I will say this, I'm thankful you weren't all "professional" about it like Justin was. Don't get me wrong, he's a really sincere lawyer and a really nice guy. But I really had to work up the nerve to talk to him about how I'm innocent, and I never would've harmed Hae. I'm about 3 sentences in when he cut me off, "Adnan, listen. I'm your lawyer. None of that stuff matters at this point. We're working on your Post-conviction petition. That's what matters." So while I appreciated his candor, eventually one day I'm gonna tell him he was a real jerk about it . . .

I hope you have a good holiday. Take care.

Sincerely,
Adnan Syed

I was hugely relieved when Adnan agreed to hand the case over to a journalist. And it was an even bigger relief when Sarah, having connected with Adnan and others and reviewed enough documents to hook her, announced she was doing the story. In order to move forward, though, she needed the rest of the documents.

I met Sarah at Adnan's parents' house. His mom led us down into the small basement to a closet filled with the kinds of boxes that are synonymous with musty legal files. There must have been close to a dozen of them.

I hadn't seen these files for almost thirteen years. I first helped the family retrieve them from a storage room where Cristina Gutierrez's case files were being held for her clients to pick up after she died. I then took the files to my parent's home and went through them. They had to be delivered to his appellate lawyers, though, and I didn't have much time.

I spent a couple of weeks, speed-reading and pulling the documents that I wanted to copy for myself, the ones that would eventually make it into the box in my car. I then delivered the full set of files back to Adnan's family and they passed them on to his lawyer. Over the years these boxes had made the rounds between the lawyers and his home, the last round being at Justin Brown's office, who had returned them a couple of years prior. Adnan's family had never gone through them.

Sarah started going through the files, and I stood by with a legal pad handy to note the ones she was going to take. After a while we both gave up and realized she needed too many to keep track. She took a few boxes that day, and then returned to get the rest.

During the first couple of months of her investigation, Sarah and I were in constant communication as I tried to get whatever she needed to her, and introduce her to the community and to people who knew Adnan, like his former attorney Chris Flohr.

Although it's hard to know exactly what convinced her that this story would be worth her time, and that there was a potential injustice here, her talk with Chris may have been what cinched it. They met at a restaurant shortly after her initial meeting with Saad and me, and she got right down to business.

She asked Chris what the deal was, was this guy really innocent, because she wasn't about to waste time on the case otherwise.

Chris reassured her that yes, this was a case that needed to be investigated and that he personally always felt Adnan was innocent. In fact, a few years prior Chris had sent Adnan a letter, his first communication with him since he had stopped representing him in 1999. For all these years he hadn't stopped thinking about Adnan. He knew that the wrong person had been convicted of this crime. The letter he sent explained a new brain-mapping technology that could determine if a person's mind had certain memories that could only be stored if they had indeed experienced an event. So if Adnan had nothing to do with Hae's murder, this technology could prove his brain had no such memories stored.

Adnan had sent me the letter, and after doing some research I learned that the technology was so new, it wasn't yet recognized by any jurisdiction as evidence. Plus, there was no way Justin would be interested in pursuing something that would distract from his PCR petition, especially something untested.

Adnan had written Chris back to thank him, but we never pursued his suggestion. Still, Adnan was deeply grateful that he still remembered him and made the effort to reach out to an old client.

It was early in 2014 when Sarah told me the great news that *This American*

Life would be committing her and other staff full-time to this story and conducting a full investigation. But I still wondered if I had done the right thing.

The problem was that I didn't know if an episode of *This American Life* was going to be able to make a dent in the case itself—it would go by like a blip, barely registering on the Baltimore legal system.

So my hope was not that her final product, the story itself, would prompt a public outcry or movement for Adnan's exoneration. My hope instead was that once she had gone through the documents, understood the weakness of the evidence and conviction, and met Adnan, she would be a reporter on a quest to find the smoking gun that would prove Adnan was innocent. I wanted to use her investigative skills, and her skills at getting people to talk, to uncover evidence that could get us a new appeal. What her story looked like at the end didn't concern me so much. It was the investigation that mattered.

But my concern remained about *This American Life*, even as an investigative tool. In a weird way, being such a big, national outlet with no local ties could prove to be its Achilles heel when it came to this case. So I asked her if she would be willing to work with a local reporter. She didn't respond immediately but a month or two later teamed up with Justin George of the *Baltimore Sun* to do some of the local work.

Before that, though, she had a breakthrough. But it was not early enough to save the appeal. The judge had made his ruling.

Sarah got the news before I did, but she didn't share it with me even though we were communicating almost daily. I hadn't heard from her in a couple of weeks and wondered what was going on. I dismissed it, thinking it was the holidays, but later she would tell me she didn't want to talk to me until I found out.

The post-conviction appeal was denied on December 30, 2013. When Justin e-mailed me the news, I was devastated, even though I fully expected it.

My eyes stung with the heat of anger and tears as I read the judge's opinion. The circuit court had dismissed both claims of ineffective assistance of counsel. The judge found that Gutierrez's failure to ask the State for a plea deal for her seventeen-year-old client did not rise to the level of incompetence, and that there was no guarantee the State would have offered a plea or that Adnan would have taken one, despite the fact that he had taken and passed a polygraph stating he would have.

As far as the court was concerned, Gutierrez didn't fumble the ball on Asia; rather she had "several reasonable strategic grounds" for not pursuing her as an alibi witness. Most interestingly, the court found that Asia's letters "did not clearly show [her] potential to provide a reliable alibi." That the court pointedly noted that Asia's only statements were through her letters is an indication that her in-person testimony may have changed the judge's mind.

But then there was the very strange assertion by the judge that Adnan himself contradicted Asia's statements. He noted that Adnan testified he never left the school campus until after track practice, whereas Asia saw him in the public library. Except (1) Adnan never testified to any such thing and (2) even if he had, the library was for all intents and purposes on the school campus.

Reading the opinion made me feel like the judge heard very little of what actually happened in his courtroom. I was bitterly upset. Didn't a man's life mean enough for the court to at least get right what he had testified to?

But I knew much of this was about Urick's testimony. Any judge who believed that a witness gave written statements under duress by the defendant or his family and friends would likely discount those statements completely. And any judge who heard this from the mouth of a prosecutor, under oath, would believe every word.

In the face of this denial, Justin did the only thing he could. He filed what's called an Application for Leave to Appeal or an ALA. Essentially this application is an appeal to the higher court, the Court of Special Appeals of Maryland, requesting one more shot at the same post-conviction claims raised earlier. In Maryland, it is granted in only 1.2 percent of cases.

While he filed the ALA, he also notified Adnan that this would probably be the end of his representation. The Court of Special Appeals would summarily deny the ALA and it would be game over. There was nowhere else to take this case.

I dreaded the inevitable call from Adnan.

What do you say?

"I'm so sorry, the one chance you had after waiting for more than a decade is now gone. Sorry that it's all over."

I didn't say anything, I just cried. Adnan's response to my teary, mumbled, snotty outpouring was to reassure me, as always.

"It's ok, it's ok. It's from Allah. He's the only Judge that counts. We'll appeal this. It's not the end."

That was the moment I knew it all came down to Sarah. Sarah had to deliver or Adnan would die in prison. The first glimmer of hope that she would came when I got a slightly dazed and dumbfounded call from her.

"Rabia. I spoke to Asia."

After numerous attempts to get a hold of Asia—who seemed as unreachable and mythic as a unicorn—Sarah finally got the call she'd been waiting for in mid-January of 2014.

Asia was timid at first, unsure about what Sarah wanted, why this case was coming back to interrupt her life, why there wasn't closure on it after all these years. Asia explained to Sarah why she didn't respond to Adnan's attorney's repeated attempts to solicit her for the appeal. As far as she knew and was concerned, a court of law had found Adnan guilty of first-degree murder. She believed in the justice system and didn't think such a conviction could stand without solid proof tying him to the murder. And now, all these years later, having never heard from Adnan after her letters in 1999, this murderer—or at least his lawyer—had found her home all the way across the country, where she lived with her children.

She freaked out, plain and simple, she told Sarah. And then she called the State's Attorney's office. How and why they connected her to Urick, a former and not current prosecutor, is unclear. Nonetheless, Urick assured her that Adnan had been convicted on irrefutable evidence and that he was now trying to game the system for a new trial.

The rub was this: Asia told Sarah that she still remembered seeing Adnan at the library after school, around 2:30 p.m., on January 13, 1999. She remembered their conversation, including his telling her that he and Hae had broken up but he still cared for her and wished her the best. She recalled her boyfriend and his friend coming to the library to pick her up, hours late to her chagrin, and her boyfriend's irritation that she had been chatting with a good-looking guy when he arrived.

Asia remembered the storm that night that left her stranded at her boyfriend's house, and that school was closed for the days following. She recalled the letters she wrote to Adnan after his arrest and that she'd concluded that there must be a reason he never responded.

Sarah called me, elated, but much to her surprise, news of her talk with Asia brought us little joy. My first reaction was tears. Not just tears of sorrow but of rage. Adnan knew, his family knew, I knew that Asia had never been pressured by anyone to write anything. I was glad that Sarah now knew that we didn't make Asia say any of it, because she clearly still stood by it.

We couldn't understand why Urick testified that Asia had told him she'd been pressured to offer her documents. Did Asia tell him that? Sarah didn't ask Asia about it either—she didn't want to scare her off. Sarah wanted to let her talk, give it time, and then circle back about that. She didn't know then that she would not get to speak to Asia again for a very long time.

It didn't really matter now. The timing of this conversation, of Asia's affirmation to Sarah of what we knew was the truth, was the final blow, the deepest cut. If it had happened a month earlier, perhaps it could have altered the course of the appeal. But now, having lost the PCR just weeks earlier, it was too late.

Sarah continued her investigation and was now routinely speaking with Adnan a few times a week. She also met with him numerous times.

I felt a certain amount of stress over their meetings and conversations, maybe from overthinking things.

I had no idea, and no way to ask without seeming ridiculous, whether Sarah personally knew any Muslims. After what happened at the bail hearing and trial, I worried: would she be able to approach our community with total objectivity? Like any human being, she might process it all through her own biases, biases that could be primed after 9/11. And while Sarah could get to know Adnan's family, Saad, and me on a human level because we could communicate with her freely and hang out with her in our homes, her access to Adnan would be controlled.

It would be through timed, awkward phone calls, or meetings across a table, divided by a half-pane of glass, surrounded by guards, bound to the stiff seats, psychologically restrained if not physically. She would see a large, hulking, built-out man with a long beard, skullcap, rolled-up prison-issue jeans, and DOC-printed sweatshirt; a man severely limited in his ability to show her who he fully was as a human being, looking instead like the archetypical prison Muslim.

She would not see the lanky kid who had been locked up in 1999, and her investigation would always be through this filter. Such concerns may seem overly sensitive, but having spent the last decade working on fighting negative perceptions of Muslims and the bigoted policies those perceptions end up producing, my fear was real. It is the fear any Muslim who visibly looks Muslim has—that we are immediately judged by others based on our appearance.

And then there was Adnan, who had never spoken to a journalist before. Who never had to answer questions about his innocence because those of us in touch with him never asked him. We knew he was innocent.

With a journalist, however, it needed to be said. Everything needed to be said. I wondered what it would be like for him to open up for the first time, to be challenged, to tell his story to a stranger, many parts of which he never told the rest of us. Remember that rule about looking the other way, not prying? It was simply not culturally acceptable even between us, between Adnan and his family or me, for him to share the intimate details of his relationship with Hae, his feelings about her disappearance and death, and to a certain extent even his private life as an inmate.

Every so often I'd ask Adnan how it was going with Sarah. What was their relationship like? Did she like him? Did he feel comfortable? His response would always be, "Alhamdulillah, everything is fine."

I would try to reassure him—and myself—that she was on "our side," that she wouldn't put this much time and effort into this story if she didn't think he was innocent. I wouldn't know until later that her discussions with Adnan showed that she wasn't ever fully convinced of his innocence.

Guilt or innocence aside, fairly early on I realized that we weren't actually on the "same side." I had misunderstood our relationship, and I had no one to blame but myself. Call me naïve, but one day I finally got it.

Sarah contacted me in May to tell me she'd be in the area and asked if she could swing by. With her would be one of her colleagues; they planned on doing the ride between the school and Best Buy to see if they could complete it within twenty-one minutes—the time between when school let out at 2:15 p.m. and the "come and get me call" from Adnan to Jay, according to the State.

I was excited. This exercise would debunk one of the most ridiculous aspects of the State's narrative: that in this short span of time, while accounting for being able to get out of a school lot crowded with buses and student cars, Adnan could somehow get into Hae's car, get her down the road to Best Buy, strangle her, move her to the trunk in the light of day in a public parking lot, then trot around the lot to make a call from a pay phone at 2:36 p.m. And I would be there when Sarah tried it and saw that it just couldn't work.

The line got drawn right then and there, though. In the nicest way possible Sarah said she couldn't take me along. She didn't explicitly say why, she was kind about it, but that's when I realized, oh wait, we aren't actually friends. She had a job to do, and my presence could impede it.

Sarah never told me the results of her experimental drive, and I didn't ask. I was too preoccupied because on that same day she came to show me a document she'd found in the police files. It was a document I'd never seen before, one that left my head pounding, my stomach twisted in knots.

It was a cultural research memo, and the name of the person and agency who wrote it was blacked out. I had no idea it existed, but it helped explain much of why the investigation in Hae's murder focused on Adnan.

Adnan:

At the end of September 2013, I received a brief letter from my attorney. He informed me that he had been contacted by a journalist named Sarah Koenig. She asked him several questions about my case, and they spoke at length. He explained to me that she was interested in investigating the case, and maybe doing a story. He advised me that I could speak with her if I wanted, and he saw no harm in it. He ended his letter by stating his understanding that she would not expend the time and resources to do a story unless she felt I was innocent. I received a letter from Ms. Koenig a day or so later. I did not know at the time, but she mentioned Rabia had reached out to her, and explained everything about the case to her. I was surprised, as Rabia had never mentioned her to me. I guess she figured I would probably say no, like I always had.

Ms. Koenig's letter was very simple and straightforward: she was considering doing an investigation into my case, and potentially doing a story. But there was no mention of her only doing a story if she thought I was innocent. So I was very confused, and really at a loss for how to proceed. I mean, her letter was very self-explanatory, but contrast it with my attorney's. She stated she wanted to review the case, but my attorney indicated she would not do anything unless she thought I was innocent . . . Two entirely different things. At least to me, anyway. I had no idea what to do. On the one hand, I had always been opposed to Rabia's suggestions of going to the media. I had been telling her no for years. And beyond making Rabia mad, I realized how hurtful it was to her. To want to help me any way she could, and I always refused. I guess she finally just went ahead and did it.

But from my attorney's letter, I have to prove to Ms. Koenig that I am innocent. Which I cannot do. So now I am heading back to a place I never wanted to revisit. And that is to be in the untenable position of having to prove to someone that I did not do something, that I did not do, and no one proved that I did it anyway.

To be honest, I did not really expect Ms. Koenig to do much. I figured she would just read the files and do a brief story or whatever. And that would be it. I thought I might have to answer a list of questions. I had no idea what my participation would entail, and I was not really looking forward to speaking with her.

But when I spoke to Rabia about it, she explained that this was what we had been waiting for. She told me that she had been working on this for a while, and that we were at a point where we had nothing to lose. The thing I remember the most is how Rabia constantly said, "we," as if she were in here with me. She has always said that, and it is something that has stuck with me throughout all these years. As I listened to Rabia, I realized I had no choice but to do it. Even if that meant having to go through all that stuff all over again.

Rabia mentioned that maybe this was God's Help that I had been waiting for. And I had not really thought about it that way. I was just thinking about the negatives this experience would have in store for me. Initially, I was hoping that maybe Ms. Koenig would find something that would prove my innocence. But I had been disappointed so many times before, that I did not really have high expectations. More importantly, I did not know how to respond to her. What to say in a reply letter? Maybe she was a crime reporter who had seen it all, and believed everyone says they're innocent. Also, I have no piece of evidence which proved my innocence. Maybe some things that make the State's case look weak, but nothing else. So what do I do? The only thing I have ever been able to hang onto and no one can disprove is that I never had any animosity towards Hae, and that I cared about her deeply. That was all I had. So I prayed about it, and that was what I wrote to her about. And that was the point where my past emotional insecurities returned.

Was she going to think I was trying to manipulate her by lying about Hae, and how I felt about her? Maybe Ms. Koenig would believe that I selected this topic in order to tug at her heart strings. Or maybe it was because our friendship was the only thing incontrovertible at trial. The State had never been able to even offer any evidence to contradict that. I do not know, it was just that everything came back, about how nobody believed me. Maybe she would be the same, and I was not eager about opening up to someone who was going to think I was just trying to manipulate her. So now I am kind of paralyzed with uncertainty. If I do not write her, I am letting Rabia down. But if I do write her, I am risking going back to that place. I did not really know what to do. So I prayed for guidance, and the next day I just wrote the letter and put it in the mail. I did not know what Ms. Koenig's reaction would be; but if nothing else, I have honored the obligation I had to Rabia. And if she were to think I was trying to manipulate her, well, there was nothing I could do about that.

So now it was out of my hands. I was done, and I just had to wait and see what happened. Secretly, I hoped she would not reply, and that would be the end of it. But then she wrote me back, and requested that I call her. I was fairly nervous at that point, as I really did not know what type of person she was. Maybe she would not give me a fair chance. I had no idea if she was a genuine person. More importantly, now I had to figure out how to deal with her.

See, in prison, I have learned that you cannot be yourself with everybody, because it may come back to hurt you. You cannot be generous with everyone, because some people will take advantage of you. You cannot be friendly with everybody, because it may cause you to lose respect in the sight of others. You cannot take the high road in all confrontations because some people will see it as an invitation to harm you. You have to approach every interaction with correct perspective. If you are in a cell with somebody, you may not be able to share your property with him (food, hygiene, etc.) because he may take advantage of it. If you are working with someone, you cannot joke around with him because it may cause problems when you are trying to be serious. If someone disrespects you, you cannot always walk away because it may be taken as a sign of weakness. Knowing the correct perspective has nothing to do with getting anything in return; rather, it is about protecting yourself when dealing with people who have the potential to harm you. And it is not just in prison, but in the outside world, too. And what I have learned is that whatever perspective you decide on, it is important to be consistent. To change the course once you set on it can have a bad effect.

So when I met Ms. Koenig, I had to decide what perspective was the correct one to take with her. Essentially, how to protect myself. Do I try to explain everything in my case that I think is wrong? Because that makes sense. The problem with that was it opens the door for me to be accused of manipulating or misleading her. And I do not want to experience that again. On the other hand, I could just remain quiet and simply answer her questions, and hope and pray she would come to find out those things for herself. I mean, everything is in the case; it is in the interviews and the transcripts. There's nothing I know that is not already in there. And I have always felt confident that if someone unbiased took a look, they would find the same troubling discrepancies. But I would be taking a risk that maybe she might miss these things. So I did not know how to protect myself with her. I prayed about it, and I decided to choose the latter approach. That I would just be as honest with her as possible in answering her questions, and hope she would see the things that I felt were not right, on her own.

I also decided that I did not want to do anything that could even remotely seem like I was trying to befriend or curry favor with her. Initially, I never addressed her by her first name, even though she asked me to on several occasions. I only called her at the times she instructed me to. I only wrote her when she would send me a letter. Other than a perfunctory "How are you?" I never inquired about her personally. And whenever she asked me how I was, I would always reply with, "I'm fine, thank you." That way I was not being personal with her. I did not want her to ever be able to accuse me of trying to ingratiate myself with her, or manipulate her. And I really tried to stick to that.

But she consistently tried to establish a rapport with me each time I called. She would always ask how I was doing, and inquire more. She would share little random things with me about her day, work, maybe what she ate for lunch. I realized that this was probably her interview style. That maybe the easiest way to get someone to open up would be to establish a familiarity. Which in turn would make a person more comfortable with opening up. She was a very kind person and seemed very compassionate. But it became very stressful, because I had every intent to be as honest with her as possible. There was no need for any strategy on her part; I just wanted to answer her questions and be done with it. And perhaps it is unfair to call it a strategy, as that may infer a negative connotation. Like I said, she is a very kind person, and I mistook her kindness to be something else. It caused me a great deal of anxiety, as I felt that I was not being true to my principles regarding how I treat people.

I had spent all these years trying to be personable towards others. But to be in a position where I am constantly speaking with someone who is kind enough to share all these things with me, and I cannot reciprocate that kindness? Because I am afraid of being accused of trying to manipulate her; I cannot ask how she is doing, or about her day. And it really hit me hard one day when she asked me why I would always reply, "I'm fine, thank you" whenever she inquired about my well-being. I felt I was being terribly rude to her, and ungrateful. It seemed as if it did not matter to me that she cared enough to ask how I was. One time, she shared with me that she had recently experienced the loss of a family member. It was heartbreaking to hear the grief in her voice, but I was afraid to express my sympathies to her because I did not want to appear as if I had an ulterior motive. I could not change my approach; my life in prison had taught me to be consistent. I mean, it was a horrible feeling. Can you imagine what it is like to be afraid to show compassion to someone out of fear that you would not be believed? Especially when that someone has been nothing but compassionate with you? She had exhibited a great deal of kindness to me, and I was afraid to treat her the same. I was so ashamed of myself at that time.

I just tried to be as honest with her as possible and I prayed that she would come to learn those things about my case. And she did. She even learned some things that I did not know. There was nothing huge, no smoking-gun. But they are things that I believe strengthen my claims of innocence. Facts and evidence that should exist if I had truly committed this crime; they were not there. And there were facts and evidence that further discredited the State's case and theory. And I was grateful for that. Because it was all in the transcripts, interviews & tapes. I did not need to point her towards anything. Like I said, I have always believed that a person could find these things out for themselves. She arrived at all her conclusions on her own. It had nothing to do with me. And no one could ever accuse me of manipulating her into any of that.

At least, I thought so up until the day when I asked her about what made her decide to do the story. She had been pretty clear with me that she could not say I was innocent. To the contrary, the tone and content of most of her questions led me to believe she felt that I was lying about many things. But the words from my attorney's letter always stayed in my mind; that she would not do the story unless she thought I was innocent. So I figured she decided to do the story because of Hae, or because the case appeared to be very wrong. But she responded that it was because of me, and that it seemed like I was a good person. And that it was difficult to reconcile the person she had spent so many hours interviewing with the person who committed this heinous crime.

To hear this was very frustrating, because it took me right back to square one. Instead of me being accused of manipulating her through the case, now I am going to be accused of being manipulative in my personal interactions with her. Which I tried to limit anyway, and I never intended to have and specifically sat out trying to avoid. And I got pretty upset when she said that. And I realize this all may sound incredibly ridiculous. Or even make me sound crazy. And maybe I am crazy. But it was so frustrating, because no matter what I do, or how many safeguards I install, I can never protect myself from being accused of manipulating someone. No matter how hard I try, or how careful I am. Also, because I'm just tired of hearing people say similar things to me. That they do not know why I am in prison, because I am such a nice guy. Guards say it, other prisoners say it. Granted, they do not know the details of my case, but still. I just wish someone would say its because of the faulty evidence, and not because of me. And I realize it makes me sound like an idiot to say that, because I should be grateful for anyone to feel that they do not believe I could commit such a heinous crime.

So now I am stressed out and just waiting for this whole interview process to be over. The very thing I have worked on all these years (just trying to be a good person) and the very thing I've always tried to avoid (being accused of manipulative behavior) have now had a cosmic collision. I am now going to be accused of demonstrating good behavior to manipulate Ms. Koenig. No matter what I do, it is as if I can never escape this. By then, I am just waiting for her to tell me we are done, and I can finally tell you I did my best. And at that point, it didn't matter to me how her story portrayed me. Guilty or innocent; I would just be glad to be done with the whole thing.

Can you imagine what it's like to never be able to be intuitive about the most important thing in your life? I could never just talk about my case with Ms. Koenig. I had to always analyze and evaluate every response I gave her, because I felt she had a general disposition to believe I was never telling the truth. It took me a long time to rid that of myself in my personal life. Prison really helped that. But I can never get rid of it when it comes to talking about my case. I am always overthinking, analyzing what I say and how it sounds. And all this thinking is not for personal gain. It is to protect myself from being hurt. Not from being accused of Hae's murder, but from being accused of being manipulative. And I know it seems crazy, but I cannot control how I feel. And it is so frustrating to know that what you're feeling is crazy but there is nothing you can do about it.

Ms. Koenig had no way of knowing, but she set the tone for me to experience this with one of the first questions she ever asked me. She stated that she had watched the video of my first trial, and she saw me sitting at the defense table during a break in proceedings. I was reading a small book, and she asked me what it was. I told her it was a *Quran* my dad had sent me. She next asked if I was reading it to make the Judge think I was religious? That triggered something in me, a hopeless feeling that I would never be able to convince her I was innocent.

I will always be grateful for the compassionate manner she demonstrated towards me. As I mentioned before, she never articulated to me her belief that I was innocent. To the contrary, I always felt she believed I had some involvement in Hae's murder. But she was always very kind to me, and I guess that caused me to respect and appreciate her even more, as a person . . .

It is not that I do not care if people believe I am innocent or not. It is just that I cannot let it affect me. When I was younger, it caused me a great deal of emotional distress to feel that everyone believed I committed this crime. Eventually, I realized I could not continue to be miserable anymore, as it was beginning to crush my spirit. I had to learn that it was destructive to allow other people's opinions to have an influence over me. It took a long while, but I was finally able to reach a point where I was not concerned with people's opinions of my innocence or guilt. I realized the emphasis must be placed on fighting my case in the proper arena. And I am grateful that God allowed me to develop that insight, because it has helped sustain me till today.

CHAPTER 9

FIFTH COLUMN

———•———

Islam began as something strange,
and it will return to being something strange,
so give glad tidings to the strangers.

Prophet Muhammad, Sahih Muslim

As of the spring of 2014, I could count on one hand the number of times I'd been left breathless by this case: when Adnan was arrested, when he was convicted, when he was sentenced, when he lost the post-conviction appeal, and when I read this cultural research memo. I scanned a paragraph, scanned another, deciding one portion was definitely the worst and then thinking, no, no, this other part is much, much worse. It was all so bad, just so very awful.

Sarah sat across the desk, looking at me expectantly, blinking every so often as I involuntarily made sounds, shook my head, uttered expletives. She looked a bit nervous.

I felt Dana Chivvis, a producer from *This American Life,* hovering somewhere in the room and I knew there was a microphone in the small space, pointed at me. But all I could see was that stupid, sick memo.

"Who the fuck wrote this?!"

Sarah and Dana exchanged looks. They had redacted the information at the top of the document; big thick black lines crossed out the name and address of whatever entity had produced it. That enraged me further.

"The woman who wrote it, she was scared, she didn't want anyone to know she wrote it, so I promised her I would keep her information confidential."

I wasn't pleased.

"Scared of what?"

Sarah hesitatingly admitted the writer was scared of retribution by the Muslim community.

On the inside all I could think was, "Are you serious? Have you seen our community? A bunch of aunties and uncles who couldn't do shit about Adnan or Gutierrez or any of this, who are too scared to challenge the police or the state, who told their kids to stay away from it all? Have you actually met our community, Sarah?"

I may have said some of this out loud, but I can't remember. I do remember wondering in amazement, does Sarah actually think this woman legitimately has something to fear?

Fear or no fear, I swore internally, I'd figure out who wrote this tripe. Then I got back to the more important business at hand—that this memo was part of the official case file.

"You're telling me this was in the *police files*? That this memo was part of the official file of the police and prosecution?"

Sarah nodded, not seeming to understand my incredulity.

The memo, dated August 24, 1999, began with the subject line, "Report on Islamic thought and culture with an emphasis on Pakistan. A comparative study relevant to the upcoming trial of Adnan Syed." It was addressed to Detectives Ritz and MacGillivary. It consisted of seven confusing and confused pages of random, and often irrelevant and unrelated, facts, conjecture, and purely invented kookery positioned as serious analysis. It covered, among other things, the following:

- "The Salafa"—that is, the generation of Muslims who lived at the time of the Prophet Muhammad
- The role of death in Islam
- A brief summary of the Shia-Sunni difference and divide
- Pakistan's political and legal systems, religious laws, ethnic groups, demographics, suffrage, agriculture (why, just why?), statistics on the condition of women in Pakistan (birth, education, crime)
- Shariah—specifically, religiously regulated criminal punishments
- Gender norms, veiling, women's roles, clothing
- "Sexual Attitudes," which included such reprehensible lies as stating that a reasonable option for a strict Muslim family, if one of its men engaged in pre-marital relations with a non-Muslim woman, would be arranging for her death.

I had no doubt that the writer was a complete bigot and quack-job posing as an Islam expert; I had come to know such people well through my work, which was spent trying to counter their damage. And this "expert," fifteen years ago, had provided the police with "research" to tie Adnan's religion and ethnicity to the crime.

I read another portion of the ridiculous document out loud, feeling my face heat up:

"Clearly Mr. Syed faced almost insurmountable odds to meet with this 'infidel or devil' in secret. Ownership is not outside of his cultural belief system. After giving her a veil, literally covering her so that only he could have her, he set her apart from all others and for him alone. For all intents and purpose he marked his territory by giving her a gift of great value within his culture and in doing so he sealed her fate with his."

I looked up at Sarah, my eyes bulging.

"What is this about?"

Sarah replied cautiously, "Well, apparently Adnan bought Hae a scarf from an Islamic conference he attended with this father."

It took a few seconds for me to make the connection.

Sarah continued.

"I mean . . . is it true?"

"Is what true?" I shot back, not wanting to accept that she had asked what I thought she had just asked.

"Is it true that when a Muslim man gives a woman a scarf, he owns her or it's like some kind of ownership?"

I don't know if I was jumping up and down in rage at that point, but at a minimum I must have been rocking back and forth, given my difficulty at hiding my temper. I remember getting up, still furiously flipping pages, glaring at her and Dana.

"You're kidding me, right? You're not actually asking me if that's true?"

Sarah stayed quiet.

"Oh my God, it's not true. You know that, right?"

She didn't look like she knew it.

At that point I had to balance my anger at the memo itself with my angry disbelief that someone as bright, educated, and sophisticated as Sarah could even entertain the thought that anything in that toxic, bigoted memo could be true. But I shouldn't have been so surprised; I had, after all, spent the last decade fighting these very lies about Islam and Muslims that have become the normative narrative in the United States.

If the cops and prosecutors thought the memo was accurate, there was no reason Sarah wouldn't.

———

Since that terrible September morning in New York and D.C., when nineteen Muslim hijackers slammed commercial planes into the crowded Twin Towers and the Pentagon, killing thousands, Muslims in America have felt besieged.

It is not by accident that half of the states in this country have either introduced or passed "anti-Shariah" legislation, a fact that may come as a surprise to those who still think the First Amendment applies to everyone. It is also no accident that neither conservative nor liberal parties welcome Muslims into their ranks. And it is completely by design that public bashing, humiliation, and outright reviling of Islam and Muslims is par for the course in the media and among our political leadership. Islamophobia is a bigotry everyone is comfortable with.

And there's a reason for this. A dedicated, well-funded, dynamic cottage industry of "Islamophobes" and anti-Muslim bigots has been operating for years under the guise of research, academia and policy-making. In 2011 the D.C. think tank Center for American Progress published a landmark report called *Fear, Inc.* It traces, in painstaking detail, the millions of dollars that annually support the very strategic creation and dissemination of misinformation about Islam and Muslims to policy makers and media and the grassroots and state-level legislative organizing against Muslims.

The impact of the work of this industry is no joking matter. Their influence has led to numerous Congressional hearings on the "radicalization" of American Muslims and a veritable witch hunt of any American Muslim engaged in policy or government work. In 2009 a group of U.S. legislators called for an inquiry into Muslim high school and college interns on the Hill, accusing them of infiltrating Congress and demanding that the Department of Justice open an investigation. A poll taken of Republican primary voters in 2015 showed that 72 percent felt a Muslim should not be allowed to be president and 40 percent felt that Islam should be outlawed writ large in the nation. A March 2016 poll showed that in all states where presidential candidate Donald Trump was the GOP frontrunner, nearly 65 percent of Republicans polled felt Muslims should be banned from the United States.

Well known and widely followed "liberals" like Bill Maher have persistently attacked Islam and Muslims; while Maher dislikes religion in general, he holds a special place of contempt in his heart for Islam, calling it the "mother lode of bad ideas."

A study by the firm Hattaway Communications found an interesting divide when it came to conservatives and liberals on the issue of Muslims and Islam: both groups generally tend to mistrust or dislike our faith group, but for different reasons. Conservatives consider Muslims a security threat, conflate Muslims with being foreign (a reason much anti-Muslim organizing is closely tied to anti-immigrant organizing), and question their loyalty and patriotism. Liberals, on the other hand, mistrust Muslims for their perceived treatment of women, religious minorities, and the LGBT community.

Either way you slice it, a lot of people don't like us. And it shows.

The Southern Poverty Law Center has been tracking the anti-Muslim industry and its impact for a number of years now. In a July 2011 piece they noted:

> *The American public psyche has undergone a subtle but profound metamorphosis since 2001, moving from initial rage at the 9/11 mass murder to fear of another devastating attack by Muslim extremists to, most recently, a more generalized fear of Islam itself. That evolution from specific concerns to general stereotyping is the customary track of racism and xenophobia—and in Muslims, those inclined to bigotry may have found their perfect bogeyman.*

But it would be a mistake to think everything was just fine for Muslims in the United States before 9/11.

It absolutely was not.

In the early 1990s, I was sitting on the Boardwalk in Ocean City, Maryland, with my best friend and siblings in tow. I was sixteen, Saad was ten. We were enjoying the last bit of summer and chowing down on Burger King as the sun went down. My dad and my best friend's dad, who also happened to be close childhood friends, had given us some cash and wandered off. The first thing I did was make a beeline to get my beloved BK chicken sandwich.

I actually saw the group of grizzled, tatted biker-looking men coming from about a hundred feet away. I assumed they would just walk by our little gaggle of brown faces. But they headed straight for us and I remember feeling slight panic as they got closer, instinctively protective of my brother and sister.

There were three of them, wearing black leather vests and sunglasses that blacked out their eyes. They stopped right in front of us and I looked up, frozen with a mouth full of my sandwich.

"Go home you fucking sand niggers, back to aye-rack."

I felt the contempt in every word—he may as well have spat at us—and my face filled up with blood and humiliation. Not the least because I wanted to say, "You asshole, we are from Pakistan, not Iraq."

They were well out of earshot when I broke out of my frozen terror, stood up trembling, and yelled something like "go to hell!" I knew they couldn't hear me, but I couldn't let my siblings think I just let that happen without a response.

It wasn't the first time I'd heard the words "sand nigger" in my life. Once, while in middle school, as I stood in the front yard of our little home in Hagerstown, Maryland, a van pulled up and the door slid open. A group of white teenagers leered out yelling "fuck you sand niggers!" and zoomed off.

That was my introduction to the idea that some people didn't like Muslims.

The first Gulf War deepened that sense when one of my teachers jokingly asked if Saddam Hussein was my uncle.

The early nineties brought us the highly popular film *Not Without My Daughter*, which came to define Muslim family dynamics for the West. To this day, over two decades later, I'm still asked by kindly old grandmothers at churches and synagogues where I guest lecture to address the implications of this movie.

"I know how Muslim men treat their women. I saw that movie, *Not Without My Daughter*."

"Why are Islamic countries so oppressive to women, like in that movie?"

"I feel terrible for you honey, the things you have to go through as a Muslim woman."

Thanks, Sally Field.

Today 80 percent of all media stories about Muslims in the United States are terrorism related.

Journalist and author of the *Fear, Inc.* report Wajahat Ali sums it up like this: "Culture is a powerful force that influences our perceptions, our mindsets and even our domestic and foreign policies. The rich, messy complexity of 1,400 years of Islamic civilization and 1.6 billion Muslims has been reduced to token stereotypes. We are either avatars of destruction or the good Muslim who helps the national security narrative. But the overwhelming majority of us live in the giant middle—the grey zone—where impressions exist in more colors than just black and white."

I knew all about anti-Muslim fear and stereotypes in the United States already, but it still didn't prepare me for this memo, which turned out to be written by Mandy Johnson of the Enehey Group, the same person brought in by Hae's uncle to help investigate her disappearance in January of 1999. This memo was written almost nine months later, long after Adnan had already been arrested. It wasn't written for the police investigation, it was written for the State's prosecution.

Some revelations are a long time coming. This was one of them.

The Enehey memo finally brought clarity as to why the police focused so strongly on Adnan, even from before it was known that Hae was murdered, and why prosecutors kept bringing up his religion throughout the case.

The narrative of the angry Muslim man worked for detectives; it fit neatly with their existing biases. During her investigation Sarah would end up speaking to a few of the jurors who confirmed our fear—that Adnan's religion and ethnicity were indeed factors considered by the jury.

One juror, remembering back to the deliberations, told Sarah, "I don't feel religion was why he did what he did. It may have been culture, but I don't think it was religion. I'm not sure how the cultures over there, how they treat their women, he just wanted control and she wouldn't give it to him." Another juror told Sarah that when the jury was deliberating, they discussed that in Arab culture it was the men who ruled, not women. It seems Gutierrez's long, impassioned soliloquy on Adnan's Pakistani roots did not clarify for the jury that he was not Arab. Adnan's faith was actual evidence against him. The State had made sure of it.

Sarah's investigation continued, with little information coming our way. Every so often I would ask her who she was speaking to. She mostly didn't indulge my nosiness, though she did tell me that neither detective MacGillivary or Ritz agreed to speak to her. I knew at that point to keep a respectful distance and hope for the best.

One day, in late February 2014, the best that I could then hope for actually happened.

Sarah called me, excited. She had reported on another case, a wrongful conviction, a number of years earlier. That reporting had put her in touch with an attorney named Deirdre Enright, who headed up the University of Virginia Innocence Project.

Feeling perhaps a bit up against a wall, Sarah had reached out to her. They met and Sarah walked her through the case, showed her some documents.

The Innocence Project has been around for decades. In 1992, nationally acclaimed attorneys Barry Scheck and Peter Neufeld co-founded the organization, which would go on to become a full-fledged nonprofit with chapters across the nation. Scheck and Neufeld, who have known each other since the mid-1970s when they were both public defenders, had been working with the newly emerging science of forensic DNA testing since the late 1980s. They based the

Innocence Project on that work. Its purpose was singular: to exonerate wrong-fully convicted and incarcerated people using DNA evidence.

To date they have helped exonerate nearly two hundred people across the country, including many on death row.

Adnan had twice applied for his case to be considered by the Innocence Project Clinic at the University of Baltimore. Both applications were summarily rejected for the same reason: the Innocence Project only worked on cases where potential DNA evidence existed—in Adnan's case there was none.

When I moved back to the D.C. area I tried getting them involved too. I left a number of phone messages, which finally resulted in a brief conversation with the director. She said there was no point in meeting, they didn't take cases like this.

Until Sarah met with Deirdre.

Deirdre shared the documents and story that Sarah brought her with her team, the law school student volunteers who were the machine that made her clinic run. They were immediately drawn in; something, they felt, was off. This story, the way the State told it, didn't make sense to them.

"Deirdre said they would take the case." Sarah marveled. We were both pretty amazed.

I made her repeat it, just to be sure.

"Can they?" she asked. "Are you ok with that, will Adnan be ok with that?"

But I didn't understand one thing—how could they take a case that had no DNA to work with? I didn't press the subject, though; I figured perhaps Sarah's existing relationship with Deirdre influenced her to take the case, or maybe not all chapters operated the same way. Regardless, Sarah and I spoke to Adnan, his family, and Justin and got permission all around. After reviewing the files, Deirdre went to see Adnan with a few other members of her team and a Maryland attorney she would work with to handle local filings. In that meeting she told Adnan something none of us ever knew: that in fact samples that could have, and should have, been tested for DNA evidence had actually been taken from Hae's body. But the prosecutor's office had put a hold on testing.

Adnan was stunned, as was I. Could there have been physical evidence that would have not only cleared him fourteen years ago, but also helped to identify Hae's killer?

I couldn't fathom Gutierrez missing something as glaring and significant as potential DNA evidence, and numerous teams of lawyers had been through these documents since without comment. Eventually Sarah's assistant sent me the files digitized on USB drives so I could take a look at what they found, but at that point I just was thankful that the IP team was going through everything with a fine-toothed comb.

According to Deirdre, those samples could still exist in a police evidence locker somewhere, and if they did, the test results could exonerate Adnan. The kinds of DNA testing available today can pick up traces that were undetectable in 1999, even in the samples the State said had no trace evidence. They could, of course, also yield nothing, no matches to anyone. For all of us the decision seemed clear—Deirdre had to find those samples and compel the State to test them.

But a storm was coming our way. In that moment we had no idea what Sarah was creating. I anticipated an hour-long *This American Life* radio broadcast, summarizing her findings, whenever she finished up her investigation. At some point over the summer she mentioned that the story would likely be told in parts, maybe six episodes, maybe ten.

Either way, I didn't care too much. The only thing that mattered to me was finding the smoking gun that could clear Adnan. So far, the closest thing that came to it was the possibility that DNA testing clearly implicated someone else.

By August I was beginning to feel low. We hadn't heard back from the Court of Special Appeals on our appeal of the PCR denial, no witness had crumbled and come forward with exonerating information, and I was starting to second-guess whether I should have taken this case to the media. For the past ten months I had juggled work, family, and managing our end of whatever was required for Sarah's investigation. The story wasn't even public yet and I was tired. It's no secret that I cry easily, but those days the tears were just under the surface. I was terrified of failing Adnan, once again.

I mentioned this to a friend, who suggested I speak to a religious or spiritual person who could give me some guidance, comfort, maybe some prayers to recite and meditate over. It just so happened that Shaykh Hisham Kabbani, an internationally known Sufi scholar, would soon be visiting the area—and my friend had the connections to get me an audience. I wasn't completely comfortable with the idea, first because I never considered myself a Sufi, and second because I had never in my entire life really asked a religious leader for help like this. Despite my prayerful ways, that had never occurred to me.

Still, I wasn't about to pass this opportunity up.

Two nights before my appointment, on the night of August 20, I had a dream. The next day I posted on Facebook about it with a picture of Adnan.

This is Adnan, my little brother's best friend and like a younger brother to me as well. He has spent over 15 years in prison for a crime he did not commit. He was 17 when arrested, is 32 now. He is serving a life sentence for a murder he is innocent of and recently lost his last appeal.

For 15 years we waited for the system to work but it failed. Now the only thing left is a public campaign to reopen his case. For the past 10 months I've been working with a journalist to investigate his case and a series of 10 radio shows will air this fall about it. I recognize without a corresponding grass-roots effort the shows will not be enough to pressure the state to reopen the case.

Last night I was discussing my emotional exhaustion with a friend and spiritual mentor, talking about whether I have the energy for the sustained push it will take to acquit and free him. I went to bed feeling demoralized.

As I slept last night I dreamt I was driving and ran out of gas. It was nighttime and I was alone. I got out of the car dejected and upset and looked around, only to realize I was within walking distance of my destination. I could see it. It was right before me.

In the dream my destination loomed right around the bend, literally a huge sign towering in the sky, all lit up. I just didn't realize how close I was when the car came to a stop in the dead of nowhere.

The dream began with fear and ended with utter relief from all my anxiety. The message it sent was clear: I might be out of gas, exhausted, but the destination was right in front of my face and I needed to start walking. Two days later I went to see the Shaykh.

Shaykh Hisham is a small man who wears a large white turban, and he has a long flowing beard to rival any childhood Father Christmas fantasy. He looked at me with a bit of a twinkle in his eye as I walked in, full of trepidation. He rose to greet me, which I found endearing—in our culture elders do not rise to greet those who are younger or less authoritative. I sat next to him at a table where we were served tea and assorted biscuits.

I said an awkward "Salaam" and began thanking him for making the time to meet me. There was a profound, quiet gentleness about him. I told him that someone near and dear to me had been in prison for fifteen years and that we were trying to exonerate him, that it was taking a toll on me, and that I was losing hope. I also told him about the dream I just had. He softly asked questions about the case, about Adnan. Then he asked to see a picture of him.

I pulled out the one photograph I had brought of Adnan, in which he was about twenty-three. The photo had been taken a few years into his incarceration, before he had been moved to the supermax prison in Cumberland. He stood with his arms around Yusuf, Saad standing by his side. He wore a white skullcap, had a short trimmed beard; his eyes were large and sad.

Shakyh Hisham took the picture in his hands while still gripping the prayer beads he held and stared at it. Then he looked up at me and said, "He is innocent, he will come home."

After the dream and meeting the Shaykh I felt hopeful that we'd get a break in the case, re-energized to keep pushing, but nothing could have prepared me for what was coming around the corner in the next few months.

On October 1, 2014, Sarah sent me a message telling me the show would be something called a podcast and be not in six, or ten, but rather twelve parts. I had two thoughts: holy moly, twelve episodes?! And, what the heck was a podcast?

CHAPTER 10

SERIAL

·

The truth was a mirror in the hands of God.
It fell, and broke into pieces.
Everybody took a piece of it,
and they looked at it and thought they had the truth.
Jalaluddin Rumi, 13th-century Sufi mystic

"Does your mom know Saad outed himself as not a virgin on the podcast?"

It was the very first reaction I got from a friend who messaged me as soon as she heard Episode 1 of *Serial*, "The Alibi." I hadn't yet heard it, but by the time I got around to listening to it I had already gotten dozens of messages from friends and colleagues asking if I was the Rabia Chaudry on the podcast.

I heard from Saad and Yusuf, who also had spent their day fielding dozens of excited messages. After sharing a bit of mortification that Sarah had aired his comment about not being a virgin, Saad quickly shrugged it off. That was minor. What mattered was that this story was finally getting told. The energy from the feedback was positive, everyone sounded pumped, and I couldn't wait to finally hear the show. Sometime in the evening of October 3, 2014, I finally sat down to listen to the first episode.

The music itself, overlaid with audio from the GlobalTel Link service through which Adnan and other inmates call family and friends, was surprising. It took what was mundane for us, years of waiting for the beep to press "0" to accept his collect call, and transformed it into something magical.

I felt hyper-aware the entire time, my shoulders tense, ears pricked. Hearing Adnan's voice—from the opening sequence, to explaining his love and respect for Hae, to his helplessness at not being able to prove his every step after school on January 13, 1999—it gutted me in a way I wasn't prepared for. I felt overwhelming sadness, grief, and hope. Finally, here it was, Adnan's story. His voice, his words. But God, it had taken so long.

And then came Asia. After all, the first episode was "The Alibi." Here was the one person we believed held Adnan's freedom in her hands, saying publicly that she still remembered being with him after school at the time Jay said Adnan had killed Hae. I felt vindicated. Asia's conversation with Sarah made it clear, despite what prosecutor Kevin Urick had testified to, that she was not pressured into making her written statements. After all these years, her memories of that afternoon were exactly the same, and while Sarah had told us long ago about their conversation, it was entirely a different experience to hear it from Asia herself.

The second episode, released simultaneously, documented Adnan and Hae's doomed Romeo-and-Juliet romance. Sarah read from Hae's diary and interviewed a number of their mutual friends, seeking clues for whether Adnan was possessive, controlling, any of the things the State alleged. She went over the homecoming dance fiasco. She spoke to Anjali, whom Adnan was dating at the time Hae disappeared. After investigating their relationship, Sarah said she didn't buy the State's version of motive. But she didn't stop with investigating how Adnan acted during and after the relationship; she also went *there*—to the idea that his religion had something to do with how he felt about and treated Hae.

In "The Breakup," Sarah says:

> Remember the setup for this crime that the State laid out was that Adnan was betraying everything he held dear for this girl. As a good Muslim he was not supposed to be dating and so he was sacrificing his religion and lying to his family all just so he could be with her and it twisted him up inside. And Hae's diary seems to be where they found some evidence for that. In fact, they had a friend of Hae's, Debbie Warren, read excerpts from it on the witness stand. "I like him, no I love him." She read at trial, dated May 15. "It's just all the things that stand in the middle. His religion and Muslim customs are the main things. It irks me to know that I'm against his religion. He called me a devil a few times. I know he was only joking, but it's somewhat true." So, yeah, anytime someone is writing stuff down like "sin" and "devil" and "religion means life" in reference to their secret relationship, that's not good. But ask the Muslim in question about it, and it all seems so much smaller.

She had asked Adnan and also Saad and me. We all said the same thing: that it was ridiculous to conclude that Adnan was so serious about his religion that it was his life, but at the same time he was partying, drinking, smoking pot, dating, and having premarital sex.

I appreciated that Sarah made it clear there was no evidence that Adnan was a domineering, dangerous ex-boyfriend, but I was decidedly bothered that she felt uneasy about the religious comments in Hae's diary. Why did Sarah think it looked bad for Adnan if he had to choose between Hae and his religion? There was no threat in this proposition other than the prospect of a broken heart. Did Sarah think that Adnan was perhaps religious enough to—in accordance with her own internal biases of what a possessive, religious Muslim man was like— kill a woman?

I couldn't shake this thought, but the first few days after *Serial* launched I could barely come up for air to think it all through.

The public reaction to the podcast snowballed; within days the dozens of messages turned into hundreds. *This American Life* had dropped two beautifully produced, narratively seductive, completely intriguing episodes, and the world of podcasting was on fire. People immediately became obsessed with the case.

The media coverage was fast and furious; social media buzzed with millions of Tweets and shared Facebook statuses: *Serial* was an instant hit, and people could not wait for the following Thursday, when the next episodes would air.

Adnan didn't yet know any of this. His family, Saad, and I began getting e-mails and calls from media outlets around the world for comment, but we held off. I decided to deal the best way I knew how—by blogging.

I did not write that very first blog post thinking, "I am totally going to undermine Sarah's story and control the narrative." My dinky little blog, hosted on Patheos, an interfaith writers' site where I mostly railed against Muslim community issues that irritated me, was hardly a platform to rival *This American Life*. But I had things to say, even as early as the first week. The plan was to fill in the blanks, to broaden the context, and address some of the things that could make people say "hmmmm" (like the homecoming incident) with specificity. I wanted, basically, to explain things from our perspective—the perspective of the community, Adnan's family, Adnan, myself.

Sarah was taking the listeners on a decidedly ambiguous journey. She presented a fact, a scene, an anecdote, showing us how it could work for Adnan or against him. Sarah had landed on why the story was fascinating—much of it, as she said herself, was spin.

And spin, whichever way you want it to go, does not rise to the level of evidence used to convict someone. There is no "beyond a reasonable doubt" when it comes to spin. There is only doubt. But doubt in the jury's conviction was not good enough; we needed an overwhelming number of people to believe in Adnan's actual innocence. And so I took to my blog, SplitTheMoon, and began writing. Every week, with every episode, I wrote. I wanted to add enough to the podcast that listeners would understand why, for all these years, I believed in Adnan's innocence.

After my first few blog posts, I got an uncomfortable call from Sarah. She was not happy.

Here she had put in a tremendous amount of work, along with her team, to craft a particular storyline, and instead of letting it unfold without interfering I was mucking things up by blogging. I understood, and the last thing I wanted to do was damage her work. We owed her a tremendous debt for taking on Adnan's story and telling it to the world. I didn't want to upset her, but at the same time I knew that the public's attention to the case would pass as quickly as the podcast. Human nature is fickle. I knew the day Sarah wrapped up this story, people would be ready for season two of *Serial*. I spoke about it with Adnan and he agreed. I already had experience with writing and public speaking, I had a platform, I knew the case, and there was no one in the family who was up to the task. He not only gave me permission to take the lead on all media, he requested that we keep his family out of the media as much as possible. And he had read the first few transcripts, heard the concern in Yusuf's voice that there was ambiguity about his innocence in the show. He knew Sarah had to tell the story not only in a way to keep the listeners compelled but also in a way that was authentic to her. But that didn't necessarily mean that after it was over, anyone would care about the case.

So I made Sarah a promise: I would never trump her story, I would never address anything she had not yet revealed (such as the involvement of the Innocence Project), and I would limit my blogs to the content of her episodes. But I wouldn't stop writing.

"You have your agenda and I have mine," I told her. My agenda was to exonerate Adnan and bring him home, and in order to do that I had to tell our side of the story.

So while I assured her that she had little to worry about, because *Serial* was reaching millions of people while my blog only reached tens of thousands, I was working on fixing that. I took to social media and put to use what I had learned in the past couple of years of organizing the New America Foundation social media trainings.

Every Thursday *Serial* would drop a new episode, and I would listen to it as soon as the girls were off to school. I'd let it marinate all day, thinking about the points I wanted to address. At night I would start going through the case files, looking for the documents I needed for the blog. I would write much of the night and aim to post the blog first thing in the morning.

And then it was all about Twitter. I found people tweeting about *Serial* and would respond to them, posting my blog with a message like "you can read more about the case here." I did this twenty, thirty, forty times a day in the first few weeks, sharing my post over and over like a slightly unhinged person. I can only imagine how irritating it must have been for the followers I already had—about twelve thousand or so who (I assume) followed me because of my writing and commentary on faith, gender, politics, and national security. And now, all of a sudden, I almost exclusively tweeted about Adnan, *Serial*, and my blogs. Despite potentially turning off my regular followers, I shared my blogs with an obnoxious frequency until one day the huge digital media outlet Slate ran a piece called "If You Love *Serial*, You Should Be Reading This." The "this" was my blog.

My readership shot up into the hundreds of thousands, and after that I shared my blogs a few times when they went live, and it was enough to get the circulation I wanted. Having been part of a number of Twitter campaigns, I knew we couldn't do without a hashtag, and so #FreeAdnan was born. I tacked it on to the end of almost all my tweets, even to pictures of my cat, Mr. Beans. More than once, #FreeAdnan ended up trending on Twitter globally.

Despite what it may have looked like, there was no organized online campaign for Adnan. It was just me constantly on my smart phone, day and night, in bed, while working, traveling, even on the toilet. I responded to every tweet; I favorited, retweeted, and replied tens of thousands of times in those months.

Rolling Stone, *The New Yorker*, *The Guardian*, *The Washington Post*, the BBC, *The New York Times*, *The Wall Street Journal*, *People*, *Time*, *Good Morning America*, MSNBC, the list went on and on and on. From the most prominent publications in the United States, to local news affiliates, to international print and broadcast media, *Serial* was everywhere. Adnan Syed, who I had once hoped would get some modest media coverage by the likes of *Dateline*, was sharing headlines with international news.

Serial didn't just give a global platform to Adnan's case, it elevated the podcast medium to astronomical heights. Suddenly the podcast was sexy. At least half a dozen podcasts about *Serial* sprung up, and I found myself listening to all of them (even some absolutely terrible ones where the hosts could barely keep the facts straight), not only to learn what others had to say about *Serial* but mostly what they thought about Adnan and the case. We, and by "we" I mean "team Adnan"—his family, me and my family—were definitely more sensitive regular listeners to Sarah's portrayal of the facts and Adnan himself. We often honed in on, obsessed even, whether a given episode made him seem guilty or innocent. But perhaps the most robust, committed, and deeply involved set of strangers anywhere online was found on Reddit, a rabbit hole we were initially only too happy to jump into.

When the *Serial* podcast "subreddit" popped up with dozens of threads, Saad, Yusuf, Tanveer, and I eagerly joined the fray. I knew about Reddit, had been a lurker long ago, but had not returned in many years. We assumed, with incredible naïveté, that we would be a welcome addition to conversations; we could answer questions, give context, and be part of a supportive community that would help us fight for Adnan's exoneration. Not completely so. On Reddit was where I first encountered not only challenges to our support for Adnan but direct hostility from strangers who were completely comfortable making the worst assumptions about us all. I never knew until then what it was like to, point-blank, be called a liar. Not just me, but Saad and Adnan's brothers, and others who supported Adnan. Among the many ridiculous and disgusting allegations were: we know Adnan is guilty but persist in trying to free him; we are milking *Serial* for fame; Rabia is in love with Adnan, or maybe Sarah is . . . actually we both are because of his "dairy-cow eyes"; we coerced Asia into her statements, alternatively Rabia paid Asia for her affidavit in 2000; we are racist for pointing out Jay's lies; Adnan confessed to us or to members of the mosque; mosque members or Adnan's mother or father killed Hae and Adnan took the fall for it; we are dishonoring or somehow smearing Hae by challenging the conviction.

The real mistake we made was taking any of it seriously. It took some time before we realized we were mostly encountering classic Internet trolls, with multiple fake accounts and nothing to do with their time. But initially their vitriol wore us down. One by one, everyone who actually knew Adnan in person, including his school friends, like Krista Meyers, and his brothers, Saad, and I left subreddit, but only after being through an emotional wringer.

While trolls didn't matter, what was relevant was the response of the actual, real-life public, especially the Muslim community. Though Adnan had never said a word to any of us about his childhood friends and community abandoning him, Saad, Yusuf, and I carried a lot of anger at the people he had been raised with. Now, with *Serial,* they were coming forward again. Friends who hadn't contacted Adnan in over a decade, elders who knew him since childhood but had written him off as a lost cause—they were coming back.

We were getting messages, sometimes sheepish ones, with apologies for being absent but also expressing gratitude for not having forgotten Adnan. Early on, as *Serial* exploded, I couldn't help but be snarky online about these friends who suddenly remembered Adnan. I reined it in quickly, though, realizing it was wrong to ostracize those who just wanted to show support now.

But Yusuf in particular finally spilled out the pain his family had held onto for over a decade. In a number of posts he pointed out how people had the nerve to come forward now that Adnan's case was all over the news, and how most of the community had just let him fade away, like he never even existed.

"The message you're sending is really messed up."

"Why?"

"Basically you're telling people, people like my kids, that it's normal for Muslim kids to sleep around, drink, smoke pot. And you're perpetuating the idea that it's the only way to prove you're a cool American, which means the Muslims who don't do that shouldn't be trusted. Like if he was actually a religious kid, then maybe he would have had motive. I don't want my kids to hear this."

I was a guest at someone else's home, meeting this man for the first time. It was Thanksgiving, *Serial* was more than halfway through, and I was not in a good place. I was already sleep deprived and stressed. I had gained twenty pounds in the past two months and had chronic back pain. As I sat there listening to him and then glanced over at his kids, both teenagers, I felt a familiar stabbing pain shoot through my side.

I gave him a piece of my mind.

"So you're telling me that what upsets you about this story is not the fact that Adnan was locked away for life because they used his religion against him, a kid your son's age, that his family has been destroyed, and that he could potentially die in prison, rather you're upset we are 'airing dirty laundry' about the lifestyles of Muslim kids."

"Yeah, but it's not true. That's not how Muslim kids live. I never did those things."

"Neither did I. And I have a teenage daughter and hope to God she doesn't either because I'd kick her ass. But I know plenty of kids who did and I know kids still do. That's reality, you don't have to accept it, you can choose willful ignorance if it makes you feel better."

"Well, I listened to the first episode and that's all I needed to hear."

Before I could bury my foot in his rear end, the friend witnessing the exchange brightly suggested that I take a walk with her.

About eight months later I was at a beautiful Pakistani benefit gala, dressed to the nines, when an excited, glamorous, older lady came over to introduce herself. Tall, slender, impeccably coiffed, and wrapped in many yards of a delicate chiffon sari, she reeked of expensive perfume and the excesses of a life very comfortably lived.

She was a fan, her daughters were fans, they all loved *Serial;* her relatives back in some posh area of Pakistan loved it too. She thanked me for my tenacity and asked for a photograph together.

She handed her phone to someone else, and we posed and took a quick picture. She grinned and texted the image to her daughter, casually said, "Even though I think he's guilty, it's rather wonderful what all you've done."

My smile evaporated.

"Why do you think he's guilty?"

"Well he was hiding the fact that he was smoking pot from his parents. . . ."

"Are you saying because he was smoking pot he could be a murderer or are you saying that because he hid his pot-smoking from his parents, which is what any kid who smokes pot would do, that makes him a murderer?"

She looked a bit flustered.

I looked around the room, a room full of very wealthy Pakistani-Americans who might never have known the kind of modest middle-class life Adnan or my family lived.

"I bet this room is full of people and their kids who've smoked weed and drink alcohol and had plenty of romances. Lots of Pakistanis drink alcohol, right? Does that mean they could commit murder? You are judging a seventeen-year-old kid for these things? Do you remember being seventeen? And do you find it a bit ironic that the State argued he killed Hae because he was religious, while you're arguing that he killed her because he clearly wasn't?"

She capitulated, probably hoping I would just let it go.

"Maybe you're right, maybe he's not guilty."

I turned and took my seat, fuming.

I had dozens of such in-person encounters with Muslims who couldn't get past their judgment of Adnan for smoking pot and dating. The deep discomfort they felt over hearing about such trespasses was not new. But I had expected that by now, by 2014, we had evolved to the point of being able to see beyond the mildly poor choices of a seventeen-year-old to what should really distress us—that the ugliest stereotypes about his religion, our religion, were used to convict him.

Others asked me to come speak to their Sunday school classes on the dangers of such things, pointing to Adnan's story as a lesson learned. I should have actually shown up at a few of those Sunday school classes so I could rail against the very premise. "Muslims are human beings too, we will mess up, even God expects that."

Ironically, as much as I had worried about this story being told at a time when polls showed that anti-Muslim bias in the United States was at its highest, my concern was unnecessary. The overwhelming public response, as *Serial* broke all records and hit over a hundred million listeners, was empathy and support for Adnan, with little attention paid to his religion other than disgust at how the State used it against him. It was an incredibly pleasant surprise, given that in the many years since 9/11, Muslim activists and organizations had pretty much failed to turn the tide of public opinion. There simply were no positive American Muslim narratives that had taken firm root in the public discourse. As I explained in the New America Foundation trainings, we had lost the narrative war to Muslim extremists and anti-Muslim bigots. The only meme we had been trying to sell for decades was "Islam is a religion of peace" and, surprise, no one was buying it.

It was one of the unintended consequences, an incredibly positive one, that *Serial* may have turned this case into the most positive story about a Muslim in America since 9/11. But as wildly popular as the story had become, there was near silence from the most prominent American Muslim figures, probably because supporting Adnan meant supporting something I cared about. And by the time *Serial* exploded, a lot of American Muslims weren't very happy with me.

In the early months of 2013 I got a call from a dear friend, Imam Abdullah Antepli, at that time the Muslim chaplain at Duke University. I knew Abdullah from our time in Connecticut—he was the coordinator of Muslim students at the Hartford Seminary, where my husband began studying in 2006. Abdullah had not only gotten us our first apartment in Connecticut, with a key ready for us the night we moved there, but also introduced us to the local Muslim and interfaith community. Over the years, Abdullah was always a willing mentor and friend and always came through when needed. Not just for me, but for everyone. That's just who he was and is.

I remember that call because it put me in a bind.

"You are going to Israel with me in May," he said.

"Uhh. Abdullah, first of all, you know my girls are in school, I can't take off and even if I could . . . Israel? No thanks," was my response.

But he went on for a while, on that call and on a few others during which he finally talked me into agreeing to be part of the very first cohort of what would become an incredibly controversial program—the Muslim Leadership Initiative, or MLI. It was a program that took American Muslim leaders to study in Jerusalem at the Shalom Hartman Institute (SHI), one of the most prominent and well-respected Jewish educational establishments in both Israel and the United States. We would be going to study not just Judaism, but the role of the state of Israel in Judaism. In other words, we would be going to study Zionism.

The life cycle of nearly every American Muslim activist begins with the Palestinian struggle; it is where nearly all of us cut our teeth. It is so central to the collective Muslim consciousness that it unites an otherwise diverse global population like no other issue. Being pro-Palestinian is not anti-Semitic. But it is anti-Zionist. This was a line that simply could not be crossed.

I also entered activism in my early twenties as an antiwar and anti-Israel protestor. I joined a small D.C. chapter of Al-Awda, the Palestinian right-of-return organization, led locally by a Palestinian Christian man and an Israeli Jewish woman. It legitimized our cause that neither of the leaders was a Palestinian Muslim—this, after all, was not a religious issue. It was a political and human rights issue.

Over the years I became deeply involved in interfaith work on various social justice issues, yet I knew that many of the Jews I worked with were strong supporters of Israel. Anytime there was unrest in that part of the world, we all retreated to our corners, only to reemerge when the latest conflict flare was over. We broke bread together, we built Habitat for Humanity homes together, we fought against poverty together, we stood against anti-Semitism and Islamophobia together. But the one thing we did not ever, ever do was discuss Israel, Palestine, and the Occupation. Beyond the pragmatics of avoiding such conversations, there was the moral imperative of not giving Zionists oxygen. We do not normalize Zionism; we do not even pretend it has an equal measure of legitimacy as Palestinian self-determination. We do not break "BDS," the "boycott, divestment, and sanctions" movement against Israel and Israeli institutions and products. This was the rule for people of conscience, no exceptions.

And here was Abdullah asking me to join him, along with almost two dozen other high-profile American Muslims, in Israel, to study Zionism, at an institute that was subject to BDS. He wanted me to break all the rules.

If it wasn't for the fact that I trusted Abdullah completely, knew his commitment to justice, and understood that nothing he did was without reason, I never would have done it. He had a vision, a mission. We had spent decades working with anti-Zionist Jews on support for Palestine—it got us nowhere. Palestinian suffering, Israeli aggression, polarization, entrenchment, and extremism on both sides only increased. It was time to figure out what this connection to Israel was about for the majority of American Jews, something I never understood. As a Muslim, I understand the attachment to holy places, but not to nation-states. I feel connected to Mecca, but no love for Saudi Arabia necessarily. The seemingly unequivocal American Jewish support of Israel always confused me. MLI was about exploring that, and also about seeing if there was space to agree with this politically influential constituency on how to end an occupation that destroyed the bodies of the occupied, and the souls of the occupiers.

I gave it a lot of thought, spoke to others who were invited, consulted mentors, and prayed about it to work my head and heart through it. And then I went.

Our group went to Jerusalem during the summers of 2013 and 2014, two weeks at a time, to study on-site as Fellows of the Shalom Hartman Institute. In the year between the two summers we met for retreats in the United States and once a month had online courses. Most of our study was centered on Torah, Talmud, and Mishnah, and included an examination of how Jews viewed themselves and the land, that rocky, inhospitable, otherwise unremarkable land, through a religious and historic lens. We visited the West Bank, spent time with Palestinians who lived in Israel proper, and visited the holy sites. Nearly every day we studied as rabbinic students did, in havruta sessions, and almost every day we trekked to the Old City to pray at the Al Aqsa mosque. And although we had gone as students, we ended up inadvertently teaching our teachers about Islam and Muslims. The SHI has brilliant scholars and academics, but the sad irony is that most of them will profess not knowing a single Muslim personally, despite being surrounded by them, or know anything about Islam. We pointed out that their daily lives were serviced by Palestinian workers. The cleaners, cooks, and repair people we saw on the campus were all Palestinian Muslims. And they were thrilled to see us there, in the middle of a Jewish educational institute holding the Muslim prayer in congregation three or four times a day.

The lessons I and other Fellows have learned from this program could fill an entire book; instead, upon returning from Jerusalem in June of 2014, I wrote an article about it for *Time* magazine titled "Seeking Common Ground in the Holy Land." The editors changed it to "What an American Muslim Learned from Zionists."

It came out shortly before Gaza erupted from "Operation Protective Edge," the Israeli assault that began in July of 2014, lasting nearly two months, including the month of Ramadan, and killing over two thousand Palestinians. As our social media feeds filled with images of dead Palestinian babies and children, my piece about spending a year studying Zionism ignited a heated, raging reaction from American Muslim activists.

We were called Zionist whores, sellouts, Trojan horses, dogs, pigs, blood suckers, traitors, normalizers, the list went on. We received thousands of ugly tweets, messages, and threats. This, despite our collective decades of work serving the Muslim community, and despite our continued public opposition to Israeli aggression. Numerous boycott petitions were launched against us, to prevent us from being invited to speak or write anywhere, and they were signed by the most prolific American Muslim activists and faith leaders.

It was truly the summer of American Muslim discontent. Collective rage had come to a head, and much of it came right at me, thanks to that article. By the time *Serial* rolled out a couple of months later, I was already exhausted from social media vitriol and had lost the backing of those who had supported my work for years. I felt terrible that Adnan wasn't getting support from high-profile community leaders because of me; there was radio silence from most of them about the case. It wasn't that they hated him, they hated me. Part of their collective punishment was that they'd not only totally ignore his case but also ignore the fact that he was humanizing Muslims in a way activists had failed to do for decades.

The stress didn't just come from dealing with Muslims, Muslim leaders, Reddit and trolls, though; it also came from the content of the podcast itself, and most importantly, from Sarah.

I got the text from Sarah late one night, around eleven o'clock. She was distressed. Yusuf, as he had a few times in the past, had sent her an angry, belligerent message, accusing her of profiting from his family's misery. She knew he was fragile and was afraid he might hurt himself. So she texted me to check in on him.

I took a deep breath and gave him a call. No answer. Then I forwarded Sarah's message to Saad, asking him to check in with Yusuf. Saad was irritated; he didn't want to deal with this. We had all been through a few bouts of Yusuf's acting out in the past few months and were losing patience.

I finally got through to Yusuf. He was fine, and he wasn't going to hurt himself, but he refused to let Sarah get away with using his family. At least a dozen times I had spoken him off this ledge, pointing out that no one had ever spent as much time and energy investigating the case as Sarah. A couple of times he had lashed out at me and Saad, saying we were responsible for not protecting Adnan, that he was a child in 1999 but we were adults and we failed him.

He was right; all the adults had failed Adnan. But because our own nerves were frayed, neither Saad nor I were very tolerant about what were clearly cries of pain from Yusuf. Our response, usually over group text, was somewhere between "You're right, fine, but we're doing the best we can now" to "Go to hell, Yusuf, it's not like you ever even looked at the files sitting in your basement for the past decade."

We were all clearly on edge. But what pushed Yusuf over the edge and what pushed me over the edge on a few occasions were two different things.

I understood the value in keeping people engaged by playing both sides of the story; what I couldn't stomach was *Serial's* failure to tell the entire story, to leave out things that were important in understanding what really happened. In the episode about the police investigation, Sarah concluded that the cops were good guys, just doing their job the best they knew how.

But these were not just good guys who never got anything wrong.

In the past decade alone, three defendants from Baltimore who were convicted of murder, Ezra Mable, Sabien Burgess, and Rodney Addison, have had their convictions overturned after serving long prison terms. All three were investigated and charged by Detectives MacGillivary and Ritz, and Sargeant Steven Lehman, or a combination thereof. Mable filed such a strong post-conviction petition that the Baltimore City State's Attorney actually joined it, asking the court for relief, which came in the form of his release. Mable then filed suit against the city (which was dismissed for lack of prosecution), naming Ritz, among others, alleging that the police "*resolved to focus entirely on Mr. Mable and did not attempt to determine the actual truth in their investigation or to develop a case based on truthful facts.*" Mable maintains that Ritz coerced two witnesses, using high-pressure tactics and threats, to get their cooperation against Mable. One of the witnesses repeatedly maintained that she saw another man commit the crime, not Mable. The other witness, who told cops she never saw who committed the murder, was threatened with having her children taken from her and finally relented, identifying Mable as the culprit. Faced with two eyewitnesses, Mable pled guilty and served ten years before filing his ultimately successful post-conviction appeal.

The Burgess case is even worse. In 1995 Sabien Burgess was charged with the murder of his girlfriend, Michelle Dyson, whom he found shot in the home they shared. A child who had been in the house when the murder took place told detectives that he had seen another man, and not Burgess, commit the crime. But Ritz and Lehman did not report this. According to the federal lawsuit brought by Burgess after his release, he was convicted based on the false testimony of another person involved in Adnan's case—Daniel Van Gelder of the

Baltimore Police Trace Analysis Unit. Van Gelder testified that he had swabbed the webbing of Burgess's hands and found gunshot residue, which could only be present if Burgess had fired the murder weapon. But Burgess maintains that Van Gelder lied; he had swabbed Burgess's palms, where such residue would naturally be found because he had touched his girlfriend's body after finding her. Burgess was convicted after a two-day trial. Two years later, a man by the name of Charles Dorsey wrote repeated letters to Burgess's attorney confessing to the murder. Ritz went to interview Dorsey a year later and dismissed him, reporting that he didn't have the kind of details the real killer would have.

In 2013 the Mid-Atlantic Innocence Project filed a petition for writ of actual innocence on Burgess's behalf; after spending nineteen years in prison, he was finally released in 2014.

In Addison's case, the testimony of a witness was used to charge and convict him of a 1996 murder, though other witnesses gave conflicting testimony that would have exculpated him. The conflicting witness statements were withheld by the State's Attorney from the defendant and he was convicted, serving nine years before those statements were discovered. In 2005 a court ordered a new trial, at which point the State dismissed charges. The investigating officer in the case was Detective MacGillivary.

In all three cases exculpatory information was withheld and wrongful convictions obtained. Sarah never mentioned any of this in the podcast. Her treatment of Gutierrez was likewise lukewarm, even sympathetic. She mentioned another important case Gutierrez was working on around the same time as Adnan's, that of Zach Whitman, an adolescent who had been convicted of the brutal murder of his brother. Gutierrez had failed to file his appeal and lied to the parents about it. They felt Gutierrez had lied to get their money. But Sarah had a generous assessment: it could be that Gutierrez didn't know how sick she was, that she was taking cases she thought she could handle, and that she didn't understand the "business side of things." Sarah point-blank disagreed with me on the podcast that Gutierrez may have thrown the case on purpose, something that not only I but Adnan and his family suspected, given her desperation for money.

In both cases, with Gutierrez and the police, I told Sarah how I felt (and blogged about it too)—that if Adnan was her son, brother, loved one, she wouldn't have gone so easy on either of them. We texted back and forth. She agreed, and I calmed down.

But I wasn't so calm when I confronted her about the clip she played in Episode 10 of Adnan discussing his relationship with Gutierrez. In it Adnan says he had a great deal of affection for her, that she only showed him compassion, and that he felt like she "had his back." He says: "The closest thing I can think of is if you combine a doctor, a nurse, a school teacher, a coach, and your parents. If you combine all of that then you may have an idea of how much I trusted Miss Gutierrez in that situation."

This episode, ironically called "The Best Defense is a Good Defense," didn't air a negative word from Adnan about Gutierrez. If all you heard was the podcast and didn't follow my blog (which was most people), you'd think Adnan was really happy with Gutierrez. I was baffled. I asked Adnan why he had only waxed eloquent about Gutierrez.

He said that he had explained to Sarah that this was how he felt about Gutierrez when she represented him, but not after he learned what she'd done and how badly she had failed him. He didn't realize Sarah had cut the rest out.

I was livid, and so was he. It wasn't so much about the public perception on this issue—it was about his having an ongoing ineffective assistance of counsel (IAC) claim. I worried that his apparent positivity about Gutierrez on the podcast could be used by the State against his claim that she was ineffective.

I didn't immediately say anything to Sarah, but a few weeks later she sent me a message; she was upset about something I had posted on my blog. I had e-mailed her to ask if her team had identified Hae's pager number, because I certainly couldn't find it in any of the files, and she responded with no, they didn't know it. I thought that was odd, considering she mentioned in the podcast that Adnan never reached out to Hae after the day she disappeared. His response to her questions about this was initially that he didn't remember. When Sarah told him his records show that he didn't page her after January 13, he tried to explain it, saying he may not have reached out because every day at school the kids were discussing it and he was getting updates from her other friends. But if Sarah was now telling me they didn't know Hae's pager number, how could they say whether or not Adnan had paged her? Did she challenge him, effectively cornering him without actually knowing whether or not he had paged her? So I took to my blog and posted about our exchange, which really pissed her off.

She called me immediately to correct her e-mail, saying that she was mistaken and they did in fact have Hae's pager number, that she was upset I shared a private e-mail, and lastly, because my blog made them seem incompetent.

But I was already angry about the Gutierrez episode and not exactly in the mood to entertain her hurt feelings at being made to look bad.

"You know who looks bad? Adnan, who looks like an idiot for saying wonderful things about Gutierrez when he's got a claim in court against her. He told me that he made it very clear to you that he had no idea how badly she was screwing up his case, and that after he found out he was upset. But all you aired was him saying lovely things about her, and that could hurt his IAC claim!"

Sarah told me that it was their editorial discretion to use his clips however they wanted, meaning yes, they had cut out the other parts of his statements, and that the IAC claim wasn't their problem, it was Adnan's lawyer's problem. I wasn't about to stand for that.

A full-on shouting match ensued. It is embarrassing, looking back on it now, but it was also a necessary purge. Having gotten our agitation with each other out of our system, we both somewhat lukewarmly apologized. I apologized for putting her private e-mail message on my blog, and she apologized for not representing Adnan's sentiments about Gutierrez fully. We called it a draw and moved on, knowing that neither of us could afford to undermine the relationship.

Negotiating this relationship was always a challenge for me and Adnan's family. We felt constantly torn between undying gratitude to Sarah and bitterness that she didn't go completely to bat for Adnan. Having such a prolonged and personal interaction with a journalist will blur lines. It makes you forget why that journalist is there and what their mission is. But it was hardest for Adnan.

My heart broke a little the first time Adnan told me how conflicted he was.

He was upset about Episode 11, "Rumors," in which Sarah gave airtime to two anonymous men who had been bugging her for weeks. They wanted to challenge the good-guy image that the rest of the community had so far painted of him. Try as Sarah would, person after person said the same thing about Adnan: he was cordial, kind, easy-going, affectionate, and just nice to everyone. But the anonymous men, who alleged that they were childhood friends of Adnan, claimed that he had a side that no one knew about. Finally Sarah capitulated, perhaps not wanting to be called biased.

Listening to "Rumors," I realized what Adnan had recognized years earlier: that many of the people he grew up with believed in the process, the system that convicted him, over their own experience of knowing him. "Ali" in the podcast was in fact Imran Hasnuddin, a friend of Adnan's growing up, who had nothing bad to say about him but was basically not allowed by his parents to publicly get involved in the case at all. Even as a thirty-three-year-old man, Imran was afraid to be interviewed with his real name and voice.

A different voice sheepishly offered as evidence of Adnan's dark side that he stole from the mosque collection box in middle school. He alleged a ridiculous figure, thousands of dollars every week, and then threw in that he himself also stole from the same collection boxes. He ended by agreeing that Adnan was a good person.

Sarah spoke to the mosque president, who said it was impossible that thousands were ever stolen. They don't even collect that much. It was an embarrassing and irrelevant sideshow. Adnan readily admitted to Sarah that he stole twenty, forty bucks here and there from the Friday collection box when he was a kid. He then got caught by his mother and stopped doing it.

If there was ever a straw that broke Adnan's back in this process, it was this episode. He didn't hide his irritation when Sarah asked him about the petty theft, and you could hear it in the podcast. The way Sarah framed it, there were only two possibilities ultimately: that either Adnan was a liar or Jay was. And if that was the case, then exploring them both in depth was only fair. Yet she gave airtime to Adnan's middle school collection-plate petty thefts while never mentioning Jay's criminal record.

Since 1999, Jay's Maryland criminal record has included assault, theft, trespassing, and domestic violence charges. This is public information easily available online, as are all Maryland criminal records. We thought Sarah would at least mention this in her commentary on Jay, especially since any of these charges should have violated the conditions of his probation, which he was on after pleading guilty to being an accessory to Hae's murder, and it was highly suspicious that they didn't. But Sarah never mentioned them. If anything, her portrayal of Jay was sympathetic and kind. She said she saw his appeal, as a person, a friend, and a witness. Which was all fine and good; after all, she said the same thing about Adnan repeatedly, that he was likeable, charming, kind, just a nice guy. But the difference between Adnan and Jay was this: Adnan's personality was and is consistent, whereas the Jay she met was not the Jay who called her late one night.

She had interviewed Jay before the podcast began, and what we heard on *Serial* was from that meeting. She had given him her contact information in case he wanted to talk further (or rather she hoped he wanted to talk more, and on tape). One night, as the podcast was well under way, she finally heard from Jay in the most unexpected way. She then called me, a little freaked out.

It was late in the evening on the East Coast when her cell phone rang. An agitated, angry man railed on for a few minutes, threatening Sarah to back off, to stop reporting on the case, cursing profanities and screaming. Then he hung up. Sarah was stunned. She knew the voice, and the man had failed to block the number he called from. So she called him back, immediately.

A calm voice answered the phone, saying "hello?"

Sarah asked, "Jay?"

He responded in the affirmative, yes, it's Jay.

Sarah asked him if he had just called her and hung up. He said no. She said that she got the call from his number, literally minutes ago. He still insisted, no, it wasn't him. His tone was even.

Sarah wasn't about to let it go so easily, of course, and then the calm, collected Jay who insisted that he hadn't called began to raise his voice. After a few minutes he was essentially using the same exact language as in the previous call, including threatening her, while at the same time maintaining that he was not the one who called.

I can't recall how the second call ended, but Sarah immediately contacted me to let me know about this exchange. Not in a gossipy way, but to give me a heads-up to be careful and be safe, because I was unequivocal in my disgust for Jay online, holding him responsible for ruining Adnan's life while protecting his own rear end. The hashtag #JayDidIt was already circulating on Twitter and the public momentum for him to come clean was building. Sarah was worried he might lash out at me.

But she was no less amazed at how easily he lied to her. It made us both wonder if he suffered from some delusional disorder—maybe he really believed his lie? Maybe he didn't remember making the call?

Either way, his ability to lie so easily and then indignantly and unflinchingly stand by his lies impressed us both.

Of course, Sarah had to keep the lines of communication open with Jay in the hopes that he would be willing to talk more. At a minimum I hoped that his behavior would impact her reporting on the case.

But she didn't say anything publicly, and neither did we. I just mildly seethed as she explored Adnan's middle school misdeeds.

Adnan didn't seethe, though; he wrestled with the relationship. Sarah and he had developed a friendship, or at least to him it was a friendship. She didn't just interview him about the case—she asked him about his life, she shared her personal stories, he learned about her family, spoke to her kids over the phone. Isn't that what friends do? But then there were these weekly shows, her public doubts, not just about his innocence, but even about his character.

Was Adnan a psychopath? Was he manipulative? These were serious considerations Sarah undertook as she tried to unravel the truth. So what was Adnan to do, cut her off? Continue to be friendly, though in reality no reasonable person could sincerely be friends with someone who publicly wondered if they were a psychopathic killer?

Serial shattered Adnan's self-contained world. He had built a life full of people who trusted him, loved him, believed him, in which he would never be accused of being manipulative again.

I always raged a bit on the inside at Judge Heard's pronouncement at sentencing that Adnan was manipulative, and I had not carefully considered the profound emotional and psychological impact it must have had on him. Here he stood, barely out of childhood, in a room packed with his community, loved ones, Hae's family, and media, with no way to fight back against the woman sitting high above us in black robes. It was official, recorded for posterity, that he was a manipulator. It broke him nearly as much as did the verdict itself.

Having been through all that, letting Sarah into his controlled emotional environment was a significant emotional risk for him.

But like any risk, this one had a shot of paying off big.

As *Serial* exploded, Adnan's mailbox filled up. I had posted his address on my blog, where some folks got it while others were enterprising enough to dig it up on their own. Adnan was deluged with letters, notes, pictures, and prayers. Some were short messages of support, others were pages and pages of personal divulgences. Adnan was stunned at the sometimes very intimate nature of the letters, people pouring out their pain and tribulations to a stranger. He realized it was sometimes easier for people to share their deepest sorrows with a stranger than with people they knew. I told him that's how the Internet mostly works.

Students who had been assigned to listen to *Serial* wrote to him. People doing their master's or PhD thesis on some aspect of the case wrote. Supporters tried to send money, music CDs, and books, all of which the prison sent back. Women infatuated with him wrote letters, sometimes proposing marriage or love, and some sent pictures of themselves, half-dressed or not dressed at all; these pictures he mailed back, feeling a bit embarrassed.

Initially he tried to respond to every letter, that was his intention. He made a stack of letters to respond to, attempting to write a couple of responses daily. The stack grew and grew, his hand began to wear down after a couple of months of painstaking writing, and eventually he gave up. He owns an ancient word processor, a machine he's had for years, which he affectionately calls his wife. The word processor, however, required reams of inked tape, and he couldn't afford to type out responses to all these letters. So he decided he would only respond to letters from kids, not wanting to disappoint them, and hope the grown-ups would understand.

There was no way the prison staff and other inmates could miss all the attention he was getting. His mail was in bundles, newspapers and magazines coming into the prison covered stories about *Serial* and his case, and local and national stations gave regular updates. More than once friends and fellow prisoners came to show him an article with his picture, and more than once he would catch updates from television. They joked and nicknamed him "Hollywood." Numerous times guards told him they were listening to the podcast; a few told him that they always knew he didn't belong in prison and now they knew why.

While Adnan could definitely tell that his case had global attention, he still had no idea of the extent of the madness. One day he said to me, "I mean, I know it's big, but it's not like as big as the West Memphis Three case, right?"

Wrong.

After Adnan was convicted he mostly lost his community, but now they were back. As word got out about the podcast, and news outlets across the globe reported on his case every week, people at the mosque began saying his name again. Women who hadn't mentioned her son in over a decade came to Aunty Shamim, telling her they supported Adnan; random people at the mosque would hug Yusuf and tell him they always knew his brother was innocent. Dozens and dozens reached out to the family to ask how they could help. Though relations were still strained, Tanveer began communicating with the family, speaking up online in support of Adnan. After all these years, they finally felt free to talk about him.

But there were also those who still kept a distance. I heard second- and thirdhand whispers that so-and-so, who knew Adnan as a kid, thought he could do it. This was new.

I realized I needed to prove that Adnan had been framed. I had to figure out how the State did it. Sarah had copied all the case files onto a thumb drive and sent them to me a few weeks after the podcast started. I began not very efficiently to review the files, documents I hadn't seen in fourteen years. There were thousands and thousands of them. Every day I reviewed a few hundred superficially, just to remind myself of what was there. Other than that, I barely had time to breathe. The three months or so that *Serial* ran, which in hindsight felt like three years, brought with it hundreds and hundreds of interview requests, article submission requests, and speaking requests. I was still blogging, working, and trying to manage the family.

Adnan had asked me to handle the public advocacy to the best of my ability—no pressure from him. But I was afraid to say no to anything while people were still interested.

I was being invited to speak at law schools that I would never have had a chance to get into, like Stanford and Yale, and law firms that would never have hired me. The legal community, from bar associations to law schools to firms, was captivated. *Serial* had taken what seemed like a routine state-level homicide case and made it something mythical, magical. The question kept coming up: why was this case so special?

"You tell me," I'd say.

One day, among the thousands of e-mails, Facebook messages, and tweets I was getting every week, I got one from a professor of digital writing and media arts named Pete Rorabaugh at the Southern Polytechnic State University.

Pete had been following my blogs and online commentary about *Serial*. He wondered if I had ever given thought about doing a discussion about the meta questions.

"The what?" I asked.

He explained. Unlike the rest of the world, Pete was interested in understanding almost everything but the case—he wanted to discuss the broader issues at play, the media dynamics, the storytelling frameworks and platforms. To be frank, I still wasn't sure what he was getting at. But I said ok.

We decided it would be best to have live conversations every Monday to parse the previous week's episode. That would give me time to do my blog, catch my breath over the weekend, think through the questions he sent me, and be prepared for another hour or more of his very thorough and thoughtful interviews.

I had thought I was being rather clever in my social media usage, but Pete forced me to take a step back and see the entire enterprise as one of storytelling. I was not fighting a case. I was attempting to shape a story, wrestling it from Sarah, from *Serial*.

Over the next couple of months we did a total of nine Hangouts, including one with a Reddit moderator, and one with an entire panel of Adnan's childhood friends. Sometimes I cried in the Hangouts—at any given moment my emotions could break free. Mondays weren't that far from Thursdays, and I often spent the weekend watching online conversations and having intense exchanges with Saad and Yusuf. Many Monday mornings I was still unsettled, raw, still processing the past few days.

And of course there was plenty happening behind the scenes. In the spirit of my pact with Sarah I hadn't uttered a peep about the Innocence Project taking Adnan's case. In early November, when the episode featuring Deirdre Enright and her team finally aired, I felt relieved and vindicated.

I kept getting asked why I believed in Adnan's innocence with such unmoving faith, but I realized my answers were colored by my personal attachment to him. Skeptics dismissed my certainty in his innocence the way atheists dismiss faith. But in Deirdre I had an unbiased expert, who by looking at just the documents could tell that something had gone very wrong.

It was a small mercy to have that information public; it provided some respite from the cynics who still pummeled me with all sorts of questions and attacks, trying hard to plant some doubt in my mind.

Still, I had a lot of bad moments when I realized there was no smoking gun that proved his innocence, and that nearly any piece of information could be interpreted in diametrically opposite ways. That Adnan never accused Jay of the crime was seen by some as proof of his innocence, that it meant he had no idea what really happened, and by others as proof of his guilt, an acquiescence to Jay's statements. That his friends saw him cry after Hae's body was found was seen by some as remorse, others as grief. That Asia never showed up at the PCR hearing to some meant that her alibi was contrived bullshit and Adnan knew it, and to others it meant that he wasn't methodical or manipulative enough to plan for an alibi.

The Asia argument, and my confusion over what had happened with her, was put to rest late one night in mid-November when I got a call from Justin Brown.

"Ok, you can't tell anyone what I'm about to tell you."

"Ok, I won't."

"No, I mean it. No posting it online or writing about it."

"Ok, I won't blog it, what is it?"

"No tweeting it."

"Oh my God, Justin, ok, I won't tweet ANYTHING."

"And . . . you can't tell Sarah I told you."

Deep breath.

"Ooookayyyyy, what the hell is going on?"

"Asia called Sarah. She's back in. She wants to give us a new affidavit and will testify that she remembers being with Adnan after school that day."

"What. What? What?!!!"

After a paralyzed "what the hell" moment, I began jumping up and down. I couldn't believe what I was hearing. I ran a few times around my dining room table, flailing my arms. Then, unsurprisingly, I began crying even before he could explain.

After calming me down, he finally did.

Asia McClain, who hadn't contacted Sarah since the one taped interview we heard on the very first episode, had listened to the podcast. She had heard the audio recording from the PCR hearing where Urick talked about getting a call from Asia, stating, "She was concerned, because she was being asked questions about an affidavit she'd written back at the time of the trial. She told me that she'd only written it because she was getting pressure from the family, and she basically wrote it to please them and get them off her back."

According to Asia, she had panicked a bit when Justin's PI showed up to talk to her about the case, and when she spoke to Urick he reassured her that Adnan had been convicted on sound evidence. After listening to *Serial,* not only did she realize how shaky the case was, and that Urick had lied to her about the veracity of the evidence against Adnan, but he had also lied to the court about their conversation. Asia had never told him she had been pressured to write her letters or affidavit, or that she had written them to get the family "off her back." And finally, Urick had all but told her not to testify, saying it was an open-and-shut case.

Late one night in November she called Sarah and told her that Urick's testimony was a lie. Sarah did something that I will always deeply respect—she immediately got in touch with Justin and put the two in contact. More importantly, she agreed with Justin's request not to report this development on the podcast.

Imagine the integrity it takes to refrain from (1) reporting a major development at the core of your story and (2) ever even hinting at your role in the development. By the time it became news a couple of months later, *Serial* had ended.

For now, Sarah was concerned about preserving Asia's current statements and realized how significantly this could impact the case. She cared about getting justice in a court of law for Adnan. It meant a tremendous amount to Adnan and all of us, then and now.

Justin had one last mini-bomb to drop on me about Asia about a month later. She had gotten her own lawyer and was going to do a new affidavit, refuting Urick's testimony and confirming her recollection of January 13, 1999. But she had one request, perhaps even a condition. The first news outlet to report this development, her new affidavit that Justin would file with the court, would have to be Glenn Beck's Web site, TheBlaze.

I thought I heard him wrong so I made him repeat it.

"She's a big fan of Beck, it is what it is."

The irony didn't escape me, that the one person who could save Adnan's appeal of the PCR denial was a fan of a media personality with a proven track record of anti-Muslim animosity.

But it proved something to me—it may be that Asia didn't care for Muslims, and maybe she even shared Beck's deeply troubling views on Islam, but she cared more about the truth. Asia wasn't even concerned about whether Adnan was innocent or guilty—that wasn't her business. Her business, regardless of his faith or culpability, was to make the truth known. This raised the value of her testimony exponentially.

It was a precarious situation, though. What if the prosecution got to her again? What if it was too late? Would the Court of Special Appeals now find credible a witness who failed to appear the first time?

Adnan, always more cautious, always aware of the thousands of ways things could go wrong (because for him, they mostly did), was less optimistic.

He said, "Look Rabia, it's a shot, but a long shot. And at this point probably our only shot."

That sobered me up. I agreed with him.

Turned out we were both wrong.

IT TAKES A VILLAGE

———— • ————

And say, "My Lord, lead me in through an entry of truth, and lead
me out through an exit of truth, and grant me from You a supporting power." And say, "The truth has come, and falsehood has
withered away; for falsehood is bound to wither away."

Holy Quran, 17:80–81

When I first got the e-mail I gasped slightly. Was this really . . . really, from the
wife of comedian Chris Rock?

Name	Dez Rock
Email	██████████
Subject	G'day
Message	Hi Rabia, I'm a 41 year old mother of 5 living in Australia, I'm also a current law student and clearly an avid podcast listener. Feel free to social media stalk me to verify who I am, yes my name really is Dez Rock and am married to Chris Rock.. side note, he's not nearly as funny, but I digress. No doubt you are getting a world wind of comments from everywhere, tainted with religion, culture, colour, verdicts, demands etc. So I don't want to talk about any of that, not that I don't have opinions and things to say, but because that is not what is motivating me to write to you. I just wanted to quietly write to support you, you as a fellow female human who is juggling all the aspects that you must juggle. I want to send you words of encouragement that you are coming across as well spoken, thoughtful, and clear. I want to whisper that you must keep strong and keep going, because your role is vital. Kindest regards, Dez
Site	http://www.splitthemoon.com

I got thousands of messages on my blog as I posted in response to *Serial* every
week. Like Adnan, I couldn't respond to everyone, but every so often a message

would make me stop, force me to respond. It could be a message from someone offering to help with their expertise, or contribute to a fund for Adnan (which I had yet to even think about setting up), or sending a surprising, feel-good message thanking me for opening the world of Muslims to them in a way they hadn't been exposed to before.

I was insanely excited when Jemima Goldstein, known as Jemima Khan to her legions of Pakistani fans, sent me a Twitter message. Jemima, the ex-wife of Pakistani cricket legend and current political leader Imran Khan, is the closest Pakistanis ever got to having their own princess. She's adored by Pakistanis, even after divorcing Khan, having gained our admiration and trust for being an outspoken critic of the U.S. drone policy in Afghanistan-Pakistan as well as for her continued public concern for the people of the country. Jemima reached out to tell me she had listened to *Serial* and how impacted she was by Adnan's story, especially given the fact that her own sons were teenaged Pakistani-British Muslim boys and Adnan reminded her of them.

I had already heard from Jemima when I got the message from Chris Rock's wife. And yes, I initally thought it was *the* Chris Rock—it took a couple of days to realize it couldn't be unless the comedian had a secret second wife stashed away in Australia. Still, I was really touched by her message, having gotten it on a particularly bad day when Internet trolls were doing a number on me.

I wrote back, and after a couple of weeks she made me an offer I couldn't refuse. Dez's Chris Rock was not only one of the most respected and well-known hackers in the world, he also ran one of the world's premier cyber-security firms, Kustodian.

Would I like Kustodian, free of charge, to protect my blog?

Why, yes, Dez, yes. I would like Kustodian to do that.

Within a matter of weeks, they took over my site and began protecting it from literally thousands of attacks a week, something I could have never have managed on my own.

Shortly before I first heard from Dez, I got another note through my blog that made me pause. A literary agent wanted to speak to me. Lauren Abramo had been reading my blogs and following my other work too. She thought I should write a book.

After talking for a bit and realizing she was really, truly interested, I finally got excited.

"Can I send you what I've written, the start of a novel? I've got a few chapters down, it's a story built on multiple stories from my life and the lives of people I've known—about a Pakistani girl who is married off by her family and ends up in the U.S. as an immigrant!"

Lauren grew silent, pausing cautiously as she tried to find the kindest way to break my heart.

"Well that sounds wonderful, Rabia, but I was thinking . . . perhaps you should write a book about Adnan's case."

It was my turn to pause.

I hadn't ever considered writing about his case, and the very thought of it filled me with dread.

I was afraid that people would think I was trying to profit from the case. I had already heard that people were saying I was trying to ride the podcast's coat-tails to fame, even though I hadn't done any fund-raising and wasn't even making money on my speaking engagements at this point. Later, because of the enormous demands on my time, I did begin asking for a small speaking honorarium, half of which I donated to Adnan's legal fees.

I didn't want to do it. It opened the door to the public considering me an opportunist, and maybe even Adnan and his family as well. But Lauren pointed out that if I didn't a write a book someone else might.

I told her I'd think about it.

I also had to think hard about it for another reason: I didn't know the case as well as she thought. I still had thousands of documents to review and would have to wait until *Serial* was over, until my project at New America was over, to really get through them. It could take at least a year to do that, and by then maybe interest in the case would be gone.

Little did I know that within the month, one of the sharpest minds I've ever encountered would enter the scene and save me.

On November 23, 2014, Susan Simpson, a lawyer I'd never heard of, put up a post on a blog I'd never heard of either, The View From LL2. I saw the link on Reddit and spent the next two hours carefully reading and re-reading the fifty-nine-page tome titled "Serial: A Comparison of Adnan's Cell Phone Records and the Witness Statements Provided by Adnan, Jay, Jenn, and Cathy."

I did a little quick Googling on Susan. Everything looked on the up-and-up—she was an associate attorney at a D.C. firm, the Volkov Law Group, and a law graduate of George Washington University. Her focus was on white-collar defense but she had a background in criminal appeals. Her previous few posts discussed maritime border laws and the Alien Tort Statute. It didn't escape me that she had also made a suit of armor for her ridiculously fluffy kitten, Ragnarok. This, I realized, was a highly talented and multifaceted woman. And she loved her cat as much I cherished my feline Mr. Beans, who graced my social media regularly and had become familiar to my followers. I liked her.

Susan also had done what I had not had the time to do—taken every phone call made from Adnan's cell that day and compared the "pinged" tower locations to every version of Jay's, Jenn's, and Adnan's stories. It was meticulous and thorough, and showed that the State's story at trial wasn't actually corroborated by the records.

Sarah had mentioned on *Serial* that the State only brought up four of the fourteen sites it had tested that day because the other ten didn't match up to Jay's story. The four that could be used to bolster Jay's testimony were all calls after 6:00 p.m., the most important ones being two incoming calls at 7:09 and 7:16—otherwise known as the "Leakin Park Pings"—because they were routed through a tower located in the park.

On these calls, Dana Chivvis concludes in Episode 5, "Route Talk," that there is little equivocation. She believes the cell phone must have been in the park at the time the calls came.

Susan Simpson writes in her first post on the case, "Of the 52 outgoing and incoming calls made to Adnan's cell phone on January 12 and 13, 1999, exactly two calls were routed through L689B, which is the tower and antenna that covers the southwest portion of Leakin Park (and covers almost nothing that isn't Leakin Park). In fact, only one other call was even routed through tower L689, despite the fact it is adjacent to the towers covering Woodlawn and Cathy's house—and that's the 4:12 p.m. call, when Jay would have been parking Hae's car immediately next to Leakin Park, at the Park-n-Ride. This is very strong evidence that the reason the 7:09 and 7:16 p.m. calls were routed from the Leakin Park tower is that the cell phone was, in fact, in Leakin Park. The odds are too much against this being a mere coincidence—because over the course of 48 hours, only two calls are routed through L689B, and both occur precisely within the one-and-a-half hour window in which we know the killer was in Leakin Park burying Hae's body. This is a sufficient basis from which to conclude that the killer had the phone while burying Hae."

Dana says something similar on *Serial*: "The the amount of luck you would have to have to make up a story like that and then have the cell phone records corroborate the key points, I just don't think that that's possible."

The Leakin Park calls were the bane of my advocacy for Adnan, the only thing I didn't know how to rebut.

The thing I could easily rebut, the issue Sarah thought most damning for Adnan, was the call made from his phone at 3:32 p.m. to Nisha Tanna, the young woman he had begun talking to after breaking up with Hae. Who would be calling Nisha in the middle of the school day from Adnan's cell phone but Adnan himself? Sarah asked. She figured that put Adnan with Jay at a time when Adnan said he wasn't with him, and at a time around when Hae went missing.

The "Nisha Call" was easy—Jay said Adnan called her after killing Hae, then gave Jay the phone to briefly chat with her too. Nisha also testified that she did indeed speak to Jay just *once* while on a call with Adnan—but she stated with specificity that this chat took place when Adnan went to visit Jay at a video store he was working at. The "Nisha Call" couldn't have have happened on January 13 though, because Jay didn't begin working at the porn video shop until January 31.

Nisha's number was saved on speed-dial on Adnan's phone. It was likely called on January 13 by mistake—a butt-dial or otherwise mistaken attempt to make a call by Jay, because he still had the phone at the time and all calls before and after the "Nisha Call" were to Jay's friends.

But the Leakin Park calls were different. According to Adnan, he was with Jay after school that evening. He had dropped Jay off at home at some point, and then headed to the mosque for evening prayers. Without a doubt, whether or not Jay was with him at 7:00 p.m., the phone definitely was. And if the phone was in Leakin Park when Adnan had it, we had a problem.

Susan's next post was a few days later, where she examines Jay's credibility and concisely articulates why he has none: because he himself admits it.

"But sometimes, it is very easy to make an assessment of a witness's inherent credibility. And that is when a witness informs you that he has none. Jay is that witness. Jay told the police and the jury, again and again, that he was willing to lie in order to avoid criminal punishment. He was not shy about this fact. Ask Jay why he lies, and he'll tell you: he lies because he didn't want to get in trouble."

Susan then challenges Sarah's agreement with the State, that while there have been some "inconsistencies" in Jay's story, the "spine" of his story has remained consistent.

"Wait, *what*?" Susan writes, "Jay tells a 'consistent' story? Jay has been 'consistent' on the main points? Koenig keeps using that word. I don't think it means what she thinks it means."

Susan spends a dozen pages listing the dozens of times Jay's story has been inconsistent. As I'm reading this, I'm thinking, *Who is this woman?*

I had to reach out. On November 26, 2014, I e-mailed her.

"Dear Susan, I've been reading your blog about Adnan's case and wanted to reach out to thank you for your tremendous work. I was going to, at the end of *Serial*, plot out Adnan's timeline as per my theory and understanding that day/evening, and you did it almost exactly as I was going to. I'm in the D.C. area too, perhaps we can get together sometime. I'd love a partner in crime on this. All the best, Rabia."

Susan wrote back the next day.

"Hi Rabia! As I'm sure you've noticed from the several documents/sources I stole from you, I'm a fan of your blog. (Am also a fan of Mr. Beans.) And I would be more than down for getting together sometime—I gotta admit, the narrative framework of *Serial* has been really frustrating sometimes, because there's just a complete absence of any legal perspective. I'd love to hear about the case from someone with a lawyer's view."

I was stoked and had already decided that I'd give her access to the files. I needed her eyes on them.

Susan's next post, on November 29, titled "*Serial:* Plotting the Coordinates of Jay's Dreams," masterfully showed the impossibility of Jay's statements like this:

> So Adnan and Jay stop in the middle of Leakin Park, blocking both lanes of Franklintown Road (or does Adnan pull over to the side? Jay says both happen, who knows). Jay and Adnan argue for a bit over whether or not Jay is going to help Adnan bury the body. Jay tells him "fuck no," and Adnan finally gives up on asking. So they drive both cars "around the corner," where they park Hae's car. Adnan gets in his car with Jay, and Jay drives back to the burial site. He pulls Adnan's car up at the spot with the "white pillar" and parks it. Adnan and Jay head back into the woods 20 yards and start digging a hole.
>
> And then, in another Jay Paradox, Jay and Adnan simultaneously dig a hole with the shovels and without the shovels:
>
>> **Detective: Do you have the digging tools at this point?**
>>
>> *Jay: No.*
>>
>> **Detective: What happens?**
>>
>> *Jay: Um, dig a small hole, put the shovels back in the back seat of his car. (Int.2 at 32-33.)*
>
> So according to Jay, he and Adnan get to the grave site and start digging. They do not have the shovels. Then they spend "20-25 minutes" digging a hole (Int.2 at 33), before putting the shovels back in the back seat of Adnan's car. Makes perfect sense. But this

From Simpson's blog viewfrom11.2.com

And this:

Finally, Jay tell the cops that after they finish burying Hae's body, "we[ ] get[ ] back in his car" and "we drive to Westview on, I told him take me home" (Int.2 at 34-35). No mention of Hae's car is made until a detective interrupts him:

> **Detective: You got 2 cars?**
>
> *Jay: Oh I'm sorry, I apologize. Um, I'm missing.*
>
> **Detective**: *Okay.*
>
> *Jay: Top spots. Um, yes I'm sorry. We leave, we we still do have 2 cars. Um, he he ah, motion for me to follow him.*

It's funny how often that happens in the second interview. Jay keeps forgetting his story — he's so lucky he has the detectives there to remind him.

Shortly after I made contact with Susan, I got a message from someone else I'd never heard of before, a man named Colin Miller.

On December 3, 2014, Colin wrote to me to share a blog he had written about the cell tower evidence in the case. Not having the trial transcript, Colin had questions about how things had transpired when the judge nearly excluded Abe Waranowitz as a cell phone expert. I took a look at the blog post he sent me and then did some background research on him.

Professor Colin Miller, I discovered, taught criminal law, criminal adjudication, and evidence at the University of South Carolina School of Law. But he wasn't just an evidence professor, he was *the* evidence professor, writing and editing a blog called, aptly, The EvidenceProf blog.

By the time Colin reached out to me, he had already done eight posts on the case and *Serial*, beginning on November 21, 2014. This was an incredibly prolific blogging rate by any standard.

I began following him and Susan and eventually realized that I needed to give them both the full case files—they both had the drive, time, experience, and brain power I lacked to analyze what had happened. What Sarah wasn't able to find, what I wasn't able to find, maybe they could.

It couldn't have come at a better time because *Serial* was wrapping up. Sarah had told me there would be twelve episodes and by my count, in early December, that meant the end was around the corner.

Here was the real test: How would Sarah conclude on his guilt or innocence? Where would a year of getting to know Adnan leave her?

Eleven episodes of *Serial* had carefully kept listeners on the fence about Adnan's guilt or innocence; maybe, we hoped, she was saving her big reveal for the last episode. Maybe she would come out and say what she hadn't so far, that she believed in Adnan's innocence.

A couple of weeks before the last episode Sarah and I met in my parents' basement, not far from Adnan's home. She recorded our conversation for about an hour, asking how I felt knowing that she had found nothing to fully exonerate him. At that point I knew there would be no big surprise at the end of the podcast.

Fine, there was no hard-and-fast proof. But what about Sarah herself, what did she think? Surely her opinion would count for so much. Unlike her listeners, she had spent time with Adnan. I didn't want to put her in a tough spot, but dammit, after all this time I wanted to know. So I finally just summoned up the courage and point-blank asked.

"In my heart," she said, "I think he's innocent."

She had no proof, of course, but for me it was enough to hear those words from her lips. I felt a rush of relief, and after she left I told Yusuf, Saad, and Adnan what she said, reassuring them that the podcast would end in Adnan's favor.

The morning of the final episode, December 18, 2014, was tense. I couldn't wait to hear Sarah's conclusion but also couldn't wait for the podcast to be over so we could focus on the actual case and bringing Asia back into it. But first there was a big surprise in the episode—out of the shadows came a person no one expected to hear from: Don Clinedinst.

When Sarah was researching the case, she had reached out to Don, and he had refused to talk to her. Then, a week before the final episode was taped, having perhaps listened to the previous eleven episodes, he contacted her and agreed to talk but not to be recorded.

I had not, in all these years, given Don a second thought. The first time he crossed my radar as a possible suspect was when I heard Deirdre Wright of the Innocence Project mention him in Episode 7. Even then, though, I figured he was part of the "big picture" excuse Deirdre thought we'd need to get a court to allow us to retrieve whatever DNA evidence may exist, nothing having been tested against Don or anyone other than Adnan and Jay all those years ago.

In the blog post I wrote after the Innocence Project episode I didn't even mention Don, but after the last episode, in which Don speaks to Sarah but refuses to have his voice recorded, I wrote a few paragraphs about him, mostly focused on entirely the wrong thing:

"Ok, I'll just be up-front here. I don't know what to do about Don. The note to him really weirded me out."

I was referring to the note found in Hae's car, the note addressed to Don in which she tells him to drive safe and that she has to run to go to a wrestling match at Randallstown High. The question I raised in my blog was when and why Hae would have written that note, because some of the language, "sorry I couldn't stay," suggested she had already seen him on the day she wrote it.

And the day she wrote it, by the State's accounts and as accepted by Sarah, was January 13, 1999, the same day Hae was killed.

Others dismissed the language as being ambiguous, that perhaps Hae was in a hurry and didn't express herself clearly. For most, the note indicated she intended to see Don that night. But that didn't sit right with me; it just didn't make sense.

Hearing Don's words about how he knew he'd be a suspect immediately and began recounting his steps raised my eyebrows. On the one hand you had Adnan, who was so clueless that even as police kept interviewing him he didn't give it a second thought, dismissing the idea as absurd.

And here you had Don, about whom Sarah said the following:

> When Hae went missing, Don was one of the first people the cops called. He says he knew immediately he'd be a suspect. "I said, 'well ok, they're going to try to blame it on me because she was with me last night. I'm the new boyfriend, I'm obviously going to be one of the first suspects, me and Adnan.'" He said he immediately made sure he knew where he was. "When someone calls you up and tells you 'have you seen this person? They went missing, they haven't been seen since school,' you automatically retrace everything you did that day."

I found Don's reaction deeply unsettling. In no universe, if my partner couldn't be located, would I begin retracing my own steps. I'd be worried sick, focused on finding that person. But I had to acknowledge that this may not be true for everyone.

The police had definitely done a shoddy job during the investigation by not confirming through paperwork that Don was really working on January 13. Despite such a glaring investigatory breach, any questions about Don could be put to rest since LensCrafters had eventually turned over his timesheets to Gutierrez prior to trial. Don was definitely at work that day, and the police considered his alibi airtight.

After Don, Sarah spoke with a former co-worker of Jay's, a man named Josh. Josh recalled Jay being terrified, paranoid about a van outside the porn shop.

Josh figured Jay was scared that Hae's killer was in the van, though Jay never mentioned that someone being Adnan.

Sarah asks Josh if Jay is scared of Adnan's "people," of Pakistani relatives, and Josh says, "Yeah, he definitely said it was somebody, the guy was Middle Eastern."

Josh goes on to speak warmly about Jay, saying he feels sorry for him and that Jay wasn't a thug, rather the opposite, and he seemed in way over his head.

Before her conclusion, Sarah asks for Dana's take on the case. Calling her the "Mr. Spock" of the podcast, Sarah lets Dana lay out her thought process in detail, which boiled down to this: in order for everything to make sense, that Adnan just happened to lend Jay his car that day, and Jay happened to turn witness against him, and there happened to be a call to Nisha that afternoon, and Adnan happened not to have an alibi or even remember where he was—well, he'd have to be the unluckiest man ever. And no one is that unlucky.

Only after this buildup, and a brief interlude from Deirdre about a possible lead and where they were on seeking to test the forensic evidence for DNA, did Sarah get to her big ending.

To the disappointment of many, certainly all of us, Sarah wasn't able to commit herself to Adnan's innocence. She said she wouldn't have convicted him because there was too much reasonable doubt, and that while most of the time she thought he was innocent, she still "nursed doubt."

I can't fault Sarah for reaching this conclusion, and neither does Adnan. Unlike myself, Saad, and Adnan's family, Sarah has no reason to put her credibility and her professional reputation on the line for a cause she didn't have full confidence in.

After *Serial* ended, Sarah assured Adnan that she would continue to follow the case. While it wasn't an endorsement of his innocence, it was good enough for us.

Sometime in the middle of December 2014, right around the last episode of *Serial*, I was asked by a friend how to donate to Adnan's legal fund.

"What legal fund?" I asked.

"Um, you didn't set up a fund? Wait, you let all of *Serial* go by and didn't do any fund-raising? Doesn't he need money to help with legal fees!?"

Indeed. Yes he does. Except I hadn't had a chance to even think about it.

There wasn't any money, there was no fund. Adnan's parents had paid out of their modest means for years, all throughout the appellate process, and it had taken almost five years to raise the money for the original post-conviction. After the PCR was denied in 2014, although Justin had been ready to finally step away from the case after representing Adnan for five years, he was now fully in again. *Serial* and the return of Asia meant he would continue to push Adnan's appeal whether or not he got paid, he told Adnan.

But it wasn't just about Justin's legal fees. It would be incredibly generous if he waived them, but it would not be fair considering the tremendous amount of work he had to put in. It was also about other expenses we anticipated, such as hiring a private investigator in the hopes of uncovering new evidence.

I knew we had to raise money, I just didn't have the mental and actual bandwidth to deal with it.

Then I received this e-mail from Dennis Robinson:

Name	Dennis Robinson
Email	⬛⬛⬛⬛⬛⬛⬛⬛@gmail.com
Subject	Referral from Chris Flohr
Message	Hi Mrs. Chaudry, My name is Dennis and I'm a friend of Chris Flohr. I hate to cold-contact you like this, and more so hate to leave a comment through your web page, but I'm hoping to talk to you ASAP about creating and implementing a plan of action for Adnan's legal defense fund. M'am, you can contact me at ⬛⬛⬛⬛⬛⬛⬛⬛ase feel free to contact Chris who will vouch for me. Just for the sake of providing bona fides (considering this is coming to you from a complete stranger), I'm a Maryland attorney and a fellow Truman National Security Project fellow (Defense Council Class of 2015). I work in a sensitive position for the U.S. government so I don't have much of an online profile. I'd like to get to work immediately on fundraising, m'am, but before doing so, I want to make sure you are comfortable with me helping out. I'm available 24/7. Please contact me when you can. Thank you. Very respectfully, Dennis
Site	http://www.splitthemoon.com

Chris and I had been discussing how to go about the fund-raising, and at some point he must have realized I needed help.

I connected with Dennis as soon as possible.

"You take care of speaking up for Adnan," he told me. "I'll take care of everything behind the scenes. I'll be your assistant, set up the fund-raising, manage the communications, whatever you need."

I cried for a couple of days, tears of happy thanks. Before I knew it, Adnan's crowd-sourced fund-raising site was up on LaunchGood.com, which went out of its way to get the account set up and promoted within a matter of days. And the donations began pouring in.

Between Dez, Dennis, Susan, and Colin, it was as if angels had been sent to lift all the burdens I wasn't capable of carrying. The podcast was over, but the quest continued. I had to figure out how to keep public interest in the case, had to figure out how to put pressure on the State and courts to help with the appeal, and had to figure out what actually happened to Hae.

Fighting Adnan's case in court based on Gutierrez's failures, coupled with Asia's allegations, seemed possible now. But without returning to the original evidence, and getting the people at the heart of the matter to talk, getting to the truth of what happened to Hae would be much, much harder.

Some people, friends from school, tried to talk to Jay and get him to come clean. But he was angry at the attention, at his life and family being disrupted. He was married with kids now, living in California, far away from it all. He told some people that strangers had located his home and driven past it, taking pictures, posting his address on Reddit, and he was (justifiably) pissed off.

But at the end of December the universe sent us a big, fat gift. Jay talked.

I was in Canada, visiting my in-laws, relieved that *Serial* was over and I could take a break. Sometime in the afternoon of December 29, 2014, I got a text from Saad.

"Jay did an interview! He said he lied, it's so effed up, read it Rabia!!!"

Within a matter of minutes the interview, written by Natasha Vargas-Cooper for *The Intercept*, was tweeted, texted, and e-mailed to me a dozen times. I pulled myself away from my mother-in-law and locked myself in a room so I could read it in peace—except I couldn't, not in peace anyway.

Every paragraph made me livid. From when he first met Adnan, to his ridiculous story of being a serious drug dealer, to admitting that he and Adnan were never friends, to completely changing the narrative of the crime, I was shocked at the ease with which he lied and transformed his story.

I couldn't get through it without tweeting my immediate reactions. I screenshot nearly every paragraph and tweeted them with exasperated comments like "#PerjuryAbounds!"

Every part of Jay's story had changed. Now he didn't know if Hae had been killed in the Best Buy parking lot, and he also never saw Hae's car there; he just picked Adnan up there after the deed had been done and didn't know where her car was. The entire ride sequence when they supposedly drove around looking for a place to leave Hae's car, the Park-n-Ride—poof, it was now gone.

Jay says after picking Adnan up, they went to Krista Vinson's house, referred to as "Cathy" in the interview since she was called "not-her-real-name-Cathy" in *Serial*, where, surprise, Jenn is present. He says it's between 3:00 and 4:00 p.m.; they hang out, smoke weed, and Adnan drops him home at 6:00 p.m. Track practice is gone. And gone is Leakin Park in the 7:00 p.m hour.

It gets more interesting. Jay says after dropping him off at home, Adnan returned with Hae's car to his grandmother's house and called Jay on the landline (there is no such call in the call records). Adnan then popped the trunk on the side of the road, showing him Hae's body. According to Jay, "she looked kinda purple, blue, her legs were tucked behind her, she had stockings on, none of her clothes were removed, nothing like that. She didn't look beat up."

This, despite the fact that when Hae was disinterred, her bra and shirt were pulled up, exposing her breasts, and her skirt was pulled above her buttocks.

Standing at the open trunk, Adnan asks Jay to just help him "dig the hole." Jay agrees after Adnan threatens to turn him in for dealing weed, as if it is a much more serious crime than accessory after the fact to murder. Then Adnan drives off with car and body.

But the night is not over. Adnan returns a few hours later, close to midnight, in his own car. This time he's back to make Jay keep that promise, but first he needs tools to dig the hole. Jay grabs some gardening tools and they go to the park, where Adnan presumably pulls over by the side of the two-lane road as it begins to rain (there was no rain on the night of January 13, 1999). Jays says: "We dig for about forty minutes and we dig and dig," until Jay finally says "fuck it" and is done digging.

They have their hole, but no body. The body is apparently still in the trunk of Hae's car, which according to Jay is up around the bend on a small hill, "parked in a strange neighborhood"—strange, despite the fact that it's the same neighborhood where one of his grandmothers lives.

They drive around the corner, up the hill, where Adnan gets into Hae's car and tells Jay to move his car "halfway back down the hill" so that after burying Hae, Adnan doesn't have to walk too far to get to his car. Why he would have to walk to get to his car is unclear, since he would have Hae's car.

Nonetheless, according to Jay, Adnan drives off with Hae's car but then returns after thirty to forty-five minutes on foot to his own car, where Jay waits for him. He says Adnan is wearing gloves, panting, saying Hae was heavy. Gone now is the entire portion of Jay's police statements and testimony in which he is sitting on a log while Adnan digs. In this new version, Jay never sees Hae in the grave at all, despite having described her position in some detail sixteen years earlier.

There is still the problem of leaving Hae's car somewhere, but apparently Jay must first drive Adnan back down the hill to get it. Jay says he then follows Adnan around (presumably Adnan is in Hae's car and Jay is in Adnan's car) for a "few minutes" and dumps the car behind some row houses.

Jay goes on to say that it took intense pressure for the police to get him to cooperate, and it was only after getting assurances that he wouldn't be prosecuted for "procurement" of weed that he agreed to talk.

The next day, December 30, the second part of the interview was published.

Again, my hackles and ire were raised sky-high, especially when Jay mentioned the grand jury hearing and testimony of a "spiritual advisor" whose name starts with a "B." Bilal. He had to be talking about Bilal.

According to *The Incercept* article, "He spoke with the police during the investigation. But when he was called to the grand jury, he pled the fifth [the fifth amendment, that is, against self incrimination through testimony]. So that whatever he knew about Adnan, he knew that if he said it in court he could also be in trouble."

The editors of the piece inserted this note: "*The Intercept* confirmed with two sources that 'Mr. B.' did plead the fifth during the grand jury testimony." This is odd and not at all accurate. Bilal and Saad, thanks to the counsel and direction of Gutierrez, filed motions to quash the State's subpoena calling them to testify, wherein they said they would "plead the fifth" if called. The motions didn't fly and both of them testified; in other words, they *did not plead the fifth*.

So not only was Jay wrong about this but the editors of the piece somehow confirmed the incorrect information as accurate, leaving people to believe Bilal hadn't testified. I was also struck by how Jay knew anything about who had testified at the grand jury—the proceedings were sealed, and there is no public access to the records. Someone from the State had to have told him, either sixteen years ago, or now.

I was a bit perplexed by all of this, and also by Jay's antagonism toward Sarah in the piece. He believed she had damaged his reputation. But overall I was thrilled with the interview, because Jay had basically undone the entire State's narrative, including his own testimony at trial. The interview was so damaging that Colin Miller was even quoted in a piece on Vox.com: "I said before that the prosecution's case was dead. With this interview, Jay has now burned the corpse."

I didn't know the reporter or her angle, but I had tremendous respect for *The Intercept*, which was known for its exhaustive investigative reporting. I thought it was pushing the envelope to publish the exchange between Jay and Sarah, which they did in full, but the exchanges weren't damaging to Sarah; if anything, they undermined Jay's allegations.

After the second part of Jay's interview, I got a message from Vargas-Cooper, who I like to refer to as "NVC," through Twitter.

Apparently Jay was already having a similar reaction to NVC as he did to Sarah. I wished NVC would tell me more about how he was acting, but I didn't ask. We exchanged a few pleasantries, but then she gave me, in retrospect, a warning when she said, "It's going to get gnarly in the coming week, regardless of what I think, just know I think you're an ass kicker."

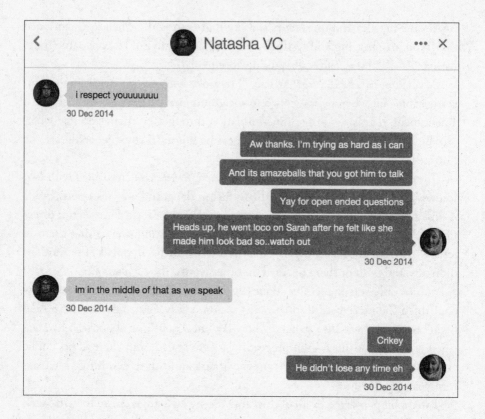

I had little reason to think that NVC was going to completely flip the script with what was to come: an interview with Kevin Urick.

Part one of the Urick interview was published on January 7, 2015. But it wasn't just an interview with him. It began as an opinion piece, with NVC making it clear that she had no respect for Sarah and the work of *Serial*. I realized with a slow sense of dread why all of Sarah's e-mails to Jay had been published.

In the prelude to the interview NVC writes:

"Serial" portrayed the case as a combination of overzealous prosecution and incompetent defense counsel. This viewpoint infused the entire podcast. While Koenig never proclaimed Syed to be innocent, she insisted the evidence didn't support his conviction. "It's not enough, to me, to send anyone to prison for life," she said in the closing of the last episode.

When a jury of 12 people comes back with a guilty verdict in two hours, you'd think that rejecting their decision would require fresh evidence. Yet the show did not produce new evidence, and mostly repeated prior claims, such as an unconfirmed alibi, charges of incompetence against Adnan's deceased

*lawyer, and allegations that information derived from cellphone records is
unreliable.*

*None of these charges has survived scrutiny. That was the conclusion of a
circuit court judge, who dismissed a defense motion that claimed such issues
compromised the fairness of the trial. Nevertheless, the 'Serial' series largely
mirrored the defense petition.*

NVC goes on for a few more paragraphs attempting to prove Sarah's bias
by showing she made little effort to contact Urick for the series—a charge I
knew was wrong because Sarah had told me how hard and how repeatedly
she had tried to get Urick—as well as detectives Ritz and MacGillivary—to
talk.

NVC goes further, stating with finality, "The justice system in America frequently doesn't work. This is not one of those cases."

I was gobsmacked, but not alone. Almost immediately I got a message from
a source at *The Intercept*. It read: "I am so disgusted by the story today . . . it is
a horrid malpractice justice wise and journalistically. Just awful pro-prosecution
garbage. The story was awful."

NVC and *The Intercept* were getting hit left and right in social media over
her embarrassingly strong defense of the State and her obvious dislike (professional jealousy maybe?) of Sarah and her listeners, who in an earlier interview
with *The Observer* NVC called "delightful white liberals who are creaming over
This American Life."

Not much was surprising in Urick's interview; the prosecutor stood by his
conviction.

Urick alleged that Gutierrez had initially submitted a witness list of eighty
people to verify that Adnan was at the mosque on the night of the 13th, but
"when the defense found out that the cellphone records showed that Adnan was
nowhere near the mosque, it killed that alibi and those witnesses were never
called to testify at the trial." NVC fails to note that this statement is unsubstan-
tiated.

Urick weds himself even more closely to the cell phone records, which may
later come to haunt him, when he is quoted in the article as saying, "Jay's testimony by itself, would that have been proof beyond a reasonable doubt? Probably
not. Cellphone evidence by itself? Probably not," but when put together "they
corroborate and feed off each other—it's a very strong evidentiary case." He
also says that "once you understood the cellphone records—that killed any alibi
defense that Syed had. I think when you take that in conjunction with Jay's
testimony, it became a very strong case."

I was squirming as I read this. How did NVC fail to ask Urick about Jay's new, improved, and completely changed timeline?

When NVC asks about Asia's potential as an alibi witness, Urick gives the same answer as before: Asia was being pressured by Adnan's family.

Urick doesn't know yet, no one in the public knows yet, that Asia heard him say all this on *Serial* and is ready to rebut under oath. He doesn't know that she is now working with Justin Brown to get a new statement in court.

A couple of days after the Urick interview, I had a dream. I was sitting in a room, not sure where, but around the corner was the bathroom. I saw that the light was on in the bathroom and heard a noise. I went to explore and found a young boy, maybe around ten years old, in a tub full of water. The boy had been left there, forgotten. It was Adnan.

He sat there, shivering and just looking at me, unable to move without the permission of a grownup, waiting for someone to come get him. I grabbed a towel, pulled him out, and wrapped him up.

It was the third time I had dreamed about Adnan. It left me a bit shaken but hopeful. I felt like the dream was a sign that Adnan was no longer forgotten, that he was close to being rescued. The possibility of getting him home was closer than ever. And I felt that between Asia and the Innocence Project, 2015 was going to be a very bad year for the State of Maryland.

Deirdre Enright at the Innocence Project was drafting a motion to request that the court order the case forensic evidence be submitted for DNA testing. The first time I spoke to Adnan about it, in late January of 2015, he sounded excited but weary.

"What's wrong?" I asked.

"I've been waiting for an opportunity like this forever, but now I don't know what to do. Deirdre wants to push forward with the motion. Justin is saying not to do it. Who do I listen to?"

I had no idea that Justin and Deirdre disagreed, but any time more than one attorney is on a case there is always the possibility of egos, agendas, and strategies clashing.

My communications with Deirdre were limited; I knew she had her own investigatory team and was pursuing leads independently, and I didn't want to interfere. But Adnan was asking for my advice, so I had to figure out what was going on.

I gave Justin a call to sort things out, and he made his case: On January 20, 2015, Justin had filed a new affidavit by Asia as an addition to the existing request to the Court of Special Appeals. The affidavit affirmed everything she had stated in her letters and earlier affidavit, explained what happened when she contacted Urick, stated that she wasn't pressured to make any of her statements, and asserted that if given the chance again, she would come to court to testify to all these things in person. On the same day, TheBlaze, Glenn Beck's Web site, published an exclusive on the new development, including both the new affidavit and an interview with Asia and her attorney.

The interview, affidavit, and new filing filled the airwaves, hitting the public (and we hoped the State) like a ton of bricks. The overwhelming coverage was a good sign; it meant that it would be hard for the court to ignore. The State opposed the filing a week later, asking the court to strike the new affidavit, but then Justin responded to the State's motion. We all knew it was a long shot, but Justin believed Asia's statement was strong grounds to reopen the PCR proceedings, hoping the court would be as incensed as the rest of us with Urick's behavior. Colin worked with Justin to get the legal research and language of the filing together.

Given these developments, Justin believed it was worth waiting to see what the court did before moving ahead with the DNA.

He explained that if the PCR didn't fly, then we still had the forensic stuff, the possible DNA to test. The truth is, he said, we don't even know if anything still exists in the police locker; all that physical evidence could be gone. Or, if it's there, it might not yield anything. In fact, it was likely we wouldn't get anything out of it. So if we moved forward with the DNA and it gave us nothing, the State would have an advantage and less incentive to negotiate. But if we held off on the DNA and focused on winning the PCR appeal, the DNA kind of hung like a sword over the State's head and also gave us one more bite at the apple if we lost.

Deirdre was adamantly against this strategy. Her plan was to get the DNA tested, show that it either matched someone else or didn't match Adnan, and file a writ of actual innocence immediately. She believed the PCR didn't have a chance. And she said so publicly, which undermined Justin and left us a bit disconcerted. Tensions ran high as we waited for the court to rule on whether we could appeal the PCR denial, and there was little communication between the attorneys. Deirdre was already speaking to state officials about filing the motion, and it seemed like she was going to go ahead whether or not Justin agreed. She just needed Adnan to say yes.

I called Deirdre and tried to explain Justin's perspective. He wasn't saying we should ditch the DNA petition altogether; he was just being his usual extremely cautious self and asking that we wait to see how the PCR appeal went. Along with Justin's strategy it was fair to say that Adnan, his family, Saad, and I all had slight misgivings, a touch of fear about the DNA testing. It wasn't unheard of that DNA could be tainted or tampered with, and I didn't trust the Baltimore City Police or the State's Attorney's office for a hot second.

Deirdre stood by her conviction that the PCR appeal was doomed and that we were wasting an incredible opportunity by not focusing on the DNA immediately.

I wrote to Justin to let him know she wasn't on board with waiting the PCR appeal out.

Justin said it was up to Adnan.

Adnan was nearly in tears. He knew if he told Deirdre to put a hold on the DNA, she would likely back out of the case altogether and he would lose the Innocence Project.

I told Adnan that if I was in his position, I'd let his lead counsel make all the legal decisions, period.

It was a good thing too, because on February 6, 2015, two days after talking to Deirdre and three days after Justin's response to the State, the Maryland Court of Special Appeals granted our application. We could appeal the denial of Adnan's post-conviction petition.

Justin's gamble paid off. Asia's new statement hadn't been thrown out; we were back in the game. The appeal was full steam ahead now.

CHAPTER 12

UNDISCLOSED

———•———

And you will obtain another blessing that you love:
help from God and a victory near at hand.

Holy Quran 61:13

Meanwhile, lawyers Susan Simpson and Colin Miller were busy trying to figure out what happened in 1999. After I gave them access to the case files, not a day went by that numerous e-mails didn't fly between us as they discovered things that had been overlooked all these years.

One of the first big eyebrow-raising findings came from Susan who, meticulous as ever, caught something I never looked at twice—the fax cover sheet from AT&T that accompanied the cell phone records provided to Detective Ritz in 1999. She sent me a screenshot of the cover sheet with the message, "Okay, I promise I'll stop doing this but *what the whatty what:* 'Outgoing calls only are reliable for location status. Any incoming calls will NOT be considered reliable information for location.'"

She noticed this tiny line in the instructions on the fax cover sheet, a line no one had ever bothered to glance at before, because really, who reads fax cover sheets?

"Why was this never discussed?" Susan asked.

"Because you're the first one who caught it," I responded.

This was big. I mean, this was really, really big. The reliability of the cell tower pings as evidence of the location of the phone was one of the big questions in the case. And now here we were, with a document straight from the horse's mouth—the phone company itself—disclaiming the use of incoming call information to pinpoint where a cell phone was at the time of the call.

A few days later Susan laid out in a blog post why, even if we were to accept that the cell site pings could identify the location of a phone, the State's case couldn't work—of the twenty-two calls made for which the State had identified cell site towers and locations, only four matched Jay's story: the 10:45 a.m. call by Adnan himself to Jay's house, the 6:07 p.m. call where Jay says he was with Adnan at Krista Vinson's apartment, and the Leakin Park calls at 7:09 and 7:16 p.m. The other calls did not match Jay's story. Of the four calls that did, three were incoming, and by AT&T's fax cover sheet, unreliable for location anyway.

Susan concluded her spectacular destruction of the State's case:

> *The prosecution's entire case has gone into a fatal loop. Why are the cellphone records accurate? Because Jay says so. Why is Jay's testimony accurate? Because the cellphone records say so. Why are the cellphone records accurate? Because . . . and so on, and so on. Except for one teeny little flaw in that premise: the cellphone records do not actually match Jay's testimony, and Jay's testimony does not actually match the cellphone records. So how can two things that do not match one another verify the accuracy of each other?*
>
> *The question we should really be asking is, "What are the odds that the incriminating portions of the prosecution's theory of the case conveniently match the cellphone records, when everything else does not?"*

It only took her a few days to figure out the answer to that last question. Her next post made me realize we were dealing with a real-life Sherlock Holmes.

Susan believed Jay was being coached by the police, and she could prove it. On January 13, 2015, she put up a post titled "Evidence That Jay's Story Was Coached to Fit the Cell Phone Records" that set my head spinning.

Susan was all about the cell tower records. Knowing them inside out, she became stuck on a detail that changed between Jay's first and second police interviews—in the first police interview Jay said that after dropping Adnan off at school in the morning, he returned home and waited for his call. But in the second interview he suddenly inserted a new detail, saying he didn't return home; instead he went to Kristi Vinson's home, aka not-her-real-name-Cathy as she was called in *Serial*, in the afternoon. But the story was easy to discredit because, according to Kristi, she wasn't home at that time and Jay had only come over once, in the evening, with Adnan.

Jay stuck with the Kristi story in the first trial. But later, by the second trial, the afternoon trip to Kristi had disappeared again. Why?

Because the police had messed up.

At the time of Jay's first interview, on February 27, 1999, the police had already obtained a list of calls made by Adnan's cell on January 13, the cell towers they pinged, and the physical addresses of those towers. A cursory look at the cell sites would have shown them that there is only one cell tower in Leakin Park, and that tower was pinged only twice that day, at 7:09 p.m. and 7:16 p.m. It was an easy conclusion to draw that the burial had to have taken place then.

But the detectives wanted to chart the route visually, and so Ritz asked for a map to be created shortly after Jay's first interview.

The map they received, Susan realized, showed that the cell tower that was pinged by two calls at 4:27 p.m. and 4:58 p.m., tower L654, was in the vicinity of Kristi's apartment and not Jay's home, which is where he originally said he was. So Jay had to change his story. He found a reason to be in the vicinity of L654 between 4:00 and 5:00 p.m. He inserted the story that he went to Kristi's after dropping Adnan at school just to accommodate the map.

Unfortunately for the police, the map itself was wrong. The address for cell tower L654 is 824 Dorchester Road in *Catonsville*, Maryland, which is close to Jay's house. But the people who created the map put the tower at 824 Dorchester Road in *Baltimore*, a location three miles south of the actual site and right next to Kristi's apartment.

The State eventually caught this error but not until after the first trial, at which Jay still maintained he was at Kristi's when the L654 calls came in. At the second trial the State had corrected the map and the cell tower locations and, like magic, Kristi disappeared from Jay's afternoon rendezvous.

All this time we were told that Jay's narrative was *corroborated* by the cell phone evidence, when it was now clear that Jay's narrative was instead *created* using the cell phone evidence.

Susan didn't just prove this by showing the evolution of Jay's story with regard to the phone calls, but also with regard to what he knew about the crime itself. When plotted chronologically, it was really quite simple to compare the details provided by Jay with what the police already knew. At the time of Jay's first interview, before the police had allegedly found the car, everything Jay knew about the crime scene matched the evidence that was visibly observable or known from evidence the police already had—pictures of the position of the body, Hae's clothing, and the reddish orange fibers found by the crime lab (perhaps prompting his story about Adnan wearing red gloves). Jay said Adnan had thrown away Hae's purse and her jacket in the first interview. By the second interview the police had found and opened up Hae's car and, lo and behold, her purse and jacket were in the trunk. In his first interview Jay told the police that he had no idea how Adnan got in Hae's car. In his second interview, after the police have interviewed Krista, who mentioned the ride Adnan asked for, Jay suddenly remembered that Adnan asked Hae for a ride. Susan had found the pattern. As the police gathered more information, Jay's story changed to match.

Sarah had said in *Serial* that trying to map out Jay's movements according to his changing statements and the cell phone records was like trying to plot the coordinates of someone's dream. The reason no one could do it, not even Jay himself, was because it wasn't his dream. It was the police's dream, and Jay was just giving them what they wanted.

In mid-January of 2015 I gave my first talk about Adnan's case and *Serial* at Stanford Law School. It was quite an honor to speak at such a prestigious institution. My friend and attorney Umbreen Bhatti had organized the event and invited me. It was a great crowd, in a room packed to the gills, and afterward I spent over an hour speaking with attendees individually. One of them was a trained economist but also a naturally sharp sleuth. Something had been bothering her and she wanted to e-mail me about it. A week later I received a detailed message from her, raising questions about different parts of the State's case and, most important, linking to a post she had made on Reddit the same day.

The title of the post was "Livor Mortis: Why Hae Could Not Have Been Buried at 7pm."

I read it with fascination. What the heck is livor mortis? I hadn't ever heard that term before. Unbeknownst to me, it was something that Susan had begun exploring a couple of weeks earlier, when an anonymous commenter on her blog alerted her to the issue. She followed up with him and he turned out to be a doctor, someone who could speak with some authority on the subject.

Susan reached out to a forensic pathologist to confirm what she had begun suspecting, and the economist was now making it plain as day in her post.

Livor mortis, or "the color of death," is the process by which blood in a deceased body becomes settled in the portions closest to, or touching, the ground, pulled by gravity. The blood seeps through the tissues and red blood cells break open, causing a dark hue, often blue or purplish, where it has settled. This settling is called lividity.

If a body is moved around after death, forensic pathologists can determine how the body was moved by following the pattern of lividity, or the blood, as it leaves a trail throughout the body, resulting in patches. For example, if a person dies on their back but after a few hours the body is turned on its left side, evidence of that movement can be found because we'll see "mixed" or "dual" lividity—some discoloration on the person's back, some on their left side. The blood becomes fixed in place only after eight to ten hours, longer in colder temperatures.

Hae's autopsy showed fixed full anterior lividity, from her face downward to her chest, stomach, and the front of her legs. But her body had been found on its right side.

In order for full, fixed anterior lividity to occur, Hae had to have been lying facedown and stretched flat for at least eight hours before she was moved to the burial site. If Hae had been buried at 7:00 p.m. on her side, the lividity would have been on the right side of her body, not on the front.

Over the next few weeks Colin and Susan would both post blogs about the issue of lividity, how it applied in other cases, and what it meant for this one.

There was no way that any of Jay's testimony, or the State's timeline of the murder, was true anymore. And it wasn't just about when Hae was buried. It was about where she was when she was killed, and where her body lay flat for at least eight hours before being moved to Leakin Park. There was the possibility, Colin posited, that Hae was left at the burial site facedown until lividity fixed, between eight to ten hours, then turned later onto her side.

Is it possible that a killer would return to the place where he's dumped a body in order to reposition it? Anything is possible, but not in this case. Because along with livor mortis there is rigor mortis.

When Hae's body was found, her right hand was sticking up through the soil with a large rock on top of it, presumably placed there by the killer to weigh it down. Why wouldn't her hand naturally just fall flat? Because it's likely that when she was buried, her body was still in rigor, and her right arm was stiffened at the elbow, forcing her hand up. The killer couldn't force it down.

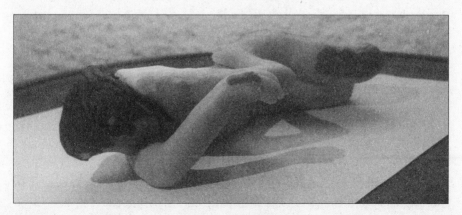

A model created by Susan to depict the position in which Hae's body was found.

Rigor mortis is the stiffening of the body after death, caused by chemical changes that occur in the muscles. It begins to set in within two to six hours after death and can last for up to a day or two. It would seem that Hae's body was already in rigor when she was placed in the grave, the reason a rock had to be placed on her hand to try and conceal it. If she had been left facedown on the ground in the same spot, then later repositioned on her side while rigor was present, both of her hands would be by her side.

Colin wrote about what the rigor in Hae's body could tell us, citing a 2014 Mississippi case, *Beasley v. State*. He notes the following:

> *Anna Savrock, a crime-scene investigator with the Mississippi Bureau of Investigation, performed an investigation of Wilkinson's home and Beasley's apartment shortly after the first responders arrived. Savrock noticed that Wilkinson's arm was hanging in the air in an unnatural position due to rigor mortis and determined that Wilkinson's body probably had been moved between ten and twelve hours after her death.*

Hae's body had also probably been moved after death.

The lividity finding, even more than the rigor, was a game-changer. It went beyond challenging the State's narrative and Adnan's conviction, and it helped point to what had actually happened to Hae.

For me, it raised the biggest question—where was Hae those eight to ten hours after death? Where could she lie flat for that long without being seen?

The new burial time Jay gave in *The Intercept* interview of around midnight was probably close to the truth, and I wondered if something signaled him to change his story. Did he know, or was he told, that if the forensics were examined more closely, the 7:00 p.m. burial would be proven bogus? I wondered if Urick contacted Jay—after all, NVC had interviewed them both, and her interview with Jay (according to NVC herself) was arranged by Jay's attorney. This was the same attorney, Anne Benaroya, whom Urick had helped retain for Jay in 1999. Would I, as an attorney, let my client talk to the media without knowing what he would say? Was Jay planning ahead, in case he had to go to court again and support another theory of the murder?

There were many more questions about the condition of Hae's body, questions sent by our readers and listeners. What about putrefaction of the body, what about evidence of insect and animal activity (one criminal law clinic professor said unequivocally that her body would have been consumed in those weeks—too many critters in a park like that, she couldn't have been there more than a couple of days), what about decomposition—why weren't any of these things visible in a corpse that was exposed to the elements for four weeks?

It didn't get any better as Susan and Colin kept digging.

I definitely felt a bit weirded out after Jay's phone rant against Sarah and her subsequent warning to me to be careful. I was publicly accusing Jay of lying and framing Adnan. Sarah and others reminded me that we didn't know what he or others in his family could be capable of, so I should tone it down.

My parents, on the other hand, were worried about the State. They both feared that publicly challenging and humiliating the State, the prosecutors, and the cops was inviting trouble. But my mother also thought that writing about social or foreign policy issues meant making enemies, and maybe one day some secret government agency would take me out for opposing drones in Pakistan and Afghanistan. I couldn't take it entirely seriously but couldn't completely shake it either.

The paranoia got stronger when we, the trustees of Adnan's legal fund, attempted to hire a private investigator. We wanted someone with a law enforcement background, maybe someone who had some contacts in the Baltimore PD, could get their foot in the door, and pick up intel in a way that non-law enforcement people couldn't.

Dennis Robinson knew just the guy, a retired former Maryland state trooper who was now doing contract PI work. He knew him from their time together at the Joint Counterintelligence Training Academy, and he was also a friend of Dennis's uncle. He was now doing some work for Baltimore City, though, but told Dennis he'd have no problem finding a PI for him, that there were lots of Maryland and Baltimore former officers doing such work.

But then Dennis got a message that made us all wonder what was going on. He e-mailed me and said the PI "appears to have cut me off cold turkey" after sending him a text that said, "Dennis, I was not able to get anyone that I would feel comfortable referring to you. Best wishes on your case." Given that he'd ignored numerous messages, Dennis said, "I am worried about what this means."

What exactly had happened here? Did the PI check with his law enforcement contacts and find out that this case would hurt their band of brothers? Or maybe he just couldn't find the right person for the case? That was an innocuous possibility, but what bothered Dennis was that this highly reliable man, a former colleague, simply stopped responding to him.

I started having trouble sleeping at night, hearing strange noises. I began saying copious prayers and blowing the prayers over my girls as they left for school, not wanting to let them go. I started noticing cars on the road that I thought I'd seen before—was someone following me? Was it the Baltimore City Police? One day I took it a bit far.

A strange car was circling the parking lot; it had blacked-out windows and a slew of antennas. I e-mailed Dennis, worried that I was being surveilled by police (band of brothers, after all). He told me to take a picture of the license plate and get back to him as soon as possible. A bit later my husband came home and I told him about the car—it turned out the car belonged to a neighbor, an officer with the Prince George's County police office, who had just gotten a new ride. Phew.

Embarrassed, I apologized profusely to Dennis, who had been legitimately concerned. But I wasn't completely out of my mind.

After all, Susan had recently found something else in the defense files that hadn't been noticed before, something that indicated serious police misconduct.

From: Susan Simpson
Date: Thu, Jan 22, 2015 at 11:39 PM
Subject: Re: Viewpoint_J-F.pdf
To: rabiachaudryesq
This one is another weird one, too. Not sure how reliable the manager of a porn store is, but if she is telling the truth . . . well, we're getting into conspiracy theory level of wrongdoing:

> *Page Two*
> *The 23-25 of February Jay was off. PD Davis was then advised that one of the days, either the 20, 21 or 22, Jay missed work when he responded to the Baltimore City Police Headquarters for an interview. Jay was questioned several times by the police at which time Sis asked Jay if they were questioning him in reference to the girl found in the Park. Jay advised that that was correct. PD Davis could not be given a reason why Sis suspected Jay to be involved in that incident. It was a hot news story and she knew Jay was heavily involved with the police at that time which prompted her to bring up the question to Jay. Jay advised that he "knew the person who did it." Jay further stated "he told me (referring to Adnan) no one thinks he did it but he did kill her."*
> *PD Davis was advised that Jay missed work to speak to the police again on February 26. He also missed work on Friday March 5 to speak to the police. After missing work on March 5, Jay advised his boss that he should not miss any more work until it goes to court. Sis was under the impression that Jay had recently moved in with his girlfriend.*

As a reminder, the official state version of events was that the Baltimore City Police first made contact with Jay on the night of February 27, after picking him up from the video store late that night. Adnan's cell phone records had led them to Jenn, who led them to Jay.

Jay gave them his first official statement on February 27, 1999, and it went into the early morning hours of the 28th, the tape being turned on after a few hours, with no "pre-interview interview" notes or record. After the interview Jay led them to Hae's car, and within a couple of hours they arrested Adnan on the morning of February 28, 1999.

But this document told a different story.

Jay's boss, a woman called Sis, told Cristina Gutierrez's private investigator Davis that at least a week prior to Jay's official "first" police interview he had already been meeting with the police, having missed work on either February 20, 21, or 22. She further specifically recalled he missed work to speak to the police on February 26, the day the cops first make contact with Jenn. Jay also missed work on March 5 to speak to police, and Sis says that Jay was questioned several times, though she did not know that Jay was interviewed on February 27 or on March 15. Despite not knowing about the official, documented dates Jay was interviewed, Sis was still able to state that he met with police several times, meaning dates other than the ones that were disclosed to the defense.

Davis had uncovered something else, though, which we connected to Sis's statements. In an interview Davis did with Ernest Carter, the same young man who apparently tried to impress a young lady on his block with a fake story of seeing a girl's body in the trunk of a car, Carter told him that he saw Jay with

> I DID NOT See Jay AGAIN UNTiL ABout ONE WEEK AFTER Hae's Body WAS found. I Saw Jay In the back of a POLICE CaR Near Jen's House. I Later spoke To

Excerpt from PD Davis 9/3/99 interview with Ernest Carter.

the cops a week after Hae's body was found, which would be around February 16. This is a day after Adnan is pulled over for a seatbelt violation and the same day AT&T is sent a subpoena for his records.

In his *Intercept* interview Jay may have been alluding to these repeated visits by the police when he said, "They had to chase me around before they could corner me to talk to me, and there came a point where I was just sick of talking to them. And they wouldn't stop interviewing me or questioning me."

The picture was getting clearer—the police had met with Jay numerous times before his first official interview, but there was no record of it. What happened in those meetings? Were those the meetings at which the police told Jay what he needed to say?

It was depressing and devastating to contemplate this. While all of these years I kept thinking the police HAD to have known Jay's stories didn't make sense, I still never thought they would have gone as far as coaching him and hiding evidence of the many times they met with him.

Now I did. And if I'm right, this was not just a conspiracy by the cops, this was straight-up corruption.

The real question was why . . . why go to such lengths to nail Adnan?

When Sarah asked Adnan's mother why she thought the police focused on Adnan, she answered, "Discrimination." I'll be honest. I knew there was bigotry in the prosecution of the case, I knew the State played the religion card against Adnan, but I wasn't so sure about whether the police felt the same way.

It was fascinating to see, during *Serial*, how Muslims and South Asians immediately picked up on the bigotry that impacted the investigation and trial, but others didn't. Sarah was openly skeptical, and when I approached Justin Brown about raising the issue in court, he likewise didn't pay much attention to it. Was it all in our head? Were we being too sensitive?

I wasn't totally sure until I heard from the most powerful organization of South Asian attorneys in North America—SABA, the South Asian Bar Association of North America.

During *Serial*, SABA representatives contacted me, alarmed at the blatant profiling and improper use of Adnan's religion against him, to inquire whether they could assist by filing an amicus curiae brief in relation to the pending PCR appeal.

An amicus brief, amicus curiae meaning "friend of the court," is generally filed by a party or organization not directly connected to litigation but concerned with the issues at hand. In this case, as a South Asian organization with many Muslim members, SABA was concerned over the treatment of Adnan based on his ethnic and religious background. They were telling us that what happened in Adnan's trial was not just unethical, it was unconstitutional, and the appellate court must be made aware of it.

After speaking with the organization, Justin decided it wasn't appropriate to file such a brief in the pending matter—after all, this wasn't an issue in front of the court at all. As such, it might have to wait and perhaps could be raised in the future, if the current appeal didn't work. I was disappointed but I understood his point.

SABA still went out of their way to publish a strongly worded OpEd in the *Baltimore Sun* on January 28, 2015, in which they stated:

> *Indeed, it appears that the prosecutor relied on ethnic and religious stereotypes in contending that Mr. Syed committed the murder because "his honor was besmirched," claiming it was the defendant's "religious beliefs" that motivated him to kill. We are not saying that arguments based on religion or ethnic background are categorically improper in criminal cases. But from our review of the record, we cannot identify any factual evidence introduced at trial to suggest that religion actually motivated the crime. While evidence was introduced that Mr. Syed's parents did not approve of his dating habits—a dynamic familiar to many parents and teenagers—the notion that Mr. Syed killed because of an honor besmirched was supported only by the prosecutor's reference to cultural stereotypes about Muslims.*
>
> *Such references to the defendant's background were persistent throughout the trial. In a recent interview with the online publication* The Intercept, *the prosecutor now suggests that domestic violence motivated the murder, but we identified no testimony about the defendant's jealousy or anger against the victim in the trial transcripts. In contrast, the prosecutor repeatedly referred to the tenets of the Islamic faith and suggested that the defendant's apparently disobeying them by dating the victim was itself proof of guilt.*
>
> *As one example among many, the prosecutor sought to convey to the jury the notion that Islam endorses harsh penalties for those who violate its scriptures. To do this, he put a teenage friend of the defendant on the witness stand and asked him: "What is your understanding of the penalty within the Islamic religion for premarital sex?" The teenager replied (evidently to the best of his theological knowledge): "That is not allowed." Many other religions have similar proscriptions that their adherents—teenagers and otherwise—routinely transgress. Would such a question be asked during the prosecution of a Catholic defendant? It seems inconceivable—at least in the absence of*

evidence that the defendant personally held hard-line religious beliefs that
led to a murder. Yet that is precisely what took place in Mr. Syed's trial.

It felt good to have the concerns of Muslims and South Asians legitimized
and substantiated; it wasn't all in our head. And if the prosecution could be so
bigoted, why couldn't the police?

The State made it seem as if they honed in on Adnan because of the anonymous tip that the Baltimore City Police received on February 12, 1999. They
lied. The police were already circling Adnan long before that tip, even before
Hae's body was ever found.

The files we had at the start of 2015 were not the complete files that existed
in the universe of Adnan's case. What we had were the defense files, the trial
transcripts from the court, and the files Gutierrez had obtained through discovery, which included police reports, forensic reports, witness statements, and
whatever the State turned over to her.

What we didn't have were the complete investigatory files of the Baltimore
City or County Police, or a copy of the State Attorney's files of the case. These
had to be obtained through the Maryland Public Information Act (MPIA),
through requests made directly to the agencies involved.

I had never made any but Sarah had, though she never supplied us with the
files. But Justin had gotten them. He passed them along in February 2015, and
finally Susan and Colin were able to take a look.

That was where evidence surfaced of the police focus on Adnan as early as
February 3, 1999, the day they first pulled his criminal records from the Maryland Interagency Law Enforcement System. It was also where the cultural research memo was found, which (I finally discovered) was written by Mandy
Johnson of the Enehey Group Investigating Services, along with evidence of
Johnson taking a strong role early on in the investigation. In a communication
with one of our researchers helping to investigate the case, Johnson admitted
she was the active lead in the case right after Hae's disappearance, since Baltimore County didn't seem to take the matter as seriously as the family would
have liked.

If Johnson was taking the lead, had come to the conclusion that Adnan did
it, had eliminated Don as a suspect, was in daily contact with Detective O'Shea,
and was literally the only movement on the case before police pulled Adnan's
records on February 3, then it seems likely that her opinion, coupled with O'Shea's
determination that Don was at work on the 13th, strongly informed the direction of the investigation.

We'll never have proof that the police focused on Adnan because of his religion, but they did indisputably focus on him. They followed no other leads; barely checked out Don; didn't investigate Hae's mother's ex-boyfriends, fiancés, and ex-husband, or Hae's uncle; didn't investigate any connection with the Jada Lambert murder—they just decided it had to be Adnan.

Now they had to make their case. They had to figure out what Adnan did that day. They knew he had a cell phone; after all, Officer Adcock called the number on the night Hae went missing. So that's where they started—with the cell phone.

In a blog post on March 2, 2015, Susan makes the case that the police were focused on Adnan before the February 12 anonymous tip. She points out that they pulled his registration records on the 11th after the visit of the black male reporting suspicious activity by another black male at Leakin Park. She also shows something remarkable with the cell phone records.

Somehow, the police had already gone through "unofficial" channels to pull Adnan's cell phone records. The first documented subpoena for Adnan's cell records from the police to AT&T was on February 16, 1999, directing them *"to furnish the name(s) address(s) for the following telephone number **and (13) cell site locations**, from January 1999 to present."*

The police already knew there were thirteen cell site locations, Susan points out, meaning that they already had some kind of records showing this information to begin with. How, we don't know and may never find out, but it's clear that they had them. They then had to get the cell tower locations, which is what they requested on February 16.

They were going to follow the cell tower pings like crumbs in a trail to figure out Adnan's movements that day, but they probably had a rude awakening when they went to speak to the person first called on the morning of January 13, 1999—Jay.

"I think the cops had no idea that Adnan didn't have this phone all day," Susan says.

Well, this was new, something I hadn't considered before. Because up until then I thought what everyone else did, that the cops started with the phone number that was called most times that day, Jenn's, which led them to Jay.

Now that we had Sis's statements, we knew the police were talking to Jay about a week before they got to Jenn.

Which made sense. If you were a cop with cell phone records trying to figure out where this phone was all day, you might start with the first number on record—a number attached to an address that would raise all kinds of red flags, given the frequent criminal charges of people living at that address.

"So the cops go to Jay to find out why Adnan called him," Susan writes. "And that's when the police realized, crap, Adnan didn't have the phone all day, Jay did."

Ok, I got it. I could see how that would happen. But what I also concluded was this: the cops must have been determined to make a case against Adnan, thinking he had his phone all day, then got completely screwed when Jay entered the scene and had to rewrite the script. Either way, I believe, Detectives Ritz and MacGillivary were going to get their man, and even, as it seems they had in other wrongful-conviction cases, produce evidence where there was none.

That's why Jay had to be coached, because the police needed him to help make their case. But it wasn't until we embarked on a new project that we figured out how they appeared to have done it.

In mid-March Susan dropped another bombshell on her blog, this one having to do with what Hae's plans were for the day she disappeared. Susan had carefully looked at Hae's employment records and noted that she was marked "no call, no show" on January 13, 1999, because she was actually scheduled to work at LensCrafters in Owings Mills from six to ten o'clock that night. This correlates with what Don had said about Hae's plans, that she was going to give him a call after work that night.

Note found in Hae's car

But much of this fact got muddled because of the infamous wrestling match the State said Hae was supposed to go to that night. In *Serial*, Sarah likewise confirmed that she missed a wrestling match that evening through her interview with a former Woodlawn student named Summer, who went on the podcast and recounted waiting for Hae that night at the match. In 1999, Inez Butler had mentioned a wrestling match to police in initial interviews, a match that she testified at the trial was against Chesapeake. But the real evidence for the wrestling match came from the note found in Hae's car.

The cops were certain the note was written the day she disappeared, and the State offered the note not just as evidence but as an emotional bullet meant to build rancor against Adnan. Sarah took the note as evidence that the match was the same day too, noting, "The local station had done a student athlete segment on [Hae]. So the note was written on the 13th, the day she went missing."

Except they all had it wrong.

Susan dug deep, finding all the school wrestling match reports in the local media, and discovered that Woodlawn High had a wrestling meet against Randallstown, as stated in Hae's note, not on January 13 but a week prior, on January 5.

The Sun : Wednesday, January 6, 1999 : Page 7D

Woodlawn 36, Randallstown 30
103—Stanley (W) p. James,
1:17; 112—Wilson (R) f.; 119
—Hatcher (R) f.; 125—Bailey
(R) f.; 130—df; 135—Df; 140
—Ervin (W) f.; 145—Harvey
(W) p. Sims, 1:40; 152—Ed-
wards (W) p. Burden, 2:16;
160—Wyche (R) p. Dwyer,
1:40; 171—Mitchell (R) f.; 189
—Webb (W) p. Cooler, 1:30;
Hwt—Powell (W) p. Aepa, :50

From the *Baltimore Sun* local school sports coverage of the matches the day prior, January 5, 1999

The note wasn't written on January 13, the match wasn't on January 13, and even the taping of the student athlete interview wasn't on January 13. It all happened a week prior.

A few days later Colin meticulously broke down Hae's day, comparing contradictory witness statements and eliminating one after the other based on Susan's findings and other inconsistencies. He boiled it down to a singular thing he was confident of: that Hae left the school having told others she "had something to do" and died when she went to do that something. In other words, Hae had somehow made plans that required her to do something or go somewhere before she picked up her cousin.

Colin told me he thought that when Hae left school she probably had her pager. But when she was found, it was gone. It seemed plausible that she may have gotten a page, which resulted in "something to do," and the killer was the one who paged her, then got rid of the evidence.

Three days later, on March 19, 2015, Susan came swinging back with a post examining Don's alibi, a post that opened the door to an entirely new set of possibilities for what happened on January 13, 1999.

Susan doesn't necessarily make the case that Don was guilty, but she makes a compelling case that the police failed fantastically in investigating him. She cites the weird seven-hour conversation he had with Debbie, which may have been the root of the rumor that Hae was thinking of going to California. Susan was the one who found the undated note on Baltimore City letterhead with the following:

"None of Hae girlfriends like new boyfr. New Boyfriend Assaulted Debbie."

It seems clear that this must refer to Don. It is not clear who wrote this note, or why Hae's friends didn't like Don. And when and why did Don supposedly assault Debbie? The police never even spoke to Don about the note found in Hae's car, which he did not know about until Sarah showed it to him. Why such neglect of the man Hae may have been going to see that day?

Having spoken to Cathy Michel, Don's manager at the LensCrafter store at the Owings Mills mall, Detective O'Shea was satisfied that Don had indeed been working on the 13th. What O'Shea didn't realize at the time was that manager Anita Baird at the Hunt Valley store, where Don allegedly temporarily filled in the day Hae disappeared, was in fact his mother. Susan points out that Gutierrez didn't know this either because the records she was sent from the store don't mention it, while the records sent to the State do note the relationship.

Susan shows how Urick stepped in to help "procure" the missing employment records for January 13th when Gutierrez made the request for Don's full employment records, even though the motion was filed under seal and ex parte with the court, meaning the other party isn't supposed to know about it. The documents LensCrafters turned over to Gutierrez didn't show that Don was working on January 13. Urick filed his own motion right after Gutierrez for the same documents, meaning he was probably somehow tipped off about the ex-parte motion. When LensCrafters produced records to both Gutierrez and Urick with no evidence of Don working on January 13, Urick gave them a call. Two days later a January 13 timecard was "discovered" and sent to Gutierrez, at which point she probably concluded that Don did indeed have an alibi. But Susan wasn't so sure.

She compared the January 13 Hunt Valley store timecard with his regular timecards from the Owings Mills store. Something did not add up.

Don's regular employee number at Owings Mills was 0162. The timecard from Hunt Valley showed his employee number as 0097. Don's mother's employee number was 0110. Beyond the oddity of his using two different employee numbers, these employee numbers are issued sequentially, and even if employees were issued a different number when filling in at other locations, Don should not have had an earlier number than his mother, who had worked there for a number of years. Don's employee number at Hunt Valley should have been sequentially a greater number than his mother's.

Susan also pointed out that while Don said he worked at Hunt Valley from 9:00 a.m. to 6:00 p.m. to fill in for another lab technician that day, there was no such shift for any other lab tech at the store. So who was Don filling in for?

Lastly, Susan notes that Don, though having worked 45.9 hours for the week when the additional Hunt Valley hours are counted, was not paid any overtime for the week—which seems to suggest that the extra hours noted on the timecard were never actually entered into the pay system.

The police's investigation was so poor that it caught none of these things, Gutierrez's representation of Adnan was so poor that she didn't either, and Sarah never gave Don's records even a cursory look.

Sarah's analysis of the documents was not much different than mine or any lay person's. The documents gave her a chronology of events and names of people associated with the events, but an investigative treatment wasn't really done, which is not surprising; she wasn't an investigator or even a crime writer, as she made clear in the very first episode of *Serial*.

Susan and Colin, on the other hand, were making connections in the case that took a keen eye and attention to every single detail. Nothing slipped past them, not even games the prosecution played as it succeeded in outwitting Gutierrez.

Though I heavily faulted Gutierrez for failing to conduct her own thorough investigation, the prosecution clearly did everything in its power to thwart discovery and withhold as much information as possible from her.

Adnan was indicted on April 13, 1999, and about a month later Gutierrez filed an omnibus request for discovery, demanding what was due to the defense from the State—all the documentation related to the crime that an attorney would reasonably need to prepare a defense for her client.

It is the State's duty to comply within ten days, but in this case Urick filed for an extension in mid-June to respond. Being stonewalled by the State, Gutierrez contacted the medical examiner's office herself, seeking the autopsy report, only to be told that they *had been directed* not to release it until the prosecutor gave permission.

On July 1, 1999, according to Susan, "The prosecution makes limited disclosures to the defense, consisting of incomplete (and illegible) police reports, partial evidence lists, and poorly scanned black-and-white photos of the crime scene that do not reasonably allow a viewer to understand what is being seen."

At this point Gutierrez hasn't seen a single police statement given by the State's witness and has no idea what the details are of the case against her client. Not only that, Urick files a Motion to Bar Discovery to prevent the defense from even knowing the identity of the State's witness. Of course, Adnan already knew the identity, as he had been told the witness was Jay by the police themselves during his interrogation.

Having filed twenty discovery requests, Gutierrez finds herself battling for every piece of information to the extent that she raises, via motion, the fact that she can't even prepare an alibi defense because of the deliberate withholding of the time the alleged crime occurred.

As the scheduled trial date of October 14, 1999, looms ahead, Gutierrez receives a single-page summary of the oral report by the State's cell phone expert,

Abe Waranowitz, on October 9—the first notice she has that the State is in fact using an expert to determine cell phone location. She has not been given any documentation by the State on the cell tower locations, so the summary (useless to begin with), is essentially meaningless. Two days later she files an urgent request with AT&T, asking for "any maps covering the cell sites discussed in his statement, any coverage maps which you have describing the different areas, and any information used by Mr. Waranowitz to distinguish the particular cell sites mentioned."

Two days before trial, Gutierrez files a motion to postpone the case, because as of this time she still hasn't gotten a single police statement made by Wilds, and has been unable to subpoena the State's cell phone witness to try and figure out what information he will bring to bear on the case. She also argues that the State gave late and incomplete disclosure on the DNA testing of the T-shirt found in Hae's car, and requests time for examination of the results by an expert.

On the morning of the scheduled trial, Urick files an opposition to the postponement, asking the court to move forward. He has every advantage at this point, having given nearly zero information on the State's theory of the crime. The defense has no idea what time the State will argue that the murder and burial took place, and is flying blind. A postponement would give the defense more time for discovery requests, and Urick has to prevent that.

But I believe there was another reason Urick wanted to proceed with the trial as soon as possible: on that same morning, he received some good news. The singular potential alibi witness Adnan had, Bilal Ahmed, had been arrested.

In March of 1999, when Ahmed was called to testify before the grand jury, he swore under oath that he recalled seeing Adnan at the mosque on the evening of January 13, 1999. His recollection was specific, because Adnan was scheduled to give a talk and prayer service for the youth the following day, January 14. On the evening of the 13th Adnan had asked Ahmed to review his notes to help him prepare for the next day.

Ahmed was the only person identifiable to the State who could place Adnan anywhere other than where Jay said he may have been—at the mosque instead of in Leakin Park.

Susan pieced together what happened next. Worried that Ahmed could throw off the State's case, the prosecution began taking a closer look at him, even issuing DEA subpoenas for his cell phone records.

Then, in August, shortly before the trial, Urick sent Ahmed a letter requesting a meeting. He singled out Ahmed only, something he didn't do with any witness other than Jay.

According to Ahmed, he went to the meeting but didn't meet with Urick. He met with a woman instead, most probably prosecutor Kathleen Murphy, but he now states he doesn't recall what they discussed.

Regardless of what was discussed at the meeting, the State seemed to have found a way to ensure his testimony would be of no use to Adnan.

On the morning of October 14, 1999, Urick issued a Brady disclosure to Gutierrez in a highly unusual move—at this point he hadn't even handed over Jay's statements and yet immediately put the defense on notice of their own witness's arrest.

The disclosure says that "the State provides the following: on this morning the State received an oral report from Baltimore County Officers that State's Witness Bilal Ahmed was arrested earlier this day and charged with a fourth degree offense."

But Susan realized something else—Ahmed never was actually charged with any crime, as a memo in Gutierrez's files shows, and shortly thereafter he disappeared from the scene altogether. This is the man who had taken a lead in organizing fund-raising, retaining counsel, and supporting the family upon arrest, who had testified at the grand jury, and was the only alibi witness the defense had managed to find with a specific recollection of January 13. Now he was suddenly, poof, gone. Ahmed didn't attend either trial and he failed to respond to the subpoena Gutierrez issued for him.

This pieced-together discovery by Susan seems to indicate something sinister: either Ahmed had some serious charges dropped in exchange for skip-

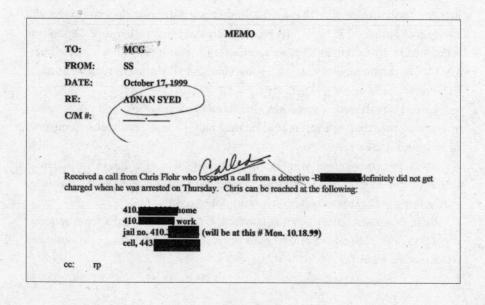

MEMO

TO: MCG

FROM: SS

DATE: October 17, 1999

RE: ADNAN SYED

C/M #:

Received a call from Chris Flohr who received a call from a detective -B[redacted] definitely did not get charged when he was arrested on Thursday. Chris can be reached at the following:

410.[redacted] home
410.[redacted] work
jail no. 410.[redacted] (will be at this # Mon. 10.18.99)
cell, 443[redacted]

cc: rp

ping out on Adnan's defense, OR the State found a way to frame him to pressure him.

Of course, this was conjecture. We had little specific knowledge of the reality behind the arrest and the subsequent failure to charge until an MPIA request was filed, which I did immediately after reading Susan's blog.

As I've noted before, Ahmed did not enjoy a great reputation in the community. Rumors abounded about his proclivity for young boys and his continued efforts to be around them. Ahmed arrived in Hagerstown, Maryland, where my family lived for many years, sometime in the early 1990s. A few years older than I was, he soon set up youth camps and overnight events for boys at the mosque, which my parents forbade my brother from attending. Something about him set off their radar, as it did for others in the community. We eventually moved from Hagerstown to Baltimore, and so did Ahmed and his mother. Community members in Hagerstown have told me now that he was forced to leave after having been caught doing something sexually inappropriate. Back then, however, I hadn't heard about this, probably because it had been buried— Ahmed's paternal uncle was a pillar of the community, a founder and leader at the mosque there, and a very well-established and influential doctor. I can only imagine that he did everything to protect Ahmed and, by extension, his family's reputation.

Once he moved to Baltimore, Ahmed resumed his youth leadership work at the ISB, Adnan's mosque, where he was eventually approached by Adnan's mom to help mentor her son. She and others had little idea about the rumors that chased him to Baltimore, but among the kids the stories began spreading.

I remember hearing them but not paying much attention, thinking they were just kids talking smack about Ahmed because he was a clearly an eccentric, effeminate man. Besides, Ahmed was married so I assumed the rumors were baseless. It turned out we should have paid more attention and taken the stories seriously.

A young man from the Baltimore community named Rashad, who was around eleven years old when Ahmed moved to the area, remembers stories other kids told about him. Ahmed would help underage kids get fake IDs, take them to bars and strip clubs, and then threaten to tell their parents if they didn't do as he said.

"What did he want them to do?" I asked.

"Just obey him I guess, not sure about anything sexual. He was just manipulative."

Ahmed's young wife, Saima, who had recently come from Pakistan where his mother had arranged their marriage, was also unaware of what was being said about her husband. But according to Saima, soon after she arrived in the United States, people started calling her older brother, scolding her family for marrying her off to Ahmed, a gay man. She had no idea these calls were happening; her family kept it from her while they tried to find out what the deal with Bilal actually was.

More troubling were the calls that told them, "He is not just gay, he is a child molester."

Saima's brother, who lived in Atlanta and didn't know the ISB community or even Ahmed well, decided to check out if any of these allegations were real. He hired a private investigator to follow Ahmed.

On the morning of October 12, 1999, the private investigator arrived at the Baltimore County Police Department to file a complaint. The complaint says that this PI, Glenn Ehasz, was conducting surveillance in a domestic case and saw what he purported to be suspicious behavior by an adult, Bilal Ahmed, who daily picked up a juvenile boy and drove him to a parking lot in the early morning hours. Ehasz observed that "Ahmed parks for about thirty minutes at a time

---

This offense has been upgraded from a Suspicious Condition to a possible 4th Degree Sex Offense.

On 10/14/99, as a result of the information learned from Glenn Ehasz, a private investigator, hired by the wife of Bilal Ahmed that her husband might be involved in an illegal relationship with the victim, ___ an underage___ surveillance was conducted of AHMED by the Woodlawn, IST.

At 0528 AM, AHMED was observed leaving his residence at 2915 Chestnut Hill Drive, Ellicott City, MD 21043 operating a 1988 Toyota Previa Van, displaying MD registration M103467. AHMED proceeded East on Rt. 40 entering into Baltimore County. At about 0533 AM, AHMED was observed arriving at ___, the apartment building where ___ lived turning his lights out as he pulled onto the court. ___ was observed exiting the building and getting into the van with AHMED. AHMED immediately pulled off and at a high rate of speed proceeded on Rolling Bend Road towards Fairbrook Rd. making a left on Fairbrook Rd. AHMED then drove to Springridge Court parking the van at the dead end of the court next to the woods line.

Detective Watkins, Detective White, Officer Welsch, and Sgt. Prothero observed that no one exited the van but obviously were not in the front seat area. At that point the van was approached and surrounded. AHMED and ___ were found in the back of the van with the seat reclined underneath a blanket. ___ was laying down facing the driver's side of the van with AHMED laying beside him facing in the same direction. Officer's lit up the van with their flashlights at the same time demanding entry into the van. It was obvious that AHMED had his pants unfastened and down and it appeared that ___ also had his pants down. It took about a minute as AHMED and ___ attempted to redress themselves and after repeated orders to do so, AHMED unlocked the van door and he was pulled from the van still attempting to secure his pants. A coat belonging to AHMED which was laying on the seat next to them was checked and a small open jar of Vaseline was found along with an open bottle of Curel hand lotion. A photograph of another young man, possibly a Highschool photo, was also found. AHMED wished to know how long he would be detained because he had to open up a daycare center. Further investigation showed that AHMED and his mother, Amtul Bashir own Little Stars Learning Center in Columbia MD.

Both AHMED and ___ were transported to Precinct Two. Sex Crimes Unit was contacted and Detective's Cross and Bonsail responded. Detective White and Detective Watkins interviewed AHMED. AHMED was advised of his Miranda rights by Detective White. AHMED advised he understood his rights and agreed to answer questions without a lawyer present and acknowledged his Miranda rights by signing, dating and noting the time as 0705 on the Miranda card. During the first interview AHMED stated he has known ___ for about 4 months. He met ___ at his Mosque on Johnnycake Road.

AHMED knows ___ 's mother and father and through his Mosque has assisted the family while they are staying here. AHMED registered ___ in school at ___ High School in the 9th grade and has assisted the family by providing clothing and food and helping them with transportation while they are here. AHMED stated that he and ___ were very close friends. AHMED stated he loved ___ and that he often hugs and kisses ___. AHMED admitted that they have engaged in mutual masturbation together and admitted to have touched ___ penis. AHMED stated he carried the Vaseline in his coat pocket because he has corns on his feet and could provide no explanation as to why his pants were down when officer's approached the van. AHMED denied engaging in oral sex or anal intercourse with ___. He indicated that this occurred in his van and at ___ apartment. He stated that he was not engaged in a sexual act when approached in the van. He indicated that the sexual contact between them had began about three weeks ago and that he used no force and had ___ consent to engage in these acts.

Victim, ___ was interviewed by Detective Watkins and Detective Cross. ___ has learned some English since being in the United States and could be interviewed with some difficulty. An effort was made to contact an appropriate translator but although translators could speak ___ there was no one who could speak in his particular dialect. ___ parents and 17 year old sister do not speak any English. ___ stated he met AHMED at the Mosque and that he was a friend, "like a brother" who had helped his family. He provided him with the tennis shoes he was wearing and had provided him with clothing and had bought him a 10 speed bike for his birthday. He had picked him up at school and at the mosque. He admitted to engaging in mutual masturbation with AHMED and in kissing and hugging him. He said that they had touched each other's penis's but denied any oral sex or anal intercourse. ___ appeared by his body language not to wish to discuss oral sex and by his manner whenever this subject was approached appeared to be deceptive in his answers in regards to those questions. ___ expressed concern over AHMED's welfare and showed concern that he was being questioned. He stated he loved AHMED and engaged in sexual contact of his own free will. ___ was asked of any other known "friends" of AHMED's. He stated he knew no one. ___ was shown the photo that was in AHMED's possession. He indicated that he knew this boy as someone else at the Mosque. He stated he and AHMED had visited the boy, ADNAN SYED at the Baltimore City Jail. Investigation revealed that SYED is incarcerated on 1st Degree Murder charges as well as Kidnaping and False Imprisonment charges for the murder of SYED's girlfriend who was buried and found in Leakin Park after being missing from the Woodlawn area. Feeling it was unusual that AHMED has this photo in his possession, Detective Watkins contacted Baltimore City Police Homicide and spoke to Detective Bill Ritz, believing that he might have some need to interview AHMED in reference to his investigation. Ritz indicated he was aware of AHMED and that AHMED had provided SYED with a cellular telephone prior to the girlfriend's disappearance and this proved to be a key element in their investigation. AHMED is not a suspect in this case and Ritz advised that AHMED was a "Mentor" for SYED as well as other young Moslem men who attend the Mosque. AHMED and others in the Pakistan community are currently raising money for SYED's court defense.

Upon reviewing the facts, the observations by officer's who approached the van, the subsequent interviews with ___ and AHMED, and after consultation with the Sex Crimes Unit and the States Attorneys office it was concluded that although probable cause existed for AHMED's arrest there was not sufficient evidence to support charging AHMED with a crime at this time. The current law does not make it a crime for a 14 year old to be involved in "Sexual Contact" with an adult if that contact is consensual and not against the will of the victim. No evidence could be found to directly show any "Sexual Acts" had occurred between AHMED and ___, although a strong suspicious exists that these acts had occurred. AHMED was released without charges to his Attorney, ___ who had been called to the Precinct by AHMED's mother and he was briefed on the officer's observations.

Detective Watkins notified Glenn Ehasz, the private investigator, of the above events. Further Detective Watkins contacted Howard County Protective Services on 10/15/99 and spoke to Sandy Patterson. She advised to contact the licensing division in Howard County for daycare providers. Detective Watkins spoke to Sandy Boyd and Janice Burris, in regards to the daycare center operated by Bashir.

with the boy and then he returns the boy to his home." The report also says that Ehasz received "third party information that there is a sexual relationship between Mr. Ahmed and the boy."

Two days later the police themselves followed Ahmed.

A grown man having sexual relations with a fourteen-year-old refugee child must be a crime. But this was a crime for which Ahmed was never charged, and the real question here is why.

According to a source, upon his arrest Ahmed called his attorney, who arrived at the station immediately. There was little to no protest by the police when the attorney requested that his client be released; it was as if they had already decided there wouldn't be any charges.

When Susan first made all these connections, we couldn't figure out how Urick learned about his arrest so quickly, and more importantly, why. Ahmed was arrested in a different county on charges that were completely unrelated to Adnan. The only possibility seemed to be that the State was somehow tracking Ahmed, but the report itself lays out very specifically the route police took to get to Urick.

But I think that part of the report is a complete fabrication. It is a whacky, convoluted story, a contrived ruse crafted to give the prosecutors cover. I just don't buy that Baltimore County Police are less interested in what was happening between Ahmed, armed with Vaseline and pants dropped, and this young boy in a rocking van, than they are in a picture found in Ahmed's pocket. Just think about that for a second, think about their priorities. Do they make sense?

The State prosecutors certainly had a hand in determining whether Ahmed got charged. The report itself states that "after consultation with the sex crimes unit and the State's Attorney's office" they decided not to charge him.

But just to make sure the point got driven home, that Ahmed was still on the hook, the police made sure he knew he was being watched. His ex-wife Saima told me that after his arrest and subsequent release, he arrived home terrified. He told her to lower the curtains and turn off all the lights. When she asked why, he pointed outside a window to show her two police cars parked directly in front of his house.

"They're watching me, they're out to get me," he told her.

They didn't "get him," but I believe they did get to him. There is no doubt in my mind that the State made Ahmed a deal—make yourself scarce for Adnan's trial and we'll let you off the hook for this heinous crime.

Shortly after this, Saima was shipped off by Ahmed to her brother's house, telling her to go visit her family while he figured some things out. There her brother told her what had happened, what their private investigator had found.

She was stunned and began making some calls herself. She called someone Bilal described as a friend, a young man who often visited the house.

"It's true, he's a sick guy. I wanted to tell you this before, but he tells us guys that if we want to have sex with his wife, we can." She was terrified and soon after filed for divorce. She never returned to Ahmed.

And Adnan lost the only alibi he had for the evening of January 13, 1999.

As *Serial* wound down, our research and writing continued, and I was giving talks about the case at law schools, law firms, and universities. I would often ask people who flocked to the events as *Serial* fans whether they read my blogs, or Susan's or Colin's blogs. About 95 percent responded in the negative. Fielding questions, it was painfully clear that Susan's and Colin's meticulous research, investigations, and prolific blogging were being largely overlooked by the general public.

I was concerned that the public's interest would continue to fade, along with the donations coming in to Adnan's fund, and Dennis Robinson, our fund-raiser, must have been worried about that too, because on March 3, 2015, out of the blue, he sent Susan and me an e-mail.

He had an idea, one that he got after attending a talk I gave at a local law firm and seeing the result of my question about how many people actually read our blogs. We needed to take all the information we were blogging and make it easier to get to people who were interested in the case—thanks to *Serial*, they were used to a podcast. We needed to make a podcast too. Not only would people get all the nitty-gritty details of the case Susan and Colin were unearthing, it would also help us fund-raise. If we got advertisers, we could use the revenue for the legal fund.

We both immediately responded by saying we were in, we were willing to do this, though I was secretly thinking, *Oh God no, I can't do it. I know nothing about podcasting. This will be a spectacular disaster.*

But I knew Dennis was right. It would be ridiculous not to take all the information Susan and Colin had found and find a way to deliver it to a broader audience. And also true was that we definitely needed more money for Adnan's legal fees.

Within two days Susan had gotten her husband on board to create the Web site; gotten a volunteer logo designer; found musician and photographer Ramiro Marquez, who was willing to create our theme music and take pictures for our Web site; tracked down a volunteer sound editor, Amar Nagi, all the way in the United Kingdom; figured out how to record via Skype together; confirmed Colin would participate; and decided on what the first few episodes would be.

Clearly, there was no backing out now.

After some initial duds on coming up with a name, Susan suggested "Undisclosed: The State vs. Adnan Syed." It sounded right, we all liked it.

We spent the next two weeks frantically picking music and a logo, drafting scripts and episode schedules, contacting potential sponsors, setting up social media accounts, trying to figure out exactly how to record everything with the three of us in different places, buying microphones and audio equipment, getting the media alerted, and building public interest.

Roughly two weeks after first agreeing to do the podcast, we issued a press release on April 3, 2015, announcing the new show and that our first episode would air on April 13. In retrospect, we were nuts. I have no idea why or how we thought we could pull this off in a matter of weeks, something professional radio people like those who work on *This American Life* took almost ten months to do.

We hadn't even recorded our first episode when the story of the new podcast made every major media outlet, from *Rolling Stone* to *Huffington Post* to the BBC. The media was framing *Undisclosed* as a *Serial* sequel, but it wasn't going to be anything like it. To be honest, we didn't exactly know what it would be like; Susan, Colin, and I didn't really even know each other, we didn't know if we could or would work well together, we didn't know if we should read from predetermined portions of a script or make it conversational, or who would do what research work to prepare. We just kind of started blind.

After the media started reporting it, Adnan gave me a call.

"You're going to do a podcast, Rabia?"

"Uh, yes. Not just me, but Susan and Colin," I responded, hoping that made me sound more responsible.

"That's kind of crazy. But also amazing. You have the time to do it?"

Well not exactly, as I was in the middle of my New America Foundation project. But both Susan and Colin had full-time jobs, so if they could handle it, so could I.

Adnan laughed and told me if anyone could do it, I could. I figured that with him on our side, being able to interview him and include the audio, we would be ahead of the game already. A wrench got thrown in that pretty quickly.

After *Serial* blew up, someone from the State's Attorney's office had contacted the prison, complaining that an inmate named Syed who was housed there was having recorded conversations with a journalist against Department of Corrections policy. His phone privileges had to be revoked or some measure taken to ensure this didn't happen again.

Adnan was summoned by the prison staffer who oversaw the inmates' phone usage and given a stern talking to, but since Adnan had good relationships with the prison staff and guards, he didn't come down too hard on him: one month of no phone calls except to his mother, and after that it was back to his regular calling list, with the understanding that there would never be another recorded conversation.

I tried hard to convince Adnan to just give us one interview, but after trying nicely to explain to me that he'd rather not, he finally broke it down: I didn't know what prison life was like. It took years to build trust and friendship in prison. One breach of that trust would not only put his phone privileges in jeopardy permanently, which he was less concerned about, but could also negatively impact that staffer and dishonor his promise to him. He couldn't do that. People respected him at NBCI, and it was important for him to maintain that trust and respect.

I finally got it, and I realized that in all these years of talking to Adnan, I really had no idea what his life in prison was like. None of us did—not his family, not Saad. Adnan had always spent his time talking to us about *our* lives, what was happening in the world, God and faith, sharing funny stories.

After it was settled that Adnan wouldn't appear on the podcast, and I had broken the news to Susan and Colin, I still went into recording the first episode feeling pretty good.

The way we envisioned it, Colin wasn't even initially going to be recording the substantive portion of the podcast with Susan and me; he was going to do short "Evidence Professor Corner"–type clips. But after the first recording we realized he needed to be in the mix. The three of us were bringing very distinctive things to the show—Colin brought his keen legal sense, Susan brought her Sherlock investigatory skills, and I was essentially the voice of the audience, the narrator moving us along and weaving the bits together, setting the stage and then closing out at the end.

I thought it worked great the first go, despite being new to recording. Susan and I (then and now) tended to do numerous takes, starting over, talking too fast, messing up, re-recording, while Colin was (and is still) a machine, barely stumbling, even when called on to improvise. Our first episode was set to flip the script on the way *Serial* framed Adnan; he wasn't someone who remembered nothing, he actually remembered most of January 13, 1999, and we were going to prove it.

I was excited to show the world the rest of the story, and also excited after the first recording session to see how it would be edited with our new music. But two days before the podcast launched we got a message. Amar Nagi, our volunteer sound editor, was suddenly sick and unavailable to do it.

I panicked. What do we do now? Susan suggested we push the launch date, but I couldn't bear the thought; we had gotten so much press coverage that postponing it would look terrible. Some of the editing had been done, and Amar and Susan had the audio files. I told Susan to send them to me and I'd see what I could do.

I know nothing about sound editing and had never even heard of Garageband in my life. But I knew my Macbook had some editing capability, and overnight I read up on and figured out how to lay tracks on Garageband. I don't think I slept that entire weekend, but by Monday, April 13, 2015, I had cobbled together a terribly edited first episode of *Undisclosed*.

I was relieved that we launched when we said we would, but I was so focused on getting it out that I didn't brace myself for what we would hear back. And what we got back was awful. This was no *Serial*, this was a low-quality, confused, poor substitute.

David Zurawik, the *Baltimore Sun* media critic, put it this way: "Unfortunately, a lot of people who followed the *Serial* podcast are going to be disappointed." His main critique was that we didn't synthesize our findings into an easily digestible narrative for the audience. Instead, we just threw everything at them (little did he know that we actually left a lot out), too many details with little storytelling. Zurawik had some great advice, though. He said *Undisclosed* needed a producer with a public radio sensibility. He was right.

Within a couple of weeks we brought Rebecca Lavoie on board; she was a crime writer and podcaster with a background in public radio. Rebecca became our production consultant and editor for every episode while Amar, once recovered, bounced back to sound edit every other week for what we called our "Addendum"—shorter episodes with additional or supplemental information.

The feedback from the public was as immediate as the feedback from the media—we got hundreds of e-mails, messages, and tweets telling us exactly what we were doing wrong: Susan talked too fast, I was biased, Colin's legal analyses were hard to understand. We did our best to take the feedback as advice and do better with every episode.

It wasn't so much the substance but the form that needed tweaking. The substance was fairly strong, especially our third episode, "Jay's Day," in which Susan showed exactly how the police could have gotten Jay to say what they needed.

When I first got the text on my phone from Susan I had to read it a few times to understand what she was saying. She had figured out how the police coached Jay? "Tap, tap, tap," was her reply. I ran to pull the audio recordings of Jay's police interviews and strained my ears. I heard it. She was right.

How on earth did you figure this out, Susan? That was my question. This was her response:

I first noticed it while I was putting Ep 1 together, so shortly before April 13th. One of the tapping sections was used in it—I think it was the one about Adnan going to track practice—and as I was (clumsily . . .) trying to put the episode together and listening to the section again and again, it just sounded off to me. Something else was going on in the room, and it, well, kinda sounded like someone was leading Jay along. But that is an insane idea and I was clearly hearing something that wasn't there, so I didn't mention it to anyone. I did make a vague reference to it in that first episode, mentioning how Jay sounds like an actor who forgot his lines, but I left out the second part of what I was starting to think: that it sounds like someone might've also been feeding Jay his lines whenever he forgot them.

Then over the next few weeks as I was going through the interviews to pull more clips to use for later episodes, I kept hearing it again and again, and as I found more examples, I became more and more convinced that it really was happening. I think the one that sealed the deal for me was the one where Jay reads out "pops" then says "Oh yeah Adnan popped the trunk."

I finally asked Amar if he could listen to the clips, and see if the taps really were there, or if they were some artifact of the recording process, or if I was going insane and hallucinating it all, or what. (He was nice about it, but I think his initial response was to go with the "Susan is insane; option.) Then he listened to the clips, and was like "yup, that's actually happening."

Episode 3 of *Undisclosed*, in which we played the police interviews with the taps in the background, clearly directing Jay, lit the Internet on fire. #Taptaptap began trending on Twitter, and the number of our listeners skyrocketed. After a rocky start we had redeemed ourselves, not only because our quality was better but because we proved that there was a lot more to this case than *Serial* had told the world.

As elated as I was about the public recognition this episode brought us, I was privately full of grief and rage. I felt a strange sense of mourning when I realized what Susan had really uncovered, the possibility that Jay actually knew nothing about the murder whatsoever.

For sixteen years I had made the argument that the reason Jay knew all these details about the crime, that it had to be because he was directly involved, and probably because he had killed her himself. Jay had been cheating on Stephanie

[03/05/2015, 23:15:45] Susan Simpson:
So this is a little conspiratorial, but I was wondering if it's something you could help me figure out. In the interviews, I swear that every time Jay screws up the story, you can hear someone go "KNOCK KNOCK" like on a table, and then Jay immediately remembers the correct answer.

Is there any way to prove that "knock knock" is actually there, and I'm not hallucinating it?

Because to me it sounds like there are papers on the table, and someone is knocking to point out the right answer.

[03/05/2015, 23:16:33] Amar Nagi:
have just got hold of all the software used by hollywood sound guys to rescue audio and fix dialogue its done a great job on this jen clip i can give it a try for sure

[[04/05/2015, 02:26:12] Susan Simpson:
I sent you the "knocking" clips

[04/05/2015, 02:26:23] Susan Simpson:
Let me know if you think there's actually something there... or if I'm being nuts.

[04/05/2015, 02:26:51] Amar Nagi:
its like a pen being **tapped** i hear it my word, your right

[04/05/2015, 02:31:25] Susan Simpson:
And then bam, Jay suddenly knows the answers!

[04/05/2015, 02:31:53] Amar Nagi:
he directly responds to one says "oh ok"

[04/05/2015, 02:32:34] Susan Simpson:
Oh wow, I didn't even pay attention to that part, I was so focused on the tapping, lol.

[04/05/2015, 02:34:15] Susan Simpson:
sent a file to Amar Nagi: Top Spots.wav

[04/05/2015, 02:34:26] Susan Simpson:
I sent the wrong "top spots" one, that's the right clip

[04/05/2015, 02:36:16] Amar Nagi:
ok I have cleaned up one audio very quickly just going to send it you this is well eery!

[04/05/2015, 02:39:55] Susan Simpson:
The police files have a document called "Jay's chronology," with a numbered list of events that occurred... I wonder if this is the one they used, and they are tapping at the number that Jay is supposed to be talking about. Also, the part about Adnan leaving Hae's car off Edmondson Avenue is on the very top of the second page.... as in, it's the "top spot" of the page....

[04/05/2015, 02:41:19] Amar Nagi:
sent a file to Susan Simpson: IBeleive_Clean.mp3

and Hae knew about it. Maybe she had confronted him and he killed her because he couldn't stand to lose the love of his life. Maybe Hae went to buy weed from Jay and they ended up in an altercation and he accidentally killed her. Maybe someone he knew and was frightened of killed her, maybe even a family member.

Over the years I had never, ever entertained the idea that he knew nothing about the crime, that he had nothing to do with any of it. I think that even considering the possibility was too painful—it meant the police set Adnan up completely and fed Jay all the details themselves. It meant the cops knew for certain that Adnan couldn't have killed Hae in the way they purported he did. I wondered if they knew he didn't do it at all, but just wanted a conviction. Knowing that in other cases they had ignored clear evidence of a defendant's guilt, I realized that there was no reason they couldn't have done the same here.

> [04/05/2015, 02:42:01] Amar Nagi:
> this clip I sent has to be the most plain obvious that something is going on
>
> [04/05/2015, 02:42:47] Susan Simpson:
> Wow that is unmistakable
>
> [04/05/2015, 02:46:52] Susan Simpson:
> Don't mention this to anyone (since I need to find more solid proof first!)
> but my leading theory right now is that Jay had nothing to dow with the murder whatsoever.

How would I tell Adnan, how would he feel? Unlike me, he had never come out and accused Jay of anything other than lying. I always thought it must be because he has a generous spirit, but when I told him about the tapping, I realized he had probably guessed what happened already.

He became quiet when I told him.

"Yeah," he said, "yeah."

Jay wasn't the only one whose statements changed, Susan pointed out.

In Debbie Warren's police interview she tells the police she is certain she saw Adnan at the guidance counselor's office around 2:45 p.m. on January 13. The detectives press her, asking her if she's positive it was that day. She responds in the affirmative.

Mac Gillivary:	Ok. You're positive you saw?
Warren:	If (inaudible) the 13th I'm talking about, yes.

Then, as it happens in Jay's interviews, Ritz announces the audio tape is going to run out and they need to flip it over. They stop the interview at 11:25 a.m. and start the tape again at 11:36, over ten minutes later. All of a sudden Debbie isn't so sure anymore when she saw Adnan.

Mac Gillivary:	Testing, one, two, three. This is Detective Mac Gillivary and it's still the 26th of March 1999, it's approximately 24 minutes of 12. Detective Ritz, Detective Mac Gillivary, and were still interviewing Debbie Warren. Um, we were talking about the guidance counselor's office and what actually everyone does there, and you indicated you were in the guidance counselor's office that day and you recall seeing Adnan, but you can't be 100% sure.
Warren:	(Inaudible) I remember the event taking place, but I'm not exactly sure, that could have been the day before or the day after, because that happened more than one time.

Something similar happened with Coach Sye, about which both Susan and Colin realized and blogged. Susan had already determined, using Sye's statements about the weather and the track practice schedule, that he had indeed seen Adnan on the 13th at practice and that he came on time and left on time. The fact that Adnan was at practice that day was never in dispute, though; even Jay stated that he dropped Adnan off at track after ditching Hae's car. The question, then, was what time track began. When interviewed on March 3, 1999, Sye told police that track practice began at 3:30 p.m. But by the time he testified the following year, track practice had moved to 4:00 p.m.

This move was rather fortuitous for the prosecution—if Adnan was on time for track practice and arrived there by 3:30, he could not have made the "Nisha call." If he arrived at four o'clock, suddenly it became possible.

In her first police statement in March of 1999, Inez Butler remembered Hae saying, as she grabbed some hot fries and apple juice, that she had to pick up her cousin before going to work. By the time Butler testified at trial, Hae was no longer headed to work, she was going to be returning to the school for a wrestling match—a detail that the State was pushing as part of the narrative because of the note they found in Hae's car.

Repeatedly Susan and Colin pointed out how witness stories had been massaged in favor of the prosecution, a pattern of deliberate manipulation. If I felt devastated at the betrayal of justice, I could only imagine how Adnan felt. They took away his life, his future, and ruined his family. Grown men, bound to protect and serve, responsible for the safety and security of the public, had framed a child by manipulating witnesses, including their eyewitness, and this was the only "evidence" they had because they could find nothing with which to tie Adnan to the murder.

What we were looking at wasn't just potential witness-tampering. The police may have taken it a step further and messed with physical evidence as well, all just to get their man.

Hae's body and car are really the only two pieces of physical evidence that can help us understand what might have happened to her on January 13, 1999. Having dissected how the autopsy contradicted the State's theory of the murder, Susan pointed out that something was also very wrong about the condition in which Hae's car was found.

The 300 block of Edgewood Drive in Baltimore is an urban area with both high crime and heavy policing. It is a sprawling neighborhood of brick row homes, and in some places the homes line up around all four sides of a vacant grassy patch, which is used as a parking lot by residents. Hae's car was found in such a lot, parked right next to rows of other vehicles.

Susan had taken a very close look at the color photograph of the car taken before it was towed and, eagle-eyed as ever, noticed things that didn't add up.

At the time the car was found, it had ostensibly sat through winter weather and storms from January 13, 1999, to February 28, 1999—six weeks. And yet, the car was remarkably clean, showing no signs of snow and ice sediment or deposit. The grass on the tires and inside the wheel wells was greenish, Susan noticed, as if it had been recently kicked up and stuck on the car. It did not look like grass from six weeks ago, which by then should have been withered, tan, and very dead looking. The grass under the car was likewise remarkably green, given that the car had apparently been standing above it for that long. In fact, the picture shows an empty space next to Hae's car with a large, brown, car-shaped patch of dead grass, a clear indication that another car had been standing in the adjacent spot, and there were dead, car-shaped patches of earth on both sides of the strip of green grass where Hae's car stood. It had actually been parked between two regular parking spots.

Then there was this: while every other car in the picture had a lock on the steering wheel, an expected measure in such a neighborhood, Hae's car had sat week after week untouched. All the items in the car, in the backseat and the trunk, were untouched. No one had broken into it; her personal items, including her purse and book bag, were in the trunk; a gold charm worth over a hundred dollars was in the glove compartment. Nothing had been stolen or stripped. This, in one of the highest-crime neighborhoods in Baltimore, with a continuous and heavy police patrol. But none of what you'd expect in this situation happened: the car wasn't damaged, stolen, or broken into; no neighbor reported the abandoned, untouched vehicle; and no cop spotted it. For six weeks.

All these things added up to one conclusion for Susan—the car most likely had not been there the entire time. It had been moved there so recently that the grass stuck to the tires was still green.

As if this wasn't enough, Colin pointed out something else.

In Jay's "first" interview, he stated that Adnan had told him that Hae had kicked the windshield wiper lever as she was being strangled, breaking it. After the police recovered the car, they took both pictures and a video of a lever that was hanging limp on the right side of the steering column. The lever itself was removed and sent to a crime lab to see if any of its edges were fractured, as they should have been if it was kicked so violently that the entire lever collapsed.

The prosecution used the video of the dangling lever to corroborate Jay's testimony that Hae was strangled in the passenger seat of her car. Except that the lever wasn't broken at all. The lab returned a result that there was no fracture anywhere along the edge of the lever. It was simply dangling down, and the video shows that the assembly behind the lever, inside the steering column itself, was loose.

In other words, the lever had not been kicked. It had been loosened at the base, where the stalk should attach to the steering column. To boot, the ignition collar was missing.

All of this could mean nothing. Or it could mean something very big if the ignition collar was missing and the lever became loose because someone was trying to move the car without any keys.

In a blog posted on March 27, 2015, Colin wrote, "If Hae's Sentra were a 1994 Sentra, removing the ignition collar would have been a good first step toward hotwiring her car, which is why the 1994 Sentra was among the 10 most stolen cars in 2011, 2007, 2006, and 2005. In the mid-1990s, however, many car companies, including Nissan, introduced new locking mechanisms. Now, removing the ignition collar would not be a good first step toward hotwiring a 'modern' car, which generally can only be done by drilling the lockpins, using a screwdriver in the ignition, or somehow powering the dash through the hood (depending on the type of car)."

Hae's car was a 1998 Nissan Sentra. The missing ignition collar may have been from a hot-wire attempt that either failed or succeeded. Colin theorized that maybe Hae was killed when interrupting an attempt to steal her car, and we all wondered if her car was hot-wired and moved recently to the location where it was eventually found.

If the car had been moved recently, and Jay didn't really know where it was the entire time, two questions now remained: why would Jay cooperate and implicate himself and, as Jay asked Sarah on *Serial*, who did it—who killed Hae?

CHAPTER 13

TRUTH AND JUSTICE

Believers, be the supporters of justice
and testify to what you may have witnessed, for the sake of God,
even against yourselves, parents, and relatives;
whether it be against the rich or the poor.

Holy Quran 4:135

"Who is this guy?"

I sent Saad a text message after he sent me a link to a podcast I had never heard of before—a new one to add to the host of many that cropped up to talk about *Serial*.

Serial Dynasty was about as obvious a name as you could come up with to get the attention of *Serial* fans, and it looked like the host was going to basically recap and cover all *Serial* and related shows out there: *Undisclosed, Serially Obsessed, Crime Writers On Serial,* and the *Serial Serial Podcast* (yes, I know).

The host was a fire chief named Bob Ruff. Born and raised in a small town in Michigan, Bob had a deep, authoritative voice to match his towering, broad frame. While true crime and criminal justice were never necessarily his interest, he loved a good mystery, had an inquisitive mind, and showed a tenacity for figuring things out. He was a die-hard follower of *Serial* and the case, but not just as a "fan." He became obsessed with the case, taking copious notes and listening to every bit of *Serial* and case-related information in the public domain. As a career arson investigator, he was committed to figuring out what really happened on January 13, 1999.

That's why, when he heard *Undisclosed*, he decided he had to get on the air and talk about it. He already hosted and produced a podcast called *Off Duty*

Podcast with a group of his firefighters. But after hearing our podcast, he decided he had to launch a second one focused on the case; he was already called crazy by friends and family for his obsession, for the hundreds of pages of notes, and for listening to *Serial* almost a dozen times. *Undisclosed* was exactly what he was looking for, a show that would dig deep and truly investigate the case.

Calling *Undisclosed* "groundbreaking," "mind-blowing," and more interesting than *Serial*, he urged everyone to listen to it immediately and then asked them to send him all theories, thoughts, suggestions, and research related to figuring out who killed Hae Min Lee.

I listened to the first episode cautiously, though I did share his show on social media since he was so positive about *Undisclosed*. But at that point, I had no idea who he was. As a fire chief he already had some credibility. He was also the director of the Fire Science Academy, owned his own training firm, and as an arson investigator he had been involved in cases as an expert witness. He had his own investigatory method and felt that Adnan's case was flawed from the beginning because of investigatory failures. I liked what I was hearing; he announced he would follow *Undisclosed*, and I decided I'd follow *Serial Dynasty*.

His second episode had a singular focus: Don. Bob found it incredibly odd and suspicious that Don hadn't reached out to Hae the night she disappeared, especially since the note found in her car seemed to indicate she had seen him or had planned to see him. But after hearing *Undisclosed* reveal that the note, and the wrestling match referred to in it, was almost certainly not written on the 13th, he backed off on Don a bit. Regardless, he was sure that the legal system had let down Adnan. The frequency of changing statements of witnesses was evidence that the detectives or prosecutor had something to do with those changes. He closed out his second episode with a clever memory experiment, showing how easy it was to manipulate someone's memories, and then showed how easily it could have been done in Adnan's case.

It was brilliant, and I was sold. Unlike other podcasts that just did recaps, with hosts giving their not-well-informed opinions on the case, Bob was taking it to an investigative level. He clearly wasn't a sensationalist, and he had a very smart head on his shoulders. A head we could use. I reached out to Bob and asked him if he wanted to delve into the case files. He said yes, and I obliged.

As our listener base grew, so did Bob's. With every episode and every revelation we disclosed, Bob developed his theories, synthesized and contextualized our findings, and interviewed Colin, Susan, and myself. But then Bob went further, doing things we were hesitant to do—like reaching out to players in the case, including the enigmatic Ernest Carter, Jay's friend who was knighted "Neighbor Boy" in *Serial*.

In my first meeting with Sarah, the two big issues I had presented to convince her to look into the case were Asia's alibi and a document that had left me confused for years—a police report about a man named Dave Hogston who called the police after his daughter came to him with some troubling information: Carter had told her he had seen the body of a young Asian woman in the trunk of a car.

This police report, which I had found in Gutierrez's files years earlier, had always haunted me. It was one of the documents I copied and kept in my private case stash as the rest of the records were passed around between attorneys and the family.

Sarah saw the importance of tracking Carter down, and did eventually speak to him, but his story left us nowhere.

Hogston's daughter, Laura, was lying, Carter essentially said. She made it all up; Carter had never said those things to her. The police had even taken him in for questioning and he had told them the same thing back in 1999. He had known Jay since childhood but he didn't know Adnan. And he told Sarah that he knew nothing about the crime or a body in a trunk, and that he wouldn't "kid around about something like that."

I didn't buy for a second that he hadn't said anything to Laura. Something prompted her father to contact the police, and a story so specific about an Asian girl's body in the trunk of a car, coming from someone with a lifetime of friendship with Jay—Laura and her father couldn't have made it up.

When Bob got a hold of Carter, a slightly different picture emerged. Carter admitted to Bob that Jay had told him a story about the crime in which Adnan had driven up to Jay's house and popped the trunk, asking him, "Yo, are you ready for this?" Adnan showed him a body, and then they drove off together to bury it somewhere. Carter recalled telling Laura something after getting drunk at a party and the next thing he knew, the cops were at his door.

At this point it became clear—"neighbor boy" wasn't such a big mystery after all. He had taken a story his friend had told him and told it to a girl, maybe in the hope of impressing her, and got caught up in something he knew nothing about. Nothing to see here, no smoking gun.

In the meantime, though, as Bob dispensed with Carter, he was already working behind the scenes on a bigger target: Jay himself.

Miracles were happening. On May 18, 2015, the Court of Special Appeals did something extraordinary. It cancelled the upcoming oral arguments that had been scheduled for the following month.

Without our even stepping into court, COSA rendered a decision to remand the case back down to the circuit court, the same court that had denied the PCR, and directed Adnan's attorney to file a motion to reopen the PCR proceedings with the lower court in order to hear Asia's testimony.

I was stunned. We were all stunned. Justin called me, full of wonderment. "Is this normal?" I asked him.

"Nothing about this case is normal, Rabia."

Adnan called, having heard it on the news.

"This is good, right?"

"Yes," I said cautiously, still in disbelief. "It's good. It's very, very good."

COSA's decision seemed a clear indication that the issues raised, the gamble that Justin took, had serious merit. It's not often that a superior court will remand a case, and when it does, it's telling the lower court that something went wrong here.

We couldn't imagine that the circuit court would refuse to reopen the case. And it didn't.

On August 25, 2015, the State foolishly referred to the cell phone records in their opposition to our motion to reopen, and Justin went full lawyer on them. Since the State raised the issue, they opened the door to the cell tower evidence, and Justin pounced, filing a supplement to our motion and raising a new issue before the court: the AT&T fax cover sheet, discovered by Susan eight months prior, that clearly indicated incoming calls were not reliable for determining the location of a cell phone.

Months earlier Susan and Justin had run the fax cover sheet past Abe Waranowitz, the State's cell expert from the trial. He said he had never seen it before, and if he had, it would have impacted his testimony.

In his filing, Justin made the only two arguments that could possibly explain how the fax cover sheet had escaped attention in 1999—either the prosecutor had hidden it from the defense and Waranowitz, which would be a a Brady violation, or Gutierrez had completely missed it, fortifying our ineffective assistance of counsel claim. It was one or the other because at the end of the day, no one had provided it to the expert who had to testify about this evidence. We were on pins and needles awaiting the State's response to this supplement. Their earlier opposition brief had been rather stomach-turning, full of dramatic, overwrought language, making rather disgusting insinuations and even reciting outright lies.

From alleging that Asia's statement had changed to become time-specific only after I'd met her (implying I fed her the time to note in her affidavit), to repeating the lie that Adnan conveniently recalled nothing of his day, to reiterating a

7:00 p.m. burial time even though Jay had drastically altered it in his *Intercept* interview, to suggesting Adnan "elected" to skip Hae's memorial service when he had actually already been arrested by that time—the brief was a disgrace by any measure.

It must have been the public reaction to the terrible brief that gave the State some difficulty in coming up with a reponse to our supplement. They missed the deadline of fifteen days after our filing, then thirty days, and finally on September 28, 2015, filed an objection to the inclusion of the fax cover issue.

The circuit court wasn't having it, though, and in record time, on November 6, 2015, Judge Martin Welch, who had denied the PCR nearly two years earlier, and now having been brought out of retirement to adjudicate the case, granted our motion to reopen. All of the State's arguments had failed.

We would get another day in court. And this time, Asia McClain would be with us.

While the wheels of the law were grinding away, Susan, Colin, and Bob were still going full steam ahead on their investigation.

As Susan and Colin broke the State's case to bits, Bob was more interested in figuring out what happened to Hae after she last left school, and who killed her.

Full disclosure: I had many times thought about Hae, shed tears of horror and grief at what the family must have gone through when she was missing, pain at thinking about her last moments, and rage at how she was discarded by some monster, but I had not given any real consideration to actually solving the crime. Not because it wasn't important, but because I seriously doubted I had the skills to do so. How are cold cases solved without the cooperation of police, without the State reopening the case? I had no idea.

But I now realized that while we might be on the road to a new trial, or a plea deal for Adnan, as long as the real killer wasn't caught a cloud would hang over him. Unless we could prove someone else killed Hae, there would still be many who'd consider Adnan a killer who got out on legal maneuverings. It made me angry but also forced me to think about the crime itself, to try and piece together what I could.

We knew that Hae's pager was never found, even though her purse and other belongings were still in her car, and Colin believed it was probably because whoever killed her had paged her, and his number appeared on that pager.

If she was paged, it had to be by someone who knew her, presumably someone not at the school.

Hae's shoes were found in the backseat of the car, which makes no sense at all if she was actually killed in either the driver-side or passenger-side seat in the front. If she had been killed in the car and her shoes had come off as the body was being moved to the trunk or the burial site, why would the killer pick them up and put them in the backseat? Why wouldn't he leave them wherever they came off? The only reasonable explanation I could think of was that either they came off as she was killed in the backseat, or they came off at another location that was tied to the killer, so he had to grab them and toss them in the backseat, like he had thrown her purse in the trunk. Women don't drive around with their purse in the trunk. Hae had to have gotten out of her car somewhere with that purse, and after she was murdered, the killer took the purse and threw it in the trunk as he was cleaning up the crime scene.

A number of listeners with backgrounds in law enforcement also contacted me about the method of the crime and suggested that bodies are moved, as was done in this case, only when the location the victim was killed in could be tied to the killer. I thought it was an interesting theory and then had a long, detailed conversation with someone who was internationally renowned for profiling criminals based on a crime scene—Jim Clemente.

Both a retired prosecutor and FBI profiler, Clemente's name is well known to crime aficionados for his work on the extremely popular television show *Criminal Minds* and many others. I kept getting suggestions from folks to try and speak to him. So I sent him a message on Twitter and, lo and behold, he responded.

Jim was incredibly gracious, explaining that despite his overwhelming work schedule he wanted very much to help us. He asked that I send him the files about the crime scene—he hadn't heard *Serial* or *Undisclosed* and wanted to keep it that way. He didn't want to know anything about any of the suspects or the investigation. He only wanted to know how and where Hae was found.

After he reviewed those documents, we set up a phone call, which basically blew my mind.

Jim explained that one thing we could almost completely rule out was that this was a third-party killer—not impossible but highly unlikely. A few things pointed to this conclusion: she was found with all her jewelry on and her purse and belongings weren't taken, so clearly this wasn't a robbery. There didn't seem to be any signs of struggle or rape either, and third-party killers generally murdered female victims in conjunction with a sexual assault or robbery. But killers who know their victim are different; they may kill in the heat of passion or for some premeditated reason like revenge.

Random killers, he also explained, had no incentive to move a body. They generally encountered their victims in an outside space not connected to either killer or victim, or in a space connected only to the victim, as in a home invasion. But generally, killers only took the immense risk of moving a body to a new location when the location of the murder itself could be tied to them.

He went on to note that he didn't think this was premeditated, that it had the hallmarks of an amateur, a young, first-time perp, of someone who panicked, leaving the body in an almost haphazard fashion with loose dirt and leaves piled on top of it, not even having the time to dig a grave.

I told him about having visited the grave site recently with a soil specialist, a woman who had done the soil survey for the entire city of Baltimore and knew the area inside and out. When we got to the site where the body was found, I showed her the depression described by MacGillivary in his testimony. She spent over an hour inspecting the area, noting that the log itself actually was lying over the depression, with half of the hollow on either side of the log.

"Unlikely someone would have dug a space out like that, doesn't make sense to dig under the log and over to the other side," she noted.

If the police had wanted to, she said, they could have easily determined if the area had actually been dug by pulling core samples of the soil from the depression and matching it to that of the slightly higher ground. It could still be done, though with less accuracy. But surveying the area and noting that the stream often rose up and flooded this part, she said the hollow was probably from the water erosion coupled with a natural dip in the earth.

She moved her shovel around the hollow, showing me that it was near rock within half an inch of the surface.

"There isn't anything to dig here," she said, "there isn't much topsoil, it's mostly rock."

As far as she was concerned, the depression was not dug, the terrain didn't allow it, and the shape of the hollow and the route of the creek at high tide all pointed to its being a naturally created space.

If anything, this explained the discrepancies in Jay's stories about the shovel (or shovels, as Jenn said). The police may also have realized that there were no shovels, which explains why they waited over a month to try and retrieve them from the dumpster where Jay said he had discarded them. But they wanted to appear to take his story seriously, so eventually they visited the dumpsters.

Jim Clemente's analysis seemed credible, then. If there was no digging, he was right—someone had just dumped Hae unceremoniously, covered her up hastily, and gotten out of there.

What then, I asked Jim, did he think happened to Hae?

She probably went to meet someone she knew, and something went badly wrong. She was killed wherever she met this person shortly after leaving the school, and late that night, after being in another location all day and much of the evening, her body was left in Leakin Park. Jim would start with the men in her life at the time: Adnan and Don, though there could be people we don't know about, people from her online life who were never discovered. From there he would look to see who had the opportunity.

There is some evidence to suggest the cops were thinking along the same lines, that she wasn't killed in a car like Jay said (or the police got him to say), and they were looking to see where the murder actually took place.

Documents emerged from the Maryland Public Information Act file, showing that the police had been trying to find out if Hae had gone to a hotel the day she disappeared. A receipt of Hae's credit card charge for a November 25, 1998, stay at the local Comfort Inn (a few minutes from the school) was part of the file, along with copies of a few business cards taken from local hotels, which had presumably been visited by a detective during the investigation.

It seemed as if these cards were collected not during the missing person's investigation but during the murder investigation. For example, the police would not have contacted Phillip Buddemeyer (bottom left), the city surveyor, until after the body was found. Buddemeyer was not part of the case until February 9, 1999, when he assisted in the disinterment of the body.

The way I saw it, if contact with these hotels was made after February 1, it means the police were seriously considering the possibility that Hae went to meet someone at a hotel after school. It may also explain why Bilal Ahmed was questioned about how, when, and for whom he booked hotels during his grand jury testimony.

Even after Adnan was arrested, the issue popped up when both Ritz and Mac-Gillivary questioned Debbie about it on March 26, 1999:

Ritz:	You said that they would go to parking lots er, once at a friend's house, er any other locations that Detective Mac Gillivary asked you about did Hae ever tell you about any hotels or motels?
Warren:	No, she never told me about any hotels or motels (inaudible).
Ritz:	How about Adnan?
Warren:	No.

Mac Gillivary:	Um, were you aware of any specific times that they had told you and locations where they had had, er intercourse?
Warren:	Um, they had um, an afternoon in the park. I don't remember which park it was. I don't who told me or not but, they did um, out in parking lots, in his car um, at one of our friends houses, at a party, er, I don't think they ever did it at his house or her house, either one, but in other places.
Mac Gillivary:	Ok, any hotels?
Warren:	No, they never went to a hotel.
Mac Gillivary:	That you're aware of?
Warren:	No, as far as I know.

This was curious, I thought. The police already had a story from Jay, the Best Buy parking lot story, but it probably rang as untrue to them as it did to anyone who has visited the area—wide open, easily viewable from both a busy main city street and the Interstate, congested in the middle of the afternoon. Or they may have realized, based on the autopsy report, that the lividity didn't match the way she was found, or Jay's story.

If they believed the Best Buy version, there would be no reason for this line of questioning with Debbie.

After speaking with Jim, who promised to keep digging through the case and asked to listen to the audio of Jay's police interviews, I couldn't stop thinking of Jay's question to Sarah: well then, who did it?

Summer was upon us and with it came Ramadan, the month of fasting for Muslims. The Islamic calendar is lunar, so the months shift around, but in recent years Ramadan has fallen on the longest, hottest days of the year.

I had recently finished up my two-year project at New America Foundation, which took me to a dozen cities across the country, and coupled with the incessant work of the podcast and the case (and lots and lots of social media advocacy), I was looking forward to taking Ramadan to unwind. The point of the month is not to starve but to learn to detach yourself from worldly needs and wants, to learn to discipline your body and soul. Like a month-long Shabbat, the point is to be more still, to be with God.

That purpose usually gets sidelined with nightly feastings, gathering with friends and family, then night prayers at the mosque. There is a special place for prayers done at night, the later the better; prayers done while fighting sleep and exhaustion are highly valued in Islam.

This is traced back to a rather mystical and magical tradition, in which the Prophet Muhammad says, "Our Lord (glorified and exalted be He) descends each night to the earth's sky when there remains the final third of the night, and He says 'Who is saying a prayer to Me that I may answer it? Who is asking something of Me that I may give it to him? Who is asking forgiveness of Me that I may forgive him?' And thus He continues until the light of dawn shines."

It's this time of night that the famous Sufi poet Rumi writes of when he says, "The breezes at dawn have secrets to tell you. Don't go back to sleep!"

This Ramadan, like many in the past, I resolved to try as much as possible to pray in the hours before dawn. My prayer was simple, it was a "*wird*," a continuous, repeated recitation, an exhortation, of one of the "ninety-nine names" (attributes, really) of God in Islam: "Ya Dhaahir," The Manifest. The One who makes things clear, who reveals what is hidden. I recited this name thousands of times on a rosary, with the intention that God please reveal what happened to Hae. Bring the truth to light.

Ramadan passed without incident, and as Muslims are wont to do, a few days after it was over I broke my abstinence from the pleasures of the world and went to see a Bollywood movie with friends late one night.

Afterward, my head full of peppy songs and flashy dance sequences, I got in my car around 1:30 a.m. The windows were down, my scarf was hanging on for its dear life, and I was singing with abandon. As I pulled onto the freeway, an incredibly strange thing happened to me. I suddenly froze, the hair on my body stood up, and a chill went through me. The Bollywood songs were slammed out of my head, replaced with an intense, screaming thought that sprung from nowhere: Don. We have to look at Don.

It may seem obvious on an intellectual level that if I didn't believe Adnan did it, I'd move on to Don. But I had no emotional impulse, in all these years, to suspect him. He was as near to a nonentity as could be to the case. I never saw him testify, I had no idea what he looked like, and there were so many other strange people like Alonzo Sellers, the streaker, involved that I dismissed Don as easily as Mandy Johnson had done in 1999.

But now I felt a strong urge to get every bit of information I could on Don. I went home and couldn't sleep all night; early in the morning I shot off an e-mail to Susan, Colin, Dennis, and Bob explaining my weird experience.

Looking back, I'm still a bit embarrassed about the e-mail. I knew I sounded nuts, but I just had to tell them that we needed to get more information about Don, immediately.

A few hours later I had to stop by Susan's place to drop off a birthday gift for her, during which time I marveled at the clay dinosaurs she made, the suits of bottle-cap armor, multiple gaming screens, and reams and reams of case documents and cell tower maps. As I was leaving, sounding sheepish, I apologized for my early morning e-mail.

Susan responded, "Oh, it's okay. I mean, you do know about the psychic, right?"

I did not. She filled me in.

As *Serial* was ongoing, a woman reached out to Sarah Koenig. Sarah had told Krista Meyers about her, and they connected. Krista had already been communicating with Susan and Colin, answering what questions she could for their investigation. So Krista told Susan about the psychic, but Susan didn't know her identity. The psychic had a story she felt compelled to tell, a story she was convinced was tied to the murder of Hae Min Lee.

It turns out she wasn't a psychic, something she explained emphatically the first time I spoke with her (I'll call her Pam). I was struck by how emotional she was, how raw it all still was for her.

Pam explained she was highly educated, had a successful career in finance, was not particularly religious, and had experienced a few odd moments in her life that she could only explain as slightly supernatural phenomena, but in no way did she consider herself psychic.

I heard her story out, shaken by it myself because of her clear sincerity. I didn't think for a second she was making any of it up, and she said that she had been carrying this experience around for the past sixteen years, having told only those closest to her, who could vouch for it.

I asked her, because it had been a long time, to give more thought to what she remembered and then send me an e-mail. She was upset after our talk from having the memories rush back at her, but said she would write it all up for me. After many months she finally did.

Here is what she said.

I wanted to document for you what I saw in the Fall of 2000 when I contacted the Baltimore police.

In November, 2000, I was a sophomore in DC, and took a southwest flight from Chicago to Baltimore after thanksgiving break. As I was about to deplane, I touched a bag in an overhead compartment at the same time as a Korean woman in the plane and felt a jolt of energy. She was in her mid to late 40s, a little plump (5'2 to 5'6 and maybe 140–150) in leather black pants and a tunic type sweater. We didn't talk but the energy was strange and left me buzzing. That night when I got back to my dorm room, I had a terrible vivid dream that disturbed me for more than a decade. I found it so disturbing I shared it with family and a few friends and actually called the Baltimore police to share my vision. I never heard back from them after I reported it. That was the one and only time I've ever contacted law enforcement about a dream or vision.

This is what I saw:

In a Baltimore motel parking lot off of a busy street with strip malls and big box stores and gas stations, etc., a young, Korean girl in her teens or early 20s is in the driver's seat of a car, the car smelled like sex . . . not sure if it was consensual sex or not, or if the sex had been in the car or motel but I didn't get the sense she'd been raped. The car had a cloth interior (like the fake crushed velvet kind) and was gray/silver. I think there was a tape deck? There was junk in the back seat and on the floor, a jacket, papers receipts and an empty 7up or Mountain Dew bottle maybe?

The girl was afraid. And a young white man in his early 20s or late teens with short dark blonde hair and piercing blue eyes that were bloodshot and crazed was in the passenger seat leaning over her, choking her with his bare hands. He may have stopped at some point and gotten some kind of cord like parachute core or a sweatshirt tie, but I'm not sure. It took a really long time, or felt like it did. It was awful and she made a gurgling cracking noise as she choked.

There was a minor struggle but the whole time I could hear her thoughts and she kept thinking "this is crazy, this isn't happening." There was a general sense of betrayal as well as shock and disbelief. She was more shocked than scared, and felt so betrayed and just shocked. She didn't fight as hard as she could have, I think because she kept thinking he was going to stop. She didn't believe for a second he was going to kill her.

It was cold out with no leaves on the trees, the heat was on in the car. You could see trees over the fence they faced. It was late afternoon. His thinking was disordered. It was almost nonsensical and manic. He didn't mean to kill her and didn't want to intellectually. I had the sense he was high on drugs or extremely mentally ill. He didn't want to kill her and just couldn't make himself stop. He really wanted to stop, but just couldn't control himself. It was terrifying being in his head. And he was so out of control and self-loathing while hurting her. It was awful. . . .

. . . After she was dead, he cried. He felt horrible and disgusted with himself and didn't know what to do. He got out of the car, which was facing a fence that was chain link with brown plastic or old brown wood, I'm not sure. Behind the car, which was gray/silver or very light blue were hotel rooms that were beige/tan with dark brown door frames and window frames like a Motel 6 or EconoLodge. They were parked by a brown dumpster that wasn't full. He put something in the dumpster. It might have been a plastic bag with something in it? I didn't see what it was but it made a light noise when it landed that sounded like something hard or heavy in plastic obviously on top of other trash, not an empty dumpster.

He opened the trunk that was also carpeted/cloth and had a dark blue or black duffle bag in it. It was late afternoon and the sun was already setting before he killed her, and he waited til just after dusk. There was basically no foot traffic or other cars. He moved her body to the trunk, folded her almost in half on her side to fit her around the duffel, and drove her to his mother's house. He didn't know what to do and drove around before taking her there but didn't know what else to do. He wasn't scared about getting caught, he was just unable to think coherently. He may have lived there too, I'm not sure, but it was definitely his mother's home.

He went inside and left her in the trunk. He didn't decide to leave her there, he just did it, which chilled me. No one else was home. When he entered the house he started to sob and shake uncontrollably. There were crosses in the house and maybe a picture of Jesus with a sacred heart? He felt intense guilt and remorse. He knew he was going to hell and this scared him very much. His mother was very Christian and he was terrified of her knowing what he had done. He went up the stairs and there were family pictures on the walls and maybe the landing on the way up. The carpet was worn and either dark gray or brown, maybe. Walls were lighter. He went into his dark room, didn't turn on the light, and fell asleep crying with terrible night-mares.

I don't know what happened next, and I didn't see the burial clearly. But he buried her with his bare hands (not a shovel) and he was wearing gloves. The ground was hard and there was a big mound of dirt like a mined patch or a construction site nearby. He was alone when he buried her in late after-noon. It was sunny and very cold. He said a prayer over the grave before he left her. He felt genuine sadness and remorse. He may have left a jacket or sweater on her? There was a red jacket too either in the car or grave. Then I stopped seeing and feeling him and could feel the dead girl.

She was in cold shallow ground. It was a wooded area near a creek or small area of flowing (not stagnant) water. But there wasn't much of it. It was frozen over. It was slightly below her and she was on a bank closer to a path or road with the water on the other side of the log. There were frozen and snowy leaves on top and she was near a rotten log that had been there at least a year, possible longer that had moss on it. There was a used condom on the ground nearby and some other trash (I didn't see any liquor bottles though). You could hear traffic muffled, and also trees rustling. It smelled like motor oil and moldy leaves. She was sad and worried about her mother who didn't know where she was. She could hear her mother crying and it made her sad and lonely. I could hear a bell of some kind ringing and saw the letters s and d or t, I'm not sure which. I have no idea what they mean. I felt like she was crying and so sad about her family not knowing where she was. She felt wor-ried and alone and betrayed.

When Pam woke from her dream, she did so screaming, soaked in sweat, as her roommate rushed to her side in the middle of the night. The dream had been so vivid that even after waking up she felt like she was in it. Finally she went to speak to a campus priest who advised her to call the Baltimore City Police. She made the call, and an officer listened impatiently, thanked her, and let her know they'd be in touch. Of course they never were. What she had seen, if it was about Hae, wouldn't have mattered then anyway; almost two years had gone by since she had been murdered, and nearly ten months since Adnan had been convicted. But over the years Pam had held on to the vision and told those closest to her about this experience she still couldn't shake. Then she heard *Serial*, and it all came together for her. She had never before heard the name Hae Min Lee, and knew nothing about this 1999 murder when she had the dream, but when the podcast ran it was as if a long-scattered puzzle came together for her. She reached out to Sarah, who spoke to her and happened to mention it to Krista, but hadn't told me about it.

The day Pam sent me the above e-mail she was also agitated. She had had another vivid and disturbing dream about the woman she saw murdered that night, and when she woke she saw online that it was Hae's birthday. She had a connection to Hae that she couldn't understand.

In an already complicated, difficult, obtuse case this added one more layer of pain and haze.

There was another psychic too, though, one that Hae's mother had consulted, according to undated notes in Gutierrez's files. The notes read: "Hae's mother went to see a psychic. Psychic said ex boyfriend did it."

So it seems there were two competing psychic visions, each pointing to a different man.

There was no reason, not a shred, to believe that Don had anything to do with Hae's death, other than he matched the profile Jim gave and now generally matched a description given by a stranger with a vision from years ago. And if we tested the Physical Evidence Recovery Kit or the fingernail clippings taken from Hae (if they still existed in a police locker somewhere) and they matched Don's DNA, then what? It wouldn't prove anything because they were dating and he had been with her the night before.

Plus, he was at work.

Or so everyone always thought. Susan had cracked open the door to the possibility that Don's timecard had been falsified, and Bob decided he was going to find out for sure.

Bob started calling around, beginning with a local LensCrafters, to get information about their time system—but they weren't talking. They referred him to "corporate" and he found an HR manager there who was much more willing to chat. What he told Bob shocked him, and all his listeners.

The manager at corporate explained to Bob that LensCrafters was not a franchise; it was and is wholly owned by Luxottica, so all of the pay comes from a central location. The way employees in 1999 logged in was the same as today, with their unique employee ID number. That number didn't change if an employee moved from store to store, even if an employee was moved to a store in a different state. When Bob asked him what an explanation for Don having two ID numbers could be, he responded, "If you're looking at two timesheets for the same employee with two different associate ID numbers on them, one of them has been falsified." Bob also asked about the missing overtime hours and the separate timesheets for the week of January 13 from the two stores. Again, the manager stated that one of the timesheets was falsified because if it was authentic, those hours would all appear on the same timesheet regardless of working at different stores. And that single timesheet would certainly contain the overtime hours.

Bob didn't stop there. He then managed to find two LensCrafters employees, a retail manager and a lab manager, both of whom worked for the Hunt Valley store in January of 1999 and were on site on January 13. The retail manager recalled Don as being a "nice enough kid." When Bob explained the situation, noting the timecard and employee number discrepancies, the manager responded that having worked at the store for many years and covered many different branches, he could confirm that employees never had more than one ID number. An employee could have had two ID numbers if that person had worked for the store previously, stopped working for them and then started again—but in that case the old employee ID was terminated.

Bob asked the lab manager the same question.

"Can you think of any possible reasonable, innocent explanation as to why these two timecards would have the different ID numbers?"

"No, I can't think of any explanation for different ID numbers," he responded.

Having put out a call for LensCrafters employees who could comment on the timesheet, about a dozen people who had worked for the chain in the late 1990s contacted Bob and confirmed what the corporate HR manager and the two Hunt Valley managers said: the Hunt Valley timesheet was falsified. Altogether, Bob had gotten confirmation with sixteen current and former employees.

It is worth noting that the only time Don ever appears to have used two different ID numbers in his employment was the week that Hae went missing. He didn't just use the different ID number on January 13; he also used it a few days later, on Saturday, January 16, 1999. A peculiarity on the 16th that also appeared on the 13th was that Don again reported working hours that no lab technician was scheduled to work. For the 16th, according to the employee work schedule in our file, one lab tech was scheduled to work at 11:00 a.m., the next at 12:30 p.m., and a third at 2:00 p.m. There was no work in the lab at 9:00 a.m., which is when Don reported being there.

Bob also asked the retail manager about why and how timecards could be changed after the fact—was this something a general employee could do? Apparently not. But in this case, the manager said, "His mother was the general manager and yes, she could have made the changes."

There are innocent, or relatively innocent, explanations as to why his mother made changes to his timecard, if indeed that is what happened. Maybe they were worried that he could become a suspect and created the timesheet just to cover for him.

Also, company policy, according to one former manager Bob spoke to, didn't allow any employee to work with anyone they had a reporting relationship to, so you could not work "under" a relative, though you could work with them. Don's mother was the manager at Hunt Valley, and it was strictly against policy for him to work there. Maybe they fudged the employee ID so no one would catch that he was working under his mother (though why would this happen only on two occasions, both in the same week?).

Yes, it could be innocent, but as Bob was airing his shows, a former manager at LensCrafters named Elizabeth went on the air with him to share something troubling.

It was true that timesheets could be retroactively changed by a manager, but only up to a point. They couldn't, for example, be changed for time worked in weeks prior. They had to be changed within a week of the end of a pay period. In this case the pay period ended on that Saturday, January 16. The changes had to have been made by January 22. That was the date of Don's interview at the Owings Mills store by Detective O'Shea.

Simply put, I am entirely convinced the timesheet was not just falsified. It was falsified at a time before anyone knew Hae had been killed.

Elizabeth noted something else: managers only have access to timesheets for their store, so it would have been odd for the Owings Mills manager to have known the exact hours and timings Don allegedly worked on January 13 at the Hunt Valley store. But that manager, Cathy Michel, did know the exact times, because she gave them to Detective O'Shea when he visited her on February 1, 1999.

Michel could have simply called Hunt Valley to get them. But if so, why wasn't she bothered by the fact that Don broke store policy by working for his mother?

Thanks to an intrepid Reddit investigator, Bob realized this: at the time that Hae disappeared, Michel was living at the same address as Don's mother, Anita

Baird. Years later the two married; Michel took her wife's last name, and together they adopted several children.

So it appears Don's airtight alibi, as one police officer called it during the investigation, was his mother, her girlfriend, and a falsified timesheet. This, along with the fact that police were not able to contact him until 1:30 a.m. on January 14, 1999, and that Debbie Warren reported the last thing Hae told her before leaving school was going to meet Don at the mall, raises serious questions about where Don was the afternoon his girlfriend, whom he never attempted to reach after that, disappeared.

Bob wasn't just digging up this information; he was in the business of going straight to the source. So he reached out to Don on Facebook, after having made sure it was the right Don, and asked him if he'd like to comment on the timesheet issues. Don told Bob he had the wrong person, though he clearly did not. Next Bob reached out to his mother, Anita, who threatened to file a complaint (presumably with the police) for harassment if he contacted her again. So Bob backed off, and shortly thereafter Don deleted his Facebook page.

Bob first reached out to Jay when he concluded that Jay had been coached on every detail of Adnan's case. He thought there might be a way to create an opening to show Jay that he had also been victimized by the State, that he had been set up to admit to being an accessory in a crime that he had nothing to do with.

But Jay was not interested.

The next time Bob reached out to Jay was to confront him with more information that might have explained why Jay got caught up in the mess.

The information was a bit of a game-changer for all of us, and it came through the most unexpected channel: Reddit.

WhenTheWorldsCollide is the Reddit handle for an ex-investigative reporter and now stay-at-home-mom who had been sucked deep into the case early on. Part of a small, private subreddit, "Worlds" and others worked with Susan to assist in investigations, pulling and reviewing documents, brainstorming theories, and sleuthing online and in real life.

Worlds is extremely talented at getting people to talk. She began looking for any connections she might have with the Baltimore Metro Crime Stoppers (MCS) to see if the rumors the community had heard long ago were true. Was someone actually paid a reward for information? It didn't seem like Sarah had checked.

She tracked down the board of the current MCS and did what investigative reporters do best, made a cold call. And she struck gold.

After a long, cordial conversation about how MCS works, Worlds asked about the Hae Min Lee case. Did this person know anything about the reward that was offered back then? Had it been paid out? The board member said they would check with someone who had been involved in 1999 and get back to her.

Three anxious days later, Worlds got an answer and immediately posted it to the private subreddit group:

> *Greetings, friends.*
> *This just in: It's true Metro Crime Stoppers of Baltimore (MCS) paid out the cash award for Hae Min Lee's murder case! Actually MCS paid out 2 rewards.*
>
> *According to my MCS source's records a call was received on the MCS hotline on February 1; the tipster apparently gave relevant information about [Hae's] disappearance (days later, murder) and was assigned tip number #6456. Reward #1 was for $575, put up by MCS from its public-donation funding pool. Reward #2 was for $2500, put up by the Korean American Safety Council. The combination prize—$3075—was paid in cash, in person (ETA: guidelines call for informant to meet with BPD detective/dept. PIO+MCS board member) on November 1, 1999.*

The February 12th anonymous tip, it seemed, must have been a cover for the February 1st tip, which had never been disclosed to the defense. Not only had this tip not been disclosed, it had not been disclosed that the tip informant was paid.

Colin, Susan, and I wondered what on earth the tip could have said. According to the MCS board member that Worlds was communicating with:

> *If a tip leads to an arrest and indictment, then the police department who made the arrest is responsible for completing the TIPSOFT program information and rating the crime for the reward potential. The MCS police representative (we call them the police council) presents the information to the board and if it meets the requirements of our by-laws we authorize a reward. We do not participate in a trial. We only provide a mechanism for getting information about the crime to the police who have the responsibility to investigate and determine the validity of the information. Defense attorneys do sometimes request information. However, all of the information that we have is provided to the police and I assume is available from them in discovery. The tip lines are not recorded. The only information we have is what the tipster provides in the call, web tip, or text tip. We give them a number. If they forget the number, then they will not get the reward.*

The tip was paid because the tipster had actual, actionable information that tied Adnan to the crime.

Crime Stoppers never knew who the tipster was; only the police had that information.

We quickly sent off a flurry of MPIA requests to Baltimore County and City police, requesting the contents of the tip, and in the meantime went back to the case files to see exactly what actions the police took after the tip came in on February 1, 1999.

On that day a big flurry of activity in the investigation took place: the police questioned Inez Butler, Gerald Russell, and Hope Schab from Woodlawn High, and Cathy Michel from LensCrafters. They placed another call to Adnan, and spoke with Hae's uncle, Tae Su Kim. The police didn't head to Leakin Park, and they didn't hunt down Hae's car. But they did narrow down on two suspects: Don and Adnan.

Michel confirmed Don's alibi, so that left Adnan.

Susan's theory on the February 1 tip is that, having hidden it from the defense and public, the police "recreated" it as the February 12 tip, which they disclosed as having been made but not paid out. The police didn't want anyone to know a tipster had been paid, never mind the identity of the tipster. At the same time they wanted to make it public that some incriminating tip had come in for Adnan, which gave them cover for their increased focus on him.

The February 12 tip must have evolved from the February 1 tip, though—while the earlier tip pointed toward both Adnan and Don, the later tip gave direct, specific information about Adnan, identifying him by name, saying he took Hae to Leakin Park for sex, naming a friend ("Baser" Ali, meaning Yaser Ali), and that he had broken up with Hae about a week before the murder.

Whoever this person was ended up getting paid $3,075 for their information.

This rang all kinds of bells for Susan and Colin, who immediately dug up the notes taken by police when they did the March 18, 1999, "ride-along" and interview with Jay. On the very first page of notes was scribbled something totally unrelated to the crime or the rest of the notes:

Mr. Brown
94 Suzuki 600 cc
9,000 Miles

At the very bottom of the twenty-six pages of handwritten notes is scribbled:

Private Invest
Going to discredit
REWARD

A few days later, on March 24, 1999, the police visited the school to interview a slew of teachers. Every single teacher on the list except one taught Adnan. The sole exception was a man named Carl Brown, who was Jay's soccer coach and had no connection with either Adnan or Hae. The police interview itinerary makes a notation next to Brown's name: "Mr. Brown—motorcycle."

Accompanying the interview itinerary in the police files were same-day printouts of the *Kelley Blue Book* value of 1994 Suzuki 600 cc motorcycles.

It seemed the police were headed to the school not just to interview teachers, but to negotiate the purchase of a motorcycle from Brown for Jay, the price of which was not much different than the amount of the Crime Stoppers reward. Just a couple of weeks later, in an April 7, 1999, interview Stephanie McPherson gave to police, she mentioned Jay was planning on buying a motorcycle and financing it, and in 2014 Jay in his *Intercept* interview mentioned that he was busy in 1999 learning to ride a motorcycle.

We put our private investigator on the case, asking him to track down Mr. Brown. It turned out he remembered talking to police about whether he knew Adnan or Hae, and remembered the bike, but he couldn't recall the police ever asking him about it. He also mistakenly told us it had been sold the previous year, when vehicle records showed us he sold it on April 9, 1999. It was entirely possible that the police didn't question him about the motorcycle, or that they asked and realized he was looking to sell it quickly, whereas Jay wouldn't get his reward until many months later.

The bike wasn't sold to Jay. But there is no reasonable explanation for this trail of documents other than that the police were going to talk to Brown about this motorcycle that had first been mentioned by Jay in the ride-along notes.

The tie-in with the Crime Stoppers tip was becoming clear. There was only one person in the entire record of the case who had incorrectly suggested, like the February 12 tip, that Hae and Adnan broke up a week before the murder when they had actually broken up about a month prior. That person was Jay. Jay also happened to know two of Adnan's mosque friends, Yaser and Tayyab. And the time of the pay-out on November 1, 1999, a few weeks after Jay's plea deal, and shortly before he finally bought a car after having spent years getting rides from friends, made it abundantly obvious who collected the reward money. After gathering all the intel we could, Susan presented us with her unified grand theory of how this all went down.

So here's my new Grand Theory of the Anonymous Call (tm). The specific details are just me randomly theorizing, but tell me what holes you see in the broader outline of it:

- Jay realizes Hae is missing sometime around 1/21 (per his and Steph's statements)
- Jay tells Jenn ridiculous stories about Adnan killing Hae around 1/22.
- Jay, Adnan, and Yaser are all at a party together on 1/23. Perhaps Yaser mentions something like "well if Adnan did it, he would dump her body in the lake."
- Jay makes anonymous call on 2/1. He says the essentials of what's in the Massey Memo, but he doesn't talk about her car. Instead he says Adnan told Yaser he would've dumped her body in a lake.
- All investigation into other avenues ceases. Searches are made with the dogs, perhaps around bodies of water. Hae's body is found 2/9, and -- as Mac testifies -- based on what O'Shea tells him, he pulls Adnan's phone records.
- BPD's finest need an excuse to investigate Adnan/Yaser. Massey receives an anonymous call -- either imaginary, or from a cell phone (perhaps by detectives out on a full-day search for Hae's car...?) -- and the 2/1 tip is recreated, with a slight difference. Instead of saying Hae's body was thrown into the lake, as the original had, it now says *Hae's car* would've been thrown into a lake. (This is a really stupid idea, when you think about it. Why the hell would Yaser or Adnan (or Jay) think of driving a car into a lake?

> On February 12, 1999, approx. 1525 Hrs., the above anonymous
> person again called the Homicide Unit. This time that caller remember about a
> year ago, the suspect informed a friend of his (Baser Ali A/M/17), if he ever hurt
> his girlfriend, he would drive her car into a lake. The caller stated the suspect's

- The cops talk to Yaser on 2/15, and ask where Adnan would ditch Hae's car. Yaser tells them he'd ditch it in the city:

> another. Adnan calls him from jail. Yasser was before the Grand Jury. Yasser
> does not think Adnan killed Hae according to Adnan's brother. He stated that
> according to Yasser the police questioned him regarding a love letter found in the
> car from Adnan which stated that if Hae was unable to get in touch with Adnan
> she should get in touch with Yasser. The police insisted that because Yasser and
> Adnan are good friends they think alike and would act alike. Yasser agreed that
> he and Adnan are very similar. The police then asked Yasser where he would
> park the car if he were to dispose of the car. Yasser replied probably the city. A
> few days later the police found Hae's car in the city.

(Side note: where the hell is this car they got the love note from?)

- The cops write in their progress report that Yaser instead said the following, because they needed Yaser's statement to match the Anonymous Call's claims about the lake:

> indicated no.
>
> All was then aked if Adnon had been involved, and he wanted to get rid of the car, where would he do
> so? All indicated somewhere in the woods, possibly in Centennial Lake or the Inner Harbor.
>
> Investigation to continue.

(Side note: this is even dumber. *Who is going to ditch a murder victim's car in the inner harbor?!* Centennial Lake may be an even dumber idea.)

- In an undated interview with Yaser -- perhaps 2/15, perhaps some other time, there's no way to tell because the notes are a single stranded page -- one of the cops slips up and records what the anonymous phone call actually said

> IF EVER HARMED HAE, WOULD DUMP BODY IN LAKE -- PER
> ANONYMOUS CALLER -- YASSER SAID THIS

- The cops subpoena all of Yaser's phone records, but they can't make anything stick against Yaser. However, they somehow already know about Jay (as shown from the list of callers, in which Jay is the sole identified phone number, and even Jenn's number is listed under her father's name), and after a period of questioning, Jay finally "comes clean" and admits to being the anonymous caller. The cops are off to the races.
- They eventually realize they have a big fat reward problem. This results in shenanigans, capers, and acquiring Benaroya to prevent Jay from spilling the beans to a public defender.
- Jay gets the very odd sized reward on 11/1/99. Perhaps this is where the car that he suddenly possesses in January comes from.

A grand theory indeed, but a theory nonetheless. Bob took it a step further and decided to challenge Jay head-on.

He sent him a message about the Crime Stoppers tip.

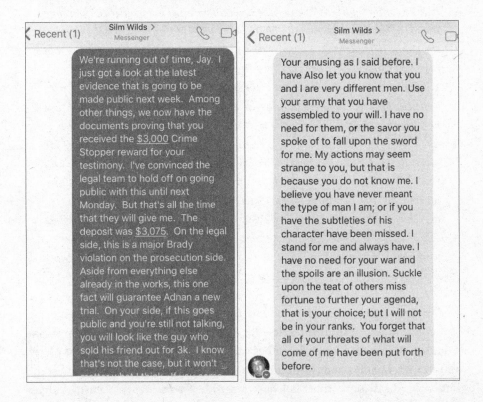

> We're running out of time, Jay. I just got a look at the latest evidence that is going to be made public next week. Among other things, we now have the documents proving that you received the $3,000 Crime Stopper reward for your testimony. I've convinced the legal team to hold off on going public with this until next Monday. But that's all the time that they will give me. The deposit was $3,075. On the legal side, this is a major Brady violation on the prosecution side. Aside from everything else already in the works, this one fact will guarantee Adnan a new trial. On your side, if this goes public and you're still not talking, you will look like the guy who sold his friend out for 3k. I know that's not the case, but it won't

> Your amusing as I said before. I have Also let you know that you and I are very different men. Use your army that you have assembled to your will. I have no need for them, or the savor you spoke of to fall upon the sword for me. My actions may seem strange to you, but that is because you do not know me. I believe you have never meant the type of man I am; or if you have the subtleties of his character have been missed. I stand for me and always have. I have no need for your war and the spoils are an illusion. Suckle upon the teat of others miss fortune to further your agenda, that is your choice; but I will not be in your ranks. You forget that all of your threats of what will come of me have been put forth before.

We couldn't have anticipated this cryptic response. The two things Bob, Susan, Colin, and I all agreed on were that Jay didn't deny having gotten the reward money, and that he had been threatened before about what could happen to him.

My own takeaway was that Jay didn't care about anyone but himself.

Not long after this, we had our suspicion confirmed: Jay had been threatened, and he feared for his life.

Sometime in the summer of 2015 Colin began corresponding with yet another curious character in the case—attorney Anne Benaroya. She had popped up on September 7, 1999, to enter Jay's plea deal as his attorney of record.

The significant thing about Benaroya, which Gutierrez raised bloody hell about at trial, was that Urick had somehow procured her for Jay pro bono. In *Serial*, Sarah covered the events like this:

> *Jay testifies that after his last interview with detectives, in April of '99, he*
> *had no contact with the cops or the prosecutors until September 6. So a long*
> *stretch where he doesn't know what's going on. He says he called the office of*
> *the public defender to try to see if he could get himself a lawyer, and they told*
> *him that unless you've been charged, we can't help you. Which is true. So Jay*
> *says the next thing that happens is the cops come to see him, on September 6,*
> *and tell him he's about to be charged with accessory after the fact and that*
> *he'll be able to get a lawyer. The next day, September 7, they come pick him*
> *up, they book him, and they take him to the State Attorney's office. He*
> *meets Kevin Urick, the prosecutor. Jay says he's never met Urick before and*
> *then he says Urick introduces him to Anne Benaroya, who can represent him*
> *for free. Jay and Benaroya talk privately for a while, and then they sign a plea*
> *agreement. Then, that same day, they all go across the street to the courthouse*
> *and present the signed plea to a judge. If you or a loved one is an attorney,*
> *your jaw is hanging open right now, correct? Prosecutors do not find attor-*
> *neys for witnesses they are prosecuting. That is not a thing.*

We never knew exactly how or why Benaroya got involved, and when Sarah had contacted her for an interview for the podcast it had not gone well. She wouldn't tell me what went down between the two, only that it was not pretty, and she never really got any questions answered. Benaroya herself called Sarah's interview "disastrous" in her conversation with *The Intercept*'s Natasha Vargas-Cooper.

But now, inexplicably, she had begun to exchange e-mails with Colin, and later Susan, in what seemed an earnest attempt to correct what people thought of her involvement with Jay and Urick. I was a bit surprised, because around the same time as the *Intercept* interview, in December 2014, Colin had written a series of blog posts about the plea deal. One in particular called attention to the fact that not only did Gutierrez find the attorney arrangement alarming but that Jay himself found it to be "fishy." On the stand during the second trial, as he was being cross-examined by Gutierrez, Jay admitted he had doubts about Benaroya.

Colin deduced on his blog that Jay felt railroaded into taking the plea and that he didn't trust Benaroya. Urick had manipulated him and Jay was deeply worried.

While I had always imagined Benaroya to be a good buddy of Urick's, someone who helped him out in this matter, it turned out from her conversations with Colin that it was nothing like that at all. According to Benaroya, Urick hated her. With a background in public interest and social justice law, Benaroya wasn't exactly the shrewd prosecutor's cup of tea. They didn't have anything close to a cordial relationship, which is why on September 7, 1999, when he found her at the courthouse and asked her to step into a room where a young black man was sitting, she was extremely surprised.

Urick explained the situation to her—this young man, Jay, had two choices: either accept a plea deal as an accessory after the fact in exchange for testifying against Adnan, or Urick would charge *him* with the murder of Hae Min Lee and prosecute the case in Baltimore County, where a majority white jury would be much more likely to find a black man guilty, and he could end up facing the death penalty.

Urick told Benaroya that Jay had no attorney, and if she didn't help him he was basically screwed. Urick was not only putting Jay up against the wall, it seems to me he was railroading Benaroya, playing on her sympathy for the young man in a precarious situation. Realizing that Jay had really no option, having given multiple on-the-record statements to police implicating himself, Benaroya advised him to take the plea deal. Her real concern was keeping him out of jail while he awaited sentencing, and she was successful at it.

This is where things are murky for me. To hear Benaroya's story, Jay was a reluctant State's witness being heavily coerced by the prosecutor. I immediately felt terrible for him.

Then I took a step back and remembered that seven months prior to the plea, Jay was already working with the police, making deals for a motorcycle and reward money. He was definitely in a bad spot—Urick hadn't charged him until now in order to prevent him from getting a public defender, but basically had charges against him secured with his statements. Jay couldn't afford a lawyer, so he was at the State's mercy and had to take the plea. Still, his cooperation, given the reward, did not seem to have come completely from being pressured by the police. But Urick needed to make the plea legit, and for that he needed Jay to have an attorney. He needed to find someone he could guilt into representing Jay for this drama. If the wool was being pulled over anyone's eyes, maybe it was Benaroya's.

One question kept coming back to challenge the theory that Jay was fed information about the crime by the police themselves: how did Jay lead the police to the car? At a minimum he must have known where the car was.

It has never been beyond the scope of my imagination that the police already knew where the car was, but the level of unethical behavior that it would take was a bit hard to swallow for some. It was even harder to accept that Hae's car could not have been where it was found for the six entire weeks, meaning it was deposited there fairly recently by someone—meaning the cops may have moved it there.

But that doesn't mean it didn't happen.

In October of 2015, after having gotten some new documents as a result of an MPIA filed with the Baltimore County Police, Susan discovered one that seemed to indicate the police had more information than they ever revealed.

It was a case report that listed a series of boxes with "factors" A through F, all of which were rated for solvability. The factors corresponded to suspect, suspect vehicle, physical evidence, stolen property, whether any type of M.O. (modus operandi or method) was present, and whether the crime could be solved with investigation at the field level. The ratings went from 0 to 12, with 12 being the highest, presumably meaning the issue was solved.

All reports leading up to February 24, 1999, have zero ratings for all the factors. But the report dated and stamped February 24, 1999, indicates that two investigatory factors were in essence solved—suspect and suspect vehicle factors were both rated 12 and stolen property was rated 4. Remember, this is ostensibly before the police have talked to Jenn or Jay, but apparently they have already "solved" who the suspect is.

"Suspect vehicle" seems to indicate they are talking about Adnan's vehicle, but if you look closely the "other" box is marked. The vehicle solvability being rated is not Adnan's—it's Hae's. How and why did Baltimore County Police determine that both the suspect in the crime and the victim's vehicle are solved, three days before the Baltimore City Police ever officially speak to Jay?

Maybe because something else pretty significant happened on February 24. Detective O'Shea, with the Baltimore County Police Department, ran a National Crime Information Center (NCIC) check for the car, an odd thing for him to do given that the case had been out of his jurisdiction since February 9, when Hae's body was found in the city. But not an odd thing to do if her car was found somewhere in the county itself, which the results of the NCIC search seem to indicate.

The last five hits on Hae's vehicle, the last five times her tags were run through the NCIC system, all placed her car in Baltimore County. Unfortunately, at the time these inquiries were made, Hae's car had not yet been linked to her missing person's report in the NCIC system, a mistake by the detective.

If patrol officers came across her car and ran the tags, they'd never know the car was connected to a missing person's investigation.

DATE	TIME	TERMINAL ID	ORI	AGENCY
011499	0248	HC69	MD013143N	Harford Co. Emergency Operation
011499	0446	ZBER	MD0030627	Baltimore Co. P. D. MDT311
011599	0324	ZBAS	MD00301N5	Baltimore Co. P. D. MDT168
012999	1027	BC4A	MD0030121	Baltimore Co. P. D.
020499	0335	ZBAK	MD00301M7	Baltimore Co. P. D. MDT160
020499	0944	ZBFT	MD0030676	Baltimore Co. P. D. MDT349

An ABC news report from the day Adnan was arrested, still found on You-Tube, mentioned that the police had "discovered her 1998 Nissan Sentra a short distance from where her killer attempted to bury her body in a shallow grave in Leakin Park, key details they had withheld as they sought out a suspect." The language of the report seems to indicate the police had told the media (perhaps the police media liason/PR office had done so inadvertently) that they already knew where her car was.

Then there's Jay himself, who on the stand agreed with Gutierrez when she stated that he'd initially taken the police to the wrong place when he led them to the car. And at his first on-the-record interview on February 28, right before Adnan is arrested, he mentions something weird.

⬛	I was....during the commute I made an effort, yeah out of my way to see if it still was there, yeah it was.
Ritz:	When was the last time that you went out of your way to see if the car was still there?
⬛	Four days ago, so the 24th.
Ritz:	When you went back to the location where he left it that night, was the car still there?
⬛	Yes.

Lastly, there's this: initial Maryland Public Information Aact results from Baltimore City Police show that a request was made on February 17 to the Maryland State Police Aviation Division to do a helicopter flyover of the area to search for Hae's car. The request was denied. Nearly a year later we received a new batch of documents from the Baltimore County Police Department showing that another request for a helicopter flyover had been made, presumably after the first one was denied. This request was made to the Baltimore County Police aviation unit and was apparently accommodated. They did a search with their helicopter, but the results of the search don't exist in the documents.

Something significant happened on February 24, it seems. It may have been the day that Baltimore County did a helicopter flyover and found Hae's car, which is why the county files a final report noting ratings of 12 for suspect and car—at this point the city police have already honed in on Adnan and are meeting with Jay off the record. And it could be that once the car was found in the county, Detective O'Shea ran the NCIC checks to see if anyone had ever spotted it. Looks like they had. If the car was found in the county, the city police would have been contacted. This was their case, after all.

So, how did Jay lead Baltimore City detectives to the car? Maybe because they told him where it was, because they moved it from the county to the city themselves after it was found on February 24. It would explain the fresh grass on the tire wells, the green grass underneath it, and the fact that it was untouched in a heavy-crime neighborhood. Is it beyond the scope of our imagination, considering these are detectives who are accused of coercing false testimony in other murder cases, that they would go this far to make their case against Adnan?

For me, the answer is no.

Thiruvendran Vignarajah, the deputy attorney general of the State of Maryland, is representing the State of Maryland in Adnan's PCR appeal proceedings. A PCR appeal is usually handled by the local-level State's Attorney's office. But the high level of scrutiny from *Serial* may have pushed it up the chain of command.

I first encountered Vignarajah when I read the brief he submitted to the Court of Special Appeals (COSA) opposing our Application for Leave to Appeal (ALA) in May 2015. I immediately loathed him.

His brief, which got dismissed less than two weeks later when COSA remanded the case back down to the circuit court, set the tone for Vignarajah's defense against the issues we raised for the PCR appeal: dramatic (the "bloom" of Hae's love for Don), misleading (saying Hae described Adnan as "possessive, jealous, and overprotective"), and pages and pages of irrelevant details where he wastes space on regurgitating the State's case at trial from fifteen years ago instead of addressing the very specific issues raised in this PCR. He calls Gutierrez Adnan's "celebrated attorney," her defense "vigorous," the State's case at trial "unimpeachable," and Adnan's accounts "vacillating."

It wasn't the harlequin-style writing that made my stomach turn, however; it was the disingenuous nature of certain arguments. Jay's interview in *The Intercept* was published six months prior, in which he says he never saw anything at Best Buy, he never saw Hae being buried, and the burial took place around midnight, but in the brief Vignarajah stuck to Jay's story from 2000, reciting the same Best Buy trunk-pop and 7:00 p.m. burial time. He tried to mask the discrepancy in a cringe-worthy way, saying, "For Syed and Wilds there were points at the burial in Leakin Park where both men seemed disturbed and disoriented by the gravity of the moment."

Jay, apparently, is still disoriented fifteen years later.

Vignarajah also depicted Adnan's behavior after Hae died as shady, saying that he tried to "thwart" Hope Schab's effort to assist the detectives' investigations, neglecting to mention her assistance was all about getting the details of Adnan and Hae's sex life.

Two of the most egregious misrepresentations Vignarajah made were these: that Adnan "elected" not to attend Hae's memorial and that Adnan fought to keep Gutierrez as his attorney. It was reprehensible—Vignarajah knew that during Hae's memorial Adnan was in prison. And he also knew that Adnan had fought to retain Gutierrez at the beginning of her representation, long before she screwed up his case.

I wanted to scream, but instead I blogged. I blogged vigorously and vociferously about the shameless fudging Vignarajah was engaged in. I knew it was only going to get worse; we had gotten calls from attorneys around the state warning us about him.

My worst fears were confirmed for me when, in November 2015, a Brady motion demanding a new trial was filed in Baltimore Circuit Court in the case of *Maryland v. David Hunter*, in which Hunter's attorney alleged that Vignarajah had withheld evidence and prosecuted an innocent man.

The gist of the claim was that Vignarajah had videotaped evidence that Hunter was innocent in the murder he was charged with, yet he proceeded to prosecute him anyway and withheld from the defense the evidence of a witness who actually saw the murder and told the police that it wasn't Hunter.

My blog in response to this news screamed, "CAN THE ATTORNEY GENERAL FIND US A SINGLE FUCKING HONEST PROSECUTOR FOR ADNAN'S CASE? Just one???"

Still, I was kind enough not to blog about a smarmy "sting" reported about a month later by *The Daily Caller*, in which Vignarajah, who is married, spilled political secrets to a pretty, blond undercover reporter in hopes of getting some action.

All of the Baltimore legal community, including Judge Martin Welch himself, according to one of my sources, knew about the misconduct allegation and the reporter scandal. Vignarajah was going to go into Adnan's PCR hearing a couple months later with some major bad publicity on his back.

I spent a month in Pakistan from late December to the end of January 2016.

During my travels I had intensified the prayers that I had recited for years for Adnan. All prayers are answered in some way, Muslims believe, but in certain conditions they are especially powerful: when a woman is pregnant, in labor, or nursing; when it's raining, in the predawn hours, in prostration; when made by a parent for a child, by a traveler, and by the victim of injustice and oppression.

I visited five Sufi shrines and five mosques. In the shrines I watched people in pain beseech their Lord, sway with prayer, light candles and incense, and scatter intensely scented rose petals over the graves of their saints. In mosques I saw people spend forever with their foreheads on the floor, backs bent in submission, rising with tears.

In every place I whispered God's names, counting on my fingers or on prayer beads, my heart and intention focused on Adnan, the appeal, and all the forces working against him.

"Ya Adl, the Most Just, Ya Raheem, the Most Merciful, Ya Muhaymin, The Guardian of all, Ya Hakam, The Judge, Ya Haqq, The Truth, Ya Hasib, The Reckoner, Ya Muntaqim, The Avenger, Ya Shaahid, The Witness, Ya Salaam, The Source of all Peace, Ya Wadud, The Most Loving, Ya Wali, The Protecting Friend, Ya Allah, The One God."

Thousands of times I recited these names and asked everyone I met to do the same, to keep Adnan in their prayers. Prayers for him have been said in Mecca, at the Prophet's mosque in Madina, at the Al Aqsa and Dome of the Rock mosques in Jerusalem, at the Ibrahimi Mosque and Tomb of the Patriarchs in Palestine, at the Church of the Nativity, at a dozen mosques in Istanbul, and at the shrine of Jalaluddin Rumi and other saints, and prayers have been said by Christians, Muslims, Jews, Hindus, Sikhs, Buddhists, and even atheists all around the world. Very few people can say the world prayed for them.

When I returned from Pakistan, the PCR appeal hearing was just a couple of weeks away, scheduled for February 3–5.

The night before the hearing, we organized a community prayer gathering at the ISB, Adnan's mosque, but a big fat wrench got thrown into our plans when we learned, two days prior, that President Barack Obama had decided to visit a U.S. mosque for the first time ever in his presidency. Not just any mosque, but the ISB.

He'd be there on the morning of Wednesday, February 3, as the PCR hearing got under way in downtown Baltimore, and Secret Service protocols demanded that the building be secured the night before—the prayer meeting wasn't going to happen there.

We moved it quickly to another local mosque and were joined by about three hundred community members. Aunty Shamim sat in the audience as Saad, Yusuf, and I sat at a table at the front. We each said some words, and I invited Bob Ruff and Michael Wood, a retired Baltimore City Police officer and whistle-blower, to say some words. Together we rallied, cried, and prayed.

The next morning around seven o'clock I arrived at Adnan's home to pick up Yusuf and Aunty Shamim. I spoke to Adnan's father, who was hanging out with my husband (who he has a special fondness for), and he gently told me he would be better off staying home and praying.

I, on the other hand, would not have missed it for the world. A couple of weeks prior Justin had broken some bad news: I might have to sit the hearing out because he had put me on the witness list as a potential rebuttal after Asia testified. Witnesses can't be in the courtroom because they might be influenced by other witness testimony; they have to be sequestered.

I protested: with Asia there, my testimony was unnecessary. Justin said he'd think about it, but when Adnan found out he said absolutely not—he wanted me in the courtroom. He asked Justin to remove me from the witness list so I could finally see Asia testify after all these years.

We met Saad and half a dozen other friends at Justin's office and walked to the courthouse together. We passed through security and marched up to the second floor, where a media room had been set up and a line was forming. Many friends and supporters had come from out of town for the proceedings; it lifted our spirits to see so many loving, familiar faces.

Sarah Koenig was also there, standing in line with others from the media as we waited for the courtroom doors to open. Aunty and I went over to greet her and I thanked her with tears in my eyes, acknowledging we would never have gotten this far without her.

The doors finally opened and I could hear a collective "bismillah" from the posse of Muslims around me as we entered. The court seating was divided into three sections. The far left was reserved for media, the center section was for Hae's family and community, and the right section was for Adnan's family and supporters. None of Hae's immediate family were able to attend, but community members close to her represented the family, their grief, and their love for Hae throughout the hearing.

We ended up being directly behind the State's table. I sat between Susan and Yusuf, in the front row right behind the prosecutors. Vignarajah and his team had walked past a few times, even smiled meekly in our direction—it turned out many people from our community knew him personally. He had, ironically, also attended Woodlawn High School and his parents lived in the same neighborhood as Adnan's in the ISB area.

I had to run to the restroom, and when I returned Adnan had already walked in and gotten seated. I frowned, knowing that he wasn't allowed to turn around (and probably couldn't because of his neck and back issues, not to mention the five-point restraints he'd have to wear the entire time), so I missed a chance of seeing him and him seeing that I was there. He sat stick-straight, face forward, directly in front of Sarah Koenig.

Next to him sat both Justin and his legal partner and co-counsel on the defense, Chris Nieto. I had never met Nieto before, but Justin trusted him and told us he was a sharp, experienced criminal defense attorney who had handled numerous high-profile cases. I said a prayer and blew it the direction of all three men.

Opening arguments began with Justin, and in the very first few minutes I realized something: we had never been so prepared before. This was not the same Justin I had seen at the PCR hearing nearly four years earlier, when he was less assertive and confident. Right out of the gate, this time Justin was taking no prisoners. His experience was showing. He wasn't the only one who was ready, I realized. All of this had happened, *Serial* had happened, when we were all as ready as possible. I had the blogging, writing, public speaking, media and social media experience to leverage *Serial*'s popularity and keep public interest high; we had a team of volunteers doing research; we had private investigators following leads; Susan was a master of the case files and cell phone evidence; Colin brought the entirety of case law precedent to us; and both of them had been working alongside Justin for the past few months to cover every base for the hearing. There was no way the State could be as prepared as our team.

In his opening Justin was concise and clear. There were only two issues to consider: whether it was ineffective assistance for Gutierrez to fail to contact Asia McClain, and was the failure of the inclusion of the fax cover sheet with the cell phone records either a Brady violation by the State or ineffective assistance of counsel by Gutierrez.

An important thing to understand about the standard of ineffective assistance is that it's not enough that Gutierrez failed to do what a reasonable attorney would do; we also had to demonstrate that her failure had a material impact on the outcome of the case.

Justin made a succinct argument that both issues could have changed the course of the trial.

The judge turned to Vignarajah and asked him to proceed. Vignarajah turned, looked straight at me, and then said to the judge that he had a preliminary matter to first attend to—he wanted all potential witnesses sequestered. Namely, me.

Justin objected, saying I was not a potential witness; he had no intention of calling me. Vignarajah, however, apparently did. He argued that he reserved the right to call me as a witness and as such I could not be present during the hearing. Judge Welch agreed.

I rose slowly, staring daggers into Vignarajah's back. I knew he wasn't going to call me; this was personal, a cheap ploy to get me back for what I'd written about him.

I walked past rows of friends, family, and community, all frowning at this new development, and took a seat outside the courtroom at the end of a long, marble hallway. I wasn't there alone, though. About an hour after I got kicked out of the courtroom Asia walked past me, holding her husband's hand.

She was as beautiful as I remembered her. Tall, immaculately dressed, bright, bold red lipstick, pregnant and glowing. We looked at each other and she smiled warmly. I wanted to hug her but instead smiled and looked away, tearing up a bit as the importance of the moment hit me, and then I watched her walk far down the hall and sit next to the courtroom to wait to be called.

After a bit of moping I headed across the street to a Dunkin' Donuts. By the time I settled in with some coffee and a donut, I had hundreds of tweets and messages waiting for me.

"Rabia got kicked out!"

"Why were you sequestered, what does that mean?!"

The media had reported it, so people were confused and many were as angry as I was at this dirty move. But I had gotten over it pretty quickly because I figured that not only could I do more damage to the State outside the courtroom, where I could use social media, but my presence wasn't going to make any difference to Adnan's case anyway, and that's what mattered.

When I had left the courtroom, Judge Welch had instructed me not to talk to any other witnesses. But he hadn't said anything about staying off of social media.

So I kept my eyes peeled for media reports. While they couldn't report directly from the courtroom, they could sprint down to the media room to tweet updates, which they did.

I also had the bright idea that if there was anyone who could find case law to get me back into court, it was Colin. And like clockwork he found Maryland case law that should have allowed my presence in the courtroom, so Justin renewed his objections repeatedly, offering Colin's findings. The judge didn't buy it.

I spent the next four days following the hearing from a corner in Dunkin' Donuts, but I knew exactly what was going on with each witness, thanks to nearly in-time tweets. The hearing couldn't have gone any better for us, or much worse for the State.

After Justin's opening, Vignarajah laid out his case, and it was no surprise.

He argued that Gutierrez was not ineffective in her representation of Adnan because she *strategically decided* not to contact Asia. It was not an oversight; Gutierrez felt that Asia would damage her case. How on earth could she do that? Well, he argued, Gutierrez's "intuition" would have alerted her to the shadiness of Asia's letters, the discrepancies in them, even how they contradicted Adnan's own accounts of his day. They were "red flags" to Gutierrez, a seasoned defense attorney who would have avoided contacting such an unreliable witness.

Framing the failure to contact Asia as a tactical decision was an important argument, because it was essentially what the judge had stated in his previous denial. The distinction is important; under the law a court cannot second-guess a lawyer's strategy. If Vignarajah could convince the court, again, that the failure to contact Asia wasn't a mistake but a choice, he would win on that issue.

On the fax cover sheet he argued that this issue simply had no merit. There was no Brady violation; how could there be when Gutierrez clearly had the fax cover sheet in her files? And he had the files, all of them, because he had won a motion in court to get them. Normally defense files are privileged, protected, confidential information, but because they had been shared with Susan, Colin, and me, Adnan had waived privilege. So Vignarajah got to sort through them.

None of this mattered, though, he said. Because in the end there was overwhelming evidence to convict Adnan of strangling Hae "with his bare hands" and burying her "in a shallow grave." He had a great lawyer, but even a lawyer as competent as Gutierrez couldn't overcome the evidence against her client. Adnan was convicted not because he got a poor defense but because "he did it."

After both sides opened, Justin called his first witness, Phil Dantes.

Dantes was a long-time friend of Gutierrez but even more importantly, he was her lawyer, both when she was fighting for admission to the bar and then many years later when she was disbarred. Vignarajah objected to nearly every-thing Dantes was there to testify to, namely Gutierrez's health and her disbar-ment, arguing that it was irrelevant. Over his many objections to Dantes' trying to explain how sick Gutierrez got, including the odd assertion that bringing up her health issues "attempts to prey on the stigma that attaches to illness," Judge Welch decided he would give Dantes' testimony the "limited weight" it warranted.

Gutierrez's declining health and the financial issues that led to her disbar-ment seem to me directly relevant to her condition when representing Adnan, but Vignarajah was successful in keeping out most evidence of these things, including her record with the Attorney Grievance Commission.

On cross, Vignarajah asked Dantes if he was aware that Gutierrez was hale and hearty enough to cross-examine Jay Wilds for a week. Dantes responded with "the shorter the better," indicating that a week-long cross-examination was actually an indicator of her incompetency.

Next to the stand was Bill Kanwisher, an unwilling witness whom Justin compelled to appear.

Kanwisher was hired as Gutierrez's assistant in 1997 and they later became close friends. While he had eventually left the firm because he couldn't deal with her increasingly erratic behavior, saying she was "hard to work with, hard to deal with," he still loved and respected her. It wasn't easy for him to revisit that time.

But, over many frequent objections by Vignarajah, he did. Kanwisher testi-fied to Gutierrez's decline, how he saw she was in pain, that she often shoveled tremendous amounts of work at him and others, and that she was managing the firm's finances badly. On Asia, he stated firmly that there could have been no tactical decision by Gutierrez to leave her off the alibi notice given to the State before the trial.

Vignarajah objected and the court sustained, striking Kanwisher's testi-mony about Asia.

At this point the prosecution moved to submit two binders, A and B, into the records. The binders were the State's collection of defense files, and Justin hadn't seen them before. He had no idea what documents they contained and didn't know how they were organized, so he objected. The court withheld making a decision on the objection, though, and they continued with the cross-examination of Kanwisher.

On cross, Vignarajah asked Kanwisher if an attorney would avoid notifying the State of "bad witnesses." Kanwisher responded yes. Vignarajah then asked a series of questions illustrating the many reasons Gutierrez may not have con-tacted Asia: that she put the defendant in a location that implicated him, that her letters contradicted Adnan's statements, and that perhaps cameras at the library showed Adnan wasn't there.

But Kanwisher pushed back on all of those reasons, saying that he would still investigate the alibi before making a determination that a witness is good or bad, and that witnesses (and clients) sometimes get things wrong or forget, but it doesn't mean you don't even contact them.

Vignarajah ended by asking Kanwisher if he was being paid to testify.

Kanwisher responded no, that he'd rather not be there at all.

Then, at the end of day one, the witness everyone had been waiting for was called to the stand—Asia McClain.

From every report I was able to glean in the outside world, Asia radiated credibility. Journalist Amelia Parry noted in an article on TheFrisky that Asia "was poised, endearing, funny, smart, and very, very clear about what she has known and SAID for the last 15+years."

Asia recalled January 13, 1999, and its aftermath as she always had: seeing Adnan in the library, visiting his family with her ex-boyfriend Justin Adger after Adnan was arrested, then reaching out to him through two letters but never hearing back. Justin went through her letters line by line, asking her to explain what she meant, what the clip art meant, and why she wrote what she wrote. She recounted my visit to her, and that I asked her if she would mind writing down what she remembered in an affidavit. She also testified to her conversation with Urick, the one she had after our private investigator had contacted her prior to the first PCR.

As luck would have it, Asia is an incredibly fastidious person. She saves, as she said on the stand, "everything." Including a hall pass from high school, which she brought to court with her to show exactly how carefully she kept track of things. And she had kept track of her call with Urick too, having taken notes during it, which were entered into evidence.

She had initiated the call because she wanted to find out what really happened in the case. She felt the prosecutor would be an "unbiased source, the good guy, the white hat."

She had lots of questions for him and wrote down all his answers. The notes read, "Bunch of witnesses ready to testify that he was @ mosque backed down after cell records. Brown is BS. Adnan lawyer not incompetent despite health issues ← No case. Plea bargain → Jay helped bury the body & testified. *Cell phone records @ time came from burial area of body."

She also wrote down a direct quote from Urick, "If I had had any doubt that Adnan didn't kill Hae, it would be my moral obligation to see that he didn't serve any time."

Asia explained that Urick told her Justin Brown was trying to "play" and "manipulate" the court system in order to win an appeal, because Adnan had exhausted all other avenues. "He killed that girl," he told her. And she believed him, which is why she never contacted the defense team.

But after hearing *Serial*, she was "in shock." She was confused by what she heard and it "weighed heavily on her heart," because she realized for the first time that her recollection of January 13 had a direct impact on the case, and that her failure to show up at the initial PCR hearing allowed Urick to misrepresent her. While Urick had said in his *Intercept* interview that their conversation lasted five minutes, she said it lasted thirty-four minutes because she had the bill. He had spent a considerable time convincing her of the strength of the case against Adnan, never once mentioning the importance of her testimony to the case.

Once she realized the gravity of the situation she contacted Justin Brown, retained her own attorney, and prepared a new affidavit for the court.

On cross-examination, which spilled into the next day, Vignarajah opened up by asking her about Sarah Koenig.

"*Serial*'s pretty good, right?"

"Sarah Koenig's good at what she does, right?"

"It's entertainment, right?"

He then went over her letters as Justin had, line by line, attempting to point out discrepancies about the timing of the letters, about how she had the information she had when she wrote them. He was implying that Asia could not have written the letters in the immediate days after Adnan's arrest—she had too many details. He asked what the name of the jail in Spokane, where she lives, was called. Asia responded, "I don't know . . . I believe it's called jail?"

Vignarajah was referring to the fact that she had used the words "central booking" in her second letter to Adnan in 1999, and was questioning how she would have known what the jail where he was being held was actually called.

The prosecutor spent a considerable amount of time asking about minute details of January 1999, getting Asia to say "I don't know" or "I don't remember" repeatedly.

He brought up my testimony from 2012, during which I recounted meeting her at the library. Asia, however, remembered my meeting at her house. Vignarajah asked if she was surprised that I had testified to a very different account of our meeting and she said yes.

My brother also remembered that we met at her house, but I have no recollection of it. It could be that we met there and then drove past the library on the way to getting her affidavit notarized. We were probably remembering different parts of the meeting, whatever stood out most to us. It was understandable that we weren't recalling it exactly the same, considering how many years had passed. After all, Asia didn't even remember that my brother was with us when we met.

After asking her what her conversation with Adnan had been in the library that day, he asked, "Would it surprise you to know that friends said Hae described him as overprotective? That friends had expressed concern over his possessiveness? Did you know that she wrote in her diary that he called her a devil?"

Asia said no, she didn't know what was in the diary. Vignarajah pressed on, over Justin's continuous objections, asking if she had read the diary or transcripts. He asked if she would be surprised to know that it was Adnan's routine to go to the school library and not the public library after school, a new tactic— suggesting that Asia had in fact seen Adnan at the public library, but it was nefariously and deliberately out of his normal routine, and she was just a pawn in his plan. Interestingly, he was doing what Urick had done in their phone call— implying there was much that Asia didn't know about the case.

His tactic throughout the cross switched between trying to show that her memory was weak, that she had made up an alibi to help Adnan, that she had written the letters to please Adnan or his family, or that her memory was correct but damaged Adnan's case, because if he was at the library around the time she saw him, he could have flagged Hae down, who would have driven past the library after leaving school. No one had ever testified to how Adnan allegedly got in Hae's car, but now Vignarajah was raising this scenario as a possibility.

On a number of occasions Asia was brought to tears as she recounted learning of Hae's death. Vignarajah did, by all measure, put her through an exhaustive and exhausting cross-examination, pushing her emotionally, attacking the veracity of her testimony from all sides. It was no surprise that she ended up crying on the stand.

On redirect Justin asked Asia to revisit all the details in her letters that the prosecutor implied she couldn't know. Then he slapped a number of *Baltimore Sun* articles, written before her letters had been sent to Adnan, onto the overhead projector. In one article about Adnan's arrest, the words "central booking" loomed large.

Justin bellowed, "How could someone have known the words CENTRAL BOOKING?" He was clearly exasperated that every detail in her letters was already public information, and that Vignarajah was grasping at straws to make the letters appear suspicious.

The rounds of redirect, re-cross, re-re-direct, and re-re-cross went on, but they ended after Justin asked whether Vignarajah had ever contacted Asia to talk about what she knew, to which she responded that her attorney had made it clear she was available for questioning but the prosecutor never contacted her.

Vignarajah came back with a single question.

"Isn't it true the last time you spoke to a prosecutor, you issued an affidavit calling him a liar?"

Despite the tenacity of Vignarajah's cross-examination, the only thing that mattered was what Asia did know for certain: on January 13, 1999, she was with Adnan at the public library until roughly 2:40 p.m.

Having presented Adnan's alibi witness to the court, Justin switched gears and moved to the cell phone evidence. He called Jerry Grant, an expert in cellular phone forensics and historical cell site analysis who works with the Innocence Project.

Before testifying, Grant had reviewed the testimony of Abe Waranowitz, the State's closing arguments from 2000, including all of the cell records, both those introduced and not introduced into evidence during the trial, and he had also spoken to Waranowitz before the hearing.

On direct examination Grant testified about how the cell evidence was used during the trial. He explained that the State had used the cell tower coverage areas to determine where Adnan's phone was; in other words, they relied on the entire sector covered by a cell tower that was pinged and placed Adnan in a location inside that sector.

Justin asked Grant to take a look at Exhibit 31 from the trial, five pages long, consisting of an "authentication" document from AT&T, the last page of a fax from AT&T noting the account details, and three pages of Adnan's call records from January 12 and 13, 1999, with cell site information visible.

Grant was asked if cell companies generally send instructions on how to read cell phone records along with the records themselves, and he responded yes, explaining that instructions varied between companies and also changed with time. He testified that as an expert he relied on such instructions.

Justin then showed Grant another set of cell records from the case file, which included a fax cover sheet from AT&T that stated incoming calls were not reliable for location status. The cover sheet was attached to a set of records titled "Subscriber Activity Reports." The title appeared on the first page. The last three pages of the document, which did not have the title, were the same three pages that appeared in Exhibit 31.

In 2000, when the State had given Waranowitz Exhibit 31 to examine right before he testified, they had not only removed the fax cover sheet but also removed the first page of the cell records that showed these were "Subscriber Activity Reports."

That was how Gutierrez also had them. Neither she nor Waranowitz had any way of knowing that this particular instruction on incoming calls and location status applied to the records the State was using to make their case against him.

Waranowitz had already submitted an affidavit that, had he seen the fax cover sheet, it would have impacted his testimony. What the State didn't know was that on day two of the hearing Waranowitz was on his way to Baltimore, ready to testify to this exact fact.

Grant testified that had he been given the instructions in the fax cover sheet, they would have factored into his analysis and he could not have plotted the calls without more information from AT&T. With the records in evidence, you simply could not pinpoint the location of the phone.

On cross, Vignarajah attempted to raise doubts about the cover sheet in every way imaginable. Susan, who took copious notes throughout the hearing, wrote, "Thiru went everywhere. Thiru tries to emphasize that AT&T is somehow a magical, unreliable unicorn."

Vignarajah tried repeatedly to point out that never before had instructions on a fax cover sheet been used to rebut the usage of records at trial, that such a claim had never been raised by an attorney before, not realizing that Maryland courts had actually granted a new trial in a 2014 case, *State v. Payne*, in which instructions had similarly been withheld from the cell expert.

Justin, on redirect, simply asked Grant if he had ever heard of an expert not being provided instructions on how to read their data. Grant said no, never.

On re-cross Vignarajah asked Grant if he knew of any reason why incoming calls wouldn't be reliable for location, and as Grant began to give an answer, he was abruptly cut off by the prosecutor, who proclaimed, "Do you want to know what the *actual* answer is? Be here tomorrow to hear our witness, and THEN you'll find out!"

Justin breathed a sigh of relief, because Grant had narrowly avoided spilling the beans on evidence Justin was planning to use to nail the State's cell phone expert, who would be testifying the next day.

Day three began with brief testimony by Justin's private investigator, Sean Gordon, who had been tasked with contacting every person on Gutierrez's 1999 alibi notice that she had given to the State, to find out if she had actually been in touch with any of them.

Gordon was able to contact forty-one out of eighty-three, and only four had ever been contacted by Gutierrez's defense team. Not a single one had been asked to be an alibi witness. A number of them had been members on the track team, which Justin showed Gutierrez's law clerk had pulled directly from the yearbook roster, a number of whom had been subpoenaed. The problem was that Gutierrez had sent the subpoenas to the school, and most of them had already graduated from Woodlawn by the time of the trial. The only one to get the subpoena actually went to the court on the date he was summoned but was never called to testify. He told Gordon he wasn't ever asked a thing, and he had no idea why he was on the witness list at all. In fact, all the track members Gordon was able to contact told him the same thing—they had never been contacted by Gutierrez.

On cross, Vignarajah pointed to memos from the defense files, noting the names of potential witnesses, but Gordon responded that just because their names were mentioned doesn't mean they were actually ever contacted. And like Kanwisher, he was asked if he was paid for his work and how much he was paid, which drew two objections, one from Justin and one from his partner Nieto. The judge called them to a bench conference, and after a few minutes they returned to the hearing.

Vignarajah again asked, "How much were you paid for your work?" and Justin loudly objected, saying, "We just talked about this, your honor!" The objection was sustained and the prosecutor moved on.

On re-direct Justin showed Gordon a twenty-four-page spreadsheet for Gutierrez's defense witnesses. Of all the witnesses listed on this spreadsheet, only a single name on that list appeared on the alibi notice she had given to the State—my brother, Saad. Neither the spreadsheet nor the alibi notice included Asia. And the spreadsheet oddly contained the names of Kevin Urick and State's Attorney Patricia Jessamy, neither of whom was called by the defense at trial, of course.

Gordon's testimony clearly showed that Gutierrez's trial preparation was disastrous.

Next on the witness stand was former Woodlawn public library manager, Michelle Hamiel.

She established that in 1999 the library did indeed have a video surveillance system, and as a matter of routine the video tapes were changed every morning, with one tape for each day of the month. At the end of the month the tapes were re-used. The video camera system was important because, according to Asia, she had inquired at the library about them after Adnan was arrested and confirmed they existed. There was no evidence in the defense files that Gutierrez had ever attempted to contact the library about the footage.

Hamiel was also asked if the library had security guards and she responded affirmatively, saying that there was a lot of chaos at the end of the school day when dozens of students would rush over. There was a "constant stream" between two and three o'clock, and the guards were supposed to help keep order.

Vignarajah's cross attempted to establish that she may have been wrong on the dates that the library had installed cameras. Hamiel stood firm. The cameras were her charge; she managed them. She knew for a fact that in 1999 cameras existed in the library.

Next, the prosecutor made a move he probably immediately regretted—he asked her about the security guards. Hamiel caused laughter in the courtroom when she responded that the guards were mostly a deterrent, so useless they were called "two-and-a-halves" because police were called "five-o's." She particularly remembered the single guard who worked there in January of 1999, who she dubbed "Useless Steve" because she did more security work than he did.

On re-direct Nieto referred to "Useless Steve" a couple more times, asking Hamiel if she knew whether he had been questioned in the case in 1999, to which she responded, "No."

At the time, none of the court spectators knew that Useless Steve would soon be called as a State's witness. Vignarajah could not have been pleased with the way his witness had already been undermined.

Justin then called his final witness, attorney David Irwin.

Irwin is a legend in the Maryland criminal defense world. A former prosecutor in Baltimore City and County, he had gone on in private practice to represent defendants in high-profile cases, including Linda Tripp, the woman who had secretly recorded White House intern Monica Lewinsky's conversations.

Judge Welch, it seemed, knew and respected him too, engaging in friendly banter when he first took the stand.

Irwin was there for one purpose, to testify as a legal expert that Gutierrez had made a fatal decision in failing to contact Asia, and that under no circumstance was her failure a legal strategy.

Irwin had watched Asia's testimony, since experts don't have to be sequestered, and he was floored by it. He recounted when he once lost a case because his client's alibi witness wasn't credible.

Since then, he said, he had been looking for an Asia McClain.

He testified that attorneys have a duty to "promptly investigate to the best of their ability" every single potential witness. Only after investigating could an attorney make a strategic decision about whether to call a witness to trial or not. There was simply no way a strategy could be decided before every witness was contacted and interviewed.

Irwin had reviewed all of Asia's documents and said he found them "powerfully credible." He said her memory would have been even stronger in 2000, and that if she was a diamond now, she would have been a diamond in the rough back then.

At that point, the State made the unusual move of requesting to cross-examine Irwin the following week. It was Friday, and the State had their own very important witness to present, who wouldn't be available the following week.

Justin and the court agreed, and Vignarajah called his first witness, FBI cell phone expert Chad Fitzgerald, to the stand.

As part of the FBI's Cellular Analysis Survey Team, Fitzgerald has testified in dozens of cases involving this technology, most infamously in the trial of Dzhokhar Tsarnaev, one of the "Boston Bombers." In that case he testified that he could track the exact cell phone locations using past data, but this claim was roundly shot down by other cell experts who said no such thing was possible, some critics calling it pure "junk science."

Fitzgerald was here to bolster the State's claim that Adnan's cell phone could have been tracked using the data provided to Waranowitz in 1999, and that the fax cover sheet was irrelevant to the case.

First, though, he explained how he had prepared to testify. He had spoken to Vignarajah for two hours previously, and in the past two days they had spoken for twenty minutes. He'd also reviewed the cell phone records in the files and said he was familiar with the fax cover sheet and the three pages attached to it, which he called a CDR, or a Call Detail Record. He said he didn't pay much attention to fax cover sheets; they were mostly identical, and he had stacks of them.

He had also reviewed Waranowitz's testimony and came to the conclusion that his analysis in 2000 had been "fully thorough," that it was "pretty good work." He saw no errors in the cell tower locations and agreed with Waranowitz on which towers were pinged by the phone.

Then the prosecutor asked what the fax cover sheet applied to, and Fitzgerald responded that it did not apply to CDRs, the documents in Exhibit 31; instead it applied to a different set of records AT&T had supplied on February 17, 1999.

Vignarajah pulled out a number of massive foam boards with partial call records blown up and asked Fitzgerald to highlight portions as he testified about them.

He went through the instruction sheet key, which has various instructions on the different columns in a subscriber activity report, and made the case that the instructions don't match up to the CDR. They match up to the February 17, 1999, records, which are subscriber activity reports.

Vignarajah then asked him why the words "subscriber activity report" appear on one page of the documents he is referring to as CDRs, and if that changed his opinion.

Fitzgerald responded no, you couldn't match up the cover sheet to the documents in Exhibit 31. In essence, the fax cover sheet was irrelevant, so even if Waranowitz had seen it before testifying it wouldn't have made a difference.

But then what, asked Vignarajah, did the language on the fax cover sheet mean? This was the moment he had told Grant to wait for, the answer to the vital question.

It had nothing to do with cell towers, Fitzgerald said. It had to do with the location of regional network "switches," and not the location of the phone. When a phone was shut off and had traveled out of its "home" area, an incoming call could hit the "home" tower and not a tower where the phone had traveled to. This was the first time such a theory had ever been floated in the case, but it still meant that the incoming call information couldn't help pinpoint a phone's actual location.

Justin caught this when he cross-examined Fitzgerald and he also caught something else. He led Fitzgerald to testify that he had first spoken to the prosecutor around January 4 or 5 and received the cell phone records a week later. But the State had filed its "expert disclosure," a statement telling the judge what their expert was going to testify to, with the court before Fitzgerald had ever seen the documents.

He admitted he had not written the disclosure or even reviewed it, and then, flustered, said that he had a pretty thorough conversation with Vignarajah and agreed with what he told him Waranowitz had testified to. Again, Justin emphasized, this was before he had ever seen any of the cell evidence.

Was it possible, Justin asked, that the disclosure was not his opinion but Vignarajah's opinion, and he had been asked to go along with it? Fitzgerald said no.

Justin moved on to catch Fitzgerald in another bind: he asked him what, if anything, Waranowitz got wrong in his testimony. Fitzgerald responded that Waranowitz had mistaken Adnan checking his voicemail with an incoming call that went to voicemail on January 13.

The rub here is that Waranowitz got that detail wrong because he didn't have the fax cover sheet, which clearly indicated how to tell when a subscriber is checking voicemail.

In other words, Justin got Fitzgerald to admit the saliency of the fax cover sheet to understanding the phone records.

Then a rather unbelievable exchange took place. Justin told Fitzgerald that the title of the records in Exhibit 31 was "Subscriber Activity Report," meaning the fax cover sheet applied to it. Fitzgerald responded that it was a CDR. Justin then pulled up a sheet that had been missing from the Exhibit itself, the first page of the cell records that should have been right after the fax cover sheet, and the sheet had written across the top: "Subscriber Activity Report."

He asked Fitzgerald to read it out loud.

Fitzgerald wouldn't do it.

Over and over Justin asked Fitzgerald to read the top of the page. But Fitzgerald wouldn't budge. The judge could have ordered the witness to answer the question but didn't. Frustrated, Justin moved on to the issue that Grant had almost spilled during his testimony.

He pulled up a page from Adnan's phone records that showed two incoming calls, twenty-seven minutes apart. The first call pinged a tower in Baltimore and the second one pinged a tower in Dupont Circle in Washington, D.C. They are forty-three miles apart, and from Dupont Circle it takes a good thirty minutes just to get to the outskirts of the capital and head to Maryland.

How, asked Justin, could Fitzgerald explain these two towers pinged twenty-seven minutes apart? Did Adnan have a helicopter? he asked.

Fitzgerald floundered and said he didn't know, maybe it was a switch issue again, maybe the phone pinged a subway tower, but he would have to do some research. He wasn't about to give Justin the answer he was looking for.

As objections flew from Vignarajah, and Fitzgerald refused to answer Justin's questions, the unhappy-looking witness suddenly raised his voice and made a dramatic declaration.

"I just found something! I want to speak to the judge!"

Judge Heard, probably tired of the theatrics, called it a day.

I was following it all online, and when the hearing adjourned on Friday I rushed over to the courthouse. The group looked a bit shell-shocked.

We gathered outside the courtroom, quietly buzzing. Susan looked alternately angry and frustrated. I was dying to pick her brain, but I knew they had been told not to speak to witnesses about the case.

Inmates who were brought for proceedings were led into the basement of the courthouse from an entrance on the right side, catty-corner to the Dunkin' Donuts where I had been camped out. We knew a van would pull up and Adnan would be quickly escorted out of the building and into the waiting vehicle. We wanted him to see us all there for him, so we huddled together in the cold across the street from the door where he would come from, waiting.

Media crews were also there, and after almost an hour Adnan finally appeared in the hallway behind the door. Everyone began waving, calling his name. He could hear us before he even came out.

The guards were kind. They let him walk out slowly so he had a chance to see us all. It was the first time I had faced him outside of a prison since the last PCR hearing. His face lit up and he smiled broadly, raising one shackled hand in a small wave to all of us.

Yusuf, hyper from the day's craziness, yelled, "Do you have a helicopter, Adnan?" as the guards helped him into the van. When it drove away, we heard him bellow, "Asalaamalaykum!"

We left then, and spent the weekend wondering what on earth Fitzgerald had found.

Monday began with Vignarajah complaining to the court that his upcoming witness, security guard Steve Mills, had been lampooned online all weekend. The phrase "Useless Steve" had become a meme, and someone online had begun selling T-shirts imprinted with the phrase, the proceeds of which she pledged to Adnan's legal fund, though we had nothing to do with the production of the shirts. Vignarajah claimed to the court that defense was selling the T-shirts, that his witness was being cyberbullied, and that his name must be kept confidential.

It was unheard of for a witness to testify anonymously. Justin vigorously objected, pointing to the hypocrisy of a press conference Vignarajah gave over the weekend in which he publicly attacked Asia's credibility.

Nonetheless, Vignarajah got the court to agree to allow his witness to appear on the record only as "Officer." The prosecutor also raised the issue of Fitzgerald and his discovery. His witness, he said, was "concerned and frankly a little indignant." He wanted a chance to address something of utmost importance.

Fitzgerald took the stand again.

Right out of the gate, he came at Justin.

The evidence he had been given to examine on the stand, he said, had been manipulated. There were "a lot of missing things." He was accusing Justin of cross-examining him using documents that had been tampered with, not a slight charge against an attorney in the middle of a hearing.

"You were trying to sway my testimony," Fitzgerald seethed.

Justin, calm as ever, said, "Right, right," and asked him if he thought the document was useless. Fitzgerald evaded answering and instead said he was offended that Justin had handed him manipulated evidence to try and trick him.

"I think you got caught in your game," he said to Justin.

Justin ignored the insults and instead went round and round with him, trying to pin him down into admitting the document was a mess, nearly impossible to understand because it was missing information. Finally he landed his blow.

The document given to Fitzgerald was the same document the State had given to Gutierrez in 1999. The manipulated documents, which had entire columns of data chopped off, weren't created by Justin. They were created by the State.

On re-direct by Vignarajah, he got Fitzgerald back to the helicopter call problem, and Fitzgerald began fleshing out the subway theory he had raised on Friday. Vignarajah asked if it was possible that someone could drive from Baltimore to drop a friend off at Glenmont, the last stop on a line that ran through Dupont Circle (which happened to be closer to Adnan's home), in twenty-seven minutes and ping the Dupont Circle tower. Fitzgerald responded that it was theoretically possible, though in reality it is not because (surprise) there weren't any AT&T towers in the D.C. subway system until the early 2000s.

After another round of re-re-cross and re-re-direct, Agent Chad Fitzgerald was finally released from his misery.

David Irwin got back on the stand to start where he had left off, being cross-examined by the State.

On cross, Vignarajah engaged in a lengthy game of hypotheticals. He asked Irwin about dozens of different scenarios in which an attorney may or may not have a duty to investigate a witness—whether he would contact a witness who may be a gossip, may be weak, may be damaging to your case, may be lying, may be "playing both sides"—on and on it went.

Finally, out of frustration, Irwin responded that if there was a witness on a space station who said they saw his client in a library, he wouldn't be constitutionally mandated to call NASA, *but* he'd at least get his law clerk to verify the witness wasn't on Earth. The courtroom erupted in giggles.

Irwin went on, saying he had been with the FBI for twelve years but wasn't like "that last witness was with Brown." He was going to answer all of Vignarajah's questions but he wasn't going to give him the answer he wanted, because no matter how many scenarios the prosecutor threw at him, the answer was always yes, you still must contact the witness. At one point, as the hypotheticals kept coming at him, Irwin said, "Stop. I said stop."

A number of other exchanges made it clear how annoyed the men were getting with each other. Vignarajah asked him to put "theatrics aside," Irwin shot back with "your theatrics, not mine," and Vignarajah responded with "my theatrics, you're just funny."

"Right," said Irwin.

Finally, Irwin had enough. He launched into a soliloquy, saying it was mandatory for the defense team to speak to Asia, a credible, unbiased alibi.

"You keep talking 'strategy.' You're begging the world to believe that Cristina Gutierrez had a strategy, but there was no strategy. You can't have a strategy without information. A strategy is a course of action. I'm saying there was no strategy."

Vignarajah attempted to cut him off, and Irwin shot back, "Are you finished? Tell me when I can talk."

On re-direct Justin went over his own set of scenarios in which he asked Irwin if he would have been prevented from contacting Asia. No, absolutely not, he said. He then asked if Gutierrez was still an exceptional lawyer at the time of Adnan's second trial.

"The jury came back in two hours. From what I reviewed, the nicest way to put it is this: she was ineffective. And constitutionally so."

The last witness of the hearing was called to the stand after Irwin, State's witness Steve Mills.

Despite Vignarajah's vigorous argument to keep his name anonymous, the very first thing Mills, a stately older gentleman, did on the stand was identify himself with his full name. Officer Mills was apparently oblivious to all the concerns the prosecutor had.

A statement written by Mills a week before the hearing had been submitted to the court. Mills had spoken to Vignarajah first and then met with a detective, who showed him photos from a yearbook. He was shown Adnan's picture as well. In his statement he said that he did not see Adnan Syed at the Woodlawn public library on January 13, 1999, and that there were no security cameras in the library either.

The prosecutor asked him if there were cameras at the public library and Mills responded, "No." But then in his very next response he said it was possible there were cameras inside he wasn't aware of. He also didn't remember being questioned in 1999 about the case.

Nieto made quick work of his cross-examination. He asked about the statement, and Mills admitted he had not written it. He had only signed it. He also admitted that while the statement said otherwise, it was possible there were cameras he wasn't aware of.

Nieto then asked him about the yearbook pictures he had been shown. They were photocopies, according to Mills, and he didn't recognize any of the kids.

Mills is then asked, "In your statement, you told the detective that you can say for certain that Mr. Syed was not in the library on January 13, 1999, seventeen years ago. Can you say that for certain?"

"No, I can't," Mills responded.

Officer Steve Mills turned out to be much more useful than Hamiel had suggested after all.

At the end of four days, the PCR hearing was finally over. Justin had presented seven witnesses: Dantes, Kanwisher, McClain, Grant, Gordon, Hamiel, and Irwin. Vignarajah had presented two: Fitzgerald and Mills.

After being sequestered for four days, I was allowed to attend the fifth day of the proceedings, the closing arguments.

Justin's closing was succinct, but he began with apologizing to the court for how heated the hearing got at times. He realized he also had gotten rather emotional and thanked the court's indulgence and patience. Justin then walked behind Adnan and put his hands on his shoulders.

He was proud, he said, of representing Adnan. He was proud of how he had comported himself throughout the hearing with quiet dignity, not even asking for his restraints to be removed. He was proud of how Adnan had carried himself for as long as Justin had represented him.

He then made a striking illustrative point about the hearing: that two witnesses were emblematic of the entire procedure—Ms. Hamiel and Officer Mills. On one hand, like other defense witnesses, Hamiel had testified to what she exactly knew from her personal knowledge. In contrast, the State offered up Officer Mills, who could testify to nothing with certainty.

The State, Justin said, spent the entire time trying to fit square pegs into round holes, offering no facts, instead hammering away in futility.

Justin then began his substantive arguments and methodically reiterated the issues at hand: ineffective assistance at failure to contact Asia, and a Brady violation on the part of the State for the way Exhibit 31 was presented to Waranowitz, a fact that hadn't been discovered until the previous October. He went over his witnesses and addressed the legal standards they were required to meet, citing a long list of case precedent that supported his issues. His closing lasted about an hour and was fairly concise.

Vignarajah's closing, on the other hand, took hours, stretching from the morning into the late afternoon.

He started out of the gate tackling what he must have thought was the biggest hurdle—the publicity and public support for Adnan. He said the case shouldn't be treated differently because of the attention it received, and that while the State "sees the wisdom" in the higher court decision to remand the case, it was really just to "clarify" the record. He said it was hard for the State to say what it believed, that Adnan was convicted based on overwhelming evidence, because the State "is aware that this is not the most popular position." The position

Judge Welch took two years ago, he urged, was correct. Still, he said, the public hearing now could help restore faith in the system, so the public could see how fairly Adnan was convicted. He cynically applauded the support Adnan had, saying, "It is inspiring, even for the State, to see so many people come together behind the defendant. And what we see now, your honor, is that the intuitions you had, the conclusions you reached, have not been diluted by the broader record. It was reinforced."

I was aghast. He was basically saying that COSA and the State were simply humoring the public, as if we had waited all these years to put on a show.

The arguments Vignarajah wanted the court to focus on were that there was no Brady violation, that there was no ineffective assistance of counsel for failing to raise an argument no attorney has ever raised before (again, mischaracterizing the case law on the fax cover sheet), and that there was no failure to investigate Asia.

Despite asking the court to focus, the prosecutor himself meandered throughout his closing, going from fierce defense of Gutierrez's abilities, to suggesting I had manipulated the defense files, to accusing Chris Flohr of helping Adnan try to solicit alibi letters, to accusing Adnan's team of smearing Gutierrez's name, which he said categorically wasn't fair and wasn't "based on the record before us."

I thought to myself, *Oh, you mean the record that exists because you fought to keep out all evidence of her illness, financial conditions, and attorney grievance commission complaints?*

He said that this case didn't just turn on a witness or two, or a piece of forensic evidence or two (or none, as the record actually shows), but on a stack of evidence that convicted Adnan. He went through a recital of the "facts" of the case as he saw it, with the same spin that his earlier briefs contained, arguing that it was much more than Jay and the cell phone records that convicted Adnan. He cited the anonymous call pointing toward Adnan, the ride he asked for, and he said Hae's diary proved that there was interpersonal violence (IPV) in their relationship.

It was all so familiar. He was not only raising the same arguments that trolls and "guilters" made on Reddit, he was even using the same language.

He said Gutierrez knew that the "offer by the alibi was not credible, in fact it was risky." He said Gutierrez was considering the fact that some witnesses had seen Hae leave the school at 3:00 p.m. and Asia would have hurt her client, putting him at a location that Hae drove past. I marveled at this, because we all knew full well that not only did Gutierrez never see those witness statements, but also in the first trial the State had already established their timeline, that Hae had left the school immediately after dismissal.

He tried to bolster his strategy argument by putting a defense memo on the projector with Adnan's recollections of January 13, 1999, which didn't mention the library, and arguing that Gutierrez knew putting him at the public library was "out of routine" because Adnan never mentioned it here, and that was dangerous. It was suspicious of him to suddenly pop up at the public library on the day of his ex-girlfriend's murder.

He also read out loud from another memo in which Hae and Adnan's sex life was described, saying it was "relevant." Vignarajah knew, again after all these years, how uncomfortable it would be for Adnan to have those details read in front of his family and community.

Vignarajah repeated his "Central Booking" claim and alleged that Chris Flohr attempted to help Adnan solicit an alibi through his friend Ja'uan, knowing full well that Ja'uan had submitted an affidavit to Judge Welch saying no such thing ever happened. He argued that Gutierrez was so effective and dogged that she issued dozens of discovery requests to the State while at the same time arguing that the State had an open-file policy in which they held no documents back. Susan rolled her eyes, furiously writing down notes that said Gutierrez needed to make so many discovery demands because the State refused to give her anything.

He went on for so long, again pulling out the large foam boards and reiterating there was never a problem with the cell records to track location, and there certainly was no Brady violation, that the judge asked, "Are we getting close?" pushing him to finish his closing already.

Vignarajah ended with a line that he must have regretted, laying out all the different reasons Asia's letters were unreliable and then saying, "Asia McClain is a charming woman and there may be a kernel of her story that is credible . . . because the defendant may have gone to the library and met up with the victim there. I don't know, it's a theory."

Justin stood up to deliver his rebuttal, forcefully reminding the court of why they were here, which wasn't because of "dumb luck or a popularity contest." The court wasn't there to rubber-stamp previous decisions and somehow "restore faith in the system" as Vignarajah claimed. The court had to make determinations on real issues.

He pointed out that Urick wasn't called to testify and rebut Asia about their conversation, and he wondered why. Then he held out a piece of paper and said here was the entire State's arguments about Asia in a nutshell: "I don't know, it's a theory."

Justin argued that none of Vignarajah's claims came from witnesses; they came only from him.

He then slapped the July 1999 memo written by Gutierrez's team, saying Vignarajah had just told the court that going to the library was a break in Adnan's routine. He then read from the July memo, "Asia and boyfriend saw him in library 2:15-3:15. Went to library often."

Justin was livid, pointing out how the prosecutor was trying to obscure and falsify facts, literally attempting to the pull the wool over the court's eyes. Vignarajah had the entire defense file, but he picked the one defense memo that didn't mention Asia or the library.

It was the perfect way to end the five long days.

The court thanked the parties graciously and adjourned the proceedings, saying he would issue a written opinion.

We headed to Justin's office, where he and Nieto were holding a press conference. During the closing arguments Adnan had been hand-writing a statement, with difficulty in his shackles, to be read at the conference.

Justin's conference room was packed with media and cameras as he read Adnan's statement:

> *"I'm incredibly grateful for the opportunity to present new evidence to the court. I'm incredibly grateful for the love of my family and friends who stood by me all this time. I'm thankful for all the support and encouragement I've received from people all over the world. The events of the past sixteen months have filled me with a great sense of hope and I intend to keep fighting to prove my innocence."*

Abe Waranowitz, who had arrived in Baltimore the day before, sat away from the crowd, back in Justin's office. It wasn't until after the press had cleared out that we finally got to meet him. Though he'd flown all the way from the West Coast to testify, the court had asked Justin to have him submit another affidavit instead. It was understandable. The hearing should have taken three days but went on much longer.

I had seen Waranowitz's trial testimony from sixteen years earlier, and in person he was as soft-spoken and unassuming as he seemed to be in the videos. He joined us for dinner on the Baltimore harbor a short while later, after we all shed some tears and gave our thanks to Justin, Nieto, and their other legal partner, Lylian Romero, for the tremendous work they'd done.

As we gathered around a table at the restaurant, Waranowitz, seated next to Aunty Shamim and Yusuf, began apologizing.

He was clearly shaken. He said he was so sorry, he had no idea that his testimony helped wrongfully convict Adnan. He looked back and forth at all of us and seemed on the verge of tears. Yusuf, Aunty, and I immediately stopped him through our own tears, assuring him it wasn't his fault. None of us blamed him, and we were deeply grateful for all he had done.

Now we just had to wait for Judge Welch's ruling.

CONCLUSION

We sent aforetime our messengers with clear Signs
and sent down with them the Book and the Balance,
that men may stand forth in Justice.

Holy Quran 57:25

Here is what I think happened:

On January 13, 1999, Adnan Syed went to school and arrived on time. He left before the lunch break to go give Jay Wilds his car so Jay could get Stephanie a gift. People who knew Jay were used to him borrowing their cars. Adnan asked that Jay drop him back at school after lunch time and then pick him up after track practice, around 5 p.m. that afternoon. Adnan had just gotten a new cell phone, which he wasn't allowed to take to school, so he left it in the glove compartment. He had shown it off to Jay and Jay was eager to mess around with it, so after dropping Adnan off he used it to make some calls. After school Adnan headed to the library; if he had his car he may have gone off campus for a bit. Because he didn't, he thought he'd check his email at the library as he often did. There he saw and chatted with Asia until her boyfriend and his friend showed up and she left with them. Adnan then headed to the locker rooms to change, and swung by the guidance counselor's office to pick up his letter of recommendation. There he saw Debbie and they briefly talked. He arrived at track practice around 3 p.m. and warmed up until the coach arrived at 3:30 p.m. He told Coach Sye that it was Ramadan and explained it to him, also telling him that he would be leading prayers the next day, something he was excited about. After track practice Jay picked him up and Adnan immediately checked the messages on his cell phone; after all, he had given all his friends and family his number the day before, someone may have tried to contact him. It was nearing the time to break his fasting so he and Jay went to McDonald's and ate. Jay had been useful during the day; he had gotten some weed. Adnan smoked some pot with Jay, and they hung out for a bit, and then he had to drop Jay off at home because it was time to head to the mosque for the nightly Ramadan prayers. He arrived at the mosque shortly after 8 p.m. and between prayers made some calls from his shiny new toy. After prayers he headed home and went to sleep.

On January 13, 1999, Hae Min Lee also arrived at school on time in the morning. She'd had a late night, having spoken to her new boyfriend, Don, for hours. She was quiet during the day, tired maybe. After school she was in a hurry. Hae left Woodlawn High School to meet someone she knew in a private place to where they'd summoned her, a place close enough to Campfield Early Learning Center that she thought she had enough time to pick up her cousin after the meeting. She was killed there in a heated moment, after being struck in the head a number of times and then strangled. She may have been unclothed or partially clothed at the time lividity set in. Her body was left facedown for the duration of livor mortis fixing, and then moved to Leakin Park in the middle of the night, hastily dumped, and barely covered. It may have taken two men to move her to the burial site. She was killed in a location that could have been traced to the murderer, so he grabbed the things Hae had brought with her, like her purse and her shoes, and threw them in the trunk of her car. Her car was abandoned somewhere in Baltimore County. The car may have been hotwired by the killer to move it, or hotwired by others who then moved it to where it was ultimately "discovered." The killer dumped or took her pager, which could have led back to him.

When Hae's family realized she was missing, they quickly pulled in Mandy Johnson and her Enehey Group, who would come to confirm (with anti-Muslim bias disguised as "expertise") that Adnan was the likely suspect based on his religion and ethnicity. Hae's mother and grandmother were already opposed to Hae's relationship with Adnan and, having consulted with a psychic, Hae's mother would be comfortable with Johnson's theory.

Johnson took the investigative lead, working closely with Detective O'Shea. The detective did some due diligence by visiting Don's workplace, and then quickly crossed him off the list as a possible suspect because Cathy Michel confirmed Don was at work at another location on the day Hae went missing.

The secret February 1, 1999, anonymous tip must have pointed to Hae's romantic interests and, having dispensed with Don, the police narrowed their focus to Adnan to the exclusion of anyone else.

The police realized that Adnan had a cell phone, got the records, and saw that even while Adnan was in school that day the phone was being used, which led them to Jay. They may not have realized that Jay had Adnan's car that day and that the two had hung out in the morning and then again in the evening, but once they did, they couldn't let him off the hook. They needed Jay to get Adnan. They really believed Adnan did it but didn't know how. Since they didn't know that, they would have to decide how he did it, and Jay would play along in exchange for reward money and protection from the police for himself and his relatives. His grandmother's home—which despite being heavily connected to drugs—was never, ever raided or searched. And Jay, despite having been charged in numerous crimes, never spent a day in jail. In an environment like Baltimore, Maryland, both then and now, these were some hard-to-come-by protections for a young black man.

Jay had no connection to the death of Hae and no knowledge of how she was killed. He was coerced into being a State's witness in order to protect himself. But at the same time he was probably also convinced by the police that Adnan, as a Pakistani Muslim (remember his comments about "Tyad," murder, Pakistanis, and Muslims?), had killed Hae out of hurt pride and religious honor.

The police began meeting with Jay long before his "first" official interview, before they ever spoke to Jenn. They had to work hard with Jay's story to make it match the cell records, because he kept saying things that could hurt their case. One of the few details he and Jenn wouldn't budge from was that the "come and get me call" happened around 3:45 p.m. I think the reason Jay insisted on this detail, and told Jenn to do so as well, was to protect himself. He realized that Hae was killed before then, so he wanted to place himself away from Adnan at that time. If the police tried to charge him with the murder, he could maintain that his statements and testimony never wavered from being at Jenn's home until 3:45 p.m.

All news footage of Hae's disappearance and murder reported she was last seen leaving school at 3:00 p.m. The police realized it too, because under the guise of the Grand Jury proceedings they subpoenaed all media coverage of the case from every single local TV station about a month after Adnan's arrest and confirmed it. Unfortunately, the police were stuck; there were no incoming calls between 3:15 and 4:27 p.m., and they knew Adnan was at track that day by 3:30 p.m., so they had to stick with the 2:36 call even though their own witness repeatedly stated it was 3:45. They got lucky, though, because Gutierrez never caught this discrepancy. And neither did the jury.

In order to get the 3:32 p.m. call to Nisha Tanna to stick, they managed to get Coach Sye, who in 1999 had told them track practice began at 3:30, to move the start of track practice to 4 p.m by the time he testified at trial a year later. They managed to get Debbie to go from being sure she saw Adnan before track practice at the guidance counselor's office on January 13th, to not being sure it was the same day. The police were frequent visitors to the school and spread information among the students and faculty that they had solid evidence, DNA evidence, proving Adnan was the killer.

Jenn had been called so many times that day that they decided she could provide corroboration for Jay's story. When initially approached by police, she had no idea what was going on. That night, Jay filled her in and she returned with her statement to help implicate Adnan. Despite confessing to helping him destroy evidence, Jenn was not charged with anything, likely having been given an off-the-record deal that she wouldn't be, and so didn't even need an official plea deal like Jay. But she was angry at having been dragged into the case and stopped talking to Jay for a long time afterward.

The State managed to pull Vinson, who had been with Jenn during her initial visit to the police, into the case. Vinson recalled that Adnan visited her on January 13th with Jay. She tied this memory to a conference she remembered returning from that day. (Susan's investigation showed there was no conference that day; the conference Vinson referred to happened on January 22, 1999.)

Because so many witnesses were asked to recall details months later, their memories were inaccurate. Phone records show that on January 22, a day with no school, Adnan did receive a number of phone calls in the evening, any of which Vinson may have been remembering if he was at her place then.

On February 24 Hae's car was found in Baltimore County, and the police in Baltimore City were alerted. They moved the car to the 300 block of Edgewood Road, and the same day took Jay by to take a look at it. A few days later, in his first on-the-record interview, he pretended to lead them to it.

When Adnan was arrested, no one at school or in the community knew the evidence against him was only Jay's word and not physical evidence as the police were suggesting. After the bail hearings, when Gutierrez took over the case, he was advised not to contact anyone and not respond to any correspondence. He didn't, which included not writing back to Asia. Adnan's silence, and the strong, continued presence of the police at the school, assuring students that they had solid evidence, made it seem to the students that Adnan must be culpable. None of his peers from Woodlawn attended his trial, further deepening the void of information on the case.

The police and prosecution avoided doing anything in their investigation that could lead to results that would harm their theory. They didn't get incoming call records for Adnan's cell phone (the very basis of their case), they didn't retrieve call records for the Best Buy payphone (if it even existed), they didn't search dumpsters for shovels for a month, they didn't retrieve Hae's pager records, they didn't search Jay's home or car, they didn't interview Jenn's brother Mark Pusateri with whom Jay said he spent the day, they didn't interview most of Adnan's peers and school friends until long after his arrest instead of before it, they didn't secure any official records of Waranowitz's drive test (indeed, they didn't even test the burial site itself), they didn't ask for work records for Don, they didn't test any evidence against Don or Alonzo Sellers, they put a hold on complete forensic testing and never tested the fingernail clippings for DNA, they didn't test Hae's trunk for evidence she had been there, they failed to test items from the crime scene (the brandy bottle, feather, and rope, which later disappeared from evidence), they didn't test three hairs found in Hae's car, they didn't retrieve Hae's online activity, they didn't pull any video footage from school, library, and street cameras, they didn't subject Jay or Adnan to a polygraph, they didn't search Sellers' residence, they didn't investigate Hae's stepfather, and the list goes on. They avoided "bad evidence," evidence that could have hurt their case.

Instead, they focused exclusively on building a case against Adnan. So they fed Jay details as they gathered them, helping him to craft a story while ensuring enough ambiguity that they could continue to change the timeline until they were certain Adnan would have no alibi. And they kept all relevant documents, from witness statements to Adnan's phone records, away from Gutierrez so neither she nor Adnan ever realized what the State's case would be. Today the State argues that the many community witnesses Gutierrez lined up to show Adnan was at the mosque that night backed out of the case when they realized the phone records showed he was in Leakin Park; but no one other than the State ever had those records, because no one realized they had anything to do with the case. Regardless, Gutierrez failed to even contact, much less create alibis from, nearly all the community members on the "alibi notice" list, which was simply a list of potential character witnesses Adnan and his family had prepared for her.

I am convinced that due to the maneuverings of the State, Bilal Ahmed, a sex offender, was released and disappeared. By the time of the trial, Gutierrez had not given notice of any other potential alibi. And to make matters worse,

Ahmed appears to have continued in his ways: In January 2016 he was arrested and charged with sexually assaulting his own dental patient while he was under anesthesia. The patient reported he woke to realize that Ahmed had forced his penis in his mouth. Ahmed is currently under investigation for this and other potential sex crimes.

On her end, Gutierrez failed to investigate and develop a defense for Adnan. Her strategy, based on the belief that it was the State's burden to prove the charges, was to try and attack whatever the State presented in court, which she failed at by not calling any expert witnesses. She also failed to raise a counter-narrative, and failed utterly at establishing with any clarity what Adnan's day looked like on January 13, 1999. Her declining health and unmanageable case-load left her incapable of meeting the standard of duty every defendant is owed by their attorney. Because she was unable to defend Adnan, like many of her other clients, he was convicted and sentenced to spend his life in prison, charged with premeditation in a crime where the State's witness stated on multiple occasions that he had no idea Adnan was planning the crime. Today that witness, Jay, says he heard the murder took place at Best Buy (from who?) but has no personal knowledge of where the crime happened or where Hae was buried because he says he was never at the site. The same witness today says they were never in Leakin Park around 7 p.m. on that day.

From witnesses who changed their testimony, to witnesses who contrived it out of whole cloth, to the cops who enabled it, to the prosecutors who withheld evidence, to the defense attorney who couldn't do her job, to the community that quietly faded away: in this case, everyone failed Adnan. And they also failed Hae.

No one could have predicted what has happened over the past two years. But to be honest, no one can predict what will happen next in this case, either.

There is every reason to believe that Adnan will finally get some measure of justice for losing nearly two decades of his life. But like so many other times, things could still go wrong for him. And if I am going to be even more honest, I don't trust the State to play fair. They haven't so far, and there are too many cases, now made public, in which prosecutors have sunk to the point of securing false testimony from jailhouse snitches or the like in exchange for deals of leniency. I'm not imagining these things. They happen. The State of Maryland wants desperately to keep Adnan in prison until he dies. The attorney general of Maryland, Brian Frosh, recently told other attorneys at a social event that the State would fight every step of the way to keep Adnan in prison. I don't know what they are willing to do to ensure that happens. We have to always keep that in the back of our minds, even as our hearts race with hope.

And we do have hope, lots of it. Because other than what has become public so far, other than what is documented in this book, and what is currently being fought in court, there are still many more revelations about the case to come. Since late 2015 a new team of crack investigators has been deep-diving into the case, speaking to witnesses who had never come forward before, and finding even more incriminating evidence of the State's misconduct and what really happened to Hae. This evidence will be brought to light sometime in the next year, when it has been properly documented and corroborated. The story is far, far from over.

If there is one takeaway from Adnan's story, it should be this—the criminal justice system is not just deeply flawed, it is broken. The law is riddled with myths and ideals that are too lofty for human attainment, from the "presumption of innocence"—a practical fiction when prosecutors are able to convict or get plea deals at alarmingly high rates (97 percent in federal cases)—to equal treatment before the law, when your likelihood of arrest and ability to secure a solid defense are completely dependent on racial-socioeconomic factors.

Criminal defense lawyers know this, which is why many of them weren't surprised by the case. It's also why Kevin Urick could so easily dismiss it as "run of the mill," ironically confirming how broken the system is.

The famous Blackstone's Formulation, that it is better that ten guilty persons escape than one innocent person suffers, has been turned on its head. We have turned into the society that supports overwhelming prosecutorial force out of fear that one guilty person will go free. The Innocence Project estimates up to 5 percent of all incarcerated people in the United States are wrongfully convicted. Given that we incarcerate more people than any nation in the world, over 2.25 million, this means up to well over a hundred thousand incarcerated people in this nation may be innocent. Studies have shown that in cases investigated by the FBI where DNA was available for testing, 25 percent of charged suspects have been cleared. A University of Texas report cites that in cases up until 1990 where DNA testing was available, 37 percent of charged suspects were excluded by the results—that means 37 percent of the time the police charged the wrong person. A more recent study by the Urban Institute shows that roughly 15 percent of *convicted* (not just charged) serious crime defendants can be cleared by DNA testing. But remember, DNA testing is only available in less than 10 percent of cases.

The system is made up of the humans who comprise it.

Every single part of the criminal justice mechanism, every cog in its wheel, is hindered by the cognitive biases of every single person who touches a case. From police officers to detectives, witnesses, prosecutors, juries, judges, and, believe it or not, even forensic and medical personnel and experts that may be involved in establishing the "scientific facts" of a case—all are prone to make dangerous mistakes based on their own preconceived prejudices.

Scientists have identified 179 different types of cognitive biases that impact and inform every decision we make. From the commonly known confirmation bias, which compels us to seek information that confirms our existing beliefs (the police seeking information only about Adnan because he was Muslim), to in-group bias in which we give people of "our group" preferential treatment (white lady Mandy Johnson quickly dispensing with the blond, blue-eyed Don), to the misinformation effect in which people suffer from less accurate memories because of post-event information given to them (every person the police interviewed after Adnan's arrest), Adnan's case was riddled with biases. The very basis of the charges against him relied on a presumption, a bias, about Muslim men. The jury itself discussed how Arab men treated their women during deliberations.

Of course, it's not just Adnan's case. The entire system is impacted by these biases. Human bias even affects the outcomes of DNA analysis and the application of "scientific evidence" in a trial. DNA and fingerprint experts who were given different information about a case or investigation were noted to reach different conclusions—which means that even the results of a "scientific" test aren't safe from human bias. A well-known study out of University College London by Itiel Dror shows that where "the human examiner is the main instrument of analysis"—including a wide range of testing and analysis, even including examinations of closed-circuit television (CCTV) images, and firearms and document investigation—human biases have a tremendous impact on outcomes because "the contextual influences are many and they come in many forms."

These are the facts we are facing as a society. The law is not blind and never has been.

This may make it seem that we are doomed when it comes to having a truly just system, free of prejudice and our internal (many times unknown) bigotries. It is why a competent criminal defense attorney, who is able to challenge and reexamine everything offered by the State, including testing results, is truly a defendant's only line of defense for now—an inordinately stressful situation for an attorney, and an ominously risky one for a defendant. And from a societal perspective, not enough, not by a long shot.

We may, however, be at a crossroads. The public has always had an appetite for true crime, but there has been an unmistakable shift recently in the focus of such stories. The last five years or so have illuminated the dark corners of criminal justice. An exponential increase in exonerations has replaced stories of how hor-rific crimes are solved with stories of how horrific practices by some law enforcement and prosecutors ensure convictions at all costs. Inequitable sen-tences for drug offenses, unequal sentences based on race, the punitive condi-tions of many prisons that destroy instead of rehabilitate, and reprehensible practices such as long-term solitary confinement are all issues receiving more and more attention.

There is also a rising awareness of police brutality and use of lethal force against people of color, most prominently against black men, and the impunity and lack of accountability of state actors.

Meaningful reform may seem a Herculean task; so much is broken, so much cries for attention. But if I could choose one issue to focus on, it would be this: full accountability of people paid by our tax dollars to protect and serve us— police officers and prosecutors.

One realistic way to achieve legitimate oversight of these institutions and state actors would be through independent, civilian-led but agency-inclusive commis-sions appointed in each state. Even as a measure to prevent wrongful convic-tions, innocence commissions that operate completely apart from the judiciary have proven effective at cutting through the onerous and severely limiting appel-late system in states like North Carolina, Pennsylvania, Connecticut, Wiscon-sin, and Illinois. These commissions review claims filed directly by incarcerated people who claim innocence, eliminating not just the systemic appellate limita-tions, but also the need for an attorney. They are, if well managed and diligently applied, an excellent and efficient model to restore justice to the wrongfully convicted. Maryland must have one; every state must have one. Likewise, inde-pendent commissions that hold prosecutors and police officers accountable should also exist. Civilians should have the power, as the ones who pay the sala-ries of these public officials, to ensure that state attorneys and cops don't abuse their authority, and even have the power to revoke that authority.

Last year, in December, I went to visit Adnan with my husband. We navigated all the hoops required to be able to sit with him, separated by a Plexiglass divider, for an hour. As we walked into the visiting room, fairly full of families sitting around the u-shaped containment area, a pen for their incarcerated loved ones to ensure they never forgot where they actually were, Adnan sat with his back to us. It was odd. He usually faced the entrance as he waited for his visitors, then would rise to greet us and make use of his one hug at the start of the visit.

I felt immediate concern. His back was stiff; he stared straight ahead, not even turning his head to look our way. I thought, *Is he angry? Is it because we haven't visited in a few months? What's going on?*

We walked around the far side of the room where he sat frozen, and he finally made eye contact with us. He stood up stiffly, smiling, and then headed toward the area where he could hug my husband. Something was definitely off.

We sat down and I immediately asked him, "Hey, what's up? Everything ok? You just sat there staring ahead when we came in."

That's when he explained what he had been going through for the past month or so, something he hadn't mentioned over the phone for fear of worrying us. A few weeks earlier, as he came out of a bronchial infection that was going through the prison, he woke up one day with pain in his neck and shoulders. He assumed he had pulled a muscle in his sleep. The pain steadily worsened and slowly traveled down his back and arms over the next few weeks. He didn't turn to face us when we entered because he couldn't—it was too painful for him to look to either side, or up and down.

The prison had given him painkillers, but he was not taking them. He had seen too many other men over the years become addicted and he wasn't about to risk it. He was just living with the pain, moving slowly or not moving at all, hoping it would go away on its own. People incarcerated at the North Branch Correctional Institution don't get MRIs or physical therapy; they get meds administered to them based on superficial assessments without any testing. Figuring out what was causing the pain was probably never going to happen.

The agony was so severe that he couldn't even look down to read or write, he could only face straight ahead. Adnan laughed, not a happy laugh, but a resigned one. All these years in prison he had been relatively healthy, barring minor issues, but he had little hope in his case. Now that his PCR was re-opened and he had a shot at a new trial, he was suddenly afflicted in a way he'd never experienced. But like always, he said "Alhamdulillah," still giving his thanks to God that he was better off than so many, and asked us not to tell his family.

I left the visit upset, knowing not much could be done, and said prayers on the ride home and in the days following.

A week later his family visited him and he could no longer hide his condition from them. Around the same time I left for Pakistan for a month-long trip. A few days into my trip I saw a Facebook post by Yusuf. He requested that people write to the governor because Adnan was in so much pain that he had fainted a few times, and one arm was now almost paralyzed.

I sat in a bit of shock. Fainting? Paralysis!? His condition must have either worsened since we visited him, or these things were happening before we visited and he didn't tell us. A ball of anger and panic began to rise inside me. What if he became paralyzed fully, what if he died? But I was sitting across the world, juggling a thousand things around me, I couldn't go visit him, couldn't go knocking on the warden's door. So I did what I could, I started tweeting about it.

I tweeted a screenshot of Yusuf's post, asking people to contact the governor to request medical attention for Adnan. Within the first hour hundreds, then thousands of others shared the tweet, and tweeted at the governor, the attorney general, the Department of Corrections. By the second hour the *Baltimore Sun* ran a story that Adnan, the famous inmate from *Serial*, was severely sick. Calls began flooding the prison, demanding that he be seen. Other outlets picked up the story, and within the day it went viral.

It went so viral that Adnan saw it on the evening news from his prison cell and immediately called Yusuf.

Adnan was livid, in a way he had never been with his little brother before. It was true, he wasn't faring well, but he didn't want any of this to be public. It made him look bad, like he was complaining about the prison and the staff to the world. He worried about how they would treat him, not necessarily fearing any real retribution, but concerned that they simply wouldn't be as nice to him anymore.

I began getting text messages from Yusuf saying he had messed up, he shouldn't have done what he did. I reassured him that he had done what any concerned loved one would do and told him not to worry.

But the incident reinforced what I came to learn about the life Adnan had created for himself inside the prison walls. That life depended on carefully negotiating relationships in which everyone, even those responsible for keeping him incarcerated, saw him as a human being and liked him as such. And they did. At the end of an earlier visit, an elderly guard leaned over and quietly asked me how my visit to Adnan went. I told him it was good, always good to see him. He smiled and nodded and said, "He's a great guy."

That was and is the world Adnan has managed to build to protect himself—positive interactions with everyone, including the guards who locked him up multiple times a day. Anything that made the prison look bad threatened those relationships, threatened to make him fade into the crowd of thousands of inmates, just one of an unruly, criminal population. But this wasn't just a calculation on his part, I realized. This was how he had been his entire life, even the short childhood from which he was snatched. Every person who has ever known Adnan can say this about him: he never wants to hurt or disrespect anyone.

Despite how clearly his own attorney damaged his defense, which he knows better than anyone, he has never spoken about her to me in a disrespectful way. He doesn't carry rancor against anyone. If there is one reason I've stood by his side it is these traits: grace, patience, and kindness through and through in the face of overwhelming injustice.

I shouldn't have been surprised at the immediate and intense public response to his health, which hasn't improved much, because without proper scans getting a diagnosis beyond "it's a pinched nerve" is impossible, but no matter how many times it happens, I can't get over the investment of people around the world in what is happening to Adnan. How do I understand and explain the support, love, prayers, and tears of strangers? How can I understand global attention to a state-level murder case? How can I understand over 500 million downloads of *Serial* and 80 million downloads of *Undisclosed*?

The only way I can process it is through my faith. That God was not going to let Adnan suffer all this in vain. Why he suffered any of it, why innocents suffer at all, is not a question mere mortals have ever been able to sufficiently answer. It's enough for me to know that all throughout history, incredibly good people have suffered terribly, and suffering is not punishment. But much suffering is followed by redemption, sometimes that redemption even coming after the death of great people. Muslims believe the tradition of the Prophet Muhammad, in which he says that nothing bad happens to a believer, not even the prick of a thorn, that if borne with patience he or she is rewarded, either by elevation in rank in heaven or by the expiation of sins.

And eventually, the wrongs committed against the innocent are perceived, acknowledged, and history makes amends.

Why all this attention to Adnan? If you ask me, God wanted the world to know what happened to him, and it started with Sarah.

Serial destroyed the silence around Adnan and ushered in Susan, Colin, Bob, Dennis, and the dozens of people who've helped with the case, the thousands who've donated, the millions who've prayed.

As important as the millions of global listeners who, having heard his story, support Adnan, is the immediate community. The same aunties and uncles who watched Adnan grow, the same friends he shot basketballs with, the same families they encountered with every trip to the mosque, that were now back.

Every so often Yusuf will be approached by someone in the community who hugs him, tells him he's been listening, that he's so glad the story is out there, and that everyone is rooting for Adnan to come home. Women whom Aunty

Shamim has known for decades but hadn't uttered Adnan's name since 2000 have come to her, held her, and asked about him.

Just saying his name to people, acknowledging he exists, is one level of healing. The second is the world knowing he is innocent. The third will be his coming home, after which it may take years to fully rectify, if it's even possible, their lives.

People ask what Adnan wants to do when he comes home. One day, when Yusuf was feeling particularly low, Adnan was trying to humor him.

He asked Yusuf how much local apartments were renting for, which set off all kinds of alarms for Aunty—what, he wouldn't come home to stay with them? Adnan was teasing them. He was going to open a bakery, he told Yusuf, and bake all kinds of pastries, cakes, cookies, mentioning beautiful sweet things to evoke positivity in his little brother.

Yusuf told me and then posted it on Facebook—his brother would open a bakery when he got out. I found it sweet and so hopeful, especially because I'd never heard Adnan ever remotely plan any such thing.

In reality, though, it's still too tenuous to plan what Adnan may or may not do when he's released. He will have the full support of his family, but it is a family that needs years to come back together. I and his other supporters will do our best to give him the financial support needed to get on his feet. In all these years, though he wasn't able to get a college degree in prison, he still developed employable skills. He's a whiz in the law library, having mastered legal research, and his knowledge of the legal system, terminology, and processes is sharp. His experience with the criminal justice system, and the workings of prisons, and prison life, position him perfectly for advocacy.

Mostly, Adnan brims with empathy for others who are struggling. He is emotionally perceptive, kind, compassionate. I see him spending the rest of his life finding a way to uplift others, whether he chooses to go to law school and defend the wrongfully convicted, or bake brownies and cookies. Maybe both, maybe all of it. That is what I wish for him, all of it.

In *Serial* Adnan explained to Sarah that while he doesn't have the life he thought he would have, he still has a life. He wasn't saying he was fulfilled. He was saying he didn't want pity, he deserved dignity, he had made the best of the worst situation. How could he not come to terms with his life when he was surrounded by thousands of others who shared that same life and struggles but have much fewer resources and support than he does? Inside the soaring, barbedwire walls of the human cages we build to keep the dangerous, unsavory, and unwanted away from our homes and towns, people continue to be people. They form friendships, find purpose, forgive, and live.

But as someone who has always felt the urgency of time, the shortness of life, the limitations of our abilities to do and experience every good thing the world has to offer, nothing makes me more sad than the thought that this may be the only life he will ever know. So when I imagine him out, I hope he is able to cram a hundred lives into the years he has left.

Thursday, June 30, 2016, was going particularly badly for me. I awoke with a migraine, fueled by sleep deprivation and dehydration as we entered the very last few days of Ramadan. It was the 25th fast, and odd nights of the last ten days of the holy month we go into worship overdrive.

The tradition holds that one of these last odd nights, the 21st, 23rd, 25th, 27th, or 29th, is the "Night of Power": the night in which God's Mercy descends like a blanket to the earth, in which all prayers are answered, in which our fates are written in the heavens for the following year. A prayer said on this night is equal to praying for a thousand months. Muslims stay up late on these nights, cramming mosques or seeking a quite corner in their home, oblivious to whatever worldly obligations will be hampered by little sleep and an empty stomach. We seek the signs we are told to look for, an extraordinarily peaceful night, pleasantly temperate, and a sun that rises gently, without any heated rays.

Many of us agreed the previous night felt like it was the one.

That afternoon, somewhat regretting my late night as my head throbbed, my phone began ringing. It was Justin. For the past few months as we awaited Judge Welch's decision he had developed the practice of texting me first, to warn me that he would be calling, but not to get excited because there was no news about the appeal.

This time, there was no text.

I answered, a lump rising from my heart to my throat, and Justin bellowed, "Rabia, Rabia, we got a new trial!"

After rendering an extraordinary 59-page opinion, Judge Martin Welch had vacated Adnan's conviction and ordered a new trial.

And while we all had our bets on winning on the issue of Asia's alibi not being investigated by Gutierrez, we instead won on the fax cover sheet: the court found that Gutierrez's failure to cross-examine Waranowitz on the cover sheet met the standard of ineffective assistance of counsel. All we needed was to win on a single issue, so this was good enough. But it didn't mean the judge dismissed Asia.

Asia, he said, was credible. Her testimony and recollection of January 13,

1999, was sound. Gutierrez had breached her duty to Adnan by not contacting her. Despite all this, the court found, that failure may not have impacted the outcome of the trail. In other words, there was no prejudice to Adnan.

Why? Remarkably, Judge Welch decided that because the State's case at trial was so obviously flawed that no one could have believed it anyway, Asia's testimony in 2000 wouldn't have mattered. Welch cited Jay's testimony at trial, noting that there was no timeline of events after school the State could have offered that wouldn't have contradicted Jay. He noted that the jury was likely more swayed by the 7 p.m. "Leakin Park pings" and not events after school. Of course, the court couldn't take into consideration statements made out of court, like Jay's *Intercept* interview, which would have rendered those pings irrelevant.

The opinion noted a number of times how "perplexed" the court was at the State's arguments, particularly with Fitzgerald's testimony. "Perplexed" was probably the nicest way the court could say, "What the hell are you talking about?" to Vignarajah.

The court's finding of facts, that Asia did see Adnan at the library and that Jay's own testimony barred the State from a workable timeline, ends up putting the State in a difficult position. While they can appeal the ruling, we can cross-appeal not winning on the Asia issue. They can argue the law in Welch's opinion, but fighting the factual findings is near impossible. The State's chances at both appeal and a new trial are dismal at best.

Regardless of whether the State appeals or decides to retry the case, Adnan is no longer a guilty man. His innocence is restored to him and he has another chance to face charges, this time a fair chance.

The night of power turned into our day of victory.

AFTERWORD

Over two years have passed since the first edition of *Adnan's Story* was published on August 9, 2016. A mere ten days earlier, Adnan's conviction was overturned on the basis of ineffective assistance of counsel—that attorney Cristina Gutierrez failed in her duty to cross-examine the cell phone expert using AT&T documents that showed incoming calls were not reliable for location status of a phone.

In overturning the conviction, Judge Martin Welch ordered the state to give Adnan a new trial, the outcome we had been fighting for for the previous seventeen years. A new trial, a fair trial. I got the news while I was alone at home hours before it broke publicly. Justin Brown called to tell me and I was nearly debilitated with tears and joy, my hands shaking for the next few hours as I called family and friends.

Later that day Judge Welch's ruling and opinion was posted online and I read it over and over and over. Ecstatically but also with a measure of surprise. We knew we had to win on only one issue, we just didn't expect it to be on the fax cover sheet. Everyone who had witnessed the PCR proceeding felt confident Asia McClain's strong testimony would be the key to a new trial.

Judge Welch expressed no doubts about Asia's veracity. Instead, he denied this issue because he felt that even if Gutierrez had contacted Asia, and Asia had testified in Adnan's original trial, it may not have made a difference in the outcome of the case. Judge Welch felt the jury convicted Adnan because of cell phone records corroborating Jay's testimony about the burial. It was the Leakin Park Pings that doomed Adnan, and a witness as to where he was after school wouldn't have mattered, according to Judge Welch.

Adnan's family, friends, supporters, and legal team all respectfully disagreed, of course. An alibi for the exact time that Hae disappeared, and was likely killed, seemed even more important than what time she may have been buried. And, of course, we knew that Jay had recanted his testimony about time of the burial in his *Intercept* interview. But the real world, and new facts, rarely ever enter the courtroom.

The ruling was highly publicized; media outlets all over the world reported that the subject, the star of the *Serial* podcast, would be getting a new trial. Adnan himself learned of his conviction being vacated from the media and we weren't able to speak for a number of days. When we finally did, it was mostly through my tears and the joy that was palpable in his voice. But his joy was cautious—he warned me that it could still take a number of years before he would come home.

And he was right. As of October 2018, two years after being granted a new trial, Adnan still sits in prison growing older, patiently waiting for the wheels of justice to grind toward a resolution. He sits in prison because the State of Maryland still isn't done with him.

Within thirty days of Judge Welch overturning Adnan's conviction, the State of Maryland appealed his decision to the Court of Special Appeals (COSA), the second highest court in the state.

But before it could be heard there, a flurry of pleadings were filed. Our very first order of business was to decide whether or not to apply for bail.

The State appealed the cell record fax cover sheet issue, saying Adnan had waived the issue by not raising it in his first post-conviction appeal, and we cross-appealed on losing the alibi witness issue.

On June 8, 2017, nearly a year after the conviction was overturned, oral arguments were held before the three-judge COSA panel. This time, I was there. This time, the prosecutor, Thiru Vignarajah, couldn't get rid of me.

On the morning of June 8, 2017, Aunty Shamim, Justin Brown, Saad, my husband, myself, and other family and friends gathered together early and walked the few blocks to the front of the courthouse in Annapolis, Maryland, to hear the oral arguments. There was already a large media presence and a line out the front door of spectators wanting to view the proceedings. If we had to get in that line, we never would have made it in. Seating was extremely limited in the courtroom, roughly a hundred chairs in a semicircular chamber.

The intimate courtroom was tense and quite. It was baffling, but Vignarajah was still handling the case on behalf of the attorney general despite now being in private practice. Justin proceeded to argue the points made in the

State's briefs, during and after which the three judges peppered them with questions.

When we spilled out of the courthouse a couple of hours later, I felt a mix of disgust at Vignarajah, deep satisfaction that the COSA judges clearly knew the trial record intimately, and pride at Justin Brown's impeccably delivered and legally solid arguments.

March of 2018, COSA reversed both of Judge Welch's opinions and in essence both the State and the defense won their appeals. COSA decided that Adnan had waived the fax cover sheet issue, giving the State a win on their appeal, and also that Gutierrez was ineffective for not contacting Asia, giving us a win on the cross appeal. Ultimately though, the end result was the same—Adnan's conviction would be thrown out and he would be granted a new trial.

The State had thirty days to file a petition for permission to appeal to the highest court in Maryland, the Court of Appeals, a process called "certiorari" or cert for short, and they did. The Court of Appeals would grant the petition, meaning the door for the State to argue one last state level appeal was now open.

On November 29, 2018, we once again filed into a courtroom to hear what would hopefully be final appellate arguments in this case. This time Justin Brown took a seat while Cate Stetson, a partner at the law firm Hogan Lovells and one of the best appellate attorneys in the nation, argued for Adnan. Once again, Thiru represented the State. And once again, he misrepresented facts to the court, a panel of seven judges that repeatedly pressed him on how it could possibly be reasonable for an attorney not to contact an alibi witness.

After an hour of arguments by both sides, we once again piled out of a courtroom to face a gaggle of reporters with messages of hope, hope that we geniunely felt given the previous two appellate wins, but also with hearts heavy for the long wait ahead for a decision.

This lengthy, unending appellate process should illustrate the uphill battle defendants face even when their conviction is thrown out of court. If the State wants to continue to throw taxpayer dollars at a case, they have vastly larger resources than the defendant to continue going to court. And they have the luxury of time and freedom.

Many have asked why Adnan is not home since two courts threw out his conviction. This answer is this: as long as the State keeps appealing the rulings they can keep him incarcerated in the same way a person newly arrested, facing charges for the first time, can be kept in prison. That is Adnan's status, like someone facing murder charges for the first time, even though he has already spent twenty years locked up for the crime. Defendants charged with first degree murder are rarely granted bail, and neither was Adnan.

He is still behind bars and will stay there until the State finally gives up.

The prosecution will give up, I'm certain of it. Other than the fact they are hurtling towards an inevitable appellate wall, the latest appeal being the last state level appeal they can file, there are more reasons to believe they will eventually wave a white flag.

One of those reasons is that, as mentioned earlier in the book, Adnan was a juvenile when sentenced and a 2012 Supreme Court decision banned life sentences without parole for juveniles. There has since been the possibility that Adnan's sentence could be revised, giving the State little reason to keep fighting the case. And then there is the possibility that more new evidence could surface, a possibility we have been doing our best to make a reality, that could push the State to throw in the towel.

Our battle to free Adnan and prove his innocence has existed outside of the courts for the past few years, with multiple podcasts, hundreds of blogs and articles, and of course, this book. But as of 2016, we began another endeavor to keep investigating deeper and find another way to tell the truth. This time, with a documentary.

Before this book was even published, we began getting offers from producers to option the film rights. One of these offers came from someone I had admired and followed from afar for decades—Jemima Goldsmith, formerly Jemima Khan.

Jemima isn't just any random producer; she is a veritable icon for Pakistanis around the world. She was the darling of Pakistan as the wife of superstar cricketer Imran Khan (who happens to currently be the prime minister of the country), a close friend of Princess Diana, and the daughter of a French billionaire. Pakistanis adored her embrace of Pakistani culture, and were devastated when the couple split after nearly a decade. She was, for many, Pakistani royalty.

Jemima went on to become a journalist and eventually a producer, founding her own production company, and creating award-nominated and -winning documentaries. In the days that *Serial* was on the air, I was shocked to receive a message of support from her as the mother of two Pakistani British teenage boys in whom she saw Adnan. She had begun following Adnan's case, was appalled at the anti-Muslim bias, and believed he was innocent.

When Jemima and her partner Henrietta Conrad made an offer to option the book, every other offer went into the bin. The quality of their films, their commitment to bringing light to important issues, Jemima's antiwar and social justice work, and her understanding of the case and our culture was everything I could have asked for. At least I thought so until she told me whom they picked to direct the documentary.

You might recall the night I decided to find a journalist to investigate Adnan's case, I had been watching a documentary called *West of Memphis*. That singular film changed every opinion I had about the West Memphis Three case and propelled me to my laptop immediately, leading me to Sarah Koenig.

That film was directed by Oscar-nominated director Amy Berg. Years later, when Jemima called me to tell me whom they hired to direct Adnan's documentary, I sat in stunned silence when she said it would be the very same Amy Berg. At that point this book had not been published and Jemima had no way of knowing yet that it was Amy's film that had changed the course of the case. But I've never believed in coincidences and this was once again divine providence bringing all the pieces of this story full circle.

In *West of Memphis,* Amy didn't just document the facts on the ground. She investigated them, challenged them, and ultimately helped find evidence to free the three incarcerated men. I hoped her taking on Adnan's case meant the same thing—that she would not be passively filming events as they took place; she would doggedly dig for new evidence, revisit old witnesses, and help truly exonerate Adnan.

I wasn't disappointed. Unlike Sarah Koenig, who maintained a journalistic distance and lack of commitment to Adnan's innocence or guilt, Amy dove in headfirst believing the wrong person was in prison for Hae's murder. I met Amy for the first time in November 2015 and by the time the PCR hearing in which Asia McClain finally testified rolled around in February 2016, the documentary crew was there to capture it. Since then, Amy and her crew were able to access witnesses no one could get to talk before, identify new forensic evidence, and capture some remarkable moments as the case continued to proceed.

Amy's hard work, investigative skills, and dedication to this case will become clear when her documentary series airs on HBO in the spring of 2019. And so will Adnan's innocence. It's my prayer that he is home to watch the series when it airs, though that is a long shot. What is not a long shot is this—Adnan's release is inevitable. Every element in the universe necessary to defend him properly has come together in the past few years and we have only ever progressed toward his freedom.

Sooner rather than later, he will be home.

ACKNOWLEDGMENTS

───────•───────

On behalf of Adnan and his family, I want to thank the many who have made the telling of his story possible, who supported him with letters, prayers, donations, and love.

I want to thank those who came to our side to help with every challenge we faced in the past two years: Amanda, Shahed, Laila, Alicia, Samantha, Patrick, Ramiro, Ballookey, Christie, Evanem, Jia, Josie, Beau, Dez, Chris, Rebecca, Amar, Ben, Amelia, Matt, Beverly, Brendan, Jim, Laura, Michael, Mital, Pete, Shaun T., Scott, Jon Cryer, the folks at Launchgood, The Magnet Program, and many, many more.

To Adnan's lawyers who have stood by his side over all these years, our deepest gratitude to Justin Brown, Chris Nieto, Chris Flohr, and Doug Colbert.

There are no words to thank Sarah Koenig and her team at *This American Life* for what they have done for Adnan. And there will never be a way to repay the diligence, time, effort, and exhaustive hours spent by Susan Simpson, Colin Miller, and Bob Ruff in investigating this case and creating podcasts to tell the world about it. Your integrity, generosity, and dedication are the rare gifts that make you incredible human beings. Thank you Dennis for steering me through all this, and continuing to show me the path ahead.

Thank you to my agent, Lauren Abramo, and editor, Elisabeth Dyssegaard, for talking me off of the many ledges, being patient during my stress-induced meltdowns, and making this book possible along with the entire team at St. Martin's Press.

I thank my loving husband, Irfan Aziz, and two beautiful daughters for their support and understanding as I've spent hundreds of hours away from them, writing, researching, traveling, speaking on Adnan's behalf. They are my foundation, my rock, my everything.

I thank my parents for raising me, my brother, Saad, and sister, Siddrah, to stand by what is right and speak up for the truth, for never forgetting Adnan, and never letting us forget him either.

Lastly I thank Saad, Aunty, Uncle, Yusuf, Tanveer, and mostly Adnan for trusting me to tell his story and to be his voice. My only fear is failing you, and my prayer is that I've honored your trust and done justice to Adnan's struggle.

INDEX